★

# Inside the Kremlin's Cold War

# Inside the Kremlin's Cold War

## From Stalin to Khrushchev

Vladislav Zubok
Constantine Pleshakov

Harvard University Press

Cambridge, Massachusetts
London, England

*Library of Congress Cataloging-in-Publication Data*

Zubok, V. M. (Vladislav Martinovich)
  Inside the Kremlin's cold war : from Stalin to Khrushchev /
Vladislav Zubok, Constantine Pleshakov.
      p.    cm.
  Includes bibliographical references and index.
  ISBN 0-674-45531-2 (alk. paper) (cloth)
  ISBN 0-674-45532-0 (pbk.)
      1. Soviet Union—Foreign relations—1945–1991.   2. Cold War.
I. Pleshakov, Konstantin.   II. Title.
DK267.Z78   1996
327.47—dc20       95-26457

# Contents

★

# Illustrations

★

# Preface

We were not even born when Joseph Stalin died in 1953 or even when Nikita Khrushchev denounced his crimes in 1956. The main characters of this book had all either died or been cleansed from the Kremlin before we began to read. By the time we started school the worst crises of the Cold War were over. The world had become more stable. But this very relative and fragile stability of what John L. Gaddis would later call the Long Peace was in fact a time of globalization of the U.S.-Soviet rivalry.[1] We were growing up with the full understanding that we could die at any moment in a nuclear blast. We learned to look for an *Enola Gay* in the skies even before we learned to brush our own teeth. Soviet middle schools would hold civil defense classes in which ludicrous survival skills were taught in preparation for all-out war. Although still half believing in Santa Claus, we were already very skeptical of gas masks and bomb shelters. We suspected that chloride cyanide, which our teachers informed us has the scent of bitter almonds, would somehow penetrate the clumsy mask and that we would be buried alive in the so-called safe havens in the basements of our apartment houses.

Our parents would frown and tell us not to worry so much about war. And yet what we overheard of their conversations reinforced our fatalism. The adults favored a very cynical nuclear age joke: What should you do in the event of nuclear war? Don't panic, just wrap yourself in a white sheet and crawl to the nearest cemetery. Having attended a lecture on the international situation, our mothers would discuss with our fathers whether they should sacrifice buying a new dress for the sake of getting a stock of canned food in case of "you know what."

The names of those who had shaped the Cold War from the Soviet shore—Stalin, Molotov, Khrushchev, Beria, and others—were taboo in the Soviet Union, for they had sinned against the Communist party. They reached us as ghosts in jokes, in old folks' stories, in books and magazines from the attic. Some magazines contained the gross political caricatures of Truman, Acheson, Eisenhower, Dulles, Adenauer, de Gaulle. Those names meant almost nothing to us. The name of John Kennedy still carried some sentiment. Our parents were saddened by his premature death, just as they would be saddened by the death of his brother Robert Kennedy, in 1968.

Very soon we learned that the places of our birth, Yalta and Moscow, were the two scenes of the most dramatic moments in the annals of the Cold War. In the czar's palace in Yalta in February 1945, Stalin, Roosevelt, and Churchill, the three quarrelsome leaders of the Great Alliance, decided the future of post–World War II Europe and Asia. Yalta was also the only town in the USSR to boast a street named after an American president, FDR, and that gave us a hint of the Soviet concept of the "lost chances" of the mid-1940s. In the Kremlin in Moscow in May 1962 Khrushchev ordered missiles sent to Cuba. When a thermonuclear crisis was provoked in October, he sat in the Kremlin many days and nights, cursing, trying to locate on a textbook-sized map where exactly his vessels were in the Caribbean and to figure out what John Kennedy in the White House was really thinking.

When Soviet tanks overran Czechoslovakia in August 1968, we were too young to know much about the Cold War, even though our parents' friends, having visited Prague during the Soviet invasion, would furtively display photographs of Czech girls in miniskirts posting anti-Soviet leaflets on the walls.

As we grew up we discovered how influenced our flamboyant youth was by international tensions. Unfazed, we would watch our first girlfriends assembling Kalashnikov machine guns; we just worried whether they would manage in twenty seconds, the time required for passing a civil defense exam. Compulsory military training brought us to the Military Department of Moscow State University once a week, after which we would go drinking with friends. During class we would mark the victorious offensive of the Soviet platoons (which we were to command in the event of war) on the maps of West Germany—and read Thomas Mann or Goethe during the break.

By the time we reached our teens we could probably be classified as "anti-Soviet elements"—just as the vast majority of the generation born in the 1950s were. Our lack of real knowledge about the complexities of the Cold War was compensated by a firm belief that the Kremlin just could not have been right, be it concerning the Berlin blockade in 1948 or the invasion of Hungary in 1956.

When we graduated from Moscow State University in the early 1980s—at the same time Soviet troops became mired in Afghanistan—and began work at the Institute of U.S. and Canada Studies in Moscow, the Cold War ghosts fully caught up with us. During the Afghan War we were not drafted into the "army in the field," though we will always remember the look in our mothers' eyes on the nights we would receive routine Cold War check-up notices from the local military registration offices. We were lucky and went through the Afghan tragedy unharmed. Instead of being conscripted into the army we were given access to the "special collections" of Moscow libraries with their impressive selections of Western books on the Cold War. The Institute of U.S. and Canada Studies itself was a kind of intellectual preserve created to supply the present and future leaders of the USSR with advice about the realpolitik. This pragmatic and infinitely cynical think tank gave us a good grasp of Soviet policy-making. Some of the veterans of the Institute had at one time briefed members of the Stalin leadership. Past and present blurred there. Having been exposed to these former Soviet intelligence agents and the Brezhnev elite, as well as Western colleagues, we finally decided to write this book. Of course the days of glasnost, initiated by Mikhail Gorbachev, proved to be a catalyst for our work: we wanted to contribute to the new freedom in our professional capacity.

Now we realize that two-thirds of our lives passed under the shadow of the Cold War, which, along with the Soviet Union, has come to an end. Yalta in the Crimea is now a territory being disputed between Kiev and Moscow. New leaders in the Kremlin, with their anti-Communist ardor gone, are talking about the unfriendliness of the United States and wondering whether there will be a new Cold War. Yet at the same time Russia's most closely guarded archives are reluctantly opening their doors a bit, and the survivors of those forty years of confrontation have begun to publish their memoirs. Diplomats, KGB operatives, generals and functionaries of the Communist party are bringing forth the submerged outlines of the Soviet giant.

This book is our personal inquiry into the Kremlin's view of the

Cold War. Growing evidence from the Russian side can help us to understand what shaped the behavior of the Soviet monolith toward the world, its confrontation with the United States, and its expansion in Europe, Asia, Africa, and Latin America. Although there have been monumental and comprehensive studies on how Stalin and his successors managed Soviet foreign policy, most of them predate the era of glasnost, and only very recently have a group of scholars begun to digest the materials available from the newly opened archives in Moscow.[2] A major, long-awaited book on Stalin by General Dmitri Volkogonov is disappointingly elusive and cursory in its description of the Soviet tyrant as a statesman and a Cold Warrior.[3]

This book is unique not only in its scope and focus but also in its content, style, and approach. Each new revelation from Soviet, East European, and Chinese archives makes it starkly clear that the history of the Cold War must be reexamined. Although the question remains as to what extent the Eastern archival findings and studies will affect the established assumptions about U.S. participation in the Cold War, there are no doubts that the history of Soviet foreign policy and the people who made it has to be rethought.

No author, as yet, has attempted to look at the Soviet view of the Cold War through the background and actions of both Stalin and his principal lieutenants and successors. Using newly declassified materials, we attempt to penetrate the Kremlin by exploring the background, psychology, motives, and behavior of Soviet rulers from Stalin to those who replaced him, and to better understand the world they helped create.

The "human factor," a favorite term of Mikhail Gorbachev, is the least understood and explained element in the history of the Cold War. Understanding means not only using keen analysis but also acknowledging barriers between diverse cultures. Knowledge of the Russian language is not enough: one needs to read between the lines of the most secret documents—to see and feel as those who had produced and consumed them. Understanding also requires a certain compassion and empathy with Russian historical roots and experience; an ability to understand imponderables such as "revolutionary faith," "nationalism," "patriotism," "memories of war"; a sensitivity to fine distinctions between fanaticism and cruel cynicism, between fear for life and hunger for power, challenging audacity and hubris, evil character and spineless cowardice.

This is a tall order in itself. But it is made even more challenging by the task of translating these perceptions into a totally different cultural language, for a foreign audience with a different national experience and attitude to political leadership. The task of making personalities in the Kremlin, their mindsets and experiences, understandable to a broader audience of Americans, not just to the initiated coterie of Kremlinologists, is daunting.

This is the first book by historians of our generation schooled under the Soviet system but with some exposure to the West. Our studies of American politics and culture at the Institute of U.S. and Canada Studies in Moscow led us to look anew at the Soviet foreign policy establishment. We viewed the old archetypes and stereotypes with skepticism. We learned that, along with the "hard power" of spheres of influence, bombs and missiles, there was the "soft power" of fear and suspicion, distorted perceptions that had driven both sides, the West and the Soviet Union, to continue the Cold War.

We began to work in the Soviet archives in the days when the only documents available were those describing the style of furniture in Soviet embassies. We could peruse at ease the files entitled "Sea Lions and Conventions on the Protection of Sea Lions." Since then, however, innumerable declassified files with "Top Secret" reports from the embassies, KGB and military intelligence, along with resolutions of the foreign ministry, the International Department of the Party Central Committee, and even the Politburo itself have been opened to scholars. Still, many doors closed in our faces, sometimes literally. But the major thoughts and objectives of the Soviet leadership in the Cold War are definitely clearer now. When we discovered a locked door, we were discouraged, but consoled ourselves with the words of Confucius: "To distinguish knowledge from non-knowledge is actual knowledge." Now it is time for the new Russian historians to bear judgment on the Cold War and those in the Kremlin who waged it.

At various stages of our research we received assistance and help from many individuals and institutions. Our gratitude to them is immense. In addition to the John D. and Catherine T. MacArthur Foundation, we would like to mention the U.S. Institute of Peace, the Fletcher School of Law and Diplomacy, the Kennan Institute for Advanced Russian Studies, and Amherst College's Loewenstein Fellowship in the Social and Political Sciences.

Among individuals we would like to thank in particular Martin

Sherwin from the Nuclear History and Humanities Project at Tufts University, John L. Gaddis, the former director of the Contemporary History Institute, Ohio University, William Taubman of Amherst College, and Robert C. Tucker of Princeton University.

James G. Hershberg, the director of the Cold War International History Project at Woodrow Wilson International Center for Scholars, helped us in many ways—by providing encouragement, transforming our presentations and papers into articles and working papers, and alerting us to newly declassified U.S. and Soviet documents.

We would like to thank Alexander Chubarian, the director of the Institute of General History, Russian Academy of Science, and Mikhail Narinsky, the deputy director of the same institute, for their keen interest in our work. We also appreciate the support of Andrei Kokoshin and Viktor Kremenyuk, former and current deputy directors of the Institute of U.S. and Canada Studies, Russian Academy of Science.

Georgi Kornienko, Oleg Troyanovsky, David Holloway, George Bunn, Robert Conquest, Kathryn Weathersby, Eduard Mark, and Alexei Filitov, among many, shared their expertise with us. Without them, there would be many more errors in this book. We are especially grateful to many archivists, particularly I. V. Bukharkin at the Archives of the Ministry of Foreign Affairs of the Soviet Union, now the Archives of the Russian Federation (AVP RF), and N. G. Tomilina, Yu. V. Afiani, and Z. K. Vodopianova of the Storage Center for Contemporary Documentation (TsKhSD). We would also like to thank K. A. Anderson, O. V. Naumov, and G. Gorskaya at the Russian Center for the Preservation and Study of Documents of Contemporary History (RTsKhIDNI). They all turned a sympathetic ear to our incessant requests and helped us overcome some of the many hurdles on our quest to uncover the mystery of the Soviet Cold War.

We are also thankful to the people at both the Institute for Advanced Studies at Princeton and the Norwegian Nobel Institute for providing us with an excellent environment in which to put the final touches on the manuscript. In particular, the book benefited from the unique resources of the National Security Archives (a nongovernmental center and library of documents on U.S. Foreign Policy) and the generosity of its researchers, including Thomas Blanton, Malcolm Byrne, and William Burr.

We could not have dreamed of better first readers for our manuscript than Melvyn Leffler and Odd Arne Westad. Their impressive knowledge of U.S. foreign policy and the diplomatic history of the Cold War, their wise and friendly comments, helped us overcome the final hurdles in preparing the book for publication.

We thank Robin R. Rone, editorial associate at the National Security Archive, for preparing the index.

Joyce Seltzer of Harvard University Press enthusiastically took on the tasks of both shaping and editing the manuscript. Without her overwhelming and generous support the book would have remained an unfulfilled enterprise.

With all that said, any deficiencies, weaknesses, errors of facts and judgments in this book are entirely our own.

Inside the Kremlin's Cold War

# Prologue: The View from the Kremlin, 1945

Soviet Russia has been looked upon as the very incarnation of all evil; hence her ideas have assumed the quality of the devilish.

Erich Fromm

Late on the morning of June 24, 1945, the golden clocks on the Kremlin's Spasskaya Tower chimed and everyone in the Soviet Union with a radio listened to those familiar sounds. The great Parade of Victory was about to begin. All along Red Square and the area surrounding it, victorious troops in decorated uniforms, with captured Nazi banners, in formations and in the turrets of tanks, all perfectly still, waited for a signal to march. Thousands of people crowded into the guest stalls. Suddenly, thunderous applause spread through the crowd as the ruling State Committee of Defense emerged from the Kremlin and began to climb the stairs of Lenin's Mausoleum. It was this group that had replaced the Communist Politburo during the four years of the most devastating war in the world's history. Leading the others, walking at some distance from them, was Joseph Stalin, the head of the USSR.

In just a few years the same leaders who celebrated the triumph over Nazi Germany would clash with their former allies, the United States and Great Britain, in a costly and protracted struggle. To understand how the Soviets perceived a conflict with the West, one has to understand what happened in the deep recesses of the Kremlin. Joseph Stalin and his lieutenants were rulers of a special type—tyrannical, cruel, and certainly loathsome in many ways—who defined their legitimacy in the terms they themselves set and harshly imposed on the people of the USSR. Nevertheless, in 1945, with the defeat of Nazi Germany still fresh in everyone's mind, these men were united in victory with the people they ruled. The Kremlin leaders and their regime experienced their golden hour representing the triumphant forces of history. They carried on the legacy of Russia as the savior of the world, a legacy willingly shared by millions of their countrymen. In order to understand the Cold War from the Soviet perspective, one must understand the importance of that moment and the larger historic legacy of Russia and the Russian Revolution, vindicated by the victory of 1945.

The Soviet worldview had been shaped by a history that was dramatically different from that of the West. The legacy of czarist history, the Bolshevik revolution, the Civil War, and the experience of World War II all contributed to a unique Soviet perspective. Another, important factor that significantly shaped the Soviet perspective was that Russia represented not only a nation but also a distinctive imperial civilization. One could argue that, with the exception of the period of the Mongol yoke (thirteenth-fifteenth centuries), Russia has always been an empire. And even during the Mongol interlude, when its land had become a province of a grandiose nomadic mega-state, Russia still remained in the imperial framework. The traditional imperial legacy was an insurmountable obstacle to Russia's becoming an "ordinary" nation-state. Despite their intentions to build a brave new world from scratch, Russian Communists simply could not break with the imperial mode of thinking.[1]

At the end of the fifteenth century the concept of Moscow as the Third Rome had emerged; two previous Romes had fallen, for they had sinned, and (after the collapse of Constantinople) it was now time for Moscow to be the eternal keeper of the Christian faith. This Russian messianism became the spiritual backbone of the expanding Russian empire, which perceived itself as nothing short of sacred. After the revolution of 1917, however, Soviet Russia assumed the responsibility of spreading the Marxist message. Now, as the keeper of the Marxist faith, it would emancipate mankind rather than Orthodox Christianity.

History gave the Russians more concrete reasons to see themselves as saviors of the world. Russians credited themselves with having rescued Europe from two invading powers—the Mongols in the thirteenth century and Napoleon's army in the early nineteenth century.

The belief that Russia was the protector of mankind against a militant anti-Christ was strongly reinforced by the victory over the Nazis in 1945. In the European war theater the Soviet contribution to victory was decisive and costly. The enormous sacrifice of the Russian people in the Second World War had led the Soviet leaders to believe that the Allies owed them a great deal.

The fact that the Soviet regime had been founded by Communist revolutionaries further alienated Russia from the West and contributed to its messianic legacy. The proletarian revolution, as envisaged by Marx and Engels, was meant to create an unprecedented universal proletarian empire. By the end of the nineteenth century, however, Marxism in Western Europe was becoming more and more national, and was being transformed into the Social-Democratic projects of a welfare nation-state. The Socialists of France and Germany and even of Russia supported World War I as a war between nation-states. V. I. Lenin, the founder of bolshevism, found himself alone when he called for transforming the imperialist European war into a civil class war. His call, after the defeat of a leftist revolution in Germany in 1918, failed to ignite any other nations. Only in Russia, where the concept of a nation-state had totally failed, did Lenin lead the people to the utopia of a universal proletarian empire without borders. The imperial implications of both Marxist thought and Russian history provide the broad background and context for understanding Soviet involvement in the Cold War.

The origins of Cold War thinking from the Soviet side are often interpreted in the West in a simplistic manner: Stalin wanted to conquer the world and so switched from cooperation to confrontation. The American revisionist school generally regards the Cold War as a bilateral process, with Stalin reacting to certain assertive actions by Washington. In the case of Stalin's leadership, however, we are facing something more complicated than just expansionism or "reactions."[2] Stalin and generations of Soviet bureaucrats who grew up with him or under his rule shared a complex attitude toward the outside world that had its roots in Russian history, Marxism, and, in its modified version, Leninism. It would be wrong to interpret Communist behavior in the world arena in terms of either geopolitics or ideology. We prefer to conceive of this conduct as the result of the symbiosis of imperial expansionism and ideological proselytism.

When Lenin came to power in 1917, he was driven by a utopian dream that the fire of the world revolution, having started in Russia, would engulf the world. In this context in 1918 he attempted to abandon the world of geopolitics.[3] If Russia were to prevail over Germany in the First World War, any regime in Russia would have to collaborate with the Allies. Instead, Lenin signed a separate peace treaty (the Treaty of Brest-Litovsk) with Kaiser Germany in which he sacrificed the most developed areas of European Russia, even those that Germany had not yet occupied. The loss of these crucial territories—a geopolitical catastrophe—could have been averted only through military cooperation with the major allies of czarist Russia: Great Britain, France, and the United States. But this was unacceptable to Lenin, for the leader of the Russian Revolution had his eyes only on consolidation of the new regime—and for a particular purpose. Preserving Russia as the headquarters of world revolution promised the spread of the revolutionary ideology around the globe, or at least in Eastern and Central Europe.

In 1922, after signing the Treaty of Rapallo with Germany, Lenin switched to a more complex model of Marxist state behavior, coming very close to elaborating the revolutionary-imperial paradigm. But the father of the Russian Revolution did not have the slightest intention of canceling ideology as a motivation in the making of foreign policy.[4] The result was a strange amalgam of ideological proselytism and geopolitical pragmatism that began to evolve in Soviet Russia in the early 1920s. Marxism was a utopian teaching, but since it proclaimed that the goal of the material transformation of the world was to be realized in a violent confrontation with its opponents, Communist proselytes developed a whole set of highly effective political institutions. Utopian ideals gave way to a ruthless and cynical interpretation of the realpolitik tradition.[5]

The combination of traditional Russian messianism and Marxist ideology produced something larger (though more fragile) than its parts taken separately. The two phenomena became completely blurred in the USSR by the 1920s and remained that way until the collapse of the Soviet regime in 1991. Together they provide a theoretical explanation of Soviet foreign policy behavior—the revolutionary-imperial paradigm.

Lenin's comrades-in-arms, such as Stalin and Molotov, and even the younger generation of Soviet leaders represented by Khrushchev, would inherit this ambivalent worldview. Each of them would make his own intricate Cold War journey, guided by the two misleading suns of empire and revolution. The story of their journeys will provide us with some new insights into their motivation and goals at various points in the Cold War. Fascinating in and of themselves, these characters are also representatives of the sunken Soviet empire, a latter-day Atlantis, the lore of which is already starting to be forgotten.

This book is constructed around key Soviet leaders. The issue of the role of personality in Soviet policy-making is a crucial one. Marxism had always asserted that the role of the leader or, for that matter, any individual was insignificant compared with the role of the masses in the class struggle.[6] The examples of Lenin, Stalin, or Khrushchev had proved just the opposite. The Kremlin had always been an Olympus—first chaired by Lenin, then terrorized by Stalin, then chaired again by Khrushchev.

Instrumental to any society, leaders were the driving force of the USSR. The changing society and the international environment at some points were even ignored by the Soviet demigods, though none of them could disregard entirely the world around them. Stalin throughout his life carefully monitored the possible dangerous consequences of Western ideological influence on his regime. Similarly, the problem of international security was never ignored during the Cold War years. The ominous and almost lethal German invasion of Russia in 1941 took the Soviet leadership by surprise and taught them a tragic lesson. The nuclear issue in particular was one of the major factors predetermining the actions of all members of the Kremlin leadership.

None of the Soviet leaders had ever approached the status Stalin zealously coveted. But every one of them was a tyrant in his own right. Gray and dull, Molotov would be Stalin's representative in the satrapy of foreign policy; the obnoxious Beria would rule over the spheres of the secret police and the atomic project. The articulate Zhdanov would bully the leaders of the East European Communist parties, while the sophisticated Malenkov would reshuffle party apparatchiks and state managers like a deck of cards. Even Khrushchev, having ousted all his rivals by 1957, would build up his own nationwide cult of personality and control everything—from emulation of American agriculture (his notorious "corn" campaign) to suppression of the intellectual opposition and the supervision of Moscow's bohemian circles.

Many questions must be asked in connection with leaders other than Stalin: What were the specific attitudes and activities of Stalin's lieutenants—such as Molotov, Zhdanov, Beria, and Malenkov—during the first years of the Cold War? What were Nikita Khrushchev's motivations throughout the international crises of 1953–1962? What can explain Khrushchev's inconsistent performance in the international arena and his eccentric escapades in his relations with Western powers? What about the Asian front of the Cold War? Was a split between Khrushchev's USSR and Mao Zedong's China just a clash of personalities, or can it be attributed to fundamentally different approaches by the leadership of the two countries toward key international issues? Should we regard the Sino-Soviet schism simply as a matter of bilateral relations or should we put it into a broad Cold War perspective?

Another major issue concerns the extent to which the Soviet Union wanted the Cold War. Without a doubt the imperial tradition of Russia, reinforced by Marxist globalism, predestined Soviet expansionism. But the Cold War emerged from the ruins of World War II, and this hard fact raises three problems. First, there was the issue of the appropriate rewards for the Soviet contribution to the war. Of paramount importance in Europe and recognized as such by Britain and the United States, the Soviet war effort had almost unimaginable costs. More than twenty-seven million people died—the majority of them young men between the ages of eighteen and thirty, but also women and children. The European sphere of the USSR was devastated by the German war machine. Shouldn't Stalin's leadership expect special treatment from Western powers after such a sacrifice? And how did this expectation affect Soviet relations with the West after 1945—be it concerning economic assistance (generous reparations from Germany, direct American aid) or recognized spheres of influence for the Soviet Union in Europe (each territory—Poland, Hungary, and Czechoslovakia—having been fertilized with Soviet blood)?

Second, given the scale of human and material losses, the Soviet Union, though it had troops almost all over Eurasia from Germany to Manchuria, could not sustain the stress of another war. In this respect, it is hard to imagine that Stalin could have deliberately chosen to pursue brinkmanship with the West. The nuclear disability of the Soviet Union in 1945–1949 also argues for the belief that Stalin's original intention of 1945–1947 was to proceed with some kind of partnership with the West.

Third, there was the issue of complete Soviet cooperation with the United States and Britain during the war. The tension this cooperation often engendered did not preclude a search for solutions and even unilateral concessions on both sides. Stalin disbanded the Comintern in 1943; Roosevelt and Churchill formally recognized the Soviet zone of security in Eastern Europe in 1943–1945.[7] Could Stalin have believed that this intense interaction was to end abruptly as soon as the war was won? Or did this new mode of understanding based upon mutual compromise imply postwar cooperation? Could Stalin—especially given his fascination with the Russian imperial past—envisage some sort of jointly managed system of international relations, not unlike that which followed the Napoleonic Wars? We do have evidence that Stalin identified himself with Alexander I, a victorious emperor and a postwar partner of his wartime allies at the Vienna Congress of 1815.

The Soviet wartime experience did not in itself regulate Stalin's attitude toward the West. There was also the xenophobic nature of Stalin's regime, which had deep roots in the past. Stalin was aware that any openness toward the outside world could mean the seeds of political opposition in the USSR. Russian czarist history taught a lesson from the Napoleonic Wars, after which Russian officers, having seen Europe, did try to abolish autocracy in their own country in the Decembrists' mutiny of 1825.

This book is limited not only in the choice of key leaders and issues discussed but also in its time frame. We have good reasons for bringing our research only up to 1962.[8] There were two distinct phases of the Cold War: first, bipolar brinkmanship; and second, multilateral permanent truce.[9] The Cold War of bipolar brinkmanship had begun amid the blooming linden trees of Berlin in 1948 and ended in the green waters of the Caribbean in 1962. It had expired for two reasons: the Cuban missile crisis had proved the insanity of brinkmanship, and the Sino-Soviet schism had eliminated absolute bipolarity by 1962. The multilateral permanent truce that dominated international relations from 1962 to 1989 provided for a more manageable confrontation that at the same time became more diversified as more nations, including Red China, became independent players.

Every one of Stalin's men discussed here was able to act as a statesman, according to his own ideas and perceptions. The time frame of this book also allows a panoramic view of the Stalinist power elite and enables us to reflect on the shaping of their worldview, under the impact of the milestone events of Soviet history—the Russian Revolution, Stalin's "revolution from above," and finally World War II. Despite the fire and blood of Stalin's purges, his inner circle, from which his successors later emerged, included men representing three generations of the Soviet elite. There was the generation of professional revolutionaries, Bolsheviks, who stormed the skies to put an end to the old world and build the new. This group of believers was represented by Molotov. His is the case of a revolutionary who became a state-builder and later a statesman. Next came the generation of the children of the Russian Revolution. Khrushchev represented its peasant-worker strand. Zhdanov was related to another strand, that of middle-class intelligentsia. Both became ardent Stalinists primarily because they were proud of the Revolution and saw the strong Soviet empire as its justification. Those from the last generation, Stalin's apparatchiks, were Beria and Malenkov. For them not the revolution of 1917 but Stalin's "revolution from above" was a formative experience. They were the cynics of power, not the dreamers. Malenkov reflected an evolution among the post-purges generation of Soviet elites from ideological fervor to techno-bureaucracy, their instincts to build a more harmonious environment out of Stalin's prison for people, to create a less dangerous environment for the Soviet empire. This generation was a direct precursor to the leadership of Leonid Brezhnev, Yuri Andropov, and Konstantin Chernenko.

A book about the Brezhnevites, however, is another story—that of a senile Cold War. It is with the earlier and more virulent Cold War that we must concern ourselves in order to understand the ways in which the Kremlin perceived the world and waged its side of the conflict in the aftermath of World War II.

# 1 Stalin: Revolutionary Potentate

What would Russia have been without me? Not
only Russia, but Europe?

> Russian czar Nicholas I, in Leo Tolstoy's
> *Hadji-Murad*

Stalin in 1945 was second only to Hitler as modern history's greatest
murderer and ruler, if greatness is measured in the destruction of
human lives and the number of territories conquered. His achievements could be matched only by his failures. In just a few years he
decimated the Russian peasantry and built on its bones Europe's
biggest war machine, rivaling that of Nazi Germany. He then viciously
destroyed the commanding core of his army, interfered with the development and production of war technologies, and massacred, in a
frenzy of political and social "cleansing," millions of loyal supporters,
skillful professionals and workers. He divided Eastern Europe with
Hitler, annexing a large part of it with its millions of inhabitants. Then
he got bogged down ignominiously in a war with tiny Finland, and
let himself be taken by surprise by Hitler's armies. During the first
months of World War II he lost three million soldiers and officers, as
well as the most industrially and agriculturally significant territories
of the country.

The Nazis were driven back from Moscow in December 1941, but
in the next year Stalin's autocratic whims triggered another military
catastrophe that brought the Wehrmacht to the river Volga and the
Caucasus. In 1943–1945 the Soviet army turned back the tide, pushed
the nine million German troops and Germany's satellite armies back
to Berlin, and occupied most of Central and Eastern Europe. In

Manchuria the Soviet army, together with the United States, thoroughly defeated a historic rival of Russia in the Far East—imperial Japan. Now the Soviet Union dominated Eurasia just as imperial Russia had after Napoleon's defeat in 1815. The price of these victories was twenty-seven million Soviet lives—a loss from which the Soviet Union would never fully recover.

The Second World War had fully demonstrated the monstrous authority of Stalin. The defeats of 1941–1942 were largely accounted for by his phobia of domestic enemies, which had led to the elimination of the USSR's best military cadres in 1937–1938, and his self-deluding euphoria over the Nazi-Soviet accord. The victories of 1943–1945, which had put an end to Hitler's pan-European invasion, proved that Stalin was able to learn from his mistakes and effectively mobilize state and society to fight to the last drop of blood.

Stalin brought the worst possible calamities on the Soviet people. Yet by the end of his life, Stalin, in the minds of party and state elites, as well as a majority of citizens, became synonymous with the Soviet state—he was considered its architect and savior. Indeed, he built the state as a tool for his own hands; he doubted anyone could manage it properly without him. His personality became the single most significant factor in the decision-making process in the USSR: a guide and a beacon for unwieldy bureaucracies.

Many who met Stalin for the first time during and after World War II were struck by the contrast between the heroic image of him projected by Soviet propaganda and the unassuming physical appearance of the man. Stalin was only five feet four and rather thin. As a child he had sustained an injury and had suffered from smallpox, which together left him with a withered left arm and a pockmarked, blotchy face. The second and third toes of his left foot had grown together. His forehead was rather low, his nose straight, and his sunken hazel eyes yellowed. A perceptive American who saw him in September 1945 compared him to "an old battle-scarred tiger." Stalin's "teeth were discolored, the mustache scrawny, coarse and streaked." He spoke haltingly, with a heavy Georgian accent, the expression on his face alternating between benign calmness and bored inscrutability. He usually wore baggy trousers and a gray, square-cut tunic that hung loosely on his body. In the presence of subordinates who did not belong to his innermost circle he was low-key, pacing soundlessly back and forth in his soft Caucasian boots, smoking or chewing his proverbial pipe, stopping to extract tobacco from cigarettes to fill it. He rarely lost his temper, but there were moments when his yellowish eyes would light up "in a flash of menace and fury," as he turned, briefly, on some unfortunate subordinate. There were other moments of "the diabolical sadism" with which he humiliated his close lieutenants in the presence of foreigners. In a word, Stalin at the end of the war was a quiet, aged, but very dangerous man.[1]

After his victory in the Second World War Stalin felt exhausted and suddenly much older. The burden of years and power became too much for him to bear. By the standards of his native land, Georgia, he was still not very old: he turned seventy-three in December 1952, two months before his death. But he was no longer the man he had been. He complained about his health, and indeed, according to those who served him daily, he increasingly suffered from arthritis, angina, and high blood pressure. During the postwar years Stalin would take a three-month vacation each fall. Then three months turned into four.[2] He did not travel abroad and rarely met any foreigners. Yet this old man in obvious poor health remained in charge. It was he who was pushing the reluctant and tired country to defy the West.

## Stalin's Universe

Stalin was an introvert who carefully guarded his speech and was quick to retreat into himself. This explains why there are so few written accounts by his contemporaries that shed light on his personality. In Stalin's letters to his mother and children there is almost nothing intimate, a total lack of candor and sharing, no thoughts, doubts, or fears. Only in his letters to his wife, Nadia Alliluyeva, did Stalin open up, until her mysterious suicide in 1932 (attributed either to Stalin's womanizing or to disagreements between the two political individuals, or both). "After Nadia's passing," Stalin wrote to his mother, "my personal life, of course, is hard. But it is nothing: a brave man should always be brave."[3] That was very likely the last time he mentioned his personal life to anyone.

Stalin's reticence explains, in part, the remarkable proliferation of interpretations of Stalin the man, the politician, and the statesman in contemporary historiography. Stalin is presented as a traditional, although exceptionally ruthless, tyrant, a devious "National Bolshevik," a realist statesman like Richelieu and Bismarck, a revolutionary leader obsessed with self-aggrandizement.[4] It is not surprising that opinions also differ greatly among Russian historians and writers. The Soviet Marxist school regards Stalin as a traitor to Marxism. Different authors see him variously as a mystical tool of "dark hierarchies," a shaping force of "metahistory," an unscrupulous schemer, a traitor, a neurotic, a follower of Peter the Great, and a real Communist (the latter definition is subject to many interpretations).[5] Probably Stalin had been all of these persons at one time of another. But there was a lodestar that guided him. It was the promise of Communist revolutionary universalism combined with the necessities of survival for the Soviet Union, the first and unique "Socialist" empire. Stalin came closer than anyone in the Soviet leadership from Lenin to Gorbachev to implementing the paradigm that balanced these two goals of Soviet policy effectively and consistently.

A devout believer in ruthless state power, Stalin was a child of the Russian Revolution with its apocalyptic belief in the catastrophic destruction of the old world in purifying flames and the emergence of a new millennium. For Stalin there were always two worlds, not one: his empire, born in the Russian Revolution and representing the Kingdom of Light and the force of the future; and the dying—therefore desperate and aggressive—world outside, against which he wanted to protect it. Any opposition to him from within was perceived as a black threat; any opposition from beyond Soviet borders represented the decadent taint of a passing order.

Today no one would deny that Stalin was the creator of one of the greatest empires in the world, which in its prime stretched from Central Europe to East Asia. But in our age it is necessary to validate the claim that Stalin was a revolutionary—an axiom one would never question half a century ago. The modern mind seeks to separate the monstrous Stalin from the notion of revolution, which still possesses the appeal of idealistic ends and utopian vision: since Stalin killed more former revolutionaries than anyone else, he must be a tyrant, not a revolutionary. There is also a desire to distinguish Stalin from Marxism itself in a futile attempt to preserve the theory from its historical incarnations.

Stalinism, of course, is not equal to Bolshevism or Leninism, as the last two are not equal to Marxism. Ideology is a dynamic phenomenon: new branches develop and others die. The tree originating in Marxism has produced a number of branches, from left-wing totalitarianism to mild and civilized Social Democracy. The Stalinist branch might look alien to the original Marxist root, but nevertheless it was an offshoot of it.

The essence of Marxism's original foreign policy doctrine was very simple: world revolution. Marx and Engels's *Communist Manifesto* (1848) had announced: "The working men have no country . . . National differences and antagonisms between peoples are daily more and more vanishing, owing to the development of the bourgeoisie, to freedom of commerce, to the world market, to uniformity in the model of production and in the conditions of life corresponding thereto . . . The supremacy of the proletariat will cause them to vanish still faster. United action, of the leading civilized countries at least, is one of the first conditions for the emancipation of the proletariat." *The Communist Manifesto* ended with a clear-cut appeal: "Working men of all countries, unite!"[6]

Yet the challenge of surviving in a world ruled by alliances of national power was great. Lenin did not have time to envisage how ideology and geopolitics might be combined: he died in January 1924 after fighting a terminal illness for two agonizing years.

Stalin was the first statesman to grasp the notion that promoting world revolution was not a goal in and of itself, but rather that it provided the rationale for building a strong Soviet Union. Indeed, a strong USSR would signify that the engine of world revolution was still on track. Stalin was determined to forge this double-edged sword of Soviet foreign policy. In 1924 he declared: "Soviet power in Russia is the base, the bulwark, the refuge of the revolutionary movement of the entire world."[7] A year later at the Fourteenth Communist Party Congress Stalin reiterated: "Our country is the base of world revolution."[8] The logic was beyond criticism: if the world revolution was to happen, the Soviet Union must become invincible; in the meantime, ideology, winning souls and space, would strengthen the USSR as a state.

It was this revolutionary-imperial paradigm that the USSR followed consistently from the early 1920s. In those years Stalin's vision of world transformation through the construction of socialism in "one, single state" had millions of admirers and eager recruits outside the Soviet Union. The global proliferation of material goods, profiteering, and capital had caused a counter-reaction. World War I with its staggering and meaningless casualties opened huge cracks in the facade of bourgeois comfort and reason. The war persuaded millions that Western "civilization" was vulnerable, perhaps even in decline. The Great Depression of the 1930s seemed to the Communists like a day of reckoning for "capitalism-imperialism"; this whore of Babylon was to be brought to the court of justice. The Soviets heralded a new dawn for their own country and the world. Lenin was a new Messiah, and Stalin was his star pupil.

Leftist visionaries abroad did not distinguish between the national interests of the Soviet Union and the interests of world revolution. Since the "evil" colonial empires, Britain and France, had spread their influence across the globe, liberation and purgation from imperialism had necessarily to be on a world scale. On October 20, 1928, the Chinese Patriotic League sent a letter to the Soviet People's Commissar of Foreign Affairs: "We would like to have your cooperation and to know how best to overthrow British imperialism in Asia." The aims of the League were to "create a United Asia," to help India, and to defeat the main imperialist power, Britain, wherever possible.[9]

There were more "believers" among Western intellectuals and artistic elites than there were actual card-carrying Communists. Many wrote enthusiastic stories about the "new Soviet civilization." In that milieu Soviet intelligence recruited its best spies. In Britain there were John Cairncross, Anthony Blunt, Donald Maclean, Guy Burgess, and Kim Philby. In the United States an illegal Soviet network in Washington consisted of informants working in various government agencies of the Roosevelt administration. The Soviets acquired important agents even in the OSS, precursor of the CIA.[10]

Without these "friends" Stalin never would have obtained the secrets of the Manhattan atomic project so quickly and efficiently. The lieutenant-general of military intelligence (GRU), Mikhail Milstein, who in 1942–1946 had supervised the North American intelligence network from Mexico to Canada, claimed that "in that period all our intelligence activities . . . relied essentially on the so-called liberal cadres, that is, the ones who sympathized with the Soviet Union . . . Those people regarded the Soviet Union as their second homeland, and worked not for cash, but for the idea [ne za strakh a za sovest]."[11]

Ethel and Julius Rosenberg, Morris and Lona Cohen, and many nuclear physicists who had shuddered at the idea of Hitler's toying with an A-bomb strongly believed that Stalin's possession of nuclear weapons would better guarantee world peace. The French physicist

Frederic Joliot-Curie offered a Soviet ambassador any information on atomic works that he and his friends possessed. His intermediary assured one of Molotov's deputies that "French scientists . . . will always be at your disposal without asking for any information in return."[12]

In sum, the ideological role of Stalin's Soviet Union was accepted by a very wide range of people. This support was one of the essential props of Soviet foreign policy. Even when Stalin betrayed these international sympathizers in 1939, with the Nazi-Soviet pact, and in 1943, with the dissolution of the Comintern, this prop did not collapse. The victory over Nazism had led to an unprecedented increase in the numbers of his—and therefore Soviet and Communist—sympathizers and admirers.

Stalin was the first statesman to direct the energy emanating from Russia's mission to spread socialism throughout the world into the building of a great empire on earth. Imperialism became part of his strategy very early. In 1922, before Stalin was able to play any role in the making of Soviet foreign policy, he defended a more imperial model of the Soviet Union, where every ethnic entity would enjoy "national-cultural autonomy," but not political autonomy. Lenin had called for the building of a union consisting of "independent" republics, with their own governments and parliaments, with borders adjacent to the outside world, and with the right to secede. Stalin would have none of that.

Although Stalin fully expected that communism would prevail over nationalism, as a native of the multiethnic Caucasus he felt it was too risky to create even the semblance of a multinational confederation. Lenin did exactly that, however, by giving the Ukrainians, Byelorussians, Turkmenians, and others the great gift of statehood. Those peoples became by the stroke of a pen "the title nationalities" with their "Soviet Republics" and seats for bureaucrats. Had Stalin prevailed in 1922, the collapse of the Soviet Union in 1991 would probably have been less predictable.

In spite of Stalin's faith in the ultimate triumph of communism, he longed for familiar patterns of state power and expansion. He reached back to the Russian state's early days to find powerful predecessors and mentors for the job of state-building. It was in Ivan the Terrible and Peter the Great that he found the kind of rulers he could respect and whom he could try to surpass. When the Lithuanian foreign minister came to Moscow in 1940 to sign the treaty that put an end to his nation's independence, Stalin took him walking along the corridors of the Kremlin late at night and said, "Here Ivan the Terrible used to walk."[13] Stalin was haunted by the imperial past, and in the last period of his life he identified himself more with the czars than with Lenin. He knew that his empire, like any empire, including Hitler's Reich, required a hierarchy of rank as well as special insignia and decorations. The first Soviet order introduced under Lenin had been the Red Banner Order—a symbol of revolutionary sacrifice and martyrdom in the name of the new millennium. Others of the same revolutionary stripe were established as well, including the highest: the Golden Star of the Hero of the Soviet Union. Stalin, by contrast, restored the old officers' regalia and reintroduced the Russian military pantheon into the Soviet gallery of fame.[14] During World War II he created new orders that he named after the czars' generals and admirals: Alexander Suvorov, the crusader of Europe; Mikhail Kutuzov, who defeated Napoleon through perseverance and the use of Russia's vast territory; Pavel Nakhimov, the hero of the Crimean War and the siege of Sevastopol; Fedor Ushakov, a buccaneer of the anti-Turkish navy campaigns who served under Catherine the Great. Stalin also created the order of Prince Alexander Nevsky, who fought the Teutonic knights in the thirteenth century.

Stalin regarded himself as the founder of the new Soviet empire as well as the heir to the traditional Russian empire. Was this a contradiction in the soul of a true believer? Only a seeming one, for the Marxist ideal was a universal empire and Russia was seen as its core. Stalin wanted to match the power and splendors of the past rulers, the czars—and surpass them. His primary task was to regain the territories lost to Russia during war and revolution from 1915 to 1921: the Baltics, Finland, Poland, and Bessarabia (Moldavia). This goal was virtually fulfilled by the end of 1945: even recalcitrant Finland fell back under the Kremlin's influence.

Never a mystic, Stalin did not believe in Russia's apotheosis as the Third Rome, an appeal of the sixteenth-century monk Phylotheus to Moscow czars to rise above the fate of the fallen empires of the past—Rome and Byzantium—and to become the only Kingdom of Light in Christian civilization. The philosophy of the Kremlin leader was based on a different kind of determinism—materialist faith in the laws of history. Yet Stalin certainly liked the idea of a "special mission" for the Russian people, a concept so dear to the hearts of the Russian intellectuals, and he adapted it to his needs. In 1945, euphoric from military victory, he again ascribed a special mission to the Russians: to be a world power, second to none.[15]

Stalin acted on a larger scale than any czar had, and he was prepared to sacrifice much more than the czars to expand Russia's power. He was determined to accomplish geopolitical tasks that they had pursued, but had been either too weak or too inept to complete. One of his primary tasks was the fulfillment of the eternal Russian dream of acquiring "the Straits," Bosphorus and the Dardanelles, which connected the Black Sea with the Mediterranean and thus Russia with Western Europe. Hence Stalin's refusal to divide Turkey with Hitler in 1940 and his demand for bases in Turkey in 1945. He was also persistent in regaining the Russian sphere of influence in Xinjiang, Outer Mongolia, Manchuria, and Korea, no matter that it meant dealing with the bourgeois and corrupt Chiang Kai-shek government or with Mao's obstreperous Communist leadership.[16]

Stalin did not need access to warm waters and control over new territories to expand trade and increase wealth. The capitalism of the British empire and even the early mercantilism of the Roman empire, with their indirect methods of integrating huge disparate territories, meant little to him. He wanted security, not cohabitation, liquidation of the bourgeoisie, not trade, and this required ultimate and undiluted control over territories and, ipso facto, control over the population, their households and minds. All of Stalin's imperial acquisitions had to be purged of old elites, potential traitors: the more strategically important the place, the more thorough the purge. Anticapitalist ideology, the rationale for purges, was invariably helping Stalin to control the space he conquered.

After the Second World War, someone sent Stalin a small, textbook-sized map of the USSR with its expanded borders as of 1945. Stalin pinned it on a wall at his dacha and began to inspect it carefully. He noted with satisfaction that the new Soviet borders in the north, west, and east offered the geographical security he had sought. "But here I don't like our border!" he said, pointing to the region to the south of the Caucasus. He was indicating the northeastern provinces of Turkey and Iranian Azerbaijan, whose borders he then determined to secure as well.[17]

Stalin's moves in the international arena until the late 1930s were both pragmatic and ideological. The concept of territorial security was the cornerstone of his regime. The pursuit of a balance of power was primary as a means to achieve this aim. Yet, unlike Richelieu and Bismarck, Stalin looked beyond this: he believed that skillful manipulation of the rules of the old world would someday allow him to sweep that world completely away—with its capitalist states and bourgeois civilization. That ultimate goal gave Stalin and his followers in the Soviet state an inimitable sense of self-righteousness and cynical resourcefulness that had already manifested itself during the Kremlin's interference in the civil war in Spain in 1935–1939. Thousands of Soviet troops, along with many volunteers and "true believers" from other countries, came to fight and die on the fields of Catalonia and the streets of Barcelona and Madrid. They saw this war as a battle of the forces of good against the forces of fascism and reaction in Europe, and they praised the Soviet "fraternal assistance" to the republican government against the military-fascist rebels of Franco. But Stalin's emissaries managed simultaneously to covertly ship the gold (valued at 518 million dollars) from the coffers of the Spanish republican government to Moscow, where it was used to cover the expenses of this "selfless aid."[18]

Stalin consistently acted to prevent Germany from aligning itself with the Western democracies against the USSR. He encouraged Hitler to destroy the system of Versailles that the Bolsheviks had always felt was directed against their regime. Then he prevented, in his opinion, a possible collusion between the Nazis, Britain, and France against the USSR, simultaneously gaining much territory in Eastern Europe in 1939–1940. If someone had told Stalin that these policies had helped Hitler unleash the Second World War, he would have smirked through his mustache: his ideology explained that world wars were the result of inter-imperialist contradictions; this explanation exonerated him and his regime of any blame and responsibility in advance.

Stalin's realpolitik was different from Hitler's aggression against his enemies. As a Marxist-Leninist, Stalin firmly believed that the most clever tactics were to let imperialist contradictions run their course and to pit his enemies against each other. When he realized that the British and French "establishments" were pushing Hitler into war against the USSR after the debacle at Munich and the dismemberment of Czechoslovakia, Stalin decided to shift to a friendly neutrality toward Hitler.[19]

This logic almost led to Stalin's downfall. The balance of power between the Allies and the Axis powers in Europe was destroyed, as France unexpectedly fell victim to the Nazi onslaught in May 1940. This upset in the balance of power brought Hitler first to Paris, and then to the gates of Moscow and Stalingrad in 1941–1942. Stalin himself took Hitler's surprise attack on the Soviet Union on June 22, 1941, as a historic and personal fiasco. "Lenin built a great state for us," he told his lieutenants in despair, "and we fucked it up."[20] But he rebounded quickly and began to push the USSR's new ally, Britain, into acceptance of the new Soviet imperial borders—previously accepted and then violated by Hitler![21] Stalin's interests and priorities in foreign policy, guided by his own realpolitik and faith in the collapse of the old world, remained clear and consistent even on the brink of military disaster.

Such was the lodestar that led Stalin. To most observers the leader appeared to be a man perfectly capable of juggling and managing the dual doctrine of proletarian triumph and imperial conquest. He looked calm, cautious, modest, impervious to emotional fits, aware of external realities and constraints. The truth was strikingly different. As so often happens with tyrants, he became self-absorbed and detached from reality. He was surrounded by adulation, half-truths, and artificiality, and the temptation was great to confuse the two suns that occupied his universe, the world revolution and the great Russian empire, with one celestial epicenter—himself. In Leo Tolstoy's novel *Hadji-Murad*, Nicholas I, hegemonic potentate of Eurasia and one of Stalin's predecessors, wonders what Russia and, indeed, Europe, would have been without him.[22] Perhaps Stalin, aging and increasingly in need of appreciation, had similar thoughts. After all, the pockmarked Georgian had more reasons than Nicholas I to put himself mentally at the hub of the world.

## The Mind of the Tyrant

Preservation and expansion of the Soviet Union at any cost were at the heart of Stalin's cruelty and ruthlessness. But shaping and strengthening these objectives was Stalin's dark mind—powerful, willful, suspicious, vindictive. Lenin and other Old Bolsheviks had overlooked, fatally, Stalin's strength. Trotsky even dismissed him as a mediocrity. Maxim Litvinov, Stalin's long-time supporter, ousted from the post of foreign minister in May 1939, lashed out at the Soviet leader for his "narrow-mindedness, smugness, ambitiousness, and rigidity." He condemned Stalin's men: "the half-wit Molotov, the careerists Kaganovich, Mikoyan, Beria, the short-sighted Malenkov, Khrushchev the fool."[23] Historians who would repeat these assessments should bear in mind that intellectual brilliance is optional for a politician; a calculating mind, strong will, and cunning are essential. Stalin brought the Soviet system to its fruition; he followed the logic of absolute power with frightening, almost impeccable precision. The combination of his mind and character was crucial to that success, and therefore we need to inquire more deeply into those forces shaping his unique persona.

Stalin's character contrasted with that of Lenin, his predecessor and teacher. Lenin was a bright, happy child, admired by his well-to-do family. As a member of the provincial elite, he could easily have become a distinguished lawyer, even a prime minister. Stalin, by contrast, was raised in a poor, uneducated family in the isolated little town of Gori in Georgia, a remote colony of czarist Russia. Later Stalin would implicitly deny that Vissarion Djugashvili, the alcoholic town cobbler, was his father. There is unconfirmed evidence that Vissarion abused Joseph and his mother, beating both of them during his drunken bouts. Joseph's visible physical defects must also have haunted him in his youth. He acquired the nickname Koba, an avenger from Georgian literature, ostracized by people, devoid of remorse.[24]

When Stalin was a student at the Tiflis Russian Orthodox Seminary, where his mother sent him to become a priest, he became a closet atheist. (Many would later note, however, that his works were influenced by a distinctly biblical style.) His atheism remained rooted in some vague idea of a God in nature. Stalin once read a book by Anatole France and was particularly impressed by the following line: "If Napoleon had to choose a religion, he would have chosen the adoration of the sun." Stalin had circled the word "sun" and written in the margin, "Good!"[25]

Stalin rejected the national identity of a Georgian and chose to be regarded as a Russian, although he continued to speak Russian with a heavy accent. In the past, empires often willingly adopted and assimilated foreign leaders. Russia had been governed by the Romanov dynasty, whose leaders by the end of the nineteenth century had virtually no Russian blood. But the Romanovs had the legitimacy of an ancient monarchy. Stalin, a parvenu in the Kremlin, had to act more Russian than the Russians.

Many of the great dictators of the twentieth century dabbled in the arts. Hitler was a painter. Mao Zedong composed poetry. Stalin was not artistic, but he was an actor. He was a *litsedei*, a man of many faces, as Khrushchev and others recalled. He could be a charming host, a modest, almost self-effacing Old Bolshevik, a magnanimous pontiff, and a vicious, yellow-eyed tyrant. Stalin, no doubt, nurtured this gift—he lived many lives in different niches. Behind these many personas, however, was a complex, somber man who was never at peace with any of the worlds he helped to create or destroy.

Stalin's identification with great heroes of the past doubtless was crucial to his successful enactment of different personas. The heroes he emulated were Lenin and the Russian czars. To identify himself with Lenin, Stalin would have to surpass the former's revolutionary deeds; to be like the czars, he would need to accomplish unabashed imperial feats. Karen Horney in her classic book *Neurosis and Human Growth* writes that "his [the neurotic's] self-idealization is an attempt to remedy the damage done by lifting himself in his mind above the crude reality of himself and others."[26] And so Stalin performed these acts of self-heroization, both in the international arena and in his own country.

People who knew him only too well, such as his daughter Svetlana Alliluyeva, saw the sharp contrast between his outstanding skills as a statesman—his unique memory, his fast reaction—and his profound discomfort with himself. Svetlana would write about his loneliness, the spiritual vacuum in which he lived, and finally, his "spiritual devastation and bitterness."[27]

At almost every stage of his youth and early revolutionary career Stalin must have felt inferior to those who surrounded him. In comparison with other Bolshevik leaders he lacked sparkling brilliance, be it erudition or a knowledge of foreign languages. He came from a remote non-Russian province of the empire and bore no conspicuous sign of being chosen for leadership. His outstanding qualification manifested itself only after the Revolution was over and it was no longer necessary to appeal to people in an immediate way. Stalin could not captivate crowds, so he learned how to manipulate individuals.

How much knowledge did Stalin have about the world he wanted to turn upside down? Along with some biblical images, he often evoked examples from Russian classical literature. Stalin even quoted Walt Whitman as a precursor to Bolshevik historic optimism: "We love, our crimson blood surges with the fire of our inexhaustible strength."[28] Stalin grasped culture as part of knowledge, and knowledge in his mind accompanied power. He had a stunning capacity for self-education and displayed an impressive command of history and literature. "A voracious reader," as Robert C. Tucker remarked, he studied the history of Russian state-building, of diplomacy, warfare, and past leaders' techniques of absolute rule.[29] In this, Stalin far outranks all his successors, from Khrushchev to Gorbachev.

All his life Stalin remained, probably owing to the inferiority he felt in comparison with the privileged and educated Russian revolutionaries, deeply xenophobic. Lenin, Trotsky, and Bukharin had never displayed a deep hostility to foreigners. They regarded the outside world, from Germany to China, as a battlefield, but they did not fear it as alien. Stalin's brief experiences abroad were negative ones. His trips to London, Stockholm, Cracow, and Vienna to attend party meetings or to see Lenin did not leave him happy. He saw himself as lonely, isolated, surrounded by strangers. He must have envied Lenin, Trotsky, and Bukharin, all of whom felt socially comfortable both in Siberian exile and in a Geneva cafe.

Soviet xenophobia had deep Russian roots, but it also found ground in Stalin's personality. During the Bolshevik trials, orchestrated by Stalin and his lieutenants, the victims were labeled as spies for foreign intelligence services. After the campaign to weed out "the fifth column" of the surrounding capitalist world in Soviet society between 1934 and 1938, Stalin's xenophobia became an institutional pillar of the state. A decade later, in May 1947, Stalin, meeting with a select group of Soviet intellectuals, lashed out at an "unjustified tradition of genuflection before Western culture" among "the mid-level intelligentsia, scientific intelligentsia, university professors, doctors." Educated people, Stalin said, should learn from a plain Russian *mouzhik* how to stop groveling before "every foreign son-of-a-bitch."[30] Those words expressed not only a calculated policy, but also Stalin's deepest feelings of rage against foreigners.

Obscene language was part of the accepted conversational style in the Kremlin's inner circle under Stalin. Crude expressions made the leader more comfortable socially, just as the general unattractiveness of his entourage made him feel better about his own physical shortcomings. Yet crude jokes also helped Stalin rid himself of feelings of inferiority toward the West and Western leaders. In 1891 the Russian painter Ilya E. Repin finished a large painting entitled *The Zaporozhye Cossacks Writing a Letter to the Sultan of Turkey*. The painting was fated to be a great success. It depicted a historical fact: in the seventeenth century, Zaporozhye Cossacks wrote a letter to the Turkish sultan in a style that expressed the bravado of the young, uncouth nation that was proud of its own ignorance and sought to challenge its powerful enemies. The Bolsheviks welcomed the painting and its sentiment, and it became a "masterpiece of Russian art." While negotiating with the British during and after World War II, Stalin, according to Molotov, carried a copy of the Cossacks' letter in his pocket and sometimes showed it to his close lieutenants, commenting, "We screwed up that England!"[31]

Usually Stalin hid his feelings well, but his presumption of animosity toward everything foreign spread down the Soviet bureaucratic pyramid. As a result, a new breed of rigid and rude xenophobic diplomats, imbued with ideological stereotypes, became a major barrier to making friends and influencing people outside the Soviet Union.[32]

Early in his political career Stalin had learned the art of looking at his enemies' cards: during his struggle for power in the 1920s he had secretly tapped the telephone system of the Politburo and eavesdropped on the conversations of his colleagues and rivals.[33] He successfully did the same in his foreign policy. As mentioned earlier, the Soviets' "friends" abroad and intelligence sources in the 1930s and 1940s supplied Stalin with a great amount of information: secret documents, unrecorded conversations, rumors from the governmental circles of London, Paris, Berlin, and later Washington. A KGB veteran recalls that Stalin and Molotov often received information about British-American talks in the 1940s sooner than it could reach the U.S. State Department or the British Foreign Office.[34] There were many cases when Stalin learned the private thoughts of Western leaders and politicians before this thinking became crystallized into policy. During the Teheran and Yalta Conference all conversations between Churchill and Roosevelt were taped, translated, and reported to Stalin daily, according to Beria's son, who participated in one of these operations.[35]

This access to Western "cards" gave Stalin a tremendous advantage in the game of international politics. It let him appear wise and omniscient, almost an oracle to his Kremlin lieutenants and Western partners. Yet it was not the intelligence that led him. On the contrary, it was Stalin's mind that employed and directed the intelligence. According to one knowledgeable KGB source, "We almost never went out looking for information at random. Instead, orders to look for certain specific things would come from above. Stalin . . . badly needed to know exactly what transpired between Churchill and Roosevelt when they met, so our agents abroad were directed to find out at all costs. This highly authoritarian style produced excellent results."[36]

Stalin's dark, cynical nature compelled him to look for similar manifestations in the minds of his Western counterparts. His suspicious character led him astray by ascribing to Western governments the same capacity for conspiring that he attributed to himself and his regime. His superior system of espionage fed Stalin's worst fears. Often those fears were not without foundation: anti-communism had always been a prevailing mood in Great Britain and the United States, and there were always powerful forces and influential individuals bent on weakening and outmaneuvering the USSR. But the problem was that Stalin, driven by suspicion and pessimism, rarely found constructive ways to neutralize those forces and people. More often the methods he chose to react to what he understood as Western ill will tended to reinforce anti-Sovietism abroad. Moreover, Stalin's reactions to the perceived plots of Western statesmen against his regime were so precipitous and so out of proportion that they were seen in the West as unprovoked, aggressive, and threatening. His excellent intelligence network did not help provide him with an inner sense of security and balance. Instead, knowledge added to his sorrow and isolation.

Stalin was enveloped by his isolation. Khrushchev said in his memoirs, "He was depressed by his aloneness and he feared it."[37] In the last years of his life Stalin clung to his minions as if they were all that stood between him and manic depression. Those who accompanied him through long nights at his country house, the Near Dacha in Kuntzevo, never included women. Stag parties were an old Georgian tradition but, unlike Georgian merry feasts, Stalin's dinners were something between post-funeral gatherings and alcoholic bouts.

Even Hitler—a tyrant of equal scale who also suffered from self-imposed isolation—did not feel so alone. Hitler perceived himself as a Wagnerian rebel who possessed the ultimate Truth. No one on earth could appreciate him because his importance transcended mankind's understanding. In Berchtesgaden, in a castle in the mountains, he communicated with the elements and felt at one with them. He might be described as an eagle in a thunderstorm. Stalin, by contrast, was more like an earthworm in constant fear of being stepped on or cut in two.[38]

Although Stalin was a prisoner of his own dark mind, like every human being he sought respect. For him, admiration from party apparatchiks like Molotov and Kaganovich did not count. He saw them as completely inferior, just puppets in his hands. It was to the world leaders abroad whom he looked for respect and under-standing—first to Hitler, then to Roosevelt and Churchill. They con-stituted Stalin's reference group and were all who mattered.[39]

Hitler must have intrigued Stalin most of all. We know that at the end of his life Hitler spoke about the Kremlin master to his close circle with admiration. Indeed, who else but Hitler could understand a leader like Stalin? Interaction with Hitler was acutely personal (who will trick whom?). Stalin almost lost the war and, after his triumph in 1945, did all he could to deny the ghost of Hitler a place in history. He even concealed from the world the remains of the führer's body, found in a bunker in Berlin. Cooperation with the leaders of Britain and the United States helped soothe Stalin's ego, which had been so wounded by Hitler in June 1941. By the end of the war the Big Three behaved almost as a private club, with shared memories and jokes that only they could understand. At last Stalin felt that he had found the company of equals, statesmen who could fully appreciate his political genius. It was an important psychological motive that pushed him in the direction of postwar cooperation.

The feeling of comfort, however, was never complete, for in order to achieve it, Stalin had to prove his superiority to himself and every-one else. In realpolitik terms Stalin regarded his partners as serious imperialist rivals. In 1944, pointing to the map of the Soviet Union, Stalin said, "They will never accept the idea that so great a space should be red, never, never!" Before his subordinates, he engaged in diminution of his opponents: "Churchill is the kind who, if you don't watch him, will slip a penny out of your pocket. Yes, a penny out of your pocket! . . . And Roosevelt? Roosevelt is not like that. He dips his hand in only for bigger coins."[40]

As long as the Alliance lasted, Stalin believed he could outsmart Western leaders and continue the redistribution of the spheres of influence—with the penny-pinching Churchill in particular. Molotov later commented with dry satisfaction: "Roosevelt . . . believed that they were so rich, and we were so poor, and would be so weakened [after the war], that we would come [begging for assistance]. But they miscalculated. They were not Marxists like us. When half of Europe abandoned them, they woke up. And Churchill found himself then in a quandary."[41]

Nineteen forty-five was a special moment in Stalin's life—even more important than 1939, when he celebrated his triumph over all his domestic opponents and expanded the western boundaries of the USSR after the pact with Hitler. At that time Stalin's victories were overshadowed by the gathering clouds of world war. But 1945 was a perfect time for pure, unmitigated catharsis. For any individual the shift from a time of great peril and tension to a moment of victory and relaxation is mentally and physically trying. Indeed, Stalin, at the peak of his career, was at the point of collapse. Svetlana, his only daughter, who saw him in August 1945 after a long separation, was struck by his haggard, worn look. Even Molotov admitted later that "Stalin . . . was overly tired."[42] A statesman in his condition generally either retires or delegates responsibility for world affairs to trusted subordinates and younger assistants. Stalin did neither. More than anything else he feared and loathed becoming irrelevant, like Lenin had during his illness in 1922–1924.

Marshal Georgi Zhukov, who led Soviet troops into Berlin, recalled that in June 1945 Stalin ordered him to open a Victory Parade on Red Square, riding a white horse. Zhukov fulfilled this mission with dignity. For Joseph Stalin, who watched the Nazi banners being thrown at the foot of Lenin's Tomb as well as at his own feet, it was the most triumphant moment of his life. Yet, as Zhukov learned from Stalin's son Vassily, the old man had wanted to open the parade himself. One night in the Kremlin he had tried to mount the horse but was unsuccessful. The story, whether true or not, implied the question: Was the emperor so old and exhausted that he was forced to leave the fruits of his triumph to others?[43]

During a huge banquet after the parade in St. George Hall in the Kremlin, surrounded by his marshals and commissars, Stalin raised his famous toast "to the health of the Russian people." He praised the legions of "screws"—average people "without whom all of us, marshals and commanders of fronts and armies . . . would not be worth a damn." Stalin never let words slip by chance. What he meant was that he appropriated the victory, every bit of it, to himself alone. He was not going to share his glory with the new Soviet elites who had risen to prominence during and after the purges of the 1930s, especially the military top brass and the captains of the military industries.[44] In 1946, to reinforce his dismissal of military leadership, Stalin had Zhukov framed and sent into semi-exile in Odessa, on the Black Sea. The Kremlin hermit clearly regarded the marshal's popularity as a war hero as an intolerable threat to his own glory, which could not be shared.

On June 27 Stalin received the title of Generalissimo. In mid-July he was making a triumphal trip on his armored train to a conference of the Big Three at Potsdam. The curtains of Stalin's car were drawn tightly. If he had looked out a window, he would have gotten a sense of how devastated the Soviet Union was and what a mad arrogance it would be to pit it against the prosperous and invulnerable United States. Even without this view, he knew only too well the price the USSR had paid for its victory and the Soviet contribution to the cause of the Allies. After the conference in Teheran in 1943, Stalin had stopped in Stalingrad and inspected its ruins. Going to Potsdam, Stalin had two ideas in mind: a new war should be prevented, and the Soviet Union should get its rightful share of the spheres of influence, that is, the outer belt of security. The United States and Great Britain had to pay for the enormous Soviet war effort.

## On the Threshold of Peace

Andrei Gromyko, the Soviet ambassador to Washington in 1943–1945, recalled, in confidential conversations with a long-time associate, that Stalin at the time of the conference in Dumbarton Oaks in September 1944 "had been definitely oriented toward a long postwar cooperation with the West, particularly with the United States."[45] During the last period of the war Stalin felt exhilaration, even euphoria. He thought of himself more as a victorious emperor than as Lenin's disciple—the closest he came to discarding the revolutionary-imperial paradigm. "After the defeat of Hitler," Khrushchev recalled, "Stalin believed he was in the same position as Alexander I after the defeat of Napoleon—that he could dictate the rules for all of Europe."[46] To a question of Averell Harriman about how it felt to divide Berlin only several years after the Germans had been standing at the walls of Moscow, Stalin replied, "Czar Alexander reached Paris."[47] Perhaps at that moment he was also thinking that at this conference Churchill could be another Clemens von Metternich at the Congress of Vienna in 1815.

New documents from the Soviet archives shed light on the options that continued cooperation with the West would have opened to Stalin's foreign policy. In late 1943 Stalin appointed Ivan Maisky and Maxim Litvinov—survivors of the earlier school of Soviet diplomacy and deputies of Molotov in the Commissariat of Foreign Affairs— heads of two special commissions: one on postwar reparations and the other on postwar peace treaties. Stalin removed both of them from practical diplomacy with London and Washington, which he considered to be his personal territory and shared only with Molotov. Litvinov in particular found himself in limbo after Molotov replaced him as foreign minister in 1939. A crusty Old Bolshevik and a Jew, Litvinov openly hated the rigidity and xenophobia (with a tinge of anti-Semitism) of the Stalin-Molotov diplomacy.[48] But once he was in Moscow under close surveillance, Stalin let him display his remarkable erudition in classified essays on the shape of the world and on Soviet interests after the war. Initially Litvinov proposed the creation of a large state committee to assess postwar strategies, headed by Molotov, which would have included Andrei Zhdanov, Anastas Mikoyan, Nikolai Shvernik (chairman of the state commission to investigate the damage done by the German invaders in the USSR), and Marshal Alexander Vassilevsky (head of the General Staff). Stalin did not support an effort of that magnitude, and reduced it to a much more modest form.[49]

Maisky and Litvinov began to discuss the postwar world in their cables from London and Washington earlier in 1943. In January 1944 Maisky summarized the first part of the discussion in a long, semiformal letter to Molotov, who read it and passed it on to Stalin and other Politburo members. Maisky wrote that the main Soviet goal after the war would be to ensure a durable peace, enough for the USSR "to become so powerful" that "no combination of powers in Europe or in Asia could even think" of threatening her. That would require, in Maisky's calculations, "about ten years for the healing of the wounds inflicted by war." More years, "thirty minimum, fifty maximum," would be necessary for Europe, at least on the Continent, "to become Socialist, thereby excluding the very possibility of a war on that part of the globe."

This goal dictated specific guidelines. First, the "borders of 1941" in the West, obtained through the Nazi-Soviet pact, had to be confirmed and, if possible, improved. Southern Sakhalin and the Kurile islands were to be annexed from Japan. Air and naval bases, as well as access to strategic routes, were to be obtained in Finland, Rumania, and the Turkish straits, via Iran to the Persian Gulf. Second, Germany had to be reduced to impotence, and the resurgence of France had to be prevented, so that the USSR would remain "the only great land power" in Eurasia. Third, in the interests of the USSR, "the state organization" of most countries after the war "should be based on the principles of broad democracy in the spirit of the ideas of the Popular Front." According to Maisky, some countries, such as Norway, Denmark, the Netherlands, Belgium, France, and Czechoslovakia, were ready for that. Other countries, such as Germany, Italy, Japan, Hungary, Rumania, Finland, Bulgaria, Poland, Yugoslavia, Greece, and Albania, would need all kinds of external inducements from the USSR, the United States, and Britain. The USSR would then become "a center of gravity for all truly democratic medium-sized and small countries, particularly in Europe."[50]

The letter is a remarkable document on the terms of Pax Sovietica in the postwar world. Yet it is imbued with the idea of a "breathing spell" between the cycles of war and revolution that was so typical of the Old Bolshevik elite. Great Britain, wrote Maisky in January 1944, was a country of "conservative imperialism" in slow retreat. The main threat to its interests after the war would come from "the dynamic imperialism" of the United States, which would challenge the privileged position of Britain in its colonies and world trade. Indeed, "The world situation in the postwar epoch will be colored by Anglo-American contradictions." To be sure, British diplomacy would try "to play the American card against the USSR and the Soviet card against the United States." But eventually "interests in the struggle for global positions will push Britain to the Soviet side." Maisky insisted that the basis of the "probable and desirable foreign policy" of the USSR would be "strengthened friendship with the United States and England."[51] He proposed that the Kremlin play a balance-of-power game between Washington and London. This was a realpolitik recipe borrowed from the Great Britain of Disraeli and the Germany of Bismarck, adapted to Soviet interests.

Litvinov, in his reports to Molotov, argued even more strongly for the possibility of cooperation. In July 1944 he wrote that "after the war an anti-Soviet bloc will be emerging around the former capitalist Allies." Should the Soviets "cooperate with [the Allies] or break off ties altogether?" His answer was: "We must seek some kind of cooperation, in order to have at least a few decades of peace."[52] Litvinov placed much hope in the apparent interest of pragmatic Western policy-makers in "a division of security zones." "One would imagine," he wrote, "that the United States would be mostly responsible for the security of the countries on the American continent and a certain part of the Pacific and Atlantic oceans." Among the supporters of this approach Litvinov named Churchill, and in the United States, Henry Wallace and Walter Lippmann.[53]

In November 1944, soon after Churchill offered Stalin "a percentage agreement" on southeastern Europe and the Balkans, Litvinov, probably not even knowing about this deal, described to Molotov a "maximum sphere of interests" that the Soviet Union should claim after the war. It included Finland, Sweden, Poland, Hungary, Czechoslovakia, Rumania, "Slav countries of the Balkan peninsula, and Turkey as well." Litvinov believed not only that Great Britain would eventually swallow these Soviet demands, but that a division of spheres of influence in Europe between the two powers—in the absence of the third—was inevitable. To avoid a clash, he suggested a zone of disengagement that included Norway, Denmark, Austria, and Italy. In this scheme the United States would have no role to play in Europe.[54]

In any future international security organization Litvinov advocated the creation of a great power club, or council, to serve as its core. For him veto power in the council would be an effective obstacle to decisions going "against the will of the USSR," a barrier to the lingering "hostility of capitalist countries."[55]

The recommendations of Maisky and Litvinov were remarkably free of Marxist-Leninist dictates. Litvinov completely omitted them. Maisky admitted that "proletarian revolutions" in Europe would lead to tense relations, even confrontation, between the USSR and the two capitalist powers. Of course, a "real proletarian revolution" in

Germany would have been a radical solution for Soviet security concerns in Europe, but if that were impossible, cooperation with the Allies would be preferable to clashing with them on ideological grounds.[56]

Advocacy for the partnership around and inside the Kremlin was boosted by the realization that the USSR had suffered grave losses in the war. In July 1944 the Emergency State Commission headed by Nikolai Shvernik put a preliminary damage figure at 375 billion rubles, not including damages to a large portion of Ukraine, Byelorussia, the Baltic countries, and the Finnish Karelia. The Maisky commission assessed that the overall damage "must be no less than 700–800 billion rubles." "Our direct material losses," commented Maisky, "surpass the national wealth of England or Germany and constitute one-third of the overall national wealth of the United States." On September 6, 1944, the chairman of the State Planning Committee (Gosplan), Nikolai Voznesensky, reported to Stalin and Molotov that the direct war losses, along with the indirect damages of war (decline of peacetime production and the costs of waging the war), amounted to 3,047 billion 1941 rubles—four times more than Maisky's estimate. In July 1944 Stalin received another memorandum from Maisky in which the head of the reparations commission argued that the amount of reparations should not be determined from this latter calculation, and suggested that one should speak at international forums only about direct damages. He insisted that $15–17 billion in reparations from Germany and its satellites would be the maximum amount the Western allies would agree to. Stalin, however, initially wanted to demand $5 billion. After Maisky argued that this figure would be too small for negotiating purposes, Stalin decided on $10 billion and proposed that amount in Yalta. Molotov recalled later that reparations were extremely important in the plans of the Kremlin, but admitted that they could not come close to covering Soviet economic needs: "We collected reparations after the war, but they amounted to a pittance." In fact, the Soviets expected to get much more unilaterally, in the form of forced labor and the dismantlement of German industries. Maisky, for instance, thought that five million Germans, if they were to work at Soviet plants for ten years, could contribute about $35–40 billion to the Soviet economy.[57]

Maisky strongly argued in 1944 that the economic power of the United States could be of great assistance to the Soviet Union, should the wartime cooperation continue. "The United States and England," he wrote, "could be a crucial source of assistance to the postwar rehabilitation of our national economy." Maisky even considered U.S. and British assistance to be one of the three principal sources for the rehabilitation of the Soviet economy, along with "our own resources" and reparations. If, however, "in the distant future" a conflict should spring up between the USSR and the United States, "America would be able to create serious problems for the USSR. For instance, it would employ various means to resurrect Germany and Japan."[58]

"It was to our benefit to stay allied with America," recalled Molotov, reflecting the spirit of the Kremlin in those days.[59] In January 1945 Molotov presented to the U.S. government a request for a $6 billion loan for postwar reconstruction. In Potsdam Stalin avoided antagonizing the United States over the issue of German reparations and, although he was not satisfied, went along with the compromise suggested by Secretary of State James Byrnes. Much of the advice tendered by Maisky and Litvinov reflected common sense, realistic estimates of Soviet interests and needs, and Stalin used it in his discussion of the world settlement at Yalta and Potsdam. His subsequent actions and attitudes toward France, Turkey, Greece, Iran, China, and Japan were often in tune with the memorandums of the two strategists.

In February 1945, in the Palace of Livadia at Yalta, the Western Allies did something that millions of people, including thousands of politicians and dozens of historians in the West, would for decades after regret and criticize: they acknowledged that the enormous Soviet sacrifices and successes in the war entitled the Soviet Union to a preeminent role in Eastern Europe. This was reflected in a number of key decisions that during the Cold War would be called "the treason of Yalta" or the "Yalta agreements." The Western Allies recognized the Soviet-made Provisional Government of National Unity in Poland on the condition that some members of the government-in-exile in London and of the Polish Home Army underground be added to it, and that free and unfettered elections take place as soon as possible. Roosevelt and Churchill also agreed to Stalin's plans to move Poland eastward by annexing the lands up to the Curzon line and compensating the Poles with Germany's Eastern Silesia, part of Saxony, and Western Prussia. This meant that Eastern Prussia would belong to the Soviet Union, a new geopolitical fact that Stalin confirmed later at

Potsdam. Even before the Soviet leader promised to join the fighting in the Far East, he found that the Western leaders supported his interest in long-sought spheres of influence there. The Yalta Conference advocated the status quo in Outer Mongolia, thus leaving it within the Soviet domain and outside China. When U.S. Ambassador Harriman asked Stalin what he wanted in exchange for Russia's entry in the war against Japan, Stalin brought out a map and said that "the Kurile Islands and the lower Sakhalin should be returned to Russia." He then "drew a line around the southern part of the Liaotung Peninsula, including Port Arthur and Dairen, saying that the Russians wished again [as before 1905] to lease these ports and the surrounding area." Roosevelt and Churchill complied with these demands as well.[60]

In expectation of this moment Stalin refrained from promoting revolutionary Marxist-oriented movements or unilateral expansion. The commitments to Soviet security interests that he extracted from the Allies in Teheran and especially Yalta for some time looked to him to be the surest way to create a protective territorial belt around the USSR, to neutralize the resurgence of its traditional geopolitical rivals, Germany and Japan. The USSR had to digest its territorial and geopolitical gains and heal its terrible wounds. Stalin, when he analyzed the world in terms of the last interwar period (1918–1939), had ample reason to expect that there would be a protracted period of "capitalist stabilization," a return of the United States to isolationism, and a struggle of European powers for preservation of their vast imperial possessions. Thus a number of considerations led him to believe after V-Day in Europe that some mode of cooperation with the United States and Great Britain could be imaginable after the war as well.

The empirical evidence confirmed for Stalin that his country had been fully recognized as a partner in managing the world. The diplomacy of the Grand Alliance of the war years seemed to have started a new chapter in international relations. The Soviet Union had been accepted as a great power, equaled only by the United States and Great Britain. This equality manifested itself in the Soviet Union's full participation in preparing the outlines for the postwar world. The Big Three were steadily coming to a mutual understanding on spheres of influence in Europe and Asia. The territories annexed by Stalin in 1939–1940 during his alliance with Hitler were recognized de facto as part of the Soviet Union. Later, in the Cold War days, the United

States would insist that it had never recognized the incorporation of the Baltics into the USSR. In 1943–1945, during the Big Three meetings, however, the three leaders and their foreign ministers had spent hours discussing the problem of elections in Poland and of the legitimacy of the Poles' "London" government, but the issue of free elections in Estonia, Latvia, and Lithuania was tacitly omitted.

As for the countries of Eastern Europe, the Allies were step by step agreeing to the introduction of Soviet influence there. These countries were not supposed to be Sovietized, but Churchill did agree with Stalin on the percentage of influence that the USSR and Britain should get in each country in Eastern Europe. The Polish issue had been the most acute one and did cause quarrels and antagonisms among the Big Three. But in Yalta and Potsdam, London and Washington were supporting the "London Poles" with much less vigor than in 1944.[61]

Even the United Nations, which was created by the Big Three, met Stalin's expectations. The permanent members of the Security Council, where the United States, the USSR, and Great Britain were to dominate (for France was hardly tolerated as a great power and China was infinitely weak), would form the elite club for managing the globe. In late 1944 to early 1945 Stalin took the task of organizing the United Nations as seriously as did Litvinov. To ensure that the U.N. Security Council would, in fact, be a club of great powers, Stalin did much to see that the United States would not stay out. With Stalin's blessing, Molotov and another Soviet diplomat, Dmitry Manuilsky, cooperated with the American drafters on the U.N. Charter—which became for decades a model document in the Wilsonian tradition. To the same end the Kremlin leader also supported New York over Geneva, Vienna, or Prague as the future headquarters of the United Nations, because he wanted the United States to be actively engaged in a future organization of united nations. Simultaneously, Stalin persistently sought and, to his satisfaction, obtained the agreement of Roosevelt and Churchill to grant the Soviet Union veto power in the U.N. Security Council.[62]

By 1945 one could find some rudiments of the revolutionary-imperial paradigm in Stalin's foreign policy, but he was fully prepared to shelve ideology, at least for a time, and adhere only to the concept of a balance of power. Stalin ardently believed in the inevitability of a postwar economic crisis of the capitalist economy and of clashes within the capitalist camp that would provide him with a lot of space for geopolitical maneuvering in Europe and Asia—all within the framework of general cooperation with capitalist countries.

Yet just one year after Yalta, in his first postwar speech in the Bolshoi Theater, on February 9, 1946, Stalin emphasized the importance of ensuring Soviet security unilaterally—through renewed mobilization of domestic resources, belt-tightening, and rearmament. There was only a dying echo of the early hopes for a possible model of peaceful coexistence. He said, "It might be possible to avoid military catastrophes, if there were a way of periodically reapportioning raw materials and markets among the countries according to their economic weight—taking concerted and peaceful decisions." But, he added, "this is impossible to fulfill in the contemporary capitalist conditions of world economic development."[63]

Stalin meant a possible settlement of disputes among the great powers through the redistribution of spheres of influence, but he could not be that explicit. This was the part of his "election" speech addressed to party functionaries, and thus Stalin's point went totally unnoticed. The American embassy in its report on the speech omitted this point completely.[64] George Kennan wrote his famous "long telegram" explaining to officials in the Truman administration that it would be simply impossible to find a modus vivendi with the USSR, the revolutionary heir to the security-obsessed czarist Russia. In another message Kennan wrote, "That suspicion in one degree or another is an integral part of [the] Soviet system, and will not yield entirely to any form of rational persuasion or assurance." From that moment many in the United States regarded Stalin's speech as the declaration of the Cold War.[65]

# 2 Stalin and Shattered Peace

Mao Zedong (commenting on a future Sino-Soviet treaty): But will it interfere with the decisions of the Yalta Conference?

Stalin: To hell with that! If we make a decision to revise treaties, we must go all the way. True, we will have to struggle against the Americans, but we have already reconciled ourselves to that fact.

Stalin-Mao talks in the Kremlin,
January 22, 1950

The shift in Stalin's attitude toward postwar cooperation in 1945–1946 can be attributed in part to his "deep and morbid obsessions and compulsions," which had lain dormant for a while but eventually pushed him to guarantee Soviet security in expectation of the total collapse of relations between the USSR and the Western democracies. These compulsions were of immense international significance, since the power to dictate Soviet foreign policy—and domestic policy as well—belonged to Stalin alone.[1]

One such compulsion was to retain his totalitarian control over the state and society once the war was over. Stalin, reflected the Soviet writer Konstantin Simonov, had "feared a new Decembrism. He had shown Ivan to Europe and Europe to Ivan, as Alexander I did in 1813–1814."[2] Indeed, many Soviet soldiers who participated in the liberation of Europe were appalled at how poorly the standard of living in the Soviet Union compared with that of Europe. Many veterans no longer feared the Soviet secret police and would not be silenced. Some, according to an NKVD (secret police) report to Stalin on January 27, 1946, made anti-Soviet remarks, clashed with local authorities, and even distributed anti-Soviet leaflets.[3]

Stalin, true to form, moved to eradicate this mood before it could develop into even the slightest threat to his power. Upon their return, millions of the Soviets who had stayed abroad, as prisoners of war or in the forces of European resistance groups, were screened—some were eventually shot, and others were sent to the Gulag to be cleansed of any European influence. All this was done when the "popular" legitimacy of Stalin's regime was at its peak, and when, for quite a few Soviet citizens, patriotism and preoccupation with Truman's America, armed with the atomic bomb, overshadowed the frustrations of everyday life.[4]

Another of Stalin's compulsions was his deep suspicion of the motives of the Western Allies. Stalin, as the Yugoslav Communist Milovan Djilas has noted, feared that "the imperialists" would never tolerate great Soviet advances during the war. As pleased as he was with the outcome of Yalta and Potsdam, he looked forward to the struggle ahead. Stalin's remarks in his private conversations with Georgi Dimitrov, a trusted leader of the Comintern, betrayed the ambiguity of his feelings. In January 1945 he told Dimitrov: "The crisis of capitalism revealed itself in the division of capitalists into two factions—one fascist, the other democratic . . . Now we side with one faction against the other, and in the future [we will also turn] against this faction of capitalists." In August he expressed to Dimitrov his satisfaction with Potsdam: "In general these decisions are beneficial to us . . . [Bulgaria] has been recognized as within our sphere of influence."[5] Stalin had decided that certain spheres of influence had to be secured by the Soviets before the Western democracies turned against Moscow.

Stalin's ambivalence seemed increasingly sinister from the Western perspective, and Washington and London began to look at the Soviet expansion sanctioned at Yalta and Potsdam in a completely different light. On June 18, 1946, Maxim Litvinov met with the CBS correspondent Richard C. Hottelet in his office, which was tapped by the Soviet secret police. Litvinov said there was nothing one could do to change the course of Soviet foreign policy. He said that the Soviet leadership had made some wrong decisions and, of the two possible paths toward building a postwar peace, the wrong one had been chosen: "the outmoded concept of security in terms of territory—the more you've got the safer you are." No Western concessions would satisfy the Soviet leadership. Litvinov concluded: "I now feel that the best that can be hoped for is a prolonged armed truce."[6]

President Truman put the minutes of the meeting in his safe, prohibiting anyone else from seeing them. But his precautions, as it turned out, were in vain. The Soviet secret service taped the conversation and informed the Kremlin about it. "Litvinov stayed alive by chance," Molotov recalled. Stalin knew that Litvinov's death would "create an international scandal, complicating relations with the Allies."[7]

Was there an alternative means to postwar collaboration that Stalin and Molotov discarded, and that could possibly have led "to more cooperative relations with the United States?"[8] Litvinov's words should be treated with caution. He was not a Cassandra, this old crusty man with great ambitions who was totally excluded from the greatest diplomatic game of the century. At no point did Stalin's demands and ambitions in 1945–1946 exceed the maximum zone of responsibility discussed by Litvinov and Maisky in their memorandums. In fact, in some cases Stalin's moves in the international arena were more modest in scope than those suggested by Litvinov. Litvinov was never a proponent of concessions to the West, particularly in Eastern Europe. The historian Voitech Mastny is correct when he says that, in principle, "there was no quarrel between Litvinov and Stalin, both ardent devotees of power politics."[9]

True, Stalin and Molotov neglected important factors in making foreign policy decisions, particularly Western public opinion, about which the diplomats of the older school tried to warn them. But Litvinov and Maisky, in their geopolitical fantasies, also missed many other important realities that greatly complicated Stalin's relations with Western leaders after the war. Litvinov's proposal of a "neutrality belt" from Norway to Italy, in combination with the dismemberment of Germany, if adopted, could have led to an even greater power vacuum in Europe that would arouse fears and competition between the East and the West.[10]

Litvinov, as well as most observers, failed to foresee the nature and direction of America's postwar involvement in the world. In fact, his knowledge of the United States led him to the incorrect assumption that Washington might return to isolationism and withdraw from international organizations. He seemed to think that it would be much easier for the USSR and Great Britain to come to an "amicable agreement" about the European settlement if the moralistic and expansionist United States would not interfere.[11]

The key difference between Litvinov and Stalin was to be found, however, in their reactions to the Allies in the postwar period. The sophisticated diplomat Litvinov believed that the Soviet leadership was making a fatal mistake by grabbing what it could instead of preserving the atmosphere of trust and authority established by the Soviets during the war against Hitler. Stalin, driven by his dark foreboding and suspicions, and picking the worst signals from his far-reaching intelligence networks, believed that a policy of partnership with the West had no future. He still did not want confrontation with his former allies, but he did not know how to avoid it.

Two events dramatically altered Stalin's view of the diplomatic landscape and loosed his demons of suspicion: the first was the death of Roosevelt; the second was America's dropping of the A-bomb on Hiroshima.

When Stalin had hoped to encourage London and Washington to resolve recurrent tensions by "redistributing spheres of influence," his dream partner had been Franklin D. Roosevelt. William Taubman correctly sees Roosevelt's death as "a turning point in Soviet-American relations," but fails to appreciate how important Roosevelt was to the Soviet dictator.[12] He was the only president whom Stalin accepted as a partner, even when he felt that FDR was scheming behind his back. In April 1945, when Soviet intelligence informed Stalin of Nazi attempts to conclude a separate peace with the Americans, his faith in the possibility of a partnership with the West was not shaken.[13] As long as the two Western leaders did not, in Stalin's opinion, "gang up" on him, there remained the chance for an international regime of cooperation.

When Roosevelt died and Churchill was not reelected—a total surprise to the Kremlin—Stalin lost his two equals, the opponents with whom he knew he could play a grand game with a good chance of success. There was no longer a common threat or the great cauldron of European war to forge a strong relationship of equals between Stalin and the new Western politicians. Truman, James Byrnes, Clement Attlee, and Ernest Bevin were obviously not powerful enough (and probably also not cynical enough) for Stalin's game. In a matter of months what looked like a classic trilateral diplomacy deteriorated before Stalin's eyes into a hopeless international morass, where many expectations were swept aside by a host of new faces and factors.[14] This must have been stunning to Stalin, who was used to dealing with a maximum of three players. During the party infighting of 1923– 1929 it was Stalin and the Kamenev-Zinoviev group against Trotsky, then Stalin and Bukharin against Kamenev-Zinoviev. This pattern of very few players had continued in the international arena in 1939– 1944.[15] Now all was changed.

Truman in particular seemed to be an unknown entity: a rookie president was easy prey for crafty manipulators. Yet Stalin did not abandon his hopes for a grand game or "détente." He tested Truman at Potsdam and, after hard bargaining, "got what [he] wanted" on two key issues: reparations from Germany and the future of Poland. Many years later Molotov admitted that, at that moment, "the Americans provided us with a way out that reduced tension between us and our Western allies."[16] Yet this was not to be.

It was the atomic bombardment of Japan and the abrupt end of the war in the Pacific that convinced Stalin that his dream of a postwar partnership was not to be fulfilled. The old demons of insecurity were back. The atomic bomb threw the Kremlin leader off balance—and eventually back into the curse of tyrants: neurotic solitude.

## The Bomb

After the American bombing of Japan, Stalin told the managers of a future Soviet atomic complex: "Hiroshima has shaken the whole world. The balance has been broken. Build the Bomb—it will remove the great danger from us."[17] This appeal from Stalin is reminiscent of his plea to Soviet "brothers and sisters" in the wake of Hitler's attack on the Soviet Union. David Holloway's understanding of Stalin's "atomic" logic concludes that before Potsdam, and perhaps even Hiroshima, "neither Stalin, Beria, nor Molotov understood the role that the atomic bomb would soon play in international relations." Like the German attack in June 1941, "the atomic bomb also caught Stalin by surprise, in spite of the detailed intelligence the Soviet Union had obtained about the Manhattan project."[18]

For all the new research and evidence, it is still not clear why the shrewd and well-informed dictator had missed the tremendous potential of the "super weapon." Some possible reasons are masterfully discussed by Holloway: Stalin mistrusted Soviet scientists and their "fantasies"; he was under enormous pressure from the war with Germany, and only those projects that helped to win the war gained top priority with him; and he and his chief of security policy, Beria, suspected that much of the intelligence on the Manhattan project could be "disinformation."[19]

Stalin, like Hitler, was suspicious of projects that did not promise fast returns. Indifferent to the loss of human lives (the Red Army had suffered appalling and unnecessary casualties even in the final battles of the war), he saved the state's money with the greed of Shylock.[20] But also, perhaps, the Kremlin leader hoped to win the war and secure the gains of peace before the mysterious uranium bomb was built. After Yalta, on February 28, 1945, Vladimir Merkulov, the commissar of the Ministry of State Security (NKGB), reported to Beria (who briefed Stalin): "No time-frame of any certainty is available for the production of the first bomb, since research or design work has not been completed. It is suggested that the production of such a bomb will require one year at least and five years at most." The first report about an imminent atomic test reached Stalin just as he was leaving for Potsdam.[21]

Had Stalin entrusted his feelings to a diary, he would have filled the whole page of August 6 with profanities, directed at the Americans in general, and Truman in particular. The Bomb was dropped on the Japanese city of Hiroshima at the worst possible moment: the Kremlin leader was in the midst of tough bargaining with the Allies. "Stalin had his doubts about whether the Americans would keep their word," recalled Nikita Khrushchev later. "What if Japan capitulated before we entered the war? The Americans might say, we don't owe you anything." Holloway cites this as evidence that Stalin feared the Americans and the British would "renege on the Yalta agreement," which was contingent on Soviet participation in the war.[22] This is another sign that the dictator was still inclined to maintain a quid pro quo relationship with Western allies.

Stalin had to be equally concerned about the future of his conquests in the East. He contemplated a Blitzkrieg against Japan that would ensure for the Soviet Union a zone of security in Outer Mongolia, Manchuria, North Korea, and perhaps even Northern Japan. The best guarantee for this was the impressive force of the Red Army. Two sea powers, Great Britain and the United States, stood no chance against the USSR as the only remaining land power. In his January 1944 letter to the Kremlin leadership, Maisky defined this as one of the most significant outcomes of the Second World War. "Two oceans," he wrote, "lie between the USSR and the United States, which make our country relatively invulnerable to American aviation (at least during the first postwar period)." (Of course, Americans could promote "the resurgence of Germany and Japan," but this was a distant threat.)[23] Maisky was actually referring to the well-known geopolitical concept of oceanic versus land nations, stressing that the geographical separation, given the current level of technology, provided for the USSR's security, with the oceans serving as a Great Divide. He knew nothing about the Bomb already on its way.

In August 1945, however, the Americans vividly demonstrated to Stalin and many Russians that they could threaten the Soviet Union in the not-so-distant future. From bases in Europe and the Middle East, the U.S. Air Force, armed with atomic bombs, could reach and destroy vital centers of the Soviet Union. It did not take much imagination to understand that further military progress would make Stalin's vast empire vulnerable to a devastating surprise attack from the air.

On August 6, Svetlana Alliluyeva recalled later, the "usual visitors" (Beria, Malenkov, Molotov, and so on) came to Stalin's dacha and told her father that the Americans had dropped a bomb on Hiroshima. Three months earlier Svetlana had had a baby—Stalin's first grandson. But on this day Grandfather Joseph hardly listened to her: "everybody was preoccupied" with the news of the atomic blast. Yuli Khariton, one of the creators of the first Soviet atomic bomb, today starkly describes the mood of that day: "The Soviet government interpreted [Hiroshima] as atomic blackmail against the USSR, as a threat to unleash a new, even more terrible and devastating war."[24]

Two days later Stalin and Molotov received Averell Harriman and George Kennan. Since Potsdam, when Truman had told him about the testing of a "new weapon," Stalin had assumed the mien of a wise statesman, which had helped him so much in his dealings with the Allies. He never tried to minimize the Bomb's global importance. In fact he admitted, in his talk with Harriman, that the Bomb could end the war in the Pacific; it could give the Japanese a pretext to surrender. Stalin also acknowledged that the Germans had failed to construct an atomic bomb, and that, had they not failed, "Hitler would never have surrendered." He told the Americans, without any prompting, that

Soviet scientists had tried to build an atomic bomb, but had also failed. He agreed that the Allies should keep the Bomb in peacetime: "that would mean the end of war and aggressors." But, he added, "the secret would have to be well kept."[25]

Stalin seemed to be saying, "You have your Bomb, I have my Red Army. Let's recognize each other's power and base our relationship on that recognition. We do not complain that you and the British kept this a secret from us." But the real Stalin understood that the Bomb placed the scepter of power in the hands, not even of Roosevelt or Churchill, but of that "petty shopkeeper" Truman and his sly advisor, Secretary of State James Byrnes. As a realist, Stalin had to reckon with this historical fact. But, being Stalin, he could never forgive it and was determined, with his usual patience, to prepare his comeback.[26]

The "absolute weapon" forced profound revisions in Stalin's thinking. The probability of an American return to isolationism, something that had seemed so crucial in the Kremlin's calculations, lost much of its sense after Hiroshima. What difference did it make if American troops returned home or not, demobilized in part or in full, if atomic capabilities and means of delivery were now available and would only increase with time? The security belt of friendly regimes around the Soviet Union acquired a new urgency—American bombers could reach into Soviet territory anyway, but at least it would take them more time to do so. Stalin decided to respond to the American atomic monopoly with deliberate scorn and arrogance. Since September 1945, he and Molotov had begun a preemptive attack against Secretary of State James Byrnes, whom they regarded as a main advocate of "atomic diplomacy" aimed at squeezing concessions from the USSR in a postwar settlement in Europe.

Stalin's major rethinking, however, concerned the small Soviet atomic project, languishing under Molotov's tutelage since May 1943. In August 1945 Stalin directed all state resources to break the American monopoly. He gave Beria, the custodian of the NKVD-GULAG machinery, extraordinary powers to marshal any resources necessary to build the Bomb. But the project "must remain under the control of the Central Committee and must work in strict secrecy," Stalin said to Boris Vannikov, a future head of the First Chief Directorate of the Council of Ministers of the USSR, a new atomic superagency. "This business must be undertaken by the entire Party."[27]

On January 25, 1946, Stalin invited Igor Kurchatov, a scientific manager of the atomic project, to his office in the Kremlin. In the presence of Beria and Molotov, the Kremlin host told the physicist that atomic work should be done quickly "on a broad front, on a Russian scale, and that in this respect all possible help will be provided." Kurchatov came away impressed most of all by "the great love of Comrade Stalin for Russia and V. I. Lenin, about whom he spoke in terms of his great hope for the development of science in our country."[28]

Stalin's decision to embark on a massive program of rearmament, triggered by Hiroshima, was a monumental shift that entailed different policies, both internal and external, from those he had been pursuing previously. Today we know that it meant an unprecedented set of decisions, on the highest state and political level, that would alter drastically the relations between Stalin's police state and the scientific community. It produced a quantum leap in the organization and technological sophistication of many sectors of the Soviet economy and ultimately created a modern Soviet military-industrial complex. In practical terms, it meant finding the ways and means to excavate hundreds of thousands of tons of uranium ore, to build huge uranium processing plants, to accumulate "pure" graphite, to build nuclear reactors, plutonium "factories," and a design bureau to deal with the theory, development, and assembly of atomic weapons. Such goals required millions of workers, billions of rubles in investment, as well as the creation from scratch of a high-tech electrochemical industry and a hasty upgrading of metallurgical, power, and other industries.

In light of this large-scale transformation, the speech Stalin gave in the Bolshoi Theater two weeks after his meeting with Kurchatov, a speech that greatly alarmed the Americans, was a significant understatement. In reality, the dictator was commanding and executing another "revolution from above": on the ashes of peasant Russia and amid the rubble of a war-torn country he ordered the creation of a nuclear superpower.

Stalin had plunged into his own atomic enterprise even before the Truman administration and the British government developed any policy on international control of atomic energy. Later, when Stalin learned through his excellent network of agents that Truman and Attlee opposed any sharing of atomic secrets with the Soviet Union, he must have felt vindicated in his worst fears. By the end of 1945 the expression "Anglo-Saxon alliance of atomic powers" became popular in communications between the Soviet embassy in Washington and Moscow.[29] Stalin publicly spoke about the possibility and desirability of international control over atomic weapons. But even if the U.S. administration, over the opposition of influential senators, the military, and those heading the atomic project, had agreed to reach a secret understanding with Moscow, it is unlikely that Stalin would have been satisfied with anything less than an equal partnership. This would have meant Washington's recognition of the USSR as another atomic power, and its consent to restoration of the "correlation of forces" that had satisfied Stalin before Hiroshima.

The Bomb destroyed Stalin's expectations of being second to none among the great powers and of promoting Soviet state interests through partnership with the Western powers. Yet the goal of building a secure periphery around the USSR remained and called for other means and new vision. On May 8, 1946, Stalin sent a letter to a leader of the Democratic party of Azerbaijan, a Soviet-sponsored organization struggling for the secession of northern areas of Iran. He admitted that there was no revolutionary situation in Iran "that would have allowed the use of Lenin's tactics of 1905 and 1917." At the same time, he wrote, if Soviet troops had decided to stay in Iran, it would have "undercut the basis of our liberationist policies in Europe and Asia. The British and the Americans would say that if Soviet troops could stay in Iran, then why couldn't British troops stay in Egypt, Syria, Indonesia, and Greece, and American troops in China, Iceland, and Denmark? So we decided to pull our troops out of Iran and China, in order to grab this weapon from the hands of the British and the Americans and unleash a movement of liberation in colonies that would render our policy of liberation more justified and efficient."[30]

For the Russian historian who published this remarkable letter, it proved that Stalin had only limited goals in Iran and did not seek territorial expansion there.[31] That is true, and Stalin in 1946 kept restraining "revolutionaries," not only in Iran, but also in Greece and other places where he did not want to provoke premature confrontation with the British and the Americans. But we see here another sign of Stalin's return, after a period of several years, to the old paradigm of Soviet security that aimed at the expansion of Soviet influence through promotion of revolutions and processes of decolonization. Stalin was back to his role of pontiff of all the world's revolutionaries.

Behind his prudent (and one must add mendacious) exhortations lurked the old stratagem: Stalin wanted a breathing spell of several years in order to rearm. The Kremlin leader knew about U.S. demobilization, and the very slow growth of the American atomic arsenal after the war.[32]

From a realpolitik viewpoint, the best tactic for Stalin would have been to avoid confrontation with the West until the Soviet atomic project started to bear fruit. At the same time, Stalin, a true Leninist, looked at his former partners in the struggle with Hitler as a shaky coalition of two imperialist powers, with conflicting priorities in many parts of the world, particularly the Middle East and Southeast Asia. For tactical reasons he preferred not to meddle in their affairs until, and only until, they stopped challenging his sphere of influence in Central Europe. But he did not mind encouraging, at no cost to himself, the collapse of British, French, and Dutch colonial domains in Asia, from Indochina and Indonesia to India, in expectation that this process would distract attention from his interests and sap the strength not only of London but eventually of Washington as well.

Stalin must have hoped that with the atomic bomb in his hands and with the revolutionary process in Asia under his control he could restore the shattered "correlation of forces" and, perhaps, divide his imperialist rivals or otherwise bend them to compromise with him on his terms. Instead, as was the case with Hiroshima, events once again forced his hand. He seemed not to expect that tensions between Moscow and Washington would flare up so quickly over the future of postwar Europe and conquered Germany. But there the Cold War started, before Stalin could get his Bomb.

## Stalin's Road to the Cold War

Stalin's diplomatic achievements at the end of the Second World War so impressed contemporaries and adversaries that many overlooked the fact that his diplomacy, when it could not be supported by the blood of millions of Soviet soldiers and civilians, was a dubious success. The Russian mystic philosopher Daniil Andreev was one of the first at the end of the 1950s to notice this: "An agent of a particular dark genius, which revealed itself in all that related to practicing tyranny, [Stalin] turned out to possess no talents of statesmanship beyond the mediocre ones. Stalin was a bad master of the land, a bad diplomat, a bad leader of the Party, a bad statesman." In a recent study the Norwegian historian Odd Arne Westad came to the conclusion that "Joseph Stalin's China policy in the fall of 1945 was as aimless and incoherent as his European policy. However much he hoped to avoid postwar confrontation with the United States, Stalin could . . . not make up his mind how to achieve his aim."[33]

This view gives important insight into the impact of Stalin's persona on the origins of the Cold War. Historians may also wonder whether the conflagration of the Cold War was at least in part caused by Stalin's poor diplomacy. Even at the peak of his international prestige, in 1945–1946, he could have performed better. He failed to obtain oil concessions in Iran just when he believed he had a deal in his pocket. His diplomatic pressure on Turkey caused him great problems with the West. Later in 1948 his attempt to remove Tito in Yugoslavia by means of "Communist diplomacy" backfired and only weakened the position of the Socialist camp vis-à-vis its imperialist adversaries.

Stalin's policy in Germany also falls into this category, if one considers the goals and the means with which the Kremlin leader had approached the issue of a German settlement, and compares them with the results he achieved by 1949, the moment Germany was divided into two states. Vladimir Semyonov and Valentin Falin, two senior Soviet experts on Germany, had always believed that throughout his life Stalin clung to the firm conviction that the security of the USSR in the West could be guaranteed not through the partition of Germany, but through the transformation of Germany as a whole into a peaceful state.[34] The experts may not be far off the mark.

At the end of the Second World War Stalin predicted, this time correctly, that Germany would be back on its feet in fifteen to twenty years. It seemed unthinkable to him that the people who had demonstrated such stunning energy in the fields of science, technology, and the economy, had conquered Europe and almost crushed the Soviet empire, would remain weak and paralyzed for long. According to the provisions agreed upon at the Yalta and Potsdam conferences, the Allies divided Germany into four occupation zones, three for themselves, and one for the Soviet Union. Yet Stalin rejected the idea of neutralizing Germany by keeping it dismembered—an idea that was supported by Litvinov and Maisky, among others. He wanted a new Germany to become his ally, and until then he was prepared to keep the Soviet zone of occupation permanently, while doing everything to neutralize any threat that the revanchist forces in West Germany could pose to the USSR. In Old Bolshevik party terms, he had "program-maximum" and "program-minimum."

On June 4, 1945, at a meeting with German veterans of the disbanded Comintern, selected by the NKVD to help the Soviets restore order in the occupied territories, Stalin said there would be "two Germanies."[35] He wanted to establish Soviet hegemony in the USSR's zone of occupation. Then he hoped to undermine British influence in West Germany, which would not be difficult, provided that American troops withdrew from Europe. As the endgame, he had in mind a unified, "friendly" Germany, leaning toward the USSR.

Between May 1945 and the fall of 1946 Stalin's strategy seemed to be playing itself out nicely. The decision of the Allies at Potsdam to treat Germany as an economic unity favored his approach. Stalin expected a quick withdrawal of Western, particularly U.S., occupational troops, a reunification of Germany under elected administrative bodies of some kind, and subsequent Allied control over the direction of Germany's future.

After the Soviets successfully restored order, by distributing food and organizing political parties and trade unions in the Soviet zone, Stalin's plan began to hit one snag after another. The chief problem was that, though Stalin seemed to want to win the Germans over with bread and Social-Democratic propaganda, many Soviet actions in Germany contradicted such a policy. Certain aspects of this behavior, like the hooliganism of the occupational troops, Stalin could not and did not want to control, since he took any criticism of the Soviet army as criticism aimed at him, the Generalissimo. But another aspect—the plight of six million German refugees who were fleeing annexed Prussia and Silesia for East Germany, disrupting life there—clearly was the result of Stalin's policies. Other negative results included the dismantling of East German industry and the forced recruitment of scientists, engineers, and workers into various Soviet-run projects, in Saxony as well as in secret laboratories inside the USSR.[36]

Soviet propagandists, the "political commissars" of East Germany, tried to explain their growing difficulties in winning the Germans' trust as the result of a lack of coordination among various arms of the Soviet state acting in Germany. But from 1946 to early 1947, Stalin, strangely enough, did little to ameliorate this situation. Perhaps he expected that the postwar crisis of capitalism would help him out by shattering U.S. power and diminishing American interest in Germany and Western Europe in general. This is plausible, but hard evidence is still missing. It is also plausible that Stalin was in a difficult position at that time. In the long run he needed the friendship of Germany, but in the short run he needed East German resources for his rearmament projects. Later, Molotov referred to this predicament: "Quietly, bit by bit, we had been creating the GDR, our own Germany. What would those people [East Germans] think of us if we had taken everything from their country? . . . After all, we were taking from the Germans who wanted to work with us. The situation should have been handled very carefully." Molotov admitted that many of the Soviet reparation policies undermined the new Germany the Soviets wanted to build, but stressed that the German booty helped the USSR.[37] Meanwhile, as Moscow's German policy came adrift, the United States began to take steps to separate West Germany economically from East Germany. The Americans wanted to restore economic life in the Western zones while preventing the refunneling of American resources from Germany to the Soviet Union through reparations.

Stalin's method of implementing Soviet occupational policies, though it reflected his bent on one-man control, was actually quite flexible and effective. In the case of East Germany, Stalin clearly could not deal personally with the myriad problems of the occupation. At the same time he did not want any powerful political figures to run those policies on his behalf. Vladimir Semyonov, a top political commissar in the Soviet military administration in Germany after the Second World War, recalls that Stalin had some success in turning SMAG into a semi-autonomous organization (autonomous, of course, from his lieutenants, not from himself). Stalin quite often called Sokolovsky and Semyonov on a high-frequency telephone in order to give them instructions, but in most cases the two men were free to act on their own initiative.[38] Yet even with the best administrative models the Kremlin leadership could not eliminate major problems that plagued their policies; nor could they foresee the unwillingness of many Germans, and certainly of the West, to let Stalin build "his own" Germany.

Stalin wanted to stop the separation of Germany into East and West. He was able to look beyond the temporary split of Germany to a time when it would be reunited and resurgent. This reunification, he thought, could take two forms: either Germany would be in the friendly but tight embrace of the Soviet Union, or it would reemerge as a militarist state, a threat to the USSR. In 1870 Otto von Bismarck had united Germany by waging a series of wars against those powers who stood in the way of unification. Stalin believed that any division of Germany would give grounds for the reemergence of "new Bismarcks" and German militarism. Therefore, in 1947 and even in 1949, he rejected proposals to adopt a program of rapid Sovietization for the Soviet zone of occupation, a policy that could divide Germany economically and, as a consequence, politically.[39]

At the sessions of the Council of Foreign Ministers in Moscow in April 1947, Molotov told Western representatives that the Soviet Union would agree to the revival of the Ruhr, if part of its production went to the Soviets in the form of reparations. But the vast majority of policy-makers in Washington categorically objected to this idea, and the conference, like that of September 1945, was in a deadlock. Stalin met with the new U.S. Secretary of State, George C. Marshall, but instead of talking about a deal, he chose to temporize. Perhaps he really expected that the West would eventually compromise with him, rather than decide on a separatist German policy. But the Truman administration had already decided to rebuild the Western zones of Germany without Stalin and, if necessary, against his will. It announced the Marshall Plan for European recovery in full expectation that Stalin and Molotov would boycott it, thereby freeing the Americans from any commitments to their former partner.

For Stalin the Marshall Plan was a watershed. He had been concerned by indications that the United States was seeking to expand its influence in Iran; by the vigorous American reaction to Soviet pressure on Turkey; and, after the proclamation of the Truman Doctrine in the spring of 1947, by the swift substitution of the British presence in Greece. All these events threw cold water on the hope that the United States and the British empire would be entangled in a protracted redivision of markets and resources after the war. The Marshall Plan was, from Stalin's point of view, a large-scale attempt by the United States to gain lasting and preeminent influence in Europe—again, contrary to all expectations of the Soviet wartime planners. Stalin also saw behind the plan a far-reaching design to revive German military-industrial potential and to direct it, as in the 1930s, against the Soviet Union. Stalin told the Czechoslovak delegation in July 1947 that the former Western Allies were now trying to restore the Ruhr, a British zone of occupation in Germany, to convert it into the industrial base of the Western bloc.[40] The Marshall Plan was a serious challenge to Stalin's vision of a future Europe, as well as to German-Soviet relations; essentially, it was a challenge on the same strategic scale as the U.S. atomic monopoly.

From the moment the Marshall Plan was proclaimed, Stalin's old xenophobia, already reawakened by the Bomb, seemed to grow stronger. When the leadership of Czechoslovakia, including some Communists, momentarily hesitated before canceling its participation in the Marshall Plan conference, Stalin was enraged. He wanted to see the Czechoslovaks in the Kremlin at once. In brutal terms, he ordered Klement Gottwald, a leader of the Czechoslovak Communists, to cancel immediately Czechoslovak plans for American aid. Gottwald, of course, complied. When Stalin met with the rest of the delegation, he had regained control of himself, and was once again benign and calm.[41]

Stalin's turn to ham-handed imperialism and an overt anti-American campaign after the Marshall Plan was made in haste, but not in panic. Like his strikes against the domestic seeds of Decembrism, this was a preemptive course, dictated by a powerful, security-obsessed mind. The Kremlin leader wanted to eliminate even the remote possibility of a threat to the Soviet zone of security in Central Europe. The best way to do this, of course, was through a show of strength: a brutal Soviet counteroffensive in response to the American politico-economic offensive.

Under these circumstances, a division of Germany into East and West would constitute for Stalin a major geopolitical defeat that would be particularly damaging in view of the continued American atomic monopoly. For Stalin, accepting this defeat would be worse than risking a confrontation with the only country to possess the Bomb. After the Western powers agreed in late 1947 to proceed with the formal foundation of a German state in their occupational zones, Stalin began to squeeze them out of Berlin by gradually imposing a blockade on the sectors under their control. Stalin's reasoning was crude and obvious: joint, four-partite administration of Germany and its capital was the result of the Yalta-Potsdam agreements; if the Western partners violated it in their zones, why should Stalin not do the same in his own? In March 1948 the Generalissimo received the leaders of the Soviet-installed Party of Socialist German Unity (SED).

One of them, Wilhelm Pieck, warned that the next elections in Berlin, scheduled for October, could end in a humiliating defeat for his party. The results might be different, however, "if one could remove the Allies from Berlin." Stalin then said, "Let's make a joint effort—perhaps we can kick them out."[42] As a tactician, Stalin left all options open. He preferred first to oust the former Allies from the city, and only then to bargain with them on a German settlement.

By June 1948 the noose around West Berlin was tightening, but the Truman administration refused again to recognize Stalin's quid pro quo in Germany. U.S. propaganda turned the Berlin blockade into incriminating evidence of the ruthlessness and inhumanity of the Soviet regime. The U.S. Air Force demonstrated its stunning superiority by supplying West Berlin for many months with everything it needed.

Stalin never planned to start a war over Berlin, but he had to accept his defeat. In May 1949 he lifted the blockade. Khrushchev called the results of Stalin's policy "a failure," and said that "an agreement was signed that made our position in West Berlin worse." He was right. Until then the Soviets could refer to the documents of the Allied Control Commission in Germany which stated that Berlin, although the place of residence for this temporary body, still remained the capital of the Soviet zone of occupation.[43] In 1949 Stalin recognized the de facto permanent Western political rights in Berlin, and agreed, in a separate protocol, to the division of the city into West and East.

Stalin's stubborn refusal to face the failure of his German diplomacy led to an even greater defeat for Soviet foreign policy in West Berlin. The outcome of the Berlin blockade, of course, was much more disastrous to Soviet security interests than Khrushchev wanted to concede. The majority of countries in Western Europe, terrified by the "red menace," turned to the United States for protection, and thus NATO, an alliance of democratic countries that outlived the Soviet Union, came into existence—and constituted the Soviet military's biggest problem for four decades. Stalin's clumsy pressure put off those Germans who otherwise would have vacillated and perhaps even followed the pied piper of the Kremlin on the road toward German reunification under Soviet tutelage.

Stalin's actions in 1947–1948 were based on the correct assumption that he was not risking a war with the West. But he had miscalculated the effect of his preventive moves. Did he expect that his pressure would only contribute to the consolidation of the Western camp around the United States? Was he a willing captive of the Marxist belief that contradictions among capitalist powers would prevent their integration into the anti-Soviet bloc? Had he underestimated the role of nuclear technology, which, by virtue of its costs, was forcing other Western countries to huddle under the U.S. atomic umbrella?

We can only guess. Stalin saw the emerging bipolarity by 1947. But, judging from what he wrote and how he acted, he definitely did not believe that this bipolarity would last long, and he still envisaged "antagonisms" in the Western camp. In any case, it is fair to suggest that from 1947 on Stalin regarded the consolidation of the two blocs and the relative growth of the U.S. influence in Europe as a foregone conclusion. On his part, he attempted brutally to force the West into some kind of settlement in Germany and began consolidating his war gains in Eastern Europe and elsewhere. Losing those gains was his primary fear; to avoid it, he was prepared to pay any price, to endure confrontation with the West.

In the categories of "good guys and bad guys," Stalin was indisputably a bad guy in the Cold War. But he was also a bad guy during World War II and before it—and the West had gladly accepted him as he was, for it needed his strength and found it easier to cope with the chaotic Europe of 1943–1945 using nineteenth-century methods, that is, regulating international relations by the concert of great powers. Stalin thought he had done well when he occupied Eastern Prussia and preserved the lands conquered before the war. But now the West perceived him as bad, and Stalin felt threatened by this shift in attitude among his former allies.

According to Molotov, Stalin had built a strict logical chain: "The First World War pulled one country out of capitalist slavery. The Second World War created a Socialist system, the third will put an end to imperialism once and for all."[44] Stalin's thinking was not, as many interpreted, an invitation to war, but rather the theoretical fatalism of the aging potentate who sought in the Laws of History the ultimate revenge on his former imperialist allies. The statement about the interconnection between War and Revolution would seem trivial even for a Marxist: Lenin had formulated this dogma already during World War I. But by the late 1940s Joseph Stalin was again turning to ideology to explain a hostile and uncertain world.

## Triumph in the East

The revival of the Soviet revolutionary-imperial paradigm had begun in early 1946, when Stalin started to shift from a postwar imperialist partnership to the search for unilateral security. But only after the announcement of the Marshall Plan, in the fall of 1947, did Stalin decide to accept the paradigm in all its implications. He began to use revolutions ("revolutions from above," in his classic style) as the chief means to build a security zone around the USSR. He began to look for new allies who would be united with the USSR in a monolithic Communist bloc, capable of withstanding the pressures of a new prewar situation.

Stalin characteristically opened this new chapter in his career with purges. His biggest target abroad, Tito, refused to be "purged," and this resulted in the Soviet-Yugoslav split in the first half of 1948. Although this rift constituted a loss for Stalin, in general he could control European "revolutionarism" as he liked. It was Asia, with its simmering revolutionary nationalism, that taught Stalin a lesson: you can make the revolutionary process serve your foreign policy, but only at your own risk and with serious, unintended consequences. Soon dramatic developments in the Far East forced Stalin in a way he perhaps had never expected or planned.

On Sunday, June 25, 1950, the North Korean army invaded South Korea in an attempt to reunify the country by force. "The North Koreans wanted to prod South Korea with the point of a bayonet," Khrushchev recalled. Molotov remembered that the Korean War "was pressed on us by the Koreans themselves. Stalin said it was impossible to avoid the national question of a united Korea."[45] The most dangerous conflict of the Cold War, which the West interpreted as blatant, Soviet-made aggression, a possible prelude to invasion in Europe, was not Stalin's brainchild. Yet the Kremlin leader supported North Korea's aggression, since he decided it would advance the geopolitical position of the Soviet Union in the Far East and strengthen the prestige of the USSR as a revolutionary vanguard.

Since the spring of 1949 Kim Il Sung, the leader of the North Korean revolutionary puppet regime, had begged Stalin for his blessing in initiating a "reunification of Korea," after the example set by the Chinese Communists in their civil war against the Guomindang. Stalin argued against this, but gradually he conceded. On January 30,

1950, after one particularly emotional plea from the impatient Kim, Stalin signaled to the Soviet representative in Pyongyang, Terenty Shtykov, his agreement to see the North Korean Communist and look upon his proposal favorably. "Such big business regarding South Korea," he wrote to Shtykov, "requires serious preparation."[46] According to this classified Soviet account, Stalin still had "reservations" about the North Korean invasion, but "did not object in principle." Kim arrived in Moscow at the end of March and stayed until April, arguing to Stalin that the regime of South Korea was weak militarily and politically, and that the "revolutionary situation" in South Korea was ripe. Massive discontent with the government of Syngman Rhee, supported by the United States, the ever-present "fifth column," and the low combat readiness of the Southern army all seemed to guarantee a quick and painless success.

After the meeting Stalin ordered the immediate fulfillment of all North Korean demands for arms and ammunition. His orders allowed the North Korean army to increase by many divisions in just two months. Soviet generals designed the plan of attack. At the outbreak of the war, the North was far superior militarily to the South. It had twice as many troops and artillery pieces, seven times as many heavy machine guns, six and a half times as many armored vehicles, and six times as many war planes. Soviet military planners, together with Kim's military, believed that North Korean troops could advance by fifteen to twenty kilometers per day and could accomplish their task in three to four weeks. By the end of May the Korean army was about to be deployed. According to one classified Soviet account, the attack was scheduled for June 25 "at [Kim's] insistence, before the rainy season could ruin the enterprise."[47]

Why did Stalin go along with Kim, when earlier, in 1945–1947, he had denied similar support to the Communist guerillas in Greece and Vietnam, and had in 1949 given a cold shoulder to Kim's plans? How had he, an experienced tactician, allowed young Kim to have his way? And why did the USSR allow the United States to legitimize the military counterstrike under the auspices of the United Nations? The main roots of Kim's aggression lay in the artificial division of the country and the simmering civil war on the Korean peninsula.[48] Yet Kim could not start the war without Stalin's agreement and Soviet supplies, training, and planning. Stalin's calculations, as well as Kim's, were responsible for this tragedy.[49]

The prelude to the Korean War came in December 1949, when Mao Zedong, the leader of the Communist party of China (CCP) and the victor of the civil war against the Guomindang, arrived in Moscow to establish a unique relationship between the Soviet Union and the newly proclaimed People's Republic of China (PRC). Until his death, Stalin dealt personally with all problems, big and small, between the Soviet Union and the Chinese Communists.[50] He was not in a hurry to support the Chinese Communist cause of Mao Zedong, the leader of a relatively independent and undeniably strong revolutionary Communist movement. He had his doubts about Mao, regarding him as excessively independent, with his roots in peasant revolt rather than proletarian revolution. In 1956 Mao complained, in conversation with the Soviet ambassador Pavel Yudin, that Stalin's "mistrust and suspiciousness may have been provoked by the Yugoslav events [the split with Tito]." Mao added in irritation that "at that time there were many rumors that the Chinese Communist party would go the Yugoslav way, that Mao Zedong was a 'Chinese Tito.' "[51]

In 1943–1946, when Stalin still nurtured his vision of a realpolitik partnership with the Western Allies, the Chinese Revolution was an unwelcome intruder into his plans. He preferred to deal with the Guomindang, while exploiting its weakness to his own advantage, until he could come to terms with Chiang and the Americans about a Soviet zone of security in Manchuria and Xinjiang.

Stalin expected to "obtain" Manchuria by virtue of its liberation by the Red Army from the Japanese. In November 1944 in Xinjiang, populated by Muslims and adjacent to Soviet Central Asia, the Soviets had supported a separatist rebellion, and since that time controlled the area.[52] Stalin received regular briefings on the Xinjiang rebellion from Lavrenty Beria, the chief of his secret police. In the Stalin-Guomindang negotiations in Moscow in July–August 1945 about a treaty of friendship and alliance, the Kremlin leader used the Red Army assault in Manchuria and his control over northern Xinjiang as bargaining chips to obtain all the concessions he wanted. He used the Chinese Communist party as his third bargaining chip, since the Guomindang officials openly wanted him to restrain Mao. In 1945 Stalin tried to invite Chiang Kai-shek to Moscow. He declined to see Mao, under various pretexts, until November 1949.[53]

In 1945–1946 Stalin reserved the same cool attitude toward lesser revolutionary movements and leaders. He called the Greek leftist rebellion "foolishness": the Anglo-Americans would never tolerate a "red" Greece threatening their vital communications to the Middle East.[54] Ho Chi Minh failed to get Stalin's support for his schemes of liberation in Vietnam, probably because this also would have threatened British interests, and because Vietnam was well beyond the reach of the Soviet Union. The Kremlin leader sent arms to the Yugoslav and Chinese Communists, but he wanted them to simmer, not boil over the real and perceived boundaries of influence existing among imperialist powers in the Mediterranean and Indochina.

Only after the beginning of the Cold War, when all chances for reconciliation with the West were lost and he faced the need to find new partners and allies, did Stalin begin to reassess Mao, who then was clearly on the winning side in the war against the Guomindang. As we learn more details about the origins of the Sino-Soviet alliance, it becomes stunningly clear that from the very beginning the relations between the two Communist giants were greatly marred by Stalin's search for one-sided security advantages for the Soviet Union, as well as a position of superiority for himself in the Communist world. Stalin's decision to shake Mao's hand in 1949 was one of hard-boiled realism, but once it happened, the partnership between the Kremlin leader and the leader of the Chinese Revolution inevitably became a test between the Soviet paradigm and a no less exceptionalist Chinese revolutionary nationalism.

Stalin began to think of Mao as a potential ally in January 1949, when the Berlin blockade had failed miserably. Still, he attempted to impose on Mao Soviet mediation between the CCP and the Guomindang (while discrediting similar efforts by the United States), and even the idea of a "coalition government" between the two. When Mao rejected or ignored these schemes, Stalin sent one of his men, Anastas Mikoyan, on a secret visit to Mao's camp (January 31–February 7). Ostensibly a mission of good will, this was, in reality, a trip to take stock of a new partner.[55]

In July–August 1949, Stalin played host to the CCP delegation, headed by Liu Shaoqi. On the eve of the visit Mao announced a "lean-to-one-side" policy; that is, he proposed to Moscow a partnership between the People's Republic of China and the USSR against the imperialist powers. Stalin paid in kind: he invited the Chinese delegation to a session of the Politburo—an unprecedented gesture, indicating a relationship of equals; he confessed that he had underestimated Mao and the potential of the Chinese Revolution "because our knowledge of China is too limited." He pleased the Chinese by proclaiming the CCP a revolutionary vanguard of Asia, "fulfilling a historic mission of unprecedented significance," becoming a hegemon for the millions in India, Burma, Indonesia, and the Philippines.[56]

Stalin was not transformed overnight from a calculating dictator into a revolutionary romantic. Behind his apparent enthusiasm for the Chinese Revolution and its implications in Asia was a hardheaded proposal for a hierarchy of influence in the Communist universe. What Stalin said and implied in essence was: Mao and the CCP would become a leader of the Asian revolutionary process. If they chose, they could even organize an Asian Cominform, in which the USSR would participate as a half-Asian country. At the same time, the Soviet Union would consolidate its gains in Europe and the Far East, defined by the Yalta-Potsdam agreements.[57]

Stalin assumed that the Chinese would recognize him as the supreme pontiff in exchange for his recognition of their role in the East. He also made clear that the Soviet Union would retain its "interests" in China (a base in Port-Arthur, railroad access to it, and exclusive rights in Manchuria and Xinjiang). These were conditions on which Stalin, for all the flexibility and new "revolutionarism," was not willing to compromise. He knew that the realities of economic and military power had cast the Soviet Union as a "big brother" to the Chinese, and that he held all the cards, including the prospect of economic assistance to Mao, Xinjiang separatism, and a "fifth column" in the Chinese leadership itself (for instance, the Communist strongman of Manchuria, Gao Gang). He wanted everything his way both as the revolutionary pontiff and as an influential emperor.

After the proclamation of the People's Republic of China in October 1949, Stalin at last agreed to receive Mao Zedong in Moscow. According to Chinese memoirs, during the first two-hour talk between the two revolutionary potentates, in the Kremlin on December 16, 1949, Mao cautiously probed Stalin to see if it would be possible to repeal the unequal Sino-Soviet treaty of 1945. He allegedly said, "I am afraid it is necessary to undergo bilateral consultations to outline certain things, [and] these things must be both beautiful and tasty." There was an awkward silence. In Mao's careful language, beautiful things stood for world revolution, and tasty things for Chinese national interests.[58]

Soviet records give a very different version of the talks. Stalin got right down to business. The old Sino-Soviet treaty, he told Mao, was concluded "with the consent of America and England. With this in mind, we in our inner circle decided not to change any articles of this treaty." Otherwise, Stalin explained, the Western powers would try to change other aspects of the Yalta agreements, "regarding the Kurile islands, Southern Sakhalin, and so on." In other words, Stalin bluntly laid Soviet geopolitical priorities on the table. The Kremlin leader did not share Mao's apparent concern over a possible war (the concern that underlay his demands for Soviet aid). "There is no immediate threat to China now," he said. "Japan is still not back on its feet, and therefore not ready for war." The United States, despite its belligerent talk, "is afraid of war" more than anyone else. Nevertheless, Stalin promised to help the Chinese Communists develop their naval and aircraft forces once they accepted his conditions. "If we were friends," concluded Stalin, "peace could be ensured not only for five to ten, but even for twenty to twenty-five years." He advised the Chinese leader to satisfy his nationalist ambitions by liberating Taiwan and Tibet.[59]

"During my first meeting with Stalin," Mao recalled to Yudin in 1956, "I submitted a proposal to conclude a [new] state treaty, but Stalin evaded a response . . . Subsequently, he avoided any meetings with me. I tried to call him by telephone, but was told that Stalin was not at home, and that it would be better for me to meet with Mikoyan." As we have seen, Stalin did not "evade" Mao's question at all. But the Chinese Communist leader was probably too proud to admit that during the first meeting, instead of resisting Stalin's geopolitical logic, he had concealed his irritation and played along. According to Soviet records, Mao humbly admitted that they in Beijing failed to see the connection between the Sino-Soviet treaty and "the position of America and England with regard to the Yalta Agreement." "We must act in a manner advantageous to the common cause," he said to Stalin. "It is clear that we should not change the treaty now." Mao also said that Soviet control over Port-Arthur (Lushun) and the Chinese Changchun Railroad in Manchuria "corresponds to the interests of China."[60]

Mao's claim that Stalin "avoided" meeting with him becomes more doubtful in the light of this new evidence. In fact, the long waiting period after their first encounter suited Mao's interests: the Chinese leader did, after all, come to the table with the firm decision to replace the old Sino-Soviet treaty with a new and "fair" one. So perhaps under various pretexts Mao delayed the start of working-level talks with the Soviets.

For several weeks Mao stewed in one of the government dachas near Moscow. Then Stalin suddenly took the first step. In Mao's estimate, Stalin conceded because Great Britain and India recognized the PRC in January. It is likely that, as in the case of the Marshall Plan, intelligence from London and Washington also contributed to Stalin's volte-face. The Kremlin leader might have suspected that he could play into the hands of the West and alienate his most promising ally in the Far East. One of Stalin's chief concerns about Mao in the mid-1940s had been his flirtation with American representatives in China. Stalin also knew that some other members of the top CCP leadership—such as Zhou Enlai—had been very enthusiastic about the prospect of balancing the influence of the USSR in China with the American presence there. The disposition of Great Britain to recognize the PRC must have aroused Stalin's old suspicions about Mao's loyalty. In late December 1949, an English news agency reported that Stalin had placed Mao under house arrest. On January 1, 1950, Mao responded, through the Soviet news agency TASS, by mentioning that the purpose of his visit to Moscow was to discuss the future signing of a Sino-Soviet treaty on friendship and alliance. The next day Mao sent a cable to Beijing: "The last two days saw important developments in our work here. Comrade Stalin has agreed to Comrade Zhou Enlai's coming to Moscow to sign a new Sino-Soviet treaty on friendship and alliance, as well as agreements on credit, trade, and aviation."[61]

On January 22, 1950, at a second meeting with Mao, Stalin "discovered" the fact that the surrender of Japan made the old Sino-Soviet treaty obsolete. When Mao spoke about the "co-prosperity" of both Communist states as the model of their future relationship, Stalin did not argue. He was apparently so forthcoming, so interested in winning Mao's trust that the Chinese leader, smelling a rat, reminded him that a new agreement between the two could touch on Soviet vital interests, sanctified by the Yalta Conference. Stalin admitted that the new Sino-Soviet treaty could cause problems between his country and the United States, but insisted that he was fully prepared to deal with the consequences.[62]

In reality, Stalin did not give much. He then allowed himself to be persuaded by Mao to keep Soviet troops in Port-Arthur, both as a guarantee against any resurgence of the Japanese-American threat, and as a base for training the Chinese navy. Economic assistance to the PRC remained minimal until his death. During tough talks he succeeded in imposing on Mao several secret agreements that were advantageous to him and extremely embarrassing to his new Chinese partner. One agreement prohibited foreigners from living in Manchuria and Xinjiang and encouraged joint Sino-Soviet economic concessions; another agreement, with no expiration date, allowed Soviet troops to move to Port-Arthur across Manchuria at any time, and without forewarning Chinese authorities. In an agreement on intelligence cooperation, Stalin asked Mao to set up a joint global network of espionage among Chinese living abroad. All these issues, embarrassing for Mao, were raised on Stalin's initiative. Other Politburo members (Molotov, Malenkov, Mikoyan, Bulganin, Beria, Kaganovich) played only a passive role in the talks.[63]

Obviously, both sides regarded the signed treaties and agreements as mere formalities. The real strength of the new Sino-Soviet alliance was in Mao's personal allegiance to Stalin as the supreme Communist leader. In return for this, Stalin presented Mao with a gift that, in his opinion, any Asian satrap would have liked: he gave away the Comintern network of Chinese informers who reported to Moscow. It was another of Stalin's many betrayals of his "fifth column" around the world; subsequently, hundreds of pro-Soviet Communists in the CCP were murdered or imprisoned.[64]

Stalin still did not completely trust Mao, however. His worldview was well organized, the picture clear and logical. But now Communist China had become a major new player on the international scene. There was no room for two supreme authorities in the Asian revolutionary world, and Stalin, in spite of his verbal recognition of Mao's predominance, was concerned that the Chinese leader might become another potential Tito by claiming a special place in the world Communist movement, outside the realm of Moscow's pontiff. Trying to allay this suspicion, Mao asked Stalin to send a comrade with a good knowledge of Marxist theory to Beijing to edit his works and look at the real situation in China. Stalin sent Pavel Yudin, his court philosopher, who had played an important role in the events preceding the Stalin-Tito split. Yudin later reported that he offered "more than three hundred suggestions, corrections, and all kinds of editorial and other alterations" for the three volumes of Mao's words. Most important, Mao "fully accepted them." Yudin told Mao after Stalin's death that the leader had asked him upon his return from China "if the Chinese comrades were [true] Marxists." Yudin had said "yes," and Stalin seemed to be satisfied with that answer.[65]

The Sino-Soviet treaty passed the ideological test. But the biggest test was still ahead. Stalin knew all too well that once a revolutionary leader becomes a state potentate, he acts according to geopolitical realities, national conditions, the logic of power itself. This knowledge was critical for explaining why Kim succeeded in getting Stalin to consent to the invasion of South Korea.

## From Victory to Defeat

During their fateful meeting in Moscow in April 1950, Stalin agreed with Kim that, though he had opposed a "reunification" of Korea before, now it could be accomplished "in light of the changed international situation."[66] Earlier, Stalin had feared that the Americans would intervene. What, then, caused him to reassess the situation?

The new alliance with Communist China must have been the biggest cause for reassessment. From Stalin's viewpoint, this treaty was a watershed: the Yalta-Potsdam agreement on the spheres of influence had been broken. The world was now open for a redivision of spheres of influence on the basis of new, ideologically drawn alliances. As a Leninist, Stalin knew that this redivision meant global war. He said to Mao: "If we make a decision to revise treaties, we must go all the way." This phrase, in a nutshell, contained the origins of the Korean War. As the world headed for its third global confrontation, the Korean peninsula acquired new strategic meaning. Stalin worried that, should the United States rearm Japan in the future, South Korea could become a dangerous beachhead for enemy forces. Therefore, it had to be captured before Japan could get back on its feet.

Several factors made the Soviet leader believe that the United States might not defend South Korea. On August 29, 1949, the Soviet Union broke the American monopoly on atomic weapons. At about the same time, the last American troops withdrew from South Korea—a development that was closely watched from Moscow. Early in 1950 some key figures in U.S. governmental circles, particularly Secretary of State Dean Acheson, made statements that excluded South Korea from the

American "defense perimeter" in the Pacific arena and even hinted that the regime of Syngman Rhee was expendable. On January 28 intelligence sources reported to Stalin that the South Korean government had "little hope of American assistance" and expected that "President Truman would leave Formosa as he had left China." The report quoted Syngman Rhee as saying that "America has shown from the very beginning that it does not intend to fight for the interests of South Korea."[67] Stalin must have felt that the Truman leadership was in disarray, incapable of mobilizing domestically. In this view, the United States failed to make use of its atomic diplomacy, could not prevent the collapse of the Guomindang, its primary ally in Asia, and now it was withdrawing from the Asian mainland altogether, returning to its traditional role of defending the islands.

Another consideration had never been spoken. Had Stalin said no to North Korea, it would have looked as if again, as during the civil war in China, he were putting the brakes on the revolutionary process in the Far East. And Mao Zedong was autonomous and unpredictable. The Chinese could start supporting Kim without the sanction of Moscow, in the same way Tito's Yugoslavia had supported the Albanians and the Greek guerillas, ignoring Moscow's objections. Taking issue with the PRC just months after the much-trumpeted conclusion of the Sino-Soviet treaty in Moscow would be unacceptable and ruinous. Equally so would be the recognition of Mao's revolutionary supremacy in Asia. That could lead the Chinese comrades to think too much about their international role, and to revive their nationalist ambitions. Stalin knew that Korea, before it was occupied by Japan in the late nineteenth century, had been a traditional sphere of Chinese imperial influence.

When, in early April 1950, Stalin supported Kim's invasion plan, he believed that he was preventing both of these developments, while maintaining the appearance of parity with Mao. He told Kim that North Korea could "get down to action" only after their plans were cleared "with Comrade Mao Zedong personally." The North Korean offensive could be postponed if the Chinese leadership objected. Kim then returned to Pyongyang and made another trip, this time to Beijing. On May 13 Mao sent Zhou Enlai to the Soviet ambassador N. V. Roshchin, asking urgently for the "personal clarifications of Comrade Filippov [a pseudonym of Stalin in correspondence among Communist leaders] on this question." Stalin's answer, a masterpiece of political astuteness, was that "the question should ultimately be decided by the Chinese and Korean comrades together, and in the event the Chinese comrades should disagree, the decision on the question should be postponed until a new discussion can take place." Never secure about communications, Stalin refused to be specific about his talks with Kim in Moscow. "The Korean comrades," he wrote, "can relay to you the details of the conversation."[68]

Stalin protected his credentials as the pontiff of world Communist revolution, responsive to the aspirations of the Korean people. At the same time he shared with Mao the burden of responsibility for the risky enterprise. Mao complained later that when he was in Moscow signing the Sino-Soviet treaty, Stalin "did not say a word about the conquest of South Korea." When Stalin invited Kim to Moscow, "nobody took pains to ask [Mao's] advice in advance."[69]

Stalin's logic provides an explanation as to why he recalled the Soviet representative from the United Nations in the spring of 1950. Stalin boycotted the United Nations because it refused to recognize the PRC as a legitimate successor to the Chinese seat on the Security Council. In Stalin's view, the risk of the Soviets' absence was less than the strategic advantages of stressing the Sino-Soviet alliance and unmasking the United Nations as a "voting machine" obedient to America. It bears repeating that Stalin's reading of the United States' withdrawal from South Korea led him to believe that the Americans would not intervene in the Korean civil war.

Stalin and Mao were completely surprised when the Truman administration took advantage of the Soviet absence in the United Nations to obtain international approval for U.S. intervention in Korea. It was, ironically, the desire in the Kremlin to make a quick and victorious war, which the Western allies "so feared would happen in Europe," that "prompted the United States to respond with precisely the intervention in Korea that Moscow wanted above all to avoid."[70] After the successful U.N. counterattack at Inchon in September 1950 and the resulting collapse of the North Korean army, American troops advanced to the Sino-Korean border.

Very soon the Kremlin leader concluded that the Inchon operation was a "strategic breakthrough by the U.N. forces fraught with fatal consequences." But he and his Soviet advisors had no control over the distant war. Kim's army got stuck south of the Korean peninsula, was cut off by enemy troops, and eventually disintegrated. Despite the gathering thunder in the Far East, Stalin took a train to his dacha at Sochi, on the Black Sea. As in June 1941, when developments went against his expectations, he took a time-out. What's more, the Generalissimo's physical condition necessitated a long rest. At Sochi, on October 1, after midnight, Stalin received an urgent cable from Pyongyang with a panicky letter from Kim Il Sung and the second-ranked man in the North Korean leadership, Pak Hong-yong. The letter informed him that the U.S.-led forces had taken Seoul and would probably capture North Korea, and that the North Korean army ceased to exist and thus would not be able to offer serious resistance. "The moment enemy troops cross the 38th parallel," Kim and Pak wrote, "we will desperately need immediate military assistance from the Soviet Union. If, for some reason, this help is not possible, then [would you] assist us in organizing international volunteer units in China and other people's democracies to provide military assistance in our struggle?"[71]

This must have been a hard moment for Stalin: Kim turned out to be a bad military leader, but he was a loyal puppet who vowed to continue a protracted war to prevent, in the name of the strategic interests of the USSR and the whole Communist camp, the emergence of an American military springboard on the Korean peninsula. In the event of defeat, Stalin faced the ultimate responsibility for the deterioration of Sino-Soviet strategic positions and, as the Communist pontiff, the blame for losing the Korean "revolutionary" regime. His whole crafty strategy in the Far East had backfired. Nevertheless, Stalin must have been expecting this moment, for he had made his tactical decision in advance. It took him only a few minutes to dictate a telegram to Mao Zedong and Zhou Enlai, advising the Chinese to "move immediately at least five or six divisions to the 38th parallel" to shield Kim's regime from the advancing U.N. troops and enable him to mobilize a new army. Stalin mentioned almost elegiacally that he was "far from Moscow and somewhat cut off from the events in Korea." He wrote that the Chinese troops "could pose as volunteers [but], of course, with the Chinese command at the helm." He left it to the discretion of the leadership in Beijing to tell "the Korean comrades" about their decision on this question.[72] In a matter of minutes, Stalin passed the buck to the Chinese, making them responsible for Kim's regime and the war.

Stalin's real "master plan" at that time was not a counterattack in

Europe, as many in the West had thought, but postponement of a head-on collision with the West. He had taken precautions: his cables to Kim and Mao were all in military intelligence codes (considered to be "safe"), and he signed them with the Chinese alias Pheng Xi. He also had forbidden Soviet advisors to travel south of the 38th parallel, and Soviet pilots, flying over Korea, to speak Russian![73] He now refused to send Soviet troops back to North Korea, because that would lead to direct war with the Americans. Let the brave Chinese fight, with Soviet arms and Soviet air cover.

Some Chinese politicians, particularly the Communist boss of Manchuria, Gao Gang, had spoken in favor of Chinese intervention, to prevent the return of the United States (and, potentially, a remilitarized Japan) to the Asian mainland. There were, however, serious reservations in Beijing about starting another war barely a year after the end of the civil war. Mao's position was ambiguous, to say the least. He argued for intervention before his colleagues at home. At the same time, on October 2, he wrote back to Stalin that the PRC could not enter the war because several Chinese divisions would not be enough to stop the Americans. Always careful to appear Stalin's loyal ally, Mao also expressed his fear that the United States might declare war on China, which would mean a Soviet-American war as well.[74] Feeling the urgency of the moment, Stalin stopped mincing words and, on October 5, dispatched to Mao the most remarkable cable in their whole correspondence, displaying the full force of his realpolitik logic.

The United States, Stalin wrote, "was not prepared at the present time for a big war," and Japan was still incapable of rendering any military assistance to the Americans. Therefore, if the United States faced the threat of such a war, they would "have to give in to China, backed by its Soviet ally, in [the settlement] of the Korean question." They would also be forced to leave Taiwan and renounce "a separate peace with Japanese reactionaries." Stalin warned that "without serious struggle and a new impressive display of its strength, China would not obtain all these concessions" from the Americans.

Stalin finished his seduction of the Chinese comrades with a stunning passage: "Of course I had to reckon with the fact that, despite its unpreparedness, the United States still may pull itself into a big war, [acting] out of prestige; consequently, China would be dragged into the war, and the USSR, which is bound to China by the pact of mutual assistance, would be dragged into the war as well. Should we fear this? In my opinion, we should not, since together we will be stronger than the United States and Great Britain. Other European capitalist states do not possess any serious military power, save Germany, which cannot provide assistance to the United States now. If war is inevitable, let it happen now, and not in a few years, when Japanese militarism will be restored as a U.S. ally, and when the United States and Japan will have a beach-head on the continent ready, in the form of Syngman Rhee's Korea."[75]

Arguably, deep down Stalin hoped for just the opposite: that the Sino-Soviet treaty would be a sufficient deterrent and that the United States would hesitate to declare war on the PRC, knowing it would automatically bring in the Soviet Union. But he made a point of demonstrating to Mao that the Kremlin "father" of the Communist world had a sober vision of World War III and was not afraid of it. In this way, also, Stalin denied Mao his strongest argument against China's intervention.

Mao seemed to have surrendered to Stalin's logic: he agreed to send nine divisions to fight in Korea. Zhou Enlai flew by Soviet military plane to Sochi, allegedly to discuss with Stalin the terms under which the Soviets would supply armaments, ammunition, and particularly air cover for the Chinese "volunteers" in North Korea. The Stalin-Zhou meeting took place on October 9–10, and here again, as in the case of the Sino-Soviet treaty, the existing Chinese versions differ significantly from the newly available Soviet documents. According to Chinese sources, including Mao himself, at some point Stalin changed his mind: he would *not* supply military equipment and provide air cover. The Chinese leadership in Beijing was stunned by this act of perfidy but, *despite* it, decided to enter the war.[76] According to Soviet records, however, Zhou told Stalin that the Politburo of the Chinese Communist party's Central Committee had decided not to send troops to Korea, restating the same old arguments. It is not clear what happened in Beijing: was Mao really facing strong opposition, or was Zhou deliberately playing the role of "bad messenger" assigned to him by Mao? One analyst of the Chinese evidence concludes that Mao and Zhou deliberately played "games" with Stalin. They were determined to send volunteers to Korea, but at the same time they were seeking the best possible deal from him. Yet another dramatic scenario is likely: the majority of Chinese leaders at that time strongly opposed the war and still hoped that Stalin was bluffing and would come to

Kim's rescue once U.S. troops moved to the Soviet borders. Stalin, at least, interpreted the Chinese "game" in this light.[77]

Stalin decided to call the Chinese bluff. The Soviet Union, he told Zhou, was not ready to fight a large-scale war in the Far East so soon after the Second World War. Besides, the Soviet–North Korean border was too narrow to allow massive troop transfers. If the U.S. actions were to jeopardize the fate of world socialism, however, the Soviet Union would be ready to take up the American challenge. Stalin began to lose his temper. The Chinese comrades should know, he said, that should they refuse to intervene, "socialism in Korea would collapse within a very short period of time." What Stalin in fact did was directly challenge the PRC's self-legitimacy from the high ground of the Soviet revolutionary-imperial paradigm. The USSR, he implied, should save itself for an ultimate battle with the forces of imperialism, whereas it is the duty of the PRC, as the major Soviet ally in Asia and the hegemon of the Asian revolutionary process, to fend off a regional imperialist offensive. In the light of the PRC's failure to perform its historic role, all Stalin could suggest was that the Soviet Union and China should work out specific plans to help the Korean comrades and their forces withdraw from North Korea and move to shelters in Manchuria and the Soviet Far East. When the stunned Zhou asked Stalin if China could count on Soviet air cover should it decide to fight in Korea, Stalin answered yes, and assured him that the Soviet Union would take care of all supplies of arms and equipment as soon as the PRC defined its actual needs. Despite all this, the Sino-Soviet talks ended without the establishment of any joint policy.[78]

This episode showed Stalin displaying, under duress, the best of his realpolitik side. He was willing to swallow a serious regional defeat and even the loss of a "Socialist" regime on the Soviet borders rather than risk a military clash with U.N. forces. He saw to it that this policy would be shared by all his lieutenants by passing several Politburo decisions. In Khrushchev's presence he once said, "So what? If Kim Il Sung fails, we are not going to intervene with our troops. Let the Americans be our neighbors in the Far East." On October 12, Stalin surprised Kim, who expected Soviet military assistance, with a letter advising evacuation of the rest of Kim's forces to the Soviet and Chinese sanctuaries. Interestingly, Stalin referred to the "recommendations" of the "conference of the Chinese [and] Soviet leading comrades" (that is, to his talks with Zhou in Sochi). He didn't forget to blame Mao for what was solely his decision! At that moment, argues one Russian historian, the Korean War could have ended in a victory for the West.[79]

The Chinese opposition to war crumbled under the weight of Stalin's stand, however. Within hours, on October 13, Mao informed the Kremlin leader that the CCP Politburo had decided to fight. Stalin, barely concealing his delight, sent another message to Kim, ordering him "to postpone temporarily" the evacuation, in expectation of "detailed reports from Mao Zedong about this matter." The next day Stalin announced to Kim that "after hesitation and a series of provisional decisions, the Chinese comrades at last made a final decision to render assistance to Korea with troops." He had quite a nerve to wish the Korean leader "luck."[80] Less than a week later, on October 19, 1950, Chinese troops crossed the Yalu River. One week later they fought their first battle with U.S. troops. This seemed to many Western observers to be the prelude to a third world war.

Soviet documents dispel the myth that Stalin had allegedly been moved to the point of tears by how "good the Chinese comrades were."[81] They reveal not a trace of revolutionary romanticism in the Soviet leader and show that, as in 1941–1945, he was even ready to act as a hard-nosed realist. The Chinese intervention, however, bore out Stalin's revolutionarism in a different way. Cynical as the Stalin-Mao bargaining may look today, its outcome was a great victory from the viewpoint of the revolutionary-imperial paradigm embraced by Stalin. The war helped wash away the ambiguity in Stalin-Mao relations: the Soviet leader accepted Mao without reservations, as long as the latter fought American power and depended on Soviet aid.

But the price of that new friendship and the continuation of the Korean War was high and tragic; it resulted in a huge setback for the USSR. The U.S. leadership adopted the view that the Sino-Soviet bloc was bent on global conquest. In turn, it was determined to destroy the aggressor and, if necessary, to embark on a large-scale campaign of mobilization and armament. The military budget of the United States quadrupled, and the arms race on the Western side did not slow down until the late 1980s.[82]

The Korean War allowed the United States to exclude the Soviet Union from a peace settlement with Japan. Incensed by the conditions insisted upon by the Americans and careful to foil Western attempts to ruin the Sino-Soviet alliance, Stalin boycotted a final peace treaty with Japan. Immediately, the United States signed a treaty of defense and alliance with Japan—Stalin's prophecy fulfilled. With Stalin's refusal to sign the Japanese peace treaty in San Francisco, Soviet territorial acquisitions did not acquire international recognition de jure.[83] Therefore, the ground remained for controversy over four tiny islands in the Kuriles—Shikotan, Kunashiri, Iturup, and Habomai, which to this day poison relations between Moscow and Tokyo.

Another of Stalin's worst nightmares came true. The hostilities in the Far East gave a decisive impulse to the rearmament of West Germany, with the help of some of Hitler's former generals—an idea unthinkable not long before. With the Bundeswehr, a new West German army, NATO was on the way to becoming a full-fledged military force in Europe. And the U.S. government, through the CIA and other means, intensified covert operations to assist the anti-Communist underground in Eastern Europe, the Baltic states, and Ukraine. In a word, the Americans began to wage the Cold War in earnest, with all available means short of outright attack on the USSR.

Did Stalin acknowledge these setbacks? He never gave any indication that he did. Several times after June 1951, when the frontline in Korea stabilized along the 38th parallel, the North Koreans, suffering mounting casualties from U.S. air strikes, begged Stalin for peace. Kim Il Sung told Stalin that the protracted war allowed "the enemy, who suffers almost no casualties, to cause continuous and terrible damage" to North Korea.[84] Yet each time Stalin advised Kim to hold on, because the enemy, according to him, would capitulate first and soon. In fact, Stalin must have believed that the war of attrition would best serve the USSR's interests: it would tie down the United States in the Far East, and it would make both North Korea and the PRC even more dependent on Soviet economic and military power, which would guarantee the Kremlin a monolithic bloc and undisputed hegemony in the Communist universe.

In the end, tiny Korea remained in a deadly trilateral embrace, between the United States on one side, determined to beat back world communism, and, on the other side, the PRC and the USSR—each guided by megalomaniac paradigms and the enormous egos of their leaders. On June 5, 1951, Stalin wrote to Mao that "one should not escalate the Korean War, for a protracted war firstly will enable the Chinese troops to study modern warfare . . . and secondly will unsettle the Truman regime in America and undermine the military prestige of Anglo-American troops."[85] One year later Zhou Enlai told Stalin that, according to Mao, "the continuation of [the Korean] war is beneficial to us, since it interferes with U.S. preparations for a new world war." Stalin agreed. The protracted war "revealed American weakness." The Americans "are generally not capable of conducting a big war, particularly after the Korean War [started]. All their strength is in air raids and the atomic bomb." Stalin again dangled the "Taiwan argument" before the Chinese comrades: they should know that the Americans are tough bargainers, "merchants," and that, if the United States "were not to lose this war, the Chinese would never obtain Taiwan."[86]

With characteristic crudeness, Stalin dismissed Chinese and Korean casualties: the North Koreans "lose nothing, except for their men." In a word, Stalin was determined to fight until the last drop of blood had been shed by Chinese and North Korean soldiers. He also insisted, as a precondition of peace, that all North Korean and Chinese POWs be returned by the enemy. Otherwise, he said, the Americans would use them as spies. ("The same happened to our POWs" during World War II, and now Americans send them to the USSR as agents; "every day we capture a few of them.")[87]

The Korean War proved to be the same for Stalin as the Crimean War had been for Czar Nicholas I a century earlier. The reign of Nicholas had started when Russia was an unquestionable great power, respected and envied in all European capitals. It ended in a shameful defeat for the czar's empire on its own territory, the Crimea, from the technologically superior coalition of Great Britain, France, and Turkey. Nicholas, however, refused to recognize defeat: only after the sudden death of the czar (suicide was suspected) did his successor end the war. Stalin had a similar decline from the Great Victory of 1945 to the deadlock on the Korean peninsula, virtually at the Soviets' doorstep. The favorable change in the international situation that he registered in his conversation with Kim turned out to be just a reprieve. The domination of American aircraft in the Korean skies, under the protection of the rapidly growing American atomic umbrella, was a sword of Damocles over Stalin's head. He found some consolation in heavy American losses in the air battles over Korea. (His lieutenants reported to him the number of planes shot down in Korea: 569 American planes as compared with 63 Soviet MIG-15s from November 1950 to December 1951.) In his talks with Zhou in

September 1952, Stalin alleviated his concerns by prodding the Chinese to join in the gigantic arms race with the West. He expected the Korean War to last a year or two, and after that "China should turn into a [military] warehouse for Asia." When Zhou shared with Stalin China's plans to create an army of 102 divisions (3.2 million troops) in peacetime, Stalin commented that it was the "minimum" number needed. Zhou spoke about 150 air regiments in the future. "That's too little," Stalin said. "One must have 200 air regiments."[88]

In December 1952, Mao Zedong warned the Kremlin leader that the U.S. president-elect Dwight Eisenhower "is currently carrying out preparations for military actions that will take place after he comes to power." He informed Stalin of a new effort in the PRC to mobilize an additional quarter of a million soldiers, to compensate for terrible losses in the war, and asked for more Soviet armament. Stalin responded almost casually, after ten days, by saying that the current preparations for military escalation in Korea reflect the plans of the Truman administration. "It is perfectly possible," he wrote, "that the Eisenhower administration will change these plans toward lesser tension in Korea." Still, he concluded, "You are right to take the worst-case scenario stemming from the possibility of an offensive by the Americans."[89]

As casual and disparaging of American land power as Stalin wanted to sound, by the end of his life, according to Khrushchev, he began to fear U.S. superiority.[90] His dark reign faded amid his fears of a premature war with the United States and dark forebodings about the future of his empire. In a sense, Joseph Stalin was also a casualty of the Korean War.

## The Long Shadow

Stalin left no testament or farewell address to his successors. The last opportunity to do so would have been at the Nineteenth Party Congress in October 1952, the last Congress he attended and the one that approved a new party program. Instead, Stalin left the whole business to Georgi Malenkov. A special panel of experts, including the apparatchiks of the International Department of the Central Committee and the young *Pravda* editor Dmitri Shepilov, wrote the foreign policy part of the program. Stalin seemed to have little interest in the result. He showed signs of rapid decline, almost senility. At the first Party

Plenum after the Congress, he angrily denounced Molotov and Mikoyan, and suddenly submitted his resignation. One witness recalled the reaction of other Kremlin leaders: "Malenkov . . . motioned with his finger (signaling that the delegates should not accept Stalin's resignation). Mikoyan was very calm. Molotov said: 'Comrade Stalin, you are our teacher.' Stalin, cupping his hand behind his ear, as he did not hear well in his last years, barked: 'All of us here are the pupils of Lenin. Of Lenin! Lenin!' "[91]

Stalin could never bring himself to consider that he might be expendable and that his system could continue to run without him. He was reluctant to accept the nature of the epoch in which he was living or its major characteristics—bipolarity and the emergence of atomic weapons. Stalin preferred to act and think in the mode of pre–Cold War history. He had one foot firmly planted in the past. His reasoning was that the confrontation between the East and the West in the military-political sphere and their balancing on the threshold of war were not new. Similar events had occurred in the 1920s and 1930s and resulted in a war in 1939–1945: the Socialist Soviet Union had attacked Finland, Lithuania, Latvia, Estonia, and Poland. Capitalist Germany attacked the Socialist Soviet Union. Even an arms race, for all its atomic dimensions, was not entirely new, either. An arms race existed not only earlier in the twentieth century, but from the times of the bow and gunpowder.

In his last pronouncements, Stalin refuted the notion that Leninist postulates and the "classic" balance-of-power lessons might no longer be valid for conducting the Cold War. "Some comrades," Stalin said in 1952, "are mistaken when they say that the contradictions between the Socialist and the capitalist camps are stronger than the contradictions between capitalist countries, that the United States of America has subdued other capitalist countries enough so as not to let them wage wars with each other and weaken each other . . . Wouldn't it be wiser to say that capitalist England, and then capitalist France, will in the end have to break away from the U.S. embrace and venture a conflict with it in order to secure independent policies and of course high profits? To think that West Germany and Japan would remain under the U.S. 'regime' . . . means to believe in miracles."[92] In September 1952, Stalin agreed with Zhou Enlai that Japan and Germany, when rearmed by the United States, could turn their weapons against the Americans at some point. Stalin also told Zhou that the United

Nations, "an American-led organization," should be quietly under-mined, and that "a separate community [of nations] for Asia, [as well as a] separate community for Europe," should be created to counter the United Nations.[93] He anticipated the struggle between the Western countries and cherished the dream of once again following the pattern of 1939–1945, when he had gambled on the contradictions inside the Western camp and won.

Robert Conquest's estimate of Stalin's conduct in the first phase of the Cold War is a good one: his actions were "sometimes carefully prepared, though occasionally erratic." Stalin's "sense of realism" was "still adequate" enough for him to avoid a headlong clash with the United States.[94] The Marshall Plan marked a watershed in Stalin's postwar foreign policy, from relative relaxation to ruthless determi-nation. The Sino-Soviet treaty of February 1950 marked another crucial development: its signing meant that Stalin changed the frame-work of thinking from the "Yalta model" of coexistence with the great powers to the coalition-strategy in response to his vision of an uncer-tain, competitive world heading toward a third world war.

In these crucial episodes one finds a strange mind at work, powerful and informed, yet suspicious and callous, cautious and calculating, ambitious and vengeful—and, in this combination, rather far from realistic. Stalin's mind played tricks on him. After the end of World War II he did not want another confrontation, but he suspected the worst and tried to grab unilaterally what he could, twisting any understanding or agreement with the Allies to suit his own best inter-ests. In sum, his built-in suspicion of the West appeared to be a self-fulfilling prophecy.

The nature of Stalin's foreign policy may be described as cautious expansionism in those areas that Stalin and his advisors defined as Soviet "natural" spheres of influence. Yet there was no master plan in the Kremlin, and Stalin's ambitions had always been severely lim-ited by the terrible devastation of the USSR during World War II and the existence of the American atomic monopoly. The transition from the Grand Alliance to the Cold War from the Soviet shore looked far less preordained and far more risky than it would later seem to a number of Western experts and historians. Had there been a more moderate regime in the USSR and a less ruthless leader in the Kremlin, the best hope for Soviet diplomacy would have been the preservation of superpower status through a series of compromises with the Western powers. Stalin, on the contrary, wanted to project the image of Soviet strength just as it had been at the time of Yalta, when Soviet victories dwarfed Western military contributions. He still wanted cooperation with the West, but always on his own terms. He believed that world trends, from an expected world economic crisis to the unexpected victory of the Chinese Revolution, worked in his favor. When the United States responded vigorously to his "probes," first into Iran and Turkey, then into Germany and Europe in general, Stalin was surprised and alarmed. When the Americans responded in Korea, he retreated into himself, torn between false optimism and gloom.

At the end of his life Stalin found refuge in "theoretical" prophecies. He wrote about the general crisis of capitalism and insisted on the irrevocable decline of the old world: "One should regard the disintegration of a single, all-embracing world market as the most important economic result of World War II and its economic consequences." He even repudiated his own old dictum about "the relative stability of markets during the general crisis of capitalism." Lenin used to admit that "capitalism in general is growing faster than before." In his last days Stalin discarded this thesis too—it did not fit his neat, logical picture of capitalist decay.[95]

Stalin was bewildered by the nature of American power, superior in a technological and military sense, but so unstable, so weak in resolve. He repeated to Zhou: "The Germans defeated France in twenty days. The United States for two years already has been struggling to overcome tiny Korea. What kind of power is this?" Stalin mentioned jokingly that "the main armament of the Americans," besides the atomic bomb, was in "goods for sale"—stockings, cigarettes, and so on.[96] On November 1, 1952, as if in response to Stalin's words, the United States tested a thermonuclear device in the Pacific that was a thousand times more powerful than the bomb dropped on Hiroshima.

In reality, Stalin never found an adequate strategy to neutralize the growing U.S. military threat. At some point, he ordered the Main Operational Directorate, the planning body of the Soviet General Staff, to prepare the deployment of superior Soviet tank forces in Central Europe. Veterans of the General Staff recalled Stalin's instructions: American pilots must reckon with the possibility that by the time they return from their missions, their airfields will be taken over by Soviet tanks. It was a crude bluff, given that the Americans stationed their strategic aircraft as far as the North African coast.[97] Stalin also prepared sabotage operations against American forward-based airfields, in case of war. Special Bureau Number One for Diversions and Intelligence of the MGB planned in 1948–1953 to do serious damage to the enemy.[98]

In the last months of Stalin's life, the "small" Committee of Information, one of the Soviet bureaus of intelligence analysis, reported to him that "the U.S. military leaders are not convinced of the practicality of using the atomic bomb in Korea. They are afraid that, if the use of atomic weapons does not ensure the real preponderance of the United States, a final blow will be dealt to U.S. prestige. What's more, in this case they believe that the existing U.S. stockpile of atomic weapons would considerably lose its importance as a means of intimidation."[99] Perhaps the dictator did not have time to read this reassuring information, which, to his suspicious, alarmist mind, would not have been very comforting.

Stalin's warnings about a future war rang in Khrushchev's ears to his last day. Stalin cast a long shadow of fear and uncertainty on his successors. Churchill and his American allies, he wrote in his last published works, were unbending, mortal enemies of the Soviet Union. They "bear a striking resemblance to Hitler and his friends . . . Other warmongers are American billionaires and millionaires who regard war as a source of profit. These aggressive forces hold in their hands reactionary governments and guide them."[100]

The emergence of relatively independent Communist regimes in China and Yugoslavia had made Stalin talk about communism as a doctrine that should reflect national interests. Speaking for the last time publicly, at the Nineteenth Party Congress, he stressed that the bourgeoisie was becoming cosmopolitan—therefore Communists should become nationalist! The power struggle with the West came to a state of balance, almost a stalemate, but national revolutions, like those in Mao's China or Kim's Korea, could help spread Soviet influence farther.

Stalin left the Cold War position of the Soviet Union in bad shape. Even worse was the shape of the Soviet leadership he left behind. Most of the party and state leaders were Stalin's creations, and, however hard they struggled to act on their own after his death, they remained in Stalin's shadow in their dealings with the outside world and their Cold War adversaries. This is true both of Molotov, who followed

Stalin to the letter, and of Khrushchev, who became the tyrant's apostate.

Stalin's idiosyncrasies did not die with him; they left an imprint upon post-Stalin foreign policy thinking. As long as the Soviet regime existed, its leaders could not rid themselves of xenophobia. Khrushchev, who was able to overcome it only in his retirement, wrote about it as "Stalin's mental disease." Every foreigner was regarded by the Kremlin "as an unmasked enemy, who came only with the goal of recruiting Soviet people for espionage."[101] Another of Stalin's gifts to his successors was a tradition of pervasive secrecy—in fact it was an extension of his xenophobia. Stalin's successors inherited a primitive understanding of the West's political system and decision-making process; just as Stalin suggested, they would look for the powerful conspiracy of "dark forces" backing the arms race and bent on the destruction of the Soviet Union in a surprise attack.

The inferiority complex that Stalin provoked in his minions was after his death reflected in their international behavior, as they became the rulers of the Soviet Union. Long-suppressed human dignity looked for outlets and sometimes, especially under Khrushchev, burst out in ugly, awkward attempts to defend the prestige and save the pride of the Soviet empire.

Most important, the Kremlin statesmen inherited the Soviet revolutionary-imperial paradigm in the form that was bequeathed by Stalin in 1953. The transformation of the world under the aegis and with the assistance of the Soviet Union remained a powerful raison d'être for the corporate mentality of Soviet power elites, however cynical they became. After Stalin's death, innovators inside the Soviet elite were outnumbered, and later, under Leonid Brezhnev, overpowered by this gray, unimaginative mass, the sinful and power-hungry Pharisees who brought necessary sacrifices to the idols of the faith that the previous, revolutionary generation had sincerely worshipped and been ready to die for.

# 3 Molotov: Expanding the Borders

> It is good that the Russian czars annexed so
> much land for us. This makes it easier for us to
> struggle with capitalism.
>
> Vyacheslav Molotov to Felix Chuev,
> January 1975

Molotov, translated literally, means in Russian "hammer-man." Like most of the leading Bolsheviks of his generation, permanently involved in conspiracies against the czarist government, Vyacheslav Mikhailovich Skryabin had to assume a party pseudonym. Like Stalin ("the man of steel"), he chose one that was well suited to aggressive proletarian revolution. The two names are now united in history forever—the steely, murderous sickle and the hard, determined hammer.

Molotov's first foreign policy initiatives were formidable. Having barely assumed the reign of foreign policy in 1939 after the Great Terror, he immediately entered the inner sanctum of European diplomacy: dealings with Nazi Germany. In August 1939 he signed the Nazi-Soviet nonaggression pact, which aimed to change the face of Europe. The document became known as the Molotov-Ribbentrop Pact and, as many believe to this day, opened the door to World War II.

In November 1940 Molotov went to Berlin on the most important mission of his life—he was to negotiate with the most dangerous and enigmatic leader in the world: Adolf Hitler. After the fall of France, the Kremlin received serious warnings from its agents in Europe that Hitler might turn to the East.[1] Following his first meeting with the

Nazi leader, Molotov communicated to Stalin late at night that "the great interest of Hitler to reach an agreement and to strengthen his friendship with the USSR about spheres of influence is obvious."[2] After a short sleep he cabled Stalin again, asking for instructions before his second meeting with the führer, during which they would discuss the main issue: the conditions on which the Soviet Union would join the "pact of three" (Germany, Italy, and Japan). These conditions, Stalin and Molotov had agreed in Moscow, should include Soviet domination in Bulgaria and the Turkish straits, a return of czarist colonial possessions in Northern China to the USSR, and recognition of the Persian Gulf and the Arabian Sea as a Soviet sphere of influence.

Molotov had the authority to sign any document with Hitler on the spot, but in his cable to Stalin he suggested that any deal on spheres of influence be delayed until the German foreign minister, Ribbentrop, came to Moscow.[3] Stalin agreed. He instructed Molotov to test Hitler on two issues: Finland and Turkey should be inside the Soviet security zone. Molotov would reject Hitler's counterproposal of a joint protectorate over Turkey as well as his attempt to divert Moscow's attention from the Turkish straits toward Iran and India.[4] (Hitler seemed to be suggesting to Stalin what Napoleon had repeated to Alexander I: quit Europe and concentrate on the Great Game with Britain in the Eurasian heartland.) As a result of Molotov's tactics, Hitler, who vacillated between the idea of attacking the Soviet Union and defeating Great Britain first (his credo, *Mein Kampf*, was also highly ambivalent in this respect), decided that Stalin, with his assertiveness, had to be crushed before he became too strong.

Valentin Berezhkov, Stalin's interpreter, writes that upon his return Molotov, like Stalin, tried to persuade himself and others that Hitler would not attack the USSR in 1941. More important, he passed on to Stalin Hitler's reassuring offer for a summit the following year.[5] (Molotov could never convincingly reject this interpretation.)[6] He and Stalin sent their drafts of an agreement to Berlin, but they never received a response.[7] Hitler had made his decision to pursue "Barbarossa," his plan for the three-pronged envelopment and elimination of Stalin's empire.

Recently, Russian historians have begun to suggest that the Molotov-Ribbentrop Pact was a great mistake, that there were alternatives—an alliance with Western democracies or neutrality. But the more we learn about Molotov the more we are convinced that he would be the last man to offer such alternatives to Stalin.

## The Character of "Iron Vyacheslav"

Molotov embodied the linkage of two epochs of international relations, the times before and after World War II. He was the only person to shake hands with Hitler, Goering, and Hess, be heartily welcomed by Franklin D. Roosevelt and Winston Churchill, cut down to size by Harry Truman, and eventually become the main diplomatic adversary of the West at the dawn of the Cold War. His life and career passed under the sign of power and humiliation, death and farce.

Molotov was born in 1890 in Kukarka, a forgotten fort between Moscow and the Ural Mountains, into a middle-class Russian family of nobility but not wealth or social prominence. The Skryabins were not related to Alexander Skryabin, the brilliant pianist and composer; they were provincial merchants. Yet Vyacheslav Molotov had every chance to establish a successful career as a professor, lawyer, or physician. Instead, he joined the Bolshevik party and built an impressive career. From 1926 to 1957 he was a member of the Politburo. From 1930 to 1941 he was the chairman of the Council of People's Commissars. From 1941 to 1957 he was the first deputy of the prime minister. And from 1939 to 1949 and 1953 to 1956 he served as foreign minister. His wife, Polina Zhemchuzhina, was a dear friend of Nadia Alliluyeva, Stalin's second wife. After Nadia's suicide the Molotovs remained very close to Stalin; Polina became a doyenne of "the Kremlin's spouses," head of the Soviet cosmetic industry, and then of fisheries.[8]

In 1948 Polina was framed by the secret police and sent to a concentration camp as "a Zionist." When the Politburo voted on his wife's sentence, Molotov did not dissent. Nevertheless, Molotov lost his master's absolute trust, and in 1949 was replaced as foreign minister by the verbose Andrei Vyshinsky, Stalin's prosecutor at the staged political trials of the 1930s. Molotov himself probably would have been a victim of Stalin's next purge, had the dictator not died. Despite all this, Molotov never complained about being mistreated. He and Polina, back from the Gulag, deeply mourned Stalin's death.[9]

In 1955 Nikita Khrushchev began to push Molotov aside. Molotov's final disgrace came in June 1957, when he tried to oust Khru-shchev from power. He was confronted by a national hero of World War II, the minister of defense, Marshal Georgi Zhukov, who said that the army would not back him. Khrushchev, with Zhukov's sup-port, sent Molotov into exile as an ambassador to Mongolia. Later, Khrushchev saw his proximity to Mao's China as a risk. There were plans to transfer Molotov to Helsinki, but the Finns objected strongly and Khrushchev decided against it.

All through the post-Stalin era, Molotov obstinately defended his past record and pestered the Central Committee with his "initiatives." Khrushchev reacted by asking the Committee of Party Control, a disciplinarian watchdog, to collect every piece of evidence on Molo-tov's past "antiparty" behavior. Despite this investigation, Molotov was sent to Geneva as a deputy representative of the Soviet Union in the International Atomic Energy Agency. In 1962 he was suddenly forced to retire and was dismissed from the Party—a sign of shame and disgrace. He outlived Khrushchev, Brezhnev, Andropov, and Chernenko, and died peacefully in 1986 in his dacha in Zhukovka, near Moscow. During the last years of his life, hosting small parties of the faithful, Molotov would raise the first glass to Lenin, the second to Stalin, and the third to his wife, Polina, victimized by the system to which both she and her husband belonged.

After Molotov died, some mysterious men (probably from the KGB) came to his dacha and took away all his papers. Their fate is still unknown. The fund of his personal papers in the foreign ministry is only partially available. Rumors were circulating in Moscow that Molotov was writing his memoirs, but they seem to be nonexistent after his death. In 1991 the Russian nationalist writer Felix Chuev published a book entitled *One Hundred and Forty Conversations with Molotov.* It consists of minutes that Chuev recorded during seventeen years of his meetings with the retired politician, from 1969 to 1986. Molotov was frank and at ease with Chuev, although he remained silent about state secrets. He stubbornly denied, for in-stance, the existence of secret protocols to the Nazi-Soviet pact of August 1, 1939.[10]

Some observers disparaged the diplomatic skills of Molotov, others exaggerated them.[11] Molotov himself admitted: "I regard myself first of all as a politician and not a diplomat."[12] This does not mean that Molotov diminished his stature; to his mind being a politician was much more important than being a diplomat.[13] He once told his American counterpart, John Foster Dulles, that his training in the politics of the Communist party, especially during the years of bitter factional struggle, had proved a remarkable advantage when he became a practitioner of diplomacy.[14] Lifelong party meetings, replete with slander, filibustering, and other smart techniques designed to upset and irritate, prepared Molotov for conference rooms and tête-à-tête diplomatic encounters. Backstage intrigue and spying on opponents were his favorite techniques. According to Molotov, the winning of trust was only a tactical ruse; flexibility on policy was a sin; and acknowledgment of mistakes was a death sentence.

For Molotov—and this endeared him to Stalin—Stalin's will, the will of the Party, and revolutionary "necessity" were all synonymous.[15] He was probably the only Robespierre-like figure in Stalin's entourage: a man morally committed to the Revolution. He believed that the Great Terror was a necessary purgative and did not fear it. He could sign the death sentences of 3,187 people in just one night and then watch Western movies with Stalin with a pure conscience.[16] To the end, Molotov and his wife, Polina, believed that with the Great Terror of the 1930s Stalin had saved the Soviet Union during the Second World War by destroying the enemies' "fifth column" inside the country. The will of the Party was the most important consideration for them. Only when the Politburo voted for Polina's expulsion from the Party and imminent arrest did the will of "iron Vyacheslav" crack. He loved Polina but could not go against the Party. Polina came to his rescue: "If the Party requires it, we will divorce," she said.[17]

Stalin and Molotov were united in the belief that the Soviet Union could be destroyed if it was not continually "cleansed" and kept in a state of permanent tension. In the Brezhnev years, the pensioner Molotov proclaimed: "When life is honey, the Bolsheviks are not needed."[18] When Khrushchev denounced Stalin for his terror against the Party, Molotov was the only one in the Kremlin who did not betray the dead tyrant.[19]

Molotov unquestionably was as much an introvert as Stalin was. Yet, when Milovan Djilas, then an enthusiastic fan of both, observed the two in 1944–1945, he was struck by how different they were. In his later memoirs Djilas describes Molotov's mind as completely "impenetrable," "inscrutable." Molotov was almost always the same, with hardly a shade of variety, unlike Stalin, who "was of a lively, almost restless temperament," "completely different in his own, the Communist, milieu." "In retrospect," concluded Djilas, "Molotov with his relativism, with his knack for detailed daily routine, and Stalin, with his fanatical dogmatism, and, at the same time, broader horizons, his driving quest for further, future possibilities . . . ideally complemented one another."[20]

There is a distinct difference in Russian between the words *vozhd* and *rukovoditel,* both of which are translated into English as "leader." The first is the master, the helmsman; the second is "one who is in charge." Stalin was the *vozhd,* the leader, and could not tolerate any challenge from minor leaders. Molotov's lack of ambition to lead may help explain his power and endurance. He subordinated his personality to Stalin's will, and from this inferior plateau he exercised his influence on him. "I maintain," wrote Djilas, "that he not only incited Stalin into doing many things, but that he also sustained him and dispelled his doubts."[21] Molotov, indeed, played this supportive role after Hitler's surprise attack in June 1941. He would continue to do so later.

Some observers mistook Molotov's subdued and inscrutable demeanor for a lack of character and sense of humor. When necessary, however, he could shed his stern appearance. As he was seeing the Japanese foreign minister off at a Moscow railway station after the unexpected signing of a nonaggression pact in 1941, the two men sealed their camaraderie by singing a Russian folk song traditionally sung by drunken party-goers: "The trees were crackling in the wind . . . And the lovers stayed awake all night."[22]

During the war Molotov did things that required great courage. He had to go to London and Washington to demand the second front from the allies. In May 1942 he flew to London on a four-engine bomber, then to Washington, and then back to London—over territory occupied by the Germans. On the way the bomber was attacked by German fighters.[23]

Unlike Stalin, Molotov never had moments when his dogmatic version of the realpolitik gave way to bolder visions. He regarded Stalin's whirlwinds of political ambition and hubris as damaging to Soviet foreign policy. He himself chose to pursue a steady and cautious path to his goals. In conversation with Chuev, Molotov often said: "It is necessary to stay within certain limits. [If you swallow too much] you could choke."[24] Everything he did was ritualized and rationally organized to ensure a long life: his walks, exercise, reading. Long after he had been ousted from power, he meticulously followed his rite of reading—each morning *Pravda,* each evening *Izvestia,* and a trip each day to read the books and magazines in the Lenin Library, one block away from his apartment on Granovsky Street.

Every month Molotov traveled to a local bank to pay his party dues. He continued to do so for twenty-three years after he was expelled from the Party. In the summer of 1984 Constantine Chernenko, Gorbachev's predecessor, invited Molotov to the Kremlin and told him about his restoration to the party ranks. Molotov, then ninety-three, almost started crying. He declared to the General Secretary: "You are doing things right, and for this you have the people's support."[25] When Molotov died two years later, he had only five hundred rubles (three hundred dollars) in his savings account.

Stalin often drew the ministers of defense, armament, and security, as well as senior intelligence officials, into his decision-making circle. The top three, four, or five were the members of ad hoc working panels on certain issues of foreign policy. Molotov was the obligatory member on all of them. At the peak of his career Molotov commanded several huge bureaucratic pyramids, and had two chancelleries, or secretariats. One was located in the Council of People's Commissars (since 1946 the Council of Ministers) and served his needs as a first deputy prime minister. The other, located in the Ministry of Foreign Affairs, dealt with materials on international affairs (and, in 1947–1948, also on intelligence). Molotov's routine included reading dozens of ciphered cables from embassies all over the world, as well as reports from intelligence stations. The staff divided the coded telegrams into three groups: the most important documents were reported to Molotov orally. Other documents were submitted with marginal notes, brief annotations, and also draft resolutions. Finally, the last group of documents were put into a single folder carrying a short summary on its cover, with a proposed resolution. Some documents were stamped "Top Secret. Personal," and were for Molotov alone to read. Those included notes written in Stalin's red pencil.[26]

Molotov served as Stalin's personal computer. He performed this function superbly: he was exceptionally industrious, punctilious, and stubborn about the facts he reported. Stalin, who valued all these qualities, even urged his "number one diplomat" to become an academician. While Molotov was in New York on a visit to the General Assembly of the United Nations, Stalin sent him a "top secret" cable:

To Comr. Molotov:
The academicians Vavilov, Bruievich, Volgin, Lysenko, and others are asking me to persuade you not to object to their proposal regarding your election as a member emeritus of the Academy. I support this proposal of the academicians and urge you to give your agreement.

—Stalin[27]

Molotov declined. Unlike his subordinates, the vainglorious Andrei Vyshinsky and Ivan Maisky, who eagerly donned the academic mantle, Molotov lacked personal ambition. The only genre of writing he allowed himself was that of the Central Committee's Secretariat and Politburo, for them and by them. Even after he had been ousted from the Party and maligned by his enemies, he never succumbed to the temptation, as Khrushchev did, to answer his opponents through the foreign press, especially the American press.

Stalin would not have been true to his paranoid self if he had left his foreign policy minister with a sense of safety in his own domain. Stalin assigned Vladimir Dekanozov, a man attached to Beria, as a deputy to Molotov. This short man with bulging, shameless eyes reported directly to Stalin and his dreaded NKVD master; his sphere of responsibility before 1941 covered Germany and its satellites, and in 1945 also included Iran, Turkey, Afghanistan, Mongolia, and Xinjiang, all consulates, cadres, and finances of the foreign ministry.[28] There was little doubt, however, that one of his duties was to keep an eye on Molotov. Stalin placed another stooge under Molotov, Andrei Vyshinsky, a former Menshevik. He would eventually replace the disgraced Molotov.

Although Molotov voted with the rest of the Politburo to indict his wife for "Zionist connections," Stalin began to suspect that his right-hand man was also a foreign agent, perhaps recruited during his trip to London in the spring of 1942. At one time Anthony Eden traveled with Molotov in the same train and met with him through a British interpreter—a flagrant violation of Stalin's instruction to meet with foreigners only in the presence of Soviet witnesses. In early 1953 Maisky was arrested as a British spy. Beria personally tortured him trying to extract information about Molotov's suspected betrayal.[29] Had Stalin lived longer, his stern consigliere would have been doomed.

## The Molotov School of Diplomacy

For years, many in the Soviet Union and abroad wondered how much autonomy Molotov had in his actions. According to the Soviet diplomat and Chinese expert Nikolai Fedorenko, Molotov would prepare a decision and then call Stalin by phone to clear it with him: "Only very rarely did he take his papers and go, as he put it, to talk it over in the Central Committee, which meant with Stalin."[30]

Another diplomatic veteran, Vladimir Yerofeev, gives a different description of Molotov's routine: "Hardly a day passed without Molotov's going to see him [Stalin] after midnight for reporting or for a conference and coming back, as a rule, tired and irritated, venting some of his anger on his staff."[31]

Molotov was not an automaton who merely implemented Stalin's decisions. Too often he was on his own and had to act accordingly. Molotov substituted for Stalin during meetings with most foreign leaders, and he went abroad to attend to what could be termed summits (Stalin had a notorious aversion to traveling). More often than not, he guessed the leader's thinking ahead of time and came to "correct" conclusions.[32] When Molotov went to Berlin, Paris, or New York on an especially important mission, he communicated with Stalin several times a day by ciphered cables. Yet often in the postwar years, when Stalin was on long vacations or seriously ill, Molotov would act on policy as he felt and understood it. "I knew when I had to act as a foreign minister, especially after Stalin, that many were surprised that I behaved so independently," he explained. Of course, he was quick to add, "within the limits of my instructions."[33]

By 1945 Molotov had mastered many details of the diplomatic craft, whereas Stalin obviously could not fully grasp them. A veteran of Molotov's secretariat was categorical about it: "Stalin could not read what Molotov could. He was briefed by Vyacheslav Mikhailovich and, actually, the information he got was mostly prepackaged, condensed, and simplified."[34] The latter part of this statement is wrong: Stalin had many channels of "special information" that led exclusively to his study. Intelligence services competed for Stalin's ear and sent the best bits of information directly to him. Yet the aging dictator, busy maintaining domestic security and unmasking plots among his lieutenants, was finding it increasingly difficult to stay abreast of the complicated postwar world.[35]

Molotov shared Stalin's mania for highly centralized diplomacy, his fear being that otherwise Soviet stratagems and tricks would leak to the enemy. The delegation of authority to subordinates was reduced to a bare minimum: ambassadors were only "transmission belts" for the policies that Stalin and Molotov concocted together. "I think it was not easy to fool us," Molotov recalled many times with satisfaction. "Everything was in Stalin's fist, in my fist—we could not act otherwise in that period."[36]

While Stalin and Molotov held their cards very close to their chests, they enjoyed a rare ability to look at their opponents' cards. Molotov came to be very dependent on information procured by Soviet espionage: for one thing, he eagerly sought evidence on the American-British split, which, in his unshakable Marxist opinion, was just a matter of time. In one key episode, when the Soviet delegation walked out of the Paris conference discussing the Marshall Plan, Molotov wanted to know in advance about the reactions of the British and American governments. According to a KGB veteran, "The KGB was stretched to the limit, and the demands on our agents in London were heavier than ever. [Molotov] flew into blind rages when he felt he was not sufficiently informed. 'Why,' he roared, 'why are there no documents?'"[37] One can imagine a giant web with Stalin and Molotov as two spiders in its center, ever ready to make a decisive move should a hapless foreign fly become ensnared. In reality, however, the system had as many flaws as it did advantages.

In an attempt to increase the usefulness of his diplomats, Molotov encouraged them to model themselves after the NKVD men, "the neighbors" (the nickname came from the original territorial proximity of the foreign ministry and NKVD buildings), who worked under diplomatic cover and produced invaluable information for him and Stalin. In the fall of 1947, Stalin created the Committee of Information (KI), a super-agency for intelligence and analysis that placed under Molotov's direct supervision the First Directorate of State Security (MGB) and the Main Intelligence Directorate (*Razvedupr,* or GRU). Soviet ambassadors in London and Washington were instructed to take charge of intelligence stations and even illegal networks. Molotov's dream had come true: to possess a diplomatic and aggressive spy network. Earlier he had made Soviet diplomats wear quasi-military uniforms; now he forced them to moonlight as spies.

The reform never worked, however.[38] The facade of the Molotov school of diplomacy concealed grave problems. One was that crucial information was often ignored, fell through the cracks, or was dismissed as "disinformation." Molotov, like Stalin, was pathologically mistrustful. "I believe that one cannot rely upon the intelligence officers," Molotov later said. "One should listen to them, but it is necessary to check up on them. The intelligence officers can lead you to a very dangerous position . . . There are many provocateurs here, there, and everywhere."[39]

Another problem that prevented the Stalin-Molotov diplomacy from taking advantage of its excellent intelligence was the extremely low quality of "transmission belts," their inability to implement instructions from the central power properly. After Stalin and the NKVD had destroyed a whole generation of experienced Soviet diplomats and intelligence officers, Molotov, Beria, Malenkov, and Dekanozov recruited new people to replace them. Among the new recruits were Andrei Gromyko, Iakov Malik, Fedor Gusev, Vassily Zarubin, and others who would become the counterparts of U.S. Cold Warriors. Eventually, these new men acquired field experience, but they never could achieve the level of flexibility, education, and rapport with the West that their purged predecessors had enjoyed. "There was nobody to choose from," Molotov recalled calmly. The hallmark of the selection process was "honesty" (Molotov's word), that is, the absence of independent thinking and unquestioning loyalty to Stalin and his regime.[40]

Molotov shared Stalin's fascination with state power as the only valid currency in world affairs. That is why Hitler's Reich, unlike Western democracies, impressed him with its "high degree of organization."[41] Without a strong USSR and its mighty Red Army, the world revolution had no future at all. His understanding of international relations gravitated to the Marxist-Leninist "theory of imperialism" with its conviction that under the capitalist order selfishness, expansion, and war were the key to relations among states, and that class struggle was the driving force of human history. He liked to instruct young diplomats: "You always have to keep Lenin in the back of your mind, particularly when dealing with the issue of foreign policy."[42] Molotov believed that it was always possible to exploit the immanent contradictions of capitalist countries to foil the united anti-Soviet front of capitalist powers. This became a cornerstone of his diplomacy.

Molotov, just like Stalin, never recognized the Cold War as a new stage in international relations with its specific features: bipolarity, the role of the nuclear arms race, global brinkmanship. "I don't like the expression Cold War," Molotov said at the end of his life. "It seems to me that it belongs to Khrushchev."[43]

Molotov never believed there were ways the Soviet Union could have prevented Germany's assault in June 1941. Equally, he did not see any lost chances to prevent world tensions after 1945. From Molotov's viewpoint, Western powers and leaders behaved the only way they could—as enemies of the Soviet Union and the Socialist way of life. Even during the time of the Grand Alliance, Molotov divided the Soviets' Western counterparts into two groups: smart and dangerous "imperialists," and "fools"; and he never altered his images of them. "It seems to me," Molotov once admitted, "that in general politicians in America are stupid."[44] He dismissed Dwight Eisenhower as a "benign lad." Anthony Eden, the British Conservative government's foreign secretary and then a prime minister, was "too feeble, delicate, and rather helpless." Yet Molotov preferred him to Ernest Bevin, the Labour government's foreign secretary, who had a long record of fighting Communists in trade unions.[45]

Winston Churchill alone, although "one hundred percent imperialist," evoked grudging respect in Molotov. He even seemed to have sympathy for him: "[Churchill] was the strongest of them all, the smartest . . . He admired Stalin."[46] Churchill's defeat by the Labour candidate Clement Attlee in 1945 was difficult for Molotov to understand. "Churchill was one of the organizers of the victory, and I still cannot imagine how it could happen." He humbly admitted that one "should better know the British way of life."[47] Molotov also paid homage to the Dulles brothers, John Foster and Allen. Foster "would get you by hook or by crook"; he was "a typical imperialist," "one-sided, hardened, convinced . . . That made him similar to Churchill." He and Allen were "the kind of brothers [who] would pick your pocket and chop your head off at the same time."[48]

Molotov understood well the conflicting ideologies of the proletarians and the capitalists; his deep-seated belief in the former was the basis of his unwavering conviction and self-righteousness. In Khrushchev's words: "Molotov was like a windup toy. Once he wound up and let go, his gears and wheels would turn and turn and turn until all the tension had gone out of his spring."[49] Early in his career he had even disagreed with Stalin on the crucial theoretical point of whether it was possible to build socialism in a single country; at that time Molotov perceived himself as a stronger supporter of world revolution than Stalin.[50] Later, when he became Stalin's foreign minister, their roles reversed somewhat. Stalin, as the emperor and the pontiff, could think in broader categories—of long-term trends and forces that shook and shaped the world. He could confess he was wrong about the Chinese Revolution. But on most problems of everyday diplomacy the two men saw eye to eye.

Many latter-day Russian nationalists viewed Molotov as their predecessor.[51] Molotov was indeed a fan of the great state *(derzhavnik)*. He defended the imperial and state interests of the Soviet Union; like Stalin, he saw the Russians as people with a "special mission." At the end of his life he said, "The Hungarians? They are . . . petty merchant souls. A Russian has some inner feeling. He likes to do things large-scale: if he is to fight, let it be a real fight; if he is to build socialism, then let it be on a world scale."[52] He heartily shared his boss's ambition for expanding the borders of the Soviet Union and maintaining security zones in key geopolitical areas around the USSR.[53]

Yet for Molotov, as for Stalin, Russian nationalism was only a useful tool of state policy. Molotov thought in terms of social classes and great powers, not just peoples and states. For his vision of revolution, everything that was weak, be it social movements or small states, was simply not important, and could easily be sacrificed on the altar of Soviet security and promotion of the Communist cause.

After Khrushchev ousted him from the Politburo, Molotov refused to repent and regarded Khrushchev as a right-wing deviationist. On May 21, 1959, Molotov sent a memo to the Central Committee with "theses" on the establishment of a confederation of Socialist states. This new body, as Molotov saw it, would leave to member states all matters of domestic and most questions of foreign policy, but would take upon itself the issues of war and peace, as well as common defense. To start, Molotov suggested a confederation of the USSR and the People's Republic of China—with a new transnational state with a permanent government and even perhaps a People's Parliament.[54]

As a firm Communist, Molotov seemed to believe that Socialist states were part of a supranational entity, a super-empire.

To the end of his life, Molotov regarded Soviet diplomacy after the Second World War as a total and absolute success. He recalled Stalin's words that czarist Russia used to "win wars, but could not enjoy the fruits of its victories." Molotov added that "Russians are remarkable warriors, but do not know how to make peace: they are deceived, underpaid." After the Second World War "we did a fine job," he concluded with deep conviction. "The results were not bad."[55] On the threshold of death Molotov kept repeating, "We have never been made fools of. I don't remember a single case."[56] Given Molotov's unfailing memory and the controversial record of Soviet diplomacy in the early Cold War, this was a startling statement. Was this preoccupation with "not being fooled" a scar left by the talks with Hitler? Did the "hammer" forget serious blunders in Soviet diplomacy committed under Stalin's and his guidance since 1945? Molotov cannot answer these questions, but the newly available documents from the Russian archives tell the story.

## The Stalin-Molotov Team

On May 8, 1945, an important cable arrived on Molotov's desk from the capital of Turkey. The Soviet ambassador Sergei A. Vladimirov informed the Soviet foreign minister about a proposal of Selim Sarper, a Turkish ambassador to the USSR, to conclude a bilateral treaty of friendship. During the war the Turkish government had clearly leaned toward Germany, despite its proclaimed neutrality. Now Ankara was sending a clear signal to Moscow that it was seeking special relations with the Soviet Union, even at the risk of causing the displeasure of another great power, Great Britain.[57]

Since the eighteenth century, Great Britain and other European powers had thwarted all attempts by the czarist empire to close the Black Sea to the fleets of Russia's enemies, as well as to provide the Russians with free access to the Mediterranean. Twice Russia's soft southern underbelly was struck through the Turkish straits: in the Crimean War (1853–1856), when the British-French expedition passed through it to lay siege to Sevastopol; and during World War I (1914–1918), when the German battleships *Goeben* and *Breslau* appeared on a pirating mission in the Black Sea. In the spring of 1917 the Provisional Government received from the Allies a promise of control over the straits, provided that Russia stayed in the war. The Bolshevik coup made this agreement null and void, and in 1918–1920 the Turkish straits were used again, this time to assist anti-Bolshevik forces in Russia. In 1936 the Soviet Union had to sign the Montreux Convention in Switzerland, confirming the neutrality of the straits and the disadvantaged situation of the Russian Black Sea fleet.

When Molotov was in Berlin in 1940, Hitler proposed replacing the Montreux Convention with a new agreement with four guarantors—Germany, the Soviet Union, Italy, and Japan. But Stalin instructed Molotov to demand the protectorate over Bulgaria and to reject any deal on Turkey. "I am leaving for a lunch and talk with Hitler," Molotov cabled to Moscow. "I will press him on the Black Sea, the straits, and Bulgaria."[58]

In November 1944, Litvinov suggested to Stalin and Molotov that they make a revision of the straits' control part of a larger Soviet-British deal "on the basis of an amicable demarcation of the security spheres in Europe according to a principle of geographical proximity."[59] A month earlier Stalin had raised the issue of the revision of the Montreux doctrine, during Churchill's visit to Moscow in October 1944. He raised it again at the Yalta summit in February 1945. But when Churchill and Roosevelt agreed that revision was necessary, Stalin, instead of negotiating a deal with the Allies, presented his ultimatum to Turkey. On June 7, 1945, Molotov summoned Sarper, who returned to Moscow, and demanded from the Turks the lease of a base in the straits and concession of two territories, Kars (Khan) and Ardagan, once conquered by czarist Russia and ceded by Lenin's government to Kemal Atatürk under the treaty of 1922 "because of the USSR's weakness."[60]

The Western Allies (as well as Stalin's successors) could never understand the logic of Stalin's actions in this particular case. Later many interpreted it as the first postwar sign of the Kremlin ruler's unlimited ambitions.[61] But another interpretation seems more likely. Stalin looked at the straits not only as an issue of Soviet security, but also as a matter of prestige. He had no doubts that his demands were justified: during World War II German traffic through the Dardanelles had caused great damage to the Soviet war effort, and the Western Allies knew it. Anything less than the earlier concession of Britain and France to the Provisional Government in 1917 would look like a diminution of the Red Army's great victory and Stalin's triumphant survival in 1945.

Stalin must have expected that the Turks, impressed with the victories of the Red Army, would give in to his demand for a base in the straits (it seems that he raised territorial demands only as a bargaining chip; he dropped them in August 1946)—and then Washington and London would accept it as a *fait accompli*. It was at that moment that Molotov had a minor argument with Stalin. At the end of his life Molotov admitted that Stalin had overplayed his hand and been arrogant in 1945. Soviet demands, Molotov said to Chuev, were "an ill-timed, unrealistic thing . . . Had Turkey been a Socialist state, then we could at least have talked about it." But Stalin insisted, "Go ahead, push for joint ownership!"[62]

When after the Potsdam Conference the Truman administration decided with some hesitation not to make any gifts to Stalin in the Dardanelles, the Kremlin leader did not ease his pressure on Turkey.[63] According to Yuri Modin of the KGB, Stalin ordered his intelligence sources to find out "exactly how far the West would go to defend this part of the world."[64] Many in Washington viewed Stalin's "war of nerves" against the backdrop of other developments (Iran, the future of Eastern Europe, Communist activities in France, Italy, and Greece). By December 1945 it led Truman to the conclusion that a Soviet invasion of Turkey was possible, and persuaded him to support the doctrine of containment of the Soviets in the Near East. When in August 1946 Stalin and Molotov renewed their ultimatum to Turkey, it produced the first real war scare inside the Truman administration, and prompted the Americans to prepare for retaliatory strategic bombing of the USSR, including the use of atomic bombs.[65]

Stalin obviously learned about these plans (code-named "Pincher"), for he made a number of conciliatory gestures to dispel U.S.-Soviet tensions. One KGB veteran believes that intelligence information on Truman's intentions "may have prevented the outbreak of war." Molotov later was of the same opinion: "It is good that we retreated in time," he recalled, "or [the situation] would have led to joint aggression against us."[66] When on March 12, 1947, Truman asked the U.S. Congress for support of his policy of containment of communism in Greece and Turkey, Kremlin leaders did not react strongly. They viewed the U.S. action as a direct and perhaps deserved consequence of Stalin's "Turkish probe."

The Turkish episode reveals that privately Molotov was less "tough" and even less risk-prone than Stalin—probably because he possessed a stronger sense of limits. It proves, again, that the most dangerous moves in Soviet foreign policy were linked to Stalin's character and mentality. At the same time, Molotov's dogmatism prevented him from recognizing possibly disastrous consequences of Stalin's "probes." It was Molotov's job to alert his boss to the self-defeating nature of this kind of diplomacy. But he had not done so, and not because he was afraid of angering Stalin. For Molotov, a conflict with the Western imperialists, with or without Turkey, was inevitable.

In many other episodes in postwar Soviet diplomacy Molotov's attitudes did not differ much from Stalin's. Yet some of those episodes deserve detailed attention, because they show how Molotov and Stalin worked together, and how they reached conclusions that determined the overall course of Soviet foreign policy from the wartime Alliance to the Cold War. During 1945, Stalin and Molotov continued to operate on what proved to be a false assumption in their diplomacy with the Americans: that Truman would not last long, and that he was just a tool in the hands of skillful and sly manipulators like Winston Churchill and James Byrnes (the prominent Southern politician who had been the U.S. Secretary of State since July 1945). A weak U.S. president evoked mixed feelings in the Kremlin: concerns that "reactionary forces" would push him to take an anti-Soviet line; and temptations to use his weakness to secure war gains.

It was Molotov who brought to Moscow the first impression of Roosevelt's successor. On April 22–23, Molotov visited Truman on his way to San Francisco to attend the opening of the United Nations. The U.S. president sternly lectured the Soviet foreign minister on Poland, where the Soviets had unilaterally set up a puppet (Lublin) government consisting of Communist Polish exiles and opposed to the Polish government-in-exile in London. The question of the future Polish government, after the opening of the second front in France in June 1944, remained the thorniest issue between Stalin and the Western Allies. Molotov recalled that the Western powers "wanted to squeeze us [out of Poland], to impose on Poland a bourgeois government that naturally would have been an agent of imperialism."[67] Roosevelt, careful to avoid any "ganging up" on Stalin over the question of Poland, resisted Churchill's attempts to form a united U.S.-British position on the issue. But Truman, angered by Stalin's crackdown on the London Poles and the Polish Home Army, joined Churchill on April 15 in sending a joint telegram to Stalin protesting his actions.

During the meeting in the White House, Molotov told Truman that the Soviet government was ready "to settle [contentious] issues" in the management of international relations in the way it had always done with Roosevelt—through bilateral secret talks. "However," he warned Truman, "there had never been a case where one or two governments tried to dictate their will to the other Allied government. This should not happen now. Only on this basis can the Soviet government cooperate with other governments." Truman shot back that the Soviets should first learn how to behave in the international arena (having in mind primarily the Kremlin's tightening grip on Eastern Europe). The meeting was disrupted, and Molotov left in a huff. Many years later he returned to this episode and described Truman as "a bit half-witted." He viewed Truman's rudeness as a substitute for self-confidence. According to Molotov, he definitely "was far behind Roosevelt in intellect."[68]

Upon Molotov's return to Moscow, he and Stalin decided to keep the episode quiet, and soon Truman sent the former Roosevelt advisor Harry Hopkins to Moscow, where he met with Stalin and settled the dispute. Yet the Kremlin tandem saw behind this episode a sinister trend. Through their excellent intelligence sources in London and Washington, they knew the full content of the ciphered correspondence between Truman and Churchill in April–July 1945. Churchill's telegrams gave the Soviets "clear, advance warning that the British would refuse the Hopkins-Stalin compromise on Poland at the conference in Potsdam."[69]

On the eve of the Potsdam summit Molotov and the Soviet ambassador to Washington, Gromyko, warned Stalin that Truman would be tough on Soviet demands for German reparations, the remilitarization of Germany, and Soviet decisions on Poland. At the conference the U.S. president, in Molotov's eyes, seemed petty and ignorant; after Molotov learned of the successful testing of an atomic bomb in New Mexico, he interpreted Truman's back-slapping familiarity as arrogance. Nevertheless, both Stalin and Molotov strongly believed that the U.S.-British differences would be acute enough to prevent their collusion against the Kremlin. They did their best to disrupt Truman-Churchill rapprochement before Potsdam.[70]

About the same time, Litvinov presented the final reports of his commission, in which he argued that the Soviets could use cooperation in the United Nations to claim some "trusteeships" along with the British. In June he wrote to Molotov that a trusteeship over Palestine would be desirable but "hardly feasible." "Libya, where we could establish a stronghold in the Mediterranean, would be a suitable object," he suggested.[71]

Molotov made some use of Litvinov's suggestions, but his and Stalin's tactics were quite different from those Litvinov proposed. Instead of tapping on public sympathies in the West toward the USSR, Stalin and Molotov were determined to break the united U.S.-British front on Eastern Europe. Their concerns were magnified in July–August by the American atomic monopoly, which, in their eyes, emboldened the Truman administration to dominate the postwar peace settlement, with the British as junior partners. Today it is known that in August U.S. Secretary of State James Byrnes toyed with the idea of using the American atomic monopoly as an "implied threat" to the Soviets in order to obtain concessions from them in Eastern Europe and deny them a base in the Turkish straits. Since the U.S. government was transparent to Soviet espionage, it is highly likely that this fact became known in Moscow.[72]

In September Molotov went to London for the first meeting of the Council of Foreign Ministers (CFM), the body designed to draft the outlines of peace treaties with Germany and its former satellites Hungary, Bulgaria, and Rumania. During the talks Molotov's position on Soviet policies in East European countries, satellites of Germany occupied by the Red Army, was unapologetic and blunt. On September 19 he told Byrnes: "In a defeated country, especially a neighboring country, the Soviet Union must have a modicum of influence." He blamed the U.S. government for employing a double standard: why did it not interfere in the policies of the British in Greece, but try to do so in Rumania? This did not happen "under Roosevelt," was the Russian plaint.[73] The next day Byrnes proposed a possible treaty to keep Germany disarmed for twenty to twenty-five years. But Molotov, with dogged persistence, kept pounding on the Rumanian issue. Stalin cabled his approval of Molotov's position: it made no sense to have a treaty on Germany as long as Soviet troops were there. A better idea would be to sign a U.S.-Soviet treaty to prevent the resurgence of an aggressive Japan.[74]

While rebuffing what they saw as a coordinated U.S-British attack on the Soviet positions in Eastern Europe, Stalin and Molotov raised other issues on which the positions of Washington and London differed. Litvinov's proposal on Libya caught Molotov's attention: he spoke about Libya to Byrnes and added, with dry humor, that the Soviets would probably be good as colonial administrators in Africa, since they had "considerable experience in bringing about friendly relations between nationals." He told Chuev years later how Byrnes's face fell when he heard about Libya.[75] The plot was clear: if the Americans objected to a Soviet proposal of trusteeship, they could be forced to reject some British trusteeships as well.

In pursuing these strategies, Molotov and Stalin achieved their goal: Byrnes was dismayed. How could the Soviets fail to appreciate America's good intentions? Did this mean it would be impossible to work out an understanding with the Kremlin?[76]

Molotov, with his sense of limits, felt the time was ripe for a deal with the United States before the conference broke off. "It is common knowledge," Molotov philosophized in a lengthy cable to Stalin and other members of the Politburo on September 19, "that the first half or first three-fourths of such international conferences are spent on recriminations and on probing one another's positions. Now the time has come to prepare some decisions that will most likely be made . . . on the Americans' initiative. There will be hard bargaining and attempts at a compromise." The British had already been softened up, and now the Americans seemed to be in retreat.[77]

Stalin, however, pressed on. "The failure of the conference," he cabled to London, "will be Byrnes's failure, and we should not grieve over this." The Kremlin leader probably wanted to drive the lesson home to Washington: to nip American "atomic diplomacy" in the bud. Molotov fell into line. When the London conference ended in a whimper, he sent Soviet ambassadors a letter of explanation: "We should maintain in the long run that the first session of the Council of Ministers ended in failure due to certain American and British quarters attempting to launch a diplomatic attack on the foreign policy gains of the Soviet Union made during the War for the first time since the War."[78]

As if nothing had happened, Stalin left Moscow in early October for an extended vacation on the Black Sea. He did not have to wait long for a new American initiative: Byrnes buried his dreams of "atomic diplomacy" and instructed Ambassador Harriman to meet with the Kremlin leader and talk about a quick deal on the peace treaties with Rumania and Bulgaria. Stalin was a good host. It was obvious that he and Molotov played out a favorite scenario: Molotov provoked and created a deadlock, Stalin kept his distance and re-treated into his shell, prepared—after several desperate calls from Western partners—to return and solve the conundrum in a magnani-mous and "fair" way.

In December Byrnes himself came to Moscow for the second CFM meeting, and the Stalin-Molotov team performed the same play for him again. For a short time they outsmarted the Truman administra-tion and blunted the U.S. use of "atomic diplomacy." But ultimately their strategy, along with Soviet moves in Turkey and Iran, came at a very serious cost to U.S.-Soviet relations.[79] Soon the Truman admini-stration embraced the doctrine of containment of the USSR and re-fused to compromise with Stalin ever again.[80]

## Molotov's Cold Peace

Molotov admitted at the end of his life that the tensions between the East and the West initially were the result of conflicting visions of Germany and Eastern Europe. Two generations of Soviet diplomats after him believed that the Soviet Union was entitled to special security arrangements in Turkey, Central Europe, and the Far East after the defeat of Nazi Germany, and that the United States, together with Great Britain, thwarted these arrangements. "We had to consolidate what had been conquered," Molotov himself told Chuev. "The [East-ern] part of Germany had to be transformed into our Socialist Ger-many; and Czechoslovakia, Poland, Hungary, Yugoslavia—they all had been in an amorphous state, and we had to introduce order . . . there."[81]

The truth was that developments in Eastern Europe and East Ger-many had a logic of their own. At first, Eastern Europe became the Soviet rear in the fighting against the Nazis. After a brief hiatus, it became a vital territorial buffer and frontline against the Americans and the British, increasingly hostile to the USSR. For Molotov, en-gaged along with Stalin in grand diplomacy vis-à-vis those powers, Eastern European countries, for all their current economic and poten-tial geopolitical benefits for the USSR and the Communist world, remained a major source of ideological and political turmoil. As Stalin fought with the Americans and the British to keep the Eastern European countries in the Soviet sphere of influence, he also carefully watched the indigenous leftist forces of these countries for indications of bourgeois nationalism, Right opportunism, and Trotskyism that, as he knew from his Old Bolshevik experience, would not take long to appear on the eastern terrain, from the Vistula to the Oder and from Poznan to Adriatica.

In April 1947, Molotov received Matthias Rakosi, a Hungarian Communist leader who had recently been sent from Moscow to Budapest. Rakosi asked what would happen to Hungary after the peace treaty had been enacted. He warned about the plots of "fascist reactionaries" who wanted to undermine financial stability in Hungary and let Americans in. How long were the Soviet troops going to stay in Hungary? "The current situation can be viewed as favoring you," answered Molotov. "A treaty with Austria will certainly not be signed this year." Since the Soviet troops would stay in Austria, they would also stay in Hungary and in Rumania to protect military communications.[82]

The fate of a Hungarian "progressive government," left without the support of the Red Army's tanks, was painfully clear. Rakosi asked for credit to buy new weapons; the old weapons received from the Red Army "proved to be absolutely inoperable." Molotov obviously did not like the idea of arming the Hungarians, even the "progressive" ones. Rakosi stressed that the creation of a Hungarian army, as "the experience of Yugoslavia" showed, would be a great step toward consolidating Communist positions. But Molotov did not like this comparison. He must have been suspicious of Tito and the Yugoslav Communists precisely because they had their own strong army, were too autonomous, and tried to export their own experience to Eastern Europe. For Molotov, any revolutionary experience different from his and Stalin's fell automatically under suspicion. "Is Yugoslavia popular in Hungary?" he asked. "Even more popular than the Soviet Union," answered Rakosi. "The Hungarian people are not afraid of the Yugoslavs, but the traditional fear of the Russians still lingers on."[83]

The problem of interethnic hostility posed a serious threat to peace and stability in Central Europe. Authoritarian regimes in Hungary, Rumania, Bulgaria, and various parts of Yugoslavia curbed ethnic hatred with force, and bloody attempts to settle old scores were infrequent before the Second World War. But during the years of the Nazi "new order," horrible ethnic cleansing took place and was resumed with new force under the umbrella of Soviet occupation and punishment of "war criminals."

The Czech and Slovak Communists, Rakosi complained to Molotov, had ousted thousands of Hungarians from Czechoslovakia. They claimed they had Stalin's support. Rakosi called the Czechoslovak comrades "insane" and pleaded with Molotov to stop them. But in his next sentence he asked for Moscow's assent to the eviction of one hundred thousand Swabs from Hungary and their resettlement in the Soviet zone of occupation in Germany. With disarming logic he predicted that, for Swabs who "plainly dislike the USSR in any form," the prospect of living in the Soviet zone of occupation would be a nightmare from which they would flee for the American zone without any prodding. Molotov professed to be shocked: "If we do agree to the eviction, then the Soviet zone in Germany will serve as a kind of scarecrow."[84]

Molotov seemed to understand that as Communist leaders in Eastern Europe attempted to assert their regimes, they had to rely on the Red Army, or be armed and allowed to draw on indigenous revolutionary traditions mixed with nationalism. The dilemma was: Sovietization or Titoization.

Since the spring of 1946, Molotov's attention had been focused on American and British policies in Germany, particularly with regard to the Ruhr, the biggest metallurgical complex of Europe. The Soviets desperately needed their share of production and equipment from the Ruhr to restore their own heavy industry, and to speed up construction of new military-industrial installations. But at the same time they wanted to dismantle the Ruhr altogether, to prevent it from becoming, yet again, the industrial heart of a German war machine directed against the East. By April 1946, at a meeting of the CFM in Paris, it was "more than evident" to Soviet intelligence—and to Molotov— "that the Russian proposal for a four-power mandate to govern the Ruhr . . . would be ruled out."[85] In July 1946 Molotov demanded the inclusion of Ruhr production in the Soviet reparation plans. In response, the Truman administration, aware of the pivotal role of the Ruhr in the economic rehabilitation of Western Europe, adopted new tactics: the British and American occupation zones would be united into "Bizonia," the U.S. troops would stay, and the Soviets would be excluded from control over Ruhr industry. On September 6, 1946, Byrnes delivered a speech in Stuttgart aimed at garnering public support for this policy in Germany. This proved to be the first step toward the division of Germany.[86]

In March 1947, at the CFM meeting in Moscow, again with the help of Soviet spies in London and Washington, "Molotov knew exactly what the other participants were saying to one another behind his back, and notably, that the Americans, represented by their new Secretary of State, George Marshall, would turn down all Soviet proposals for the future of Germany." Later, after the division of Germany became a reality, Molotov admitted to his staff that the United States had already been against a unified Germany in early 1946.[87]

Germany remained the centerpiece of the Stalin-Molotov peace diplomacy in 1945–1947, a part of their "high policy" targeted at the creation of a favorable balance of power in Europe. Yet Molotov understood even less than Stalin the processes that developed in the Soviet zone of occupation in Germany. The Soviet military administration (SMAG) was in charge of the day-to-day transformation of the zone into a "peaceful and democratic" Germany. On the issues of this "low policy" Molotov was just one of many to advise Stalin, along with Beria, Malenkov, Mikoyan, Voznesensky, and Matvei Saburov, with their bureaucratic priorities and interests. Sometimes Molotov was not even informed of important decisions of Marshal Vassily Sokolovsky, the head of the Soviet military administration, that led—with the steps of Sokolovsky's American counterpart, General Lucius Clay—to the economic division of Germany into two halves.[88]

Molotov was in charge, however, as far as Moscow had to oppose American plans in Germany. And, strangely enough, the American presence in Germany and Europe in general at first did not bother Molotov too much. This attitude was reflected in an important policy assessment, written under Molotov's supervision and known to historians as "Novikov's telegram."

In late August–early September at the Paris conference, Molotov requested a memorandum on current and prospective American intentions from Nikolai Novikov, Gromyko's replacement in Washington. Novikov noticed that Molotov was taking an extraordinary interest in the memo and dictated changes to it. The final document, sent from the Soviet embassy in Washington to Moscow on September 27, 1946, reflected Molotov's thinking rather than the views of the ambassador.[89]

The text of Novikov's cable with Molotov's blue pencilled marks on it is in the Moscow archives. The United States, the telegram said, abandoned its prewar tradition of isolationism and was now driven by the desire for world supremacy. This transformation, underlined Molotov, would allow the Americans to "assume the role of the most powerful force in resolving the fundamental questions of the postwar world." He then stressed that American influence would to a large extent depend on "prospects for enormous shipments of goods and the importation of capital" into the countries hungry for consumer goods. But what kinds of policies could one expect from the American colossus? Molotov did not doubt that those policies would be virulently anti-Soviet, given the retreat of the New Deal Democrats and the increasing influence on U.S. foreign policy of "the most reactionary circles of the Democratic party" in the alliance with Republicans.[90]

The Molotov-Novikov cable predicted that in the countries of Eastern Europe and the Middle East the American government would stop at nothing "to limit or dislodge the influence of the Soviet Union." It drew attention to the fact that American "expenditures on the army and navy have risen tremendously" in comparison with the years prior to World War II, and that the Americans maintained their old military bases and began constructing new ones thousands of miles away from the United States, on the periphery of the USSR.[91]

Nevertheless, Novikov and Molotov were confident that the correct Marxist-Leninist response to this growing strategic threat was to exploit contradictions among imperialist powers. The telegram pointed out "a secret agreement" between the United States and England "concerning the partial division of the world on the basis of mutual concessions [all underlined by Molotov]." The British tolerated American control over China and Japan "and the United States follows a similar line with regard to the English sphere of influence in the Far East."[92] But the authors of the memorandum expected that U.S.-British contradictions would eventually flare up. The Middle East, according to the cable, "will become a center of British-American contradictions that will undermine the agreements now reached between the United States and England." The tensions between the two powers would grow when the United States increased its own presence there, "attracted by the area's natural resources, primarily oil." When Molotov read the memorandum in Moscow, he underlined the word "oil"—that was the hidden spring of American aspirations, according to Marxist-Leninist theory.[93]

This document was the hallmark of Molotov's postwar "realism." The telegram left two options open: either Britain would remain America's "greatest potential competitor" or the two powers would reach strategic alliance—no doubt on a platform of anti-Sovietism. Understandably, each of these scenarios would mean a different turn in world politics and a different level of threat to the Kremlin. But the premises for superpower diplomacy still existed, at least in Molotov's eyes. Indeed, the possibility of joint management of the system of international relations survived until the announcement of the Marshall Plan.

## Responding to the Marshall Plan

In November 1947 Molotov, along with other Politburo members, received a letter from Tarasenko, a counselor in the Soviet embassy in Washington. He harshly criticized the estimates of America's foreign policy strategies that embassy officials, particularly the retiring ambassador Novikov, had been sending to Moscow. The counselor wrote that those estimates stemmed from "a rather limited . . . [interpretation] of the policy of the United States." According to this interpretation, "the essence of this policy was that all . . . political and diplomatic actions of the United States toward the Soviet Union are allegedly based on [the idea] of blackmail." A detailed analysis of U.S. foreign policy "for the last year" leads, according to Tarasenko, to another conclusion: that all serious undertakings of Washington focus on "the direct preparation for war against the Soviet Union."[94]

This letter was aimed at the Novikov-Molotov analysis of late 1946 and other reports from the embassy that had reflected a relatively benign interpretation of international affairs. Similar letters accompanied all radical shifts of policy under Stalin and indicated a search for scapegoats. Novikov, however, was not arrested for his political shortsightedness, he just resigned from the post of ambassador. One reason for his luck was that his former co-author was still in Stalin's good favor; another was that both Stalin and Molotov found nothing wrong with the embassy's estimates until the Marshall Plan.

George Marshall's speech, unlike many other U.S. initiatives, took Molotov by surprise. His first reaction to the Marshall Plan was quite positive. "I had agreed [to the plan] in the beginning," he recalled later, "and . . . sent a suggestion to the CC [Central Committee] that we should participate. Not only we, but also the Czechs and the Poles."[95] "The idea was to accept the proposal and make an attempt, if not to eliminate, at least to keep to a minimum all its negative aspects," Vladimir Yerofeev recalls. In a word, it should be something like "Lend-Lease," that is, no-strings-attached assistance to the anti-Nazi Allies.[96] On June 21, 1947, Stalin approved the idea of a reconnaissance mission to Paris with Molotov as its head.

The danger of American economic blackmail of the Soviet Union (the potential use of economic aid as leverage) was very much on Molotov's mind.[97] At the same time, the desire to obtain long-term American loans and credit was stronger than arrogance and suspiciousness. During the trial of Nazi war criminals at Nuremberg, Stalin and Molotov made a last effort to obtain U.S. economic and financial aid without begging: the Soviet prosecutor passed a memorandum to the U.S. representative. The request was "lost" somewhere in the U.S. State Department.[98] Only six months later, on February 21, 1946, did Secretary of State James Byrnes respond, but he spoke about a "one billion dollar" loan and bluntly linked it to the settlement of several contentious issues between the two countries.[99] No doubt, the foreign policy leaders in the Kremlin kept this episode in mind when they heard about the Marshall Plan. But Molotov, as his first reaction to the plan proves, still thought of using the discussion of American aid to promote his favorite goal—exploiting contradictions among Western countries to drive a wedge between the United States and a number of West European nations. And he still did not exclude the possibility that the Soviets would benefit from American generosity, which would result, as his Marxist instincts told him, from fears of an imminent crisis of overproduction.

On June 24, 1947, Molotov hastily formulated the initial task for the Soviet delegation to Paris as the procurement of data from the ministers of England and France about the "character and conditions" of American economic aid. Molotov wanted to seek a joint platform with the French and the British regarding American aid, so that it would be given to the countries most devastated by the recent war. He was determined to repudiate attempts to reduce German reparations in exchange for American generosity.[100] Among the experts of the large Soviet delegation, representing all major branches of Soviet economic planning, the expectation was that the United States would offer something along the lines of a "Lend-Lease" program of assistance.[101]

But the intent of the Marshall Plan, as they quickly learned, was to deprive the Soviet Union of its influence in Germany and Central Europe. On June 29–30, Soviet intelligence agents, with information from London sources, reported to Moscow that Undersecretary of State William Clayton (known since early 1945 as an advocate of "dollar diplomacy" with regard to the USSR) and British officials negotiated how to bring the Western zones of Germany into the plan and keep the Soviet Union out of it. In Paris, Molotov received a cable from Moscow that Britain and the United States considered Germany the "basis of any plan for the rehabilitation of the continent." British Foreign Minister Ernest Bevin and his French counterpart, Georges Bidault, denied to Molotov that they had any insight into U.S. designs. Molotov read this as a "behind-the-scenes collusion of the United States and Great Britain" against the Soviet Union. Later Molotov also received and approved an important report from the Soviet ambassador in Washington, according to which the American plan consisted of building "a strategic circle around the U.S.S.R., passing in the West across West Germany and West European countries; in the North—over the network of bases on Northern islands in the Atlantic Ocean, and also in Canada and Alaska; in the East—across Japan and China; and in the South—over the countries of the Middle East and the Mediterranean."[102]

These estimates were prescient, but Molotov was wrong to look at the American plan as a foregone conclusion. The success of the Western powers' plot was by no means certain. At that time the hard-liners in the Truman administration did not even hope to achieve this stupendous geopolitical goal. But with such adversaries as Stalin and Molotov they needed no friends. "We used to say," Dean Acheson wrote to Harry Truman years later, "that in a tight pinch we could generally rely on some fool play of the Russians to pull us through."[103]

Had the Soviet Union in July 1947 agreed to participate in the Marshall Plan, the American plan for European rehabilitation would have been seriously jeopardized.[104]

Molotov was good at diplomatic wars of attrition, but not at brilliant propagandist coups and the persuasion of opponents. "Since our stand differs radically from that of Britain and France," Molotov cabled to Stalin on July 1, "we can hardly expect any joint decisions on the substance of the issue in question."[105] He laid his hopes on contradictions between the United States and its West European allies. The absence of the Soviets in Paris, Molotov seemed to think, would help exacerbate the tension in the emerging Western bloc. "I changed my mind," he recalled later, "and sent a second memorandum: Let's reject [the plan]!"[106]

The next day, Molotov denounced the Marshall Plan and the Soviet delegation walked out of the conference. In the cascade of hectic events that followed, the Soviet foreign minister had to focus his attention on the areas he had considered to be of secondary or no strategic significance—the small countries of Eastern Europe. As Bevin and Bidault issued invitations to the governments of these countries to take part in the European economic conference, Molotov advised Stalin that they should go to Paris and "give a rebuff to America and its satellites, Britain, and France." The next step would be to "leave the conference, taking . . . as many delegations of other countries as possible." On July 5–6, Molotov cabled instructions to Soviet ambassadors in Warsaw, Prague, Bucharest, Sofia, Belgrade, Budapest, Tirana, and Helsinki to share his plan with the Communists in those countries. He ordered the Poles and the Yugoslavs to come to Moscow "to adopt a coordinated stand" on the conference.[107]

Just a few hours later Molotov, in another cable, overruled himself. "Things were vague back then," he acknowledged later.[108] Molotov and Stalin wanted, on the one hand, to throw a monkey wrench into the American plan, but, on the other hand, they sensed it was too risky, since the Eastern European "fifth column" might defect suddenly to the West, lured by economic gains and the prospect of national self-determination. At that time the Kremlin had yet to consolidate its total control over the Communist parties, not to mention other political forces, in those countries.

The days following the Soviets' rejection of the Marshall Plan were hard for Molotov: like everyone in the Kremlin, he had to guess

Stalin's new mood, and guess it right. By the fall of 1947, as Tarasenko's letter indicated, the danger of being denounced as "too soft" on the United States emerged among the ranks of Soviet diplomats. Molotov was not one to acquire such a reputation. On the contrary, after a moment of hesitation, he enthusiastically supported the new, tougher line.

In September, Molotov dropped out of sight: Stalin invited his consigliere to share his vacation on Lake Ritsa near the Black Sea—a sign of trust, but also probably because the two had much to talk about. In November, after a long vacation with Stalin, Molotov rushed back into diplomatic battle. By that time the U.S. government had made clear that it would not tolerate a neutralized unified Germany that might gravitate toward the Kremlin. It launched preparations for the creation of a separate West German state, and the CFM held its last meeting in London on this question, the Marshall Plan, and other issues.[109] The Soviet Union was isolated. Still, Molotov, with the assistance of intelligence sources, remained very much involved in the game; he was eager to detect splits and contradictions among the Western participants on the future of Germany. According to one KGB veteran's recollections, Molotov "clamored for fresh information every day." He was particularly eager to see that the British and the Americans disagreed about the future status of West Berlin. "Do what you like," he ranted in his office, "but I must know what [foreign ministers are] saying to their chiefs. And I also need to know what London and Washington are telling them to do next. And I want this information by six o'clock tonight." Guy Burgess, a Soviet spy in the British embassy in Washington, passed the desired information on to Molotov even before it reached Truman.[110]

This timely knowledge did not help the Kremlin rulers understand their gross misperception: the harder they drove against Western policies, the more their resistance contributed to the implementation of American separatist plans in Germany and Europe. On the contrary, the intelligence from Washington made the Kremlin leaders believe even more that they could destroy Western unity by retaliating in West Berlin.

If anyone had suggested to Molotov that the West would have been more responsive to the Soviets had he and Stalin behaved differently at international conferences, he probably would have rejected this suggestion as un-Marxist and naive. "If they [the West] believe it to be our mistake to reject the Marshall Plan," Molotov said several decades later, "it means that we had done the right thing."[111] This rationalization became a litany for the two generations of Soviet Cold Warriors: if your enemy criticizes you, it means you have won; beware when your enemy praises you.

## A True Believer

By the end of Stalin's life, the security fears of the Soviet statesman became self-fulfilling prophecies. Stark geopolitical realities, such as the Soviets' control in the heart of Europe or their new power in the Far East, became implacable security dilemmas: consolidation of these positions versus a possible compromise with Western powers. Perhaps it would have required an uncanny combination of Metternich and Bismarck to reach both ends. Molotov's vision and skills were of quite another quality.

For Molotov, life did not contain any riddles—there were no contradictions in his system of values. One difference between him and post-Stalin innovators and challengers may be crudely compared to the difference between a physicist in the days before Albert Einstein and those after his theory of relativity. The physics of Sir Isaac Newton was basic and all-encompassing. Similar was the world of revolutionaries. For the postrevolutionary elites the world was full of dilemmas and demanded new choices every day. They, like any post-Einstein physicist, lived in a more complicated universe and knew no stability.

As Molotov grew older, he was even more of a true believer. He felt the need to be "stronger" and more orthodox in his foreign policy thinking than the new generation of rulers. With Stalin dead, Molotov was the person to defend the revolutionary-imperial paradigm, nearly destroyed by both of them in 1939–1945. This paradigm became his keep. The innovative approaches of the post-Stalin elites were unacceptable to him, and he would ardently worship the sun of revolution, which was increasingly neglected by realpolitik-minded apparatchiks. "It was the right thing to send troops to Czechoslovakia, and many support this, but they support it from a superpower position, and I—from a Communist position."[112]

Molotov would repeatedly oppose Khrushchev. The leader's quest for some informal permanent truce with the West, first of all with the Americans, greatly angered Molotov. In terms of Bolshevik party history, he was quite right in defining Khrushchev's approach to both domestic and foreign affairs as a "rightist deviation" ("less revolution, more stability, even at the cost of certain ideological concessions" became the motto of the day).

"Khrushchev was not alone," Molotov remarked. "There were thousands of people like him."[113] Molotov's intuition was absolutely correct. He sensed the gradual, slow, uneven, but final sunset of ideology in Soviet foreign policy, and the evaporation of Communist self-legitimacy in Soviet elites. The rays of the revolutionary sun would be felt for years and would contribute, for instance, to the Soviet invasion in Afghanistan, which Molotov approved to the end. But after Stalin's death the dictator's doctrine started to lose its universalist glint.

# 4 Zhdanov and the Origins of the Eastern Bloc

> The average Soviet man has certain shortcomings, but he also has distinctions that no average Western European or American possesses.
>
> Andrei Zhdanov, November 6, 1946

In late September 1947, Stalin was on vacation with Molotov. The Soviet ruler and his foreign policy minister enjoyed the sun, sumptuous food, and delicate wines of Georgia. But late in the evening, refreshed after a nap, Stalin would read secret cables sent by a special scrambled radio transmission from the small town of Szklarska Poremba, in the Southern Sudetenland, which became a territory of Poland after 1945. The names of the addressee and the senders were replaced by aliases, similar to those used in the days of the Comintern for interparty correspondence. The first cable from "Sergeev and Borisov" to "Comrade Filippov" reported that "tonight, September 22, the conference began its work. Participants of all invited parties are taking part in [it]." Filippov was Stalin; the senders were the Politburo members Andrei Zhdanov and Georgi Malenkov. Six days later the conference ended and they sent the message: "Tomorrow, the morning of the 29th, we will fly to Moscow. On all documents of the conference we will report personally."[1]

Not until forty-four years later were historians granted access to the documents of this secret and important conference, but some facts about it the world learned immediately. What took place in Szklarska Poremba was the creation of the Informational Bureau of Communist Parties, the Cominform. This event formally signaled the beginning of a new and often brutal Soviet policy: the consolidation of the Soviet sphere of influence in Eastern Europe. This new policy entailed the transformation of five countries into Soviet satellites under the control of Communist regimes cloned from the regime in Moscow.

For many East European intellectuals, the report that Zhdanov gave on the new Soviet foreign policy at the meeting in Poland was a signal of doom; among the advocates of the Communist millennium it was received as a new gospel after several years of ideological famine. On November 1, 1947, Zhdanov received encomiums from Alexandra M. Kollontai, the Old Bolshevik and retired Soviet ambassador (and the only woman prominent in the Soviet diplomatic service). "Your presentation," wrote Kollontai in her letter, "is not only a brilliant, in-depth analysis of the global situation, particularly of the United States, but also a document of historic significance . . . Recently many of us succumbed to pessimism, but your analysis and clear direction to the subsequent phases of our policy and liberation movement in the whole world open yet another door into the future. The soul rejoices and brightens. The instruction of our Party, so colorfully conveyed in your presentation, firm and clear, is the most impressive answer to the warmongers."[2]

Kollontai's praise, sincere or not, did not exaggerate the importance of Zhdanov's report. This report, even more than the creation of the Cominform, clearly marked a watershed in the history of Soviet foreign policy. It signaled Stalin's failure to abandon the revolutionary-imperial paradigm and switch to a purer realpolitik mode. Stalin pursued, among other things, the goal of providing the Soviet satellites and the whole Communist world with a clear-cut ideological perspective on global confrontation with the United States. To achieve this goal he did not need to recreate the Comintern—a too flagrant demonstration of the revolutionary facet of Soviet foreign policy. Everything he needed from that organization had stayed intact after its dissolution in 1943: the core staff in Moscow, a network of agents and sympathizers linked up with Soviet intelligence and spread over Eurasia. The Cominform of 1947 was a sketch of the future Soviet regional bloc with its affiliations in Western Europe—not a replica of the dead Communist International.

Andrei Alexandrovich Zhdanov, a Soviet keynote speaker at the conference in Poland, became the main mouthpiece of the new worldview that turned the iron curtain into a tragic reality for many millions to the east of the Elbe River. Among Stalin's lieutenants, Zhdanov was responsible for shaping a Cold War mentality inside the Soviet Union as well as for Communist followers and sympathizers all over the world. He was a trumpeter of the Cold War in the Soviet leadership.

## Stalin's Most Favored Ideologist

Stalin liked Zhdanov more than anyone else in his inner circle. He even encouraged his only daughter, Svetlana, to marry Zhdanov's son.[3] Indeed, the Zhdanov family seemed to embody what Stalin gradually grew to like and cultivate among his bureaucrats: blind loyalty, spineless obedience, and meticulous adherence to ideological dogma.

Andrei Zhdanov was born in 1896 in Mariupol, Ukraine, into a middle-class Russian family. His family was almost Chekhovian, passionate patriots of a small, cherry-blossomed town. Zhdanov's mother belonged to the nobility and graduated from the Moscow Musical Conservatory. His father, like Lenin's, was an inspector of public schools in the area. Zhdanov's three sisters, unlike Chekhov's heroines, plunged into revolutionary activities, motivated by the world war and the collapse of the Romanov dynasty. Two of them never married and devoted all their energy to the "enlightenment of the masses." Their influence on Andrei remained strong even later, when he built a career in the Party; the two women lived in his house, with his wife and son, until his death. Zhdanov never received a formal higher education; as in many Russian families like his, this was compensated by early random reading and pretensions to be "part of the Russian intelligentsia."

Zhdanov did not belong to the cohort of revolutionary heroes. At the end of the civil war he was only a young deputy of a local soviet in a town in the Urals. His career progressed quickly after that, however: from 1922 to 1927 he was a city administrator in the old Russian cities of Tver and Nizhni Novgorod and a delegate to congresses of the Communist party. He first attracted Stalin's attention with his fiery speech against Grigory Zinoviev, the leader of an anti-Stalin "Leningrad opposition" (the most threatening anti-Stalinist group in the Party, joined even by Lenin's widow, Nadezhda K. Krupskaya). In 1927 he became a secretary of the Central Committee. In 1934 Zhdanov replaced Sergei Kirov, after his mysterious assassination, as head of the Leningrad party organization, second only in importance to that of Moscow. In 1935 he became a candidate, and in 1939 a full member, of the Politburo. From 1941 to 1944, during the ferocious German siege of Leningrad, Zhdanov was in the city, both as a party secretary and as a political counselor of the Northwestern (later Leningrad) front. In 1944–1945 he was the Allied Commissioner in Finland. At the end of 1945, Stalin transferred him to Moscow, to the Central Committee apparatus. Zhdanov stayed there until his sudden death after two heart attacks in August 1948.

Some American historians have suggested that Zhdanov's rise and disappearance after the Second World War had something to do with the emergence of the Communist proselytes in the Soviet apparatus for the first time since the great purges of the 1930s. Stalin allegedly was under pressure from the new cadres, proud of the Soviet victory in the war and pushing a more radical, ideological line in domestic and foreign affairs.[4]

Ideology had several related functions in the Stalinist state. Its paramount goal was to promote the "monolithic unity of the Soviet people," that is, to suppress any antagonisms between state and society, authority and individual, and also between different groups within the USSR (interethnic tensions were just one of the potential powder kegs). Ideology also had a foreign policy function. In the framework of the revolutionary-imperial paradigm it was one more dimension of political and physical control. In the Socialist countries, the Soviet ideology imposed by Moscow and its puppet regimes strengthened Soviet influence over its territory, be it Poland or Hungary. Outside the Soviet camp, Soviet ideology was recruiting a "fifth column" for the purpose of undermining the enemy's control over Europe and Asia.

Thus, ideology to an extent had retained its revolutionary glory and importance. The ideologues did not fare quite so well. Bolshevism could be interpreted only in the form canonized by Stalin in the 1930s—all innovations were initiated by the pontiff himself, and even the leading ideologues, from Zhdanov to his successor, Mikhail Suslov, were just librarians responsible for finding the proper quotation at the right time and for keeping the credo in strict order. No creativity or ardor from an ideologue was tolerated. The keepers of the Bolshevik shrine were deprived of any true revolutionary passion and any real interest in ideology as such.

By 1947 it had become crystal clear that the Western leaders regarded their cooperation with Stalin during the war years as an unfortunate episode that was to be followed by considerable detachment. But "detachment" during the fragile peace of 1945–1947 had to be transformed into something more definite. Thus many Western intellectuals and propagandists, ranging from the Trotskyites and the anti-Communist Socialists to Catholic theologians, contributed to the ideological, cultural, and doctrinal justification for a Cold War. In the United States, the philosopher and sociologist Hannah Arendt, the theologian Reinhold Niebuhr, the Socialist Norman Thomas, and many others finished what the diplomat George Kennan had started: they explained to a public that had been sympathetic to the Soviet Union as the main fighter against the Nazi threat or as an "interesting social experiment" that the Stalinist state and Hitler's regime had one common denominator—they were totalitarian states. The motto of the Western Cold Warriors became "free world versus totalitarianism."

Stalin clearly felt a need to resuscitate ideology as a prop for his regime and its foreign policy. An ideological component was required to give legitimacy both to the Moscow sphere of influence in Eastern Europe and to Yalta and Potsdam, undermined by the collapse of the Grand Alliance. Coordination among "fraternal" parties in the Cominform guaranteed Soviet domination much better than any system of bilateral state treaties, and at the same time dispelled negative associations with traditional imperialist practices, such as the domination of Poland by czarist Russia in the nineteenth century. But at the same time Stalin *did not* want the Cominform to be in any way an ideological headquarters of the revolutionary movement. The Yugoslav Communists tried to perceive it as such and were unceremoniously expelled from the Cominform in June 1948.

Stalin made sure that the ideology of his Cold War system of alliances would not dissent or deviate from the Kremlin's view. According to this view, the world was again, as in 1917, shattered by world war. The second phase of the terminal crisis of capitalism had begun. It was characterized by the world's split into two "blocs," one of imperialism and war, led by the United States, and one of peace, democracy, and socialism, led by the Kremlin.

The main paradox was that this new ideology was the product not of the zealous faith of "party resurrectionists," as one American historian claimed, but of the meticulous work of gigantic bureaucratic machinery, manned by Soviet ideologists and propagandists. The distance between them and true Communist zealots supporting the Soviet cause over the world was immense. Even a very brief portrait of Zhdanov is enough to substantiate this point.

Zhdanov belonged to the first generation of Soviet apparatchiks. Admiration and utter loyalty were his feelings toward Stalin that he shared with Khrushchev and hundreds of ranking party organizers in the 1930s. Initially just a young party idealist, Zhdanov was quickly disciplined by the deadly realities of Stalin's rule. He was extremely close to Stalin all the way through the bloody miasma of the great purges. His signature was next to Stalin's on a famous cable from Sochi in 1936 that unleashed the secret police on millions of new victims. Zhdanov's primary focus, however, was party propaganda and agitation. He helped Stalin to edit a new and falsified history of the Party entitled *The Brief Course.*

Zhdanov's papers reveal one important feature that he shared with many of his colleagues under Stalin: the bureaucratic perfectionism of a workaholic. His notes betray a man with a huge, almost oppressive, sense of duty and meticulousness. When Zhdanov was an Allied commissioner in Finland, he operated with mountains of Finnish statistics, driven by the duty to extract as much in reparations as possible from the defeated country. When he supervised Finland's politics, he turned into a walking encyclopedia of "who's who in Helsinki." He left many drafts of every policy: each of them written in longhand, every succeeding draft changed, reformulated.

People who worked with Zhdanov then and later could not remember anything remarkable, noteworthy, or anecdotal about the man. In Stalin's inner circle, however, he was regarded as "a man of culture." As part of his education, he learned to play the piano and the accordion, and from time to time would entertain the tyrant and his drunken guests. Zhdanov's early habit of reading Russian literature served him well when in 1946, on Stalin's order, he denounced two writers, the bearers of the free-spirit tradition of Russian literature, Mikhail Zoshchenko and Anna Akhmatova. Here as well, Zhdanov did not do his job perfunctorily; he dug deep into literary criticism, reading everything he could find on the two selected victims. No one else in Stalin's circle could do this work better.

Did Zhdanov remain as sturdy and one-dimensional as Molotov?

We know that he did not. He was not physically strong enough. The siege of Leningrad in 1941–1944, along with the years spent within Stalin's court, took its toll: from a vibrant, physically attractive person Zhdanov turned into an overweight, pasty-faced man, prone to severe asthmatic attacks.[5] Outward diligence, the working habits of a brilliant clerk, contrasted with sudden drinking bouts. He was a splintered person, pitiful or tragic. Zhdanov concealed his true disposition behind a turgid facade.

Stalin valued and liked Zhdanov's punctuality and perfectionism. But sometimes it irritated him, and he turned the "ideologically correct" Zhdanov into the object of his fits of rage. There are rare traces of this in the memoirs of Stalin's daughter, Svetlana Alliluyeva. "Once, shortly before Andrei Zhdanov's death," she writes, "knowing that the man suffered from recurrent heart attacks, my father, angered by Zhdanov's silence at the table, suddenly turned on him viciously: 'Look at him, sitting there like little Christ as if nothing was of any concern to him.' Zhdanov grew pale, beads of perspiration stood out on his forehead."[6]

Zhdanov's biggest feat in the service of Stalin's doctrine, the report on the international situation at the creation of the Cominform, he performed impeccably, with the maximum passion of which he was capable, although without any personal "theoretical" imprint: the pivotal ideas of the document had been formulated under Stalin's guidance. But again, that was what Stalin valued Zhdanov for.

For most of his career, Zhdanov was in charge of ideology. Ideology in all its terrifying splendor, a utopian teaching leading to Armageddon, could be guarded or regulated only by the supreme pontiff—Stalin. But ideology as a set of "correct" and simple clichés based upon well-developed institutions was Zhdanov's responsibility. He had to be both opportunistic, to find propagandist justifications for the realpolitik, and dogmatic—to preserve the original ideological credo, in spite of changing political winds and currents.

## On the Margins of Grand Diplomacy

Zhdanov's Cold War experience began in Finland, where he served as an Allied commissioner after the war. One year of negotiations with Finland, from October 1944 to November 1945, helped to shape what later became known as "Finlandization," the transformation of a hostile country into something Stalin could be comfortable with, a friendly neighbor of the USSR—not a satellite, but not quite independent in the security sphere. The Finnish experiment, along with other scenarios, was very much on Zhdanov's mind in the months following the conclusion of his tenure there in November 1945, as he and other Soviet rulers, along with Stalin, searched for ways to deal with the countries that fell into the Soviet sphere of influence.

At that time Stalin was prepared to outline most of his general political goals and let others work out a policy. Probably influenced by Roman history, he appointed a proconsul to each new Soviet satellite. (The experience of the Russian empire was also not lost on him, since under the czars "the Polish kingdom," as a special case, was governed by an especially trustworthy person, a member of the royal family. Nicholas II had a proconsul in the Far East, Admiral Alexeev, during the active phase of Russian expansion in the area.) Stalin appointed other proconsuls besides Zhdanov: Voroshilov in Hungary, Zhukov and Semyonov in Germany, Vyshinsky in Rumania.[7] In Germany there was a group of proconsuls whom Stalin entrusted with the micromanagement of domestic situations; they were to use every means possible, including, of course, the Communist carpetbaggers trained in the Comintern schools and returned to their respective homelands.

The power of the proconsuls was curbed once the Stalin-Molotov foreign policy came into play. In January 1945, Zhdanov was conducting talks on a Soviet-Finnish settlement. His Finnish counterpart was Field Marshal Carl von Mannerheim, a former officer of the czar's court and a father of independent Finland. On January 18, Zhdanov informed Stalin and Molotov that Mannerheim agreed to sign a bilateral defense treaty, but "would defend the interior of the country himself." "He asked if there were standard treaties, and I replied that the one with Czechoslovakia might be taken as such. I am waiting for instructions."[8]

The Soviet-Czechoslovak treaty of alliance was a sign that, of all the countries in the Soviet sphere of influence, Czechoslovakia enjoyed the most favorable relations with Moscow. The treaty was a product of successful efforts by Eduard Benes to alleviate Moscow's concerns about the Czechoslovak government-in-exile in London.[9] More important, perhaps, in 1944 Stalin had needed the Czechoslovak model to encourage other countries, particularly Hitler's allies, to surrender to the Red Army on its march to the West. This was no longer necessary, especially not with prostrated Finland.

The Finnish attempt to obtain an early, better deal in comparison with the general terms of armistice ran contrary to the Stalin-Molotov grand diplomacy in Europe. It would certainly have been a violation of the principle to settle a postwar world in the concert of three great powers, something that Stalin still highly valued. Zhdanov, who was on the margins of this grand diplomacy, failed to see this obvious fact. Therefore, Molotov sent him a terse reply: "You have gone too far. A pact with Mannerheim of the sort we have with Czechoslovakia is [the] music of the future. We have to reestablish diplomatic relations first. Don't frighten Mannerheim with radical proposals." And then: "You were too emotional."[10]

Zhdanov swallowed Molotov's remonstration. "Finland is on probation," he told Mannerheim, "and it still cannot have relations of a different kind with the USSR." Of course, the whole Soviet-dominated zone from the Baltic Sea to the Black Sea was on probation. But later, in 1948, the Finns escaped the common fate and did not become subdued satellites in the Soviet bloc. Zhdanov hardly played any role in this decision—its real underpinning was revealed by Molotov in his conversations with Chuev: "We did the right thing. It would have been an open wound."[11]

These words showed that the Kremlin leaders had learned a lesson from the Finns' stubborn and courageous resistance to the Soviet Army during the Winter War of 1939–1940 and come to the correct conclusion that the "Sovietization" of Finland would be a bloody, protracted struggle. There were too many "open wounds" already inside the Soviet Union, such as Western Ukraine and the Baltic, where the nationalist guerillas had fought with regular troops for years.

Still, the activities of High Commissioner Zhdanov give another clue to the special luck of the Finns. His declassified papers contain hundreds of pages dealing with Finland's postwar economic life and politics. First and foremost, Zhdanov was responsible for the smooth flow of reparations from Finland to the Soviet Union. In 1945 the official Kremlin emphasis was still on the political alliance of all anti-Nazi forces, including the Social-Democratic and Agrarian parties. But, as a security measure, several key ministerial positions in the Finnish government were given, at Moscow's insistence, to the Communists. Zhdanov had a "special channel" to them, and advised them how to preserve their power through various tactical alliances with other parties. In the process he got to know many bourgeois politicians: he preferred to deal with the most conservative among them (Mauno Pekkala, Urkho Kekkonen) rather than with Social Democrats (who were traditionally regarded as treacherous heretics, and once labeled "worse than fascists" by Stalin in the early 1930s).

From the very beginning Stalin, through Zhdanov, kept two options open: as long as Finland behaved well and fulfilled the reparations plan, a deal with the traditional, conservative leadership remained a preferred option. But he kept another option open as well—a possible Communist junta—in case things should not work out with the existing leadership. Relations between the two countries continued to go well, however, and, instead of a Communist coup, the Finns received a friendship treaty.[12]

In December 1945, the Generalissimo returned from his Black Sea dacha to Moscow and held a meeting of the Politburo, the first after a five-year interlude. At about the same time he summoned Zhdanov back from the margins of Soviet diplomacy. Zhdanov returned to his preeminent role of propagandist-in-chief.

Zhdanov's administrative "empire" in the central party apparatus was greater than in the prewar years. Again he was responsible for institutionalized ideology. He presided over two departments of the Central Committee: the Department of Agitation and Propaganda and the Foreign Policy Department (the latter would change its name and even its functions in the future, and would eventually become known as the International Department). Included were Sovinformburo, with its experienced wartime staff in charge of the dissemination of all public information; the Telegraph Agency of the Soviet Union (TASS); some divisions of the Committee on Broadcasting; and a publishing house dealing with foreign literature. The structures of "public diplomacy," extremely effective during the war, included the Jewish Anti-Fascist Committee, the All-Slavic Committee, and the All-Union Society for Cultural Ties Abroad (VOKS).

The Foreign Policy Department in particular is worth examining in some detail. After Stalin decreed the dissolution of the Comintern in 1943, its staff continued to work in various Soviet state and party structures, mainly in military intelligence and propaganda. The central apparatus had been transferred to the Central Committee, but remained under the command of the former Comintern's leader, the

Bulgarian Communist expatriate Georgi Dimitrov. In December 1945, the "Ghost Comintern" had become part of his administrative fiefdom. Dimitrov, who returned to Bulgaria to build a coalition government, was replaced by Mikhail Suslov and his deputy, Alexander Panyushkin, two Russian apparatchiks with no exposure to international Communist movements. They both reported to Zhdanov as their direct boss.

The Foreign Policy Department continued to run several secret "institutes" of the disbanded Comintern that maintained old operative and informational contacts with the world Communist movement. "Institute-205" dealt with the assessment and analysis of information. "Institute-99" specialized in the recruitment of cadres for operative Communist work among the POWs. "Institute-100" dealt primarily with radio broadcasting and maintained a network of radio agents scattered around Europe. The Foreign Policy Department and its old Comintern cadres could hardly constitute a bureaucratic rival to the Ministry of Foreign Affairs run by Vyacheslav Molotov, but in the field of information this was a very impressive complex.

The Comintern people had always been a very valuable part of Soviet political and especially military intelligence networks. The information from chiefs of Comintern stations and sympathizers around the world was not just an addition to the regular intelligence collected by MGB, GRU, and Soviet diplomats; those informers provided a fresh and different angle—reflecting the faith and illusions of various social movements primarily belonging to Popular Fronts.

In 1945, when Soviet leaders were busy haggling with the Allies over peace treaties, this network was almost completely disbanded and left without instructions. No coordination of activities existed among foreign Communist parties. Some of them, including the American and the British parties, had almost no ties with the Foreign Policy Department.

In 1946 the role of Zhdanov's bureaucratic empire was very limited as far as foreign policy was concerned. It published a top-secret bulletin of international information, a few copies of which were prepared by the secret "institutes" and reserved for those at the top of the central party apparatus. Zhdanov was personally responsible for the content and dissemination of this bulletin, but in all other respects he and his departments and secret "institutes" were completely subservient to the needs of foreign policy directed by Stalin and Molotov. This was the pattern in the relationship between the Comintern and Soviet foreign policy before World War II, and the events in Iran, which coincided with Zhdanov's new nomination, demonstrated that the pattern had not changed.

Since czarist times the northern part of Iran (Persia) had been regarded by Moscow as part of a legitimate perimeter of security. The importance of Iranian oil, fisheries, and other resources was on the minds of the new Soviet rulers, who extracted many concessions from the weak Iranian government even before World War II. In August 1944 Lavrenty Beria signed and sent to Stalin and Molotov a memorandum about the growing importance of Middle East oil and the possible American-British struggle for it after the war. In 1944–1945 the Kremlin leadership attempted to use the presence of Soviet troops in Iran (made possible through a wartime agreement with the British to prevent Germany from penetrating into the Middle East) to secure these concessions, particularly on oil. But the Truman administration feared the Soviets might reach out as far as the Persian Gulf, and regarded a delay in the withdrawal of Soviet troops from Northern Iran as the first evidence of Stalin's aggressive intentions after the war.[13]

Indeed, larger concerns about the security of the southern underbelly of the USSR could not have been far from the minds of Stalin and Molotov. But even so, they seemed to be content with manipulating the Iranian government rather than subverting it. They completely ignored the Iranian Communist party (the Tudeh), setting up a separatist puppet party of Iranian Azerbaijan (ADN). As events showed, Stalin was ready to trade the ADN and the Soviet presence in Iranian Azerbaijan for oil and other privileges. The Tudeh's influence in this region was effectively undermined.[14]

The old Comintern network had informants in Teheran, very close to the Tudeh, who tried to use this channel to change Moscow's policies. One agent, for instance, indicated the possibility of striking a deal with Shah Reza Pahlevi, who seemed then not hostile to the idea of a behind-the-scenes alliance with the Soviets and the Tudeh against Prime Minister Quavam. The Tudeh pushed for establishing a separate revolutionary government in Iranian Azerbaijan, along the lines of the base of the Communist party of China in Yanan. This information streamed into the Department of Foreign Policy and landed on Zhdanov's desk.

It was then sent to Molotov, who was very angry at the Tudeh's intervening in Soviet foreign policy. In February 1946, on Molotov's explicit orders, the officials of the Foreign Policy Department secretly brought to Moscow a very active leader in the Tudeh, Avanesian (Ardashir). They explained to him that the Tudeh's proposals were "mistaken and harmful": the Kremlin would not tolerate any autonomy of or initiative from its Communist allies as far as Soviet policies in the Middle East were concerned.[15]

Avanesian still hoped to revive the old Comintern network in the Middle East. On May 27, 1946, he sent a report to Zhdanov and Suslov in which he proposed "having representatives from the Foreign Policy Department in each country in order to maintain through them contacts with Communist parties and groupings."[16] This idea clearly interfered with the Stalin-Molotov centralized diplomacy.

Stalin and Molotov rarely shared their strategic deliberations with Zhdanov. They dismissed the timid attempts of Zhdanov's subordinate Mikhail Suslov to gain access to more sensitive information on international affairs, in addition to inadequate and ideologically biased party sources, and to start the campaign of "screening" Soviet diplomatic cadres abroad. Having met with cold disapproval in the Kremlin, Zhdanov never pursued that line. As a result, the functionaries of "party diplomacy" remained, in Suslov's words, "virtually without access to the materials of the Ministry of Foreign Affairs."[17]

Still, it is instructive to read Zhdanov's bulletins of international information, for they reflect the common wisdom, level of knowledge, and ideological stereotypes regarding international affairs and leaders among the rest of the high Soviet elite outside the narrow policy-making and intelligence-procuring circles. In the summer of 1946 the bureau issued a reference book on world leaders with the following descriptions:

> *Truman, Harry:* Under heavy influence of reactionary imperialist circles of American monopoly capital striving to achieve U.S. world domination . . . Started his working life as a small clerk [then was] the owner of a haberdashery shop . . . [A promoter of] the bloc with British imperialist circles.

> *Byrnes, James:* Under his guidance a comedy was played out about the alleged "interference" of the USSR in the domestic affairs of Iran . . . At the Paris peace conference he is continuing the policy of

ensuring the interests of American aggressive circles, directed against
the USSR and other democratic countries.[18]

These sharply negative characteristics of American policy-makers
contrasted with the more tolerant portraits of some "realistically
minded" European politicians—among them Jukho Paasikivi of Finland, George Bidault of France, Jan Massaryk and Eduard Benes of
Czechoslovakia. Describing the orientation of Prime Minister Benes
of Czechoslovakia, however, the bulletin's editors noted that he "sur-
reptitiously supports and covers reactionaries," and that he "advocates a pro-England orientation, although officially he comes out for
the cementing of friendship with the USSR."[19] The inimitable party
clichés disseminated by Zhdanov and his staff later grew into the
full-fledged Cold War mentality of the Soviet elites.

Some in the West had long believed that Stalin started the Cold War
as a pretext for domestic repression, to fan the mood of so-called
Soviet patriotism. Documents from Zhdanov's files, however, show
that the main thrust of the campaign for "Soviet patriotism" against
pro-Western "cosmopolites" initially had nothing to do with plans for
confrontation with the West. Rather, in 1945–1946 Stalin was looking for an ideology for domestic consumption that would help him
both to eradicate Western influences spread during the war and to
extract more resources from the impoverished and exhausted USSR
and its people. In other words, it looked as if Stalin and Zhdanov had
carefully read George Kennan's "long cable" of February 1946 and
started to eliminate those "seeds of decay" on whose growth and
proliferation the American diplomat laid a principal hope in his fer-
vent desire to see Stalin's state crumble and disappear.

Thus Zhdanov, with his jeremiads against wayward composers,
writers, and poets, remained on the margins of grand diplomacy,
managed, as before, by others. On April 18, 1946, he held the first
postwar conference of the Central Party apparatus on propaganda.
He unleashed the Department of Propaganda of the Central Committee against literary journals. On April 26, Zhdanov repeated the
performance at another session devoted to the situation in cinematog-
raphy.[20] Then it was the composers' turn.

The universalist language of Marxism-Leninism was not a sufficient
booster for domestic mobilization and propaganda. So much of the
campaign, orchestrated by Stalin and Zhdanov, found its food in the

annals of czarist Russia. The propaganda about the Russians as "senior brothers," the leaders of all Slavs as well as all other, "smaller" peoples of the Soviet Union, was nothing but a secularized version of the czarist myth about "god-bearing people" *(narod bogonosets)* and the official Pan-Slavism of the 1870s. Rooted in xenophobia, which was instilled by Stalin and his apparatus of terror, this propaganda was sure to erect a Great Wall between the Soviet people and the West.

The first victims of the new Russian patriotism were Jews. In the spring of 1946 Stalin ordered the cleansing of state structures, from intelligence and the security police to propaganda and education, of Jewish cadres. On June 1, 1946, Suslov, responding to commands from the top, reported to Zhdanov that "the staff of authors and technicians in the Sovinformburo is cluttered with unqualified people without political clearance." He suggested bringing new people into the Sovinformburo and "Institute-205."[21] He also advised against using the Jewish Anti-Fascist Committee, created during World War II to marshal support for the USSR among the world's Jewish population, in field propaganda in Poland, Austria, and Rumania, given the "considerable demonstrations of anti-Semitism there."[22] The heads of both institutions, Solomon Lozovsky and Boris Geminder, were Jews. About the same time, Zhdanov summoned Boris Ponomarev, a Russian and party propagandist who organized the wartime broadcasting beamed on the Resistance movement in the "Slav" countries. "We want to send you to the Sovinformburo. [The head of the Sovinformburo, Solomon] Lozovsky turned it into some kind of synagogue," Zhdanov told him.[23]

Zhdanov and his people knew that Western societies were demobilized and did not represent a threat. The American economy was heading for a postwar slump, and Truman was not up to the formidable tasks that faced him.[24] When Winston Churchill made his "iron curtain" speech in Fulton on March 5, 1946, Zhdanov's secret bulletin presented the speech as a failure. It "fell short of evoking in the masses of the American people (except for its reactionary minority) the kind of response Churchill expected . . . Americans quite sensibly discerned in the speech . . . an appeal to maintain and restore the might of the British empire with support from the United States." The party and military informers reported negative reactions to Churchill's speech in Germany, Poland, and other European countries.[25] Stalin evidently shared this estimate. On March 14 and 23, Stalin ridiculed Churchill in interviews, claiming that he was running against the trend of history. "It is necessary," Stalin said, "for the public and the ruling circles of the states to organize a broad [program of] counterpropaganda against the propagandists of a new war and for the safeguarding of peace."[26] This was a clear directive to Zhdanov's apparatus. At that time, however, Stalin still felt no need for an overarching ideology of confrontation—a Soviet analogue to Kennan's "containment" or Churchill's "iron curtain" speech. The Kremlin's foreign policy was still based on the assumptions of the realpolitik, balancing among powers, and trying to use British-American contradictions. Zhdanov and his ideological bulldogs had already been barking loudly—but Stalin still kept them away from the international arena.

## Why the Cominform?

Two factors prompted the establishment of the Cominform: the Soviets' perceptions of a threat from the West to their zone of security in Europe, and the conviction of Stalin and Molotov that the Soviets could manage this zone only with iron ideological and party discipline. The events of 1946–1947 that shaped and rocked the Communist movement in France and Italy, the Balkans, and the Soviet "security zone" of Eastern Europe explain to a large extent the emergence of the "Soviet camp" and the sudden demand for a unifying ideological message for this camp—the demand that brought Zhdanov to prominence.

In the Balkans, the lack of coordination between the activities of indigenous Communist movements and Moscow's foreign policy contributed to misunderstandings and conflicts of interest between the Kremlin and the Yugoslav leadership, as well as to Stalin's suspicion of, and then fury against, Tito.

In 1945–1946 the Yugoslav Communists, bolstered by their victories over Germany and its satellites in the Balkans, acted in the area with little or no restraint from Moscow. At first Stalin supported the ambitions of the Titoists, recognizing their predominant role in the Balkans. In 1946 he agreed that Yugoslavia should eventually annex Albania. Free for a moment from his insecurity, he seemed to trust Tito. Belgrade became the second most important hub of the Communist network after Moscow. When Italian, Greek, and often French

Communists reported to Stalin and Zhdanov, they had to communicate through Belgrade or use Yugoslav messengers.

Nor was Stalin dismayed at first by the conflict between the regional ambitions of Tito and his comrades-in-arms and Soviet postwar peace goals. There were mutual goals, to be sure, when Molotov supported Yugoslav claims on the area of Trieste, the territory disputed between Yugoslavia and Italy. At that time Stalin and Molotov wanted to "punish" Italy, using it as a bargaining chip against the Allies' interference in Eastern Europe.

Revolutionary guerillas in Greece, supported by Belgrade, were only a minor nuisance to Stalin in 1945–1946. As early as the fall of 1944 Stalin observed "the percentage agreement" with Great Britain, according to which London had a right to impose order on the Greek peninsula. Later he forbade Dimitrov to grant exile to the defeated Greek guerillas, probably since he did not want to give the British a reason to argue against Soviet domination in Eastern Europe. The Soviets seemed to be content with probing the British influence in the Balkans, most likely knowing that it was coming to an end.[27] In any case, in November 1946 Zhdanov did not mention Greece in his address on the anniversary of the Bolshevik Revolution.

There is no indication that Zhdanov's Foreign Policy Department and other party propaganda structures had daily contact with Belgrade. This is all the more remarkable, given that many Soviet and Yugoslav Communists had developed strong mutual sympathies. The siege of Leningrad and the guerilla battles in Serbia evoked common memories of the hardships and horrors of war. The youngest member of Stalin's Politburo and head of the State Planning Committee (Gosplan), Nikolai Voznesensky, and his brother were acquaintances of Milovan Djilas, then Tito's close lieutenant. Some attempts at collaboration were evident between them on various "theoretical" and practical questions of "Socialist construction."[28]

The Pan-Slavic campaign Zhdanov sponsored in the Russian part of the Soviet Union also made him look to the Serbs in the Yugoslav leadership as friends and propagandists of the historic Russo-Serbian alliance. In a word, Zhdanov was the man who could find a common language with the Titoists and prevent a conflict between them and Stalin. But Stalin never even let him try.

Meanwhile, the crisis in the Balkans began to evoke security concerns in Moscow. In Greece the Communists (KKE), rearmed and instigated by the Yugoslavs, resumed the civil war against the British-backed government. The Titoists bragged about the impending fall of Greece in the presence of Western diplomats and politicians.[29] Perhaps people in Belgrade and the Greek Communists believed they could appeal to Stalin's revolutionary instincts. Nicos Zachariades, a dedicated Stalinist from the KKE, went to Moscow via Belgrade and Sofia to talk Stalin into supporting this venture.

But by the time Zachariades arrived in Moscow, Harry Truman had already made a dramatic address on March 12, 1947, to both Houses of the U.S. Congress asking for emergency aid and military involvement in Greece and Turkey to save those countries from imminent Communist takeover. The Truman administration feared that the Greek Communists would align Greece with the Soviet Union. Any suggestion that it was Tito, not Stalin, who operated behind the scenes would have been taken at the time as a bad joke.[30] But it was clear in Moscow that the Yugoslavs imprudently triggered the U.S. intervention in the Balkans.

Zachariades met Zhdanov on May 22, 1947. The Greek Communist painted an overly optimistic picture of the civil war and was quick to dismiss the importance of the Truman Doctrine. American involvement would be "as bankrupt" as the British had been. He complained then that the Soviets could have been more active in Greece. "The [Soviet] embassy is silent." The All-Union Society for Cultural Ties Abroad (VOKS), over which Zhdanov had control, "is of no help." Zachariades reminded Zhdanov that Russian and Greek Orthodox hierarchies had their ties, too. "One can do something through the Church," he begged.[31]

Zachariades tried hard to persuade Zhdanov that Soviet aid to the guerillas would tip the scales in the Communists' favor. Heavy artillery was needed to drive the government troops out of the cities. Knowing well how cautious Stalin was, he promised that the Greeks "would do everything themselves": given Soviet financial aid, they could buy and ship illegally the required weaponry from Palestine, Egypt, and France.

Zhdanov's response was a firm "no." "There are still big battles ahead," he said. Using the language of the combatants for world revolution in the 1920s, he implied that the Greek Communists were just a small flute in the Red orchestra of the future, conducted by the powerful Soviet Union. "The big reserve has to be spared for big

X business." "Not everybody realizes," he continued, "that one has to pick a moment to unleash all the forces of the USSR." Zhdanov then said that he understood the impatience of the Greek Communists. He stressed that they should be "the fighters for a national idea" against the corrupt regime, bought by the Americans and the British, thus playing down the Communist component of the Greek leftists' offensive and enhancing their role as the bearers of progressive nationalism.

Zhdanov seemed to fear becoming involved with the Greek Communists, but also with the Yugoslavs. It would be embarrassing and harmful for the Soviets if it became known that they were aiding the guerillas. "Sometimes indifference can be a more considerate thing than attention," he said to Zachariades.[32]

Zachariades decided to appeal directly to Stalin. There are no records of this meeting, but immediately after it the Soviets asked the KKE to send a wish-list of armament needs. From Belgrade another Greek party leader informed the comrades in Athens that there were reasons to be "completely satisfied" about the meeting. On June 16 a special courier of "Institute-100" brought a letter of Zachariades from Belgrade with a joint request from him and the Yugoslavs to send much more than had been promised in Moscow: rifles and machine guns, mountain and air-defense guns, millions of rounds of ammunition.[33]

This time Stalin allowed them to force his hand. Was it because he did not want Tito to look like a good revolutionary supporting the Greek leftists, while he himself, Stalin, was actually forsaking the Communist cause? If so, it did not add sympathy to the Stalin-Tito relationship.[34]

Stalin's ideas about Tito's Yugoslavia, whatever they were, remained hidden and did not affect Soviet policies until the summer of 1947. Until then Stalin tolerated the special role of Belgrade and the growing informal influence of the "Yugoslav model" on other East European Communists, especially in Bulgaria and Hungary. Zhdanov and Suslov, however, may have been given some instructions on how to handle Yugoslavia and its influence, since they systematically discouraged all attempts to implement the idea of "Slavic solidarity" in any specific form, be it the conference of "friends of Slavs" or a confederation of the Danube countries.

From July 30 to August 1, 1947, Dimitrov and Tito met in Sofia and issued a joint declaration about their intent to conclude a bilateral

Yugoslav-Bulgarian treaty of friendship, cooperation, and mutual assistance. Neither Stalin nor Zhdanov and Molotov were informed. This time Stalin reacted sharply. In a ciphered cable flashed to Belgrade and Sofia he denounced the meeting as a mistake that might be used by "reactionary British-American elements" in order "to expand military intervention in Greek and Turkish affairs against Yugoslavia and Bulgaria." He made a particular point of the fact that neither culprit had consulted the Soviet government.[35]

This Yugoslav-Bulgarian declaration appeared even before the peace treaty with Bulgaria was implemented on September 15. Stalin had other plans for the order and hierarchy of relations between the Soviet Union and the countries of Eastern Europe. Tito inadvertently intervened in Stalin's domain just at the time when the dictator, his xenophobia returning, was seeking to deflect the effects of the Marshall Plan on the Soviet sphere of influence.

It was at this moment that Stalin began to get impatient with the anarchy and the nationalist deviations in the European Communist movement. And Zhdanov's time had come. In May 1947 Zhdanov was forced to focus attention on an area that had not been his concern at all—Western Europe. French and Italian Communists, increasingly isolated in their coalition governments, suddenly decided to go into opposition—without any prior consultations with Moscow. The reaction in the Kremlin was one of disbelief and consternation. It was Zhdanov whom Stalin asked to send an urgent letter to Maurice Torez, General Secretary of the French Communist party.

The Soviet leadership, wrote Zhdanov, cannot understand "what has happened in France" and "what motives guided the Communist party." "Many think that the French Communists coordinated their actions" with Moscow, he wrote in a draft of the letter. "You know this is not true. Your steps were a total surprise to us."[36] The chief of the "Ghost Comintern" admitted his ignorance of the situation. He was asking for information in addition to what he could cull "from the mass media." This remarkable admission highlights how sporadic communication between Moscow and the West European Communists was.

From Stalin's viewpoint, the Western European countries were closing their ranks, supported by U.S. resources, while the Soviet strategic rear in Central Europe and the Balkans was in turmoil. Sometime in August he summoned Zhdanov to his vacation site in Ritsa, near the

Black Sea, and instructed him to work out, in complete secrecy, the blueprints of a new organization—the Information Bureau of the Communist Parties. To the foreign Communists it was announced that an emergency conference of "some European parties" would be held in the fall. After reading the Yugoslav and Soviet records, one historian came to the conclusion that Stalin and Zhdanov wanted "to invite them to a seemingly innocent meeting and then ambush them by imposing something quite different on them."[37] The most important months in the Cold War history of Europe were about to begin. These would also be the last months of Zhdanov's life.

Zhdanov's report to the conference of the European Communist parties and the emergence of the Cominform in September 1947 have often been regarded as a clear example of Stalin's dual approach to foreign policy. There is little evidence that before the Marshall Plan Stalin had any master plan for immediate expansion. He had to digest what he had already gained during the war. But later, when the Americans were aiming at the whole of Europe, how did Stalin's foreign policy change? Did he want first of all to organize Eastern Europe? Or did he seriously expect to use the Cominform to revive "party foreign policy" and to take advantage of the political and economic chaos in Western Europe to get the Americans out of there?

The newly available Russian sources suggest the emphasis was on the former: building up the Soviet-led bloc. This was the practical thrust of the "Six Points" formulated by Zhdanov in his memorandum to Stalin in early September for the upcoming conference in Poland. Zhdanov suggested that a report on the international situation should be "devoted primarily to":

1. an analysis of the postwar situation and the unmasking of the American plan for the political and economic subjugation of Europe (the Truman-Marshall plan);
2. the tasks of organizing forces for counteraction to new plans of imperialist expansion and for the further strengthening of socialism and democracy on both a national and an international scale;
3. the increased role of Communist parties in the struggle against American serfdom;
4. The decisive significance of the USSR as the most powerful force and a reliable bulwark of the workers of all countries in their struggle for peace, socialism, and real democracy;

5. a critique of errors committed by some Communist parties (French, Italian, Czechoslovak, and so on), in part because of a lack of communication and cooperation;

6. the urgent necessity of coordinating the actions of Communist parties in the modern international situation.[38]

Stalin's decision to boycott the Marshall Plan meant for the Soviet Union the end of a wait-and-see attitude toward neighboring countries and, for the "transitional" regimes in Eastern Europe, a death sentence. Seemingly, Stalin faced a simple choice—to create a bloc using either formal diplomatic or "formal-ideological" instruments: proclaiming a Warsaw Pact in 1947 or restoring the new Comintern. He did neither. Instead, he chose another route that fit his needs remarkably well: he used the common ideology of Communist parties to organize Eastern Europe into a "security buffer" for his state.

Even before Stalin decided to boycott the Marshall Plan, Zhdanov expressed uncertainty and fear about the impact of U.S. economic aid on the geopolitical orientation of Finland. On June 30, 1947, Zhdanov told the Finnish Communists Ville Pessi and Hertta Kuusinen that the Finnish Communist party should intensify a struggle for national independence against the threat of "economic enslavement to America." American credit to Finland, he said, had to be unmasked as a result of the "collusion of the Finnish bourgeoisie with American imperialist circles."[39]

On July 1, 1947, the day Molotov walked out of the conference in Paris, Zhdanov taught the Finnish Communists a new line on "blocist" politics: "Communists will gain nothing through peaceful cooperation within a coalition. On the contrary, they may instead lose what they've got." "It is impossible to avoid bloodshed in relations with one's partners," he continued, if they are opposing more radical means of political mobilization. "One has to act so that Communists, instead of awaiting a strike, strike first." When the Finns dared to say they lacked hard evidence of U.S.-Finnish "collusion," Zhdanov scoffed at this punctiliousness: "How Truman intimidated you! If you keep following this rule—that you should use only decent means with the enemies who use dishonest means—then you will never win . . . Paasikivi [the prime minister of Finland] must have sold friendship with the Soviet Union for the first ten billion [dollars] the Americans had promised him."[40] Later, in August, Zhdanov warned the Finnish

Communists that the Americans, if unopposed, might buy Europe wholesale, and that foreign Communists were blind enough to overlook this fact.[41]

Zhdanov had real reasons to be worried. Only under strong Soviet political pressure did the government of Finland prudently decide against any participation in the Marshall Plan, to the great satisfaction of Moscow. But Finland's defiance of Moscow grew so rapidly that in 1948 Stalin and Molotov had to accommodate the Finns to make them accept what Mannerheim had wanted from the very beginning: "the Czechoslovak model of the defense treaty with the USSR." The tragic irony was that by that time Czechoslovakia's independence had been crushed and the country transformed into a Stalinized Soviet satellite.[42]

At the conference in Szklarska Poremba in September 1947, Zhdanov focused his attacks on "the errors" of the French and Italian Communists, who proved unable to fight back when faced with the offensive of the Right, supported by Americans. "Do you have a plan for a counteroffensive against the . . . government of [Alcide de] Gasperi [the Christian Democratic Prime Minister of Italy]?" Zhdanov asked Luigi Longo of the Italian Communist party. "Or do you intend only to defend your rears and retreat, till they, perhaps, will ban you altogether? . . . de Gasperi carried out a coup against the biggest party in the nation, and you leave the field without battle!" Longo lamely cited the "objective difficulties" of fighting against government forces, but Zhdanov pressed on: "Does the Communist party of Italy believe that general strikes, militant demonstrations of workers, the struggle for the return of Communists to the government— that this is 'adventurism'?" Zhdanov's fiery comments were in sharp contrast to Stalin's efforts in 1945 to check radical impulses among French and Italian Communists. In 1947 the revolutionary-imperial doctrine was back, hope for cooperation with the Western leaders over the heads of the Western Communists proved to be unrealistic, and Moscow needed the ideological "fifth column" in Western capitals— just as the classical mode of Stalin's doctrine suggested.

The instructions from Moscow to West European Communists, relayed by Zhdanov and Malenkov, were "to destroy the capitalist economy and work systematically toward unity of live national forces" against American aid. The focus of party work had to be the creation of combat units and warehouses of arms and ammunition. Through August and September, Zhdanov worked hard on a text of his report on the international situation, which he presented to the conference at Szklarska Poremba on September 25. The most famous thesis of the report was that the world was now divided into "two camps"—which was an objective fact by that time, for Stalin and the West had proved to be unable to maintain the integrity of 1941–1945. The phrase strongly implied that there would be no neutral parties in the Cold War. Foreign Communists, who in 1944–1946 were quite autonomous in charting their national ways toward a "new democracy," were suddenly forced to return to the ranks under Stalin's command, to oppose the common enemy. Drafts of Zhdanov's speech in his personal archives in Moscow tell only part of the story of how the speech was drafted. In its earlier versions the words "two camps" were missing. Who added these crucial words? The most probable explanation is that Stalin introduced this concept—thereby giving a required rigidity to the future structure of the Soviet sphere of influence in Eastern Europe.[43]

All conference participants understood the implications of Moscow's ultimatum. Jacques Duclos, a French Communist leader, returned to Paris to tell his colleagues (some of whom reported it back to Zhdanov and Stalin through the Yugoslavs) that he "faced an alternative—to subdue or to break off."[44] The steel discipline of the Communist movement came to be applied to the relationships among states. Thereby Stalin's doctrine became a truly international phenomenon that soon would become embodied in the Soviet bloc.

The idea of the Information Bureau of Communist Parties was another surprise that Stalin and Zhdanov had prepared for East European Communist parties. The conference participants did not even know that this organization of the Cominform was on the agenda. The Poles, when they learned about it, were defiant. A Polish participant at the conference tried to argue that perhaps the whole shift of tactics was erroneous and that it would be better to maintain national People's Fronts, that is, alliances with Social Democrats and Labourists. Zhdanov snapped back: we in Moscow know better how to apply Marxism-Leninism.[45] On September 25, Zhdanov and Malenkov (together again, each reluctant to assume full responsibility) telephoned Molotov, who instructed them that the meeting must by all means adopt a decision on the establishment of an Informburo. And Stalin pressed further: the new structure should be fully vested with control over European, and primarily East European, parties.

## Zhdanov's Last Target

The Titoists, unlike all others, enthusiastically supported the idea of the conference, and then the Informburo. Tito was at the head of the mailing list of the Kremlin for all things relating to the conference, coming before Dimitrov, Georgiu Dej (Rumania), Gottwald (Czechoslovakia), and Rakosi (Hungary).[46] Tito, Kardel, and Djilas took an active part in logistical efforts. During the conference Zhdanov worked hand in hand with the Yugoslav delegation, orchestrating a vicious "trial" of the French and Italian Communists. Zhdanov in his cables to Stalin saved his best compliments for the Yugoslavs.[47]

Yet beneath this smooth surface was Stalin's growing displeasure with Tito. He was already receiving, through Molotov, reports from Lavrentiev, the Soviet ambassador in Yugoslavia, about the complaints the Yugoslav Communists spread around on the insufficiency of Soviet support in Trieste and Macedonia. Initially, Stalin wanted Zhdanov to plan a strike in two directions at the conference in Poland. In addition to the rightist "mistakes" of the French, Italian, and Czechoslovak Communists (who betrayed their desire to take part in the Marshall Plan), another salvo was reserved for the "leftist mistakes" of the Yugoslav leadership.

In the first drafts of Zhdanov's report to the conference, the sins of the Titoists were described as "the criticism of allegedly inadequate aid that the Soviet Union provides for friendly states and the presentation of inordinate claims as to the size of this aid . . . the assertions that the USSR, reputedly for considerations of big politics, out of unwillingness to spoil relations with great powers, slackens up on its struggle to satisfy the demands of smaller countries, particularly Yugoslavia."[48] The Yugoslavs put their finger on a sore spot: Stalin's cynical disregard of national Communist movements in 1944–1946 and his preference for reaching an imperialistic agreement with the United States and Britain were a cardinal sin against the universal Communist cause.

Zhdanov wanted to rebuke the Yugoslavs for their "underestimation of the great meaning and role of the Soviet Union, which cannot and should not waste its strength, crucial for bigger battles." The conclusion of the passage left no doubt that Stalin inspired it: "The pretenses to make the Soviet Union support in all cases and under all circumstances any demand [of a smaller state], even to the detriment  of its own positions—those pretenses are unfounded."[49]

Later Stalin decided to drop those charges. The Yugoslavs protected their flanks by resisting the Marshall Plan from the very beginning. In a familiar pattern, tested in his fight against opposition from various corners in the 1920s, the Kremlin tyrant reasoned that it would be easier to deal with "deviations" one by one, first using the "leftist" Yugoslavs in an effort to discipline the French, Italians, and East Europeans. But even Tito's enthusiasm for the Cominform must have looked suspicious in Stalin's eyes. No, he had not created this structure so that the Titoists could use it for the expansion of their influence and their "model." On the contrary, he was preparing to use the Cominform against Tito.

From December 1947 Stalin began, step by step, to tighten the noose around Yugoslavia. On February 10, 1948, Stalin and Molotov lashed out at the Bulgarian and Yugoslav delegation for "reckless independent actions." Then Stalin revealed that behind his lack of enthusiasm for the Greek civil war was his growing animosity toward Tito. He accused the Yugoslavs of being afraid of the Russian advisors in Albania (read: the Balkans), and expressed his lack of belief in any success of the Greek Communist party, issuing an instruction to stop aid to a guerilla movement in Greece—a blow to any imaginary vision of a Yugoslav-Bulgarian sphere of influence in the Balkans.[50]

Zhdanov was involved in this final stage of the drama, and there is no evidence that he or his "faction" expressed support and sympathy to the Titoists. In fact, Zhdanov brought to Stalin's attention more proof that the Titoists were getting out of hand: their attempts to remove Soviet advisors from the Balkans in order to reassert their domination there. Zhdanov began corresponding with Tito and Kardel about this incident. After Stalin's meeting with the Yugoslavs, Zhdanov drafted a letter to them, probably after consulting with Stalin. He reminded Tito and Kardel that they had approved enthusiastically the French and the Italians' subjection "to the Bolshevik critique." Why did the Yugoslavs not want to surrender now, to repent? Because "they began to think they were the salt of the earth" and considered themselves "exceptional." Later Zhdanov would temper the language, but Stalin's hatred for Tito was unmistakably there.[51]

Stalin, as a great psychologist of the intraparty factional strife of the 1920s, expected the Yugoslavs to give up rather than decide to break the ranks of the "united front of People's democracies and the USSR." In Tito's case, this plot backfired.

It has been proposed that the Stalin-Tito split led to the decline of the "Zhdanov faction" and perhaps to the sudden death of Zhdanov on August 30, 1948. In fact, Zhdanov's health was never strong after the war and began to fail quickly in 1947. After the creation of the Cominform he had to go to the Black Sea dacha, where he stayed until early December, often paying visits to the vacationing Stalin. His vicious treatment by the irritable and neurotic dictator did not aid his health. The voice of the man whose fiery speeches made foreign Communist veterans tremble became faint when near his boss.

Until his death Zhdanov persisted in a remarkably cheerful mood— his official trademark as propagandist-in-chief. On December 12, 1947, he received an Italian Communist and was feisty: What is the mood of the masses—ready for combat? Are they rushing forward to struggle? His assessment of the Cold War dangers also called for optimism. The West was barking, but could not bite, as "elements of blackmail prevail over the real preparation for war." "Everybody understands that we forced them [the imperialists] into defense." After the conference in Poland, the "situation changed in our favor, which gives us reason to look even more confidently toward our future."[52]

Rumors about Zhdanov's unexpected death at the age of fifty-four suggested that it was the work of Beria and Malenkov, his old rivals inside the Kremlin power circle. But the simple truth was that Zhdanov, suffering from grave cardiac atherosclerosis, died on August 31 as the result of two heart attacks he had while in a sanatorium far from Moscow. The Kremlin doctors, who flew to the sanatorium to help him, made an incorrect diagnosis, which contributed to his premature death.

If there was an overwhelming reason for Zhdanov's early death, it was the enormous stress of being a workaholic and the terrifying proximity of his master. Three years after Zhdanov died, Stalin managed to use him as a tool to discipline his lieutenants and terrorize the country. He blamed his death on a "conspiracy" of the Kremlin's doctors, and unleashed a vicious witch-hunt against the "Zionists" and "agents of foreign intelligence services."[53]

In a sense, Zhdanov's death had a symbolic meaning: the era of the faceless politicians, the valets of the master, was nearing its end. Other, more ruthless and robust players were to survive a few remaining years of terror and to attempt to construct the post-Stalin world. Two of the most intriguing figures among them were Lavrenty Beria and Georgi Malenkov.

# 5 Beria and Malenkov: Learning to Love the Bomb

> It is not true that humanity is faced with a
> choice between two alternatives: either a new
> world war, or the so-called Cold War . . . The
> Soviet government . . . decisively opposes the
> Cold War, since that policy is the policy of pre-
> paring a new world war, which with modern
> weapons means the end of world civilization.
>
> Georgi Malenkov, March 12, 1954

On March 5, 1953, Stalin, paralyzed by a stroke, died in his dacha near Moscow. Less than six months later, on August 12, the USSR tested the world's first deliverable hydrogen bomb, equivalent to 400,000 TNT. Together, the death of the universal Communist leader and the appearance of this weapon of global destruction constituted, perhaps, the most far-reaching event in the course of the early Cold War.

The steps taken by both the Soviet Union and the United States toward producing the "super-weapon" on a massive scale (the United States had tested the first thermonuclear device in November 1952) led to the possibility that any conflict between the two could result not only in another devastating world war but in the destruction of the human race. This new reality would have been a severe test for the foreign policy of any state. For Soviet foreign policy, locked into the revolutionary-imperial paradigm in the last years of Stalin's rule, it represented a seemingly impossible challenge.

The death of Stalin shattered the foundations of Soviet domestic and foreign policy. The Soviet empire, personified by one man, was in serious danger. Its fate very much depended on who would pick up the fallen scepter of the universal Communist cause and what means would be used for its preservation and strengthening. Throughout his rule Stalin had undercut deep faith in Marxist-Leninist ideological universalism and killed its genuine advocates; he had reduced the party ideologues to propagandist pawns in his global schemes. He became the only person to reconcile the promise of a Communist "brotherhood of nations" with the Soviets' shamelessly imperialistic performance in the international arena. After his death no figure in the Kremlin could personify the dualism of the revolutionary-imperial paradigm as Stalin had. Nor would anyone have wanted to.

As a result, the year following Stalin's death became the biggest window of opportunity since 1943–1945 for those in the Soviet leadership prepared to move away from the universalist ideology of communism and the practice of global confrontation. At this time, Soviet foreign policy was almost taken over by two politicians prepared to sacrifice, for various reasons, the new millennial vision of the world. These two were Lavrenty Beria and Georgi Malenkov.

Western diplomats and scholars immediately noticed the changes in Soviet international behavior after Stalin's death. But, because of scanty knowledge about the power struggle within the Kremlin, they could never fully understand what those changes were and who stood behind them.[1] While some in the CIA bet on Malenkov, few knew what to make of Beria, an invisible but omnipresent character close to Stalin.[2] At the Yalta Conference, Franklin Roosevelt had asked Stalin who the man in the pince-nez sitting across from Ambassador Gromyko was. "Ah, that one," Stalin had answered. "That is our Himmler. That is Beria."[3] At that time, however, the West's knowledge of Beria's personality and actions was limited, giving them little clue to the role he would play in the spring of 1953.

Most Western analysts felt that the Kremlin's initiatives after Stalin's death were either new, improved Soviet tactics in waging the Cold War or the implementation of a policy designed to reduce international tensions gradually.[4] Both of these estimates hinted at reality but failed to take into account the impact of Beria and Malenkov on Soviet foreign policy during a time when it was undergoing change. Amy Knight has recently revealed that Beria, the chief of the Soviet secret police, became a very active advocate of this change after the death of his boss.[5]

The rise of Beria and Malenkov was as quick as their fall. On June

26, 1953, Beria's colleagues arrested him in the Kremlin, confined him in the military prison, interrogated him for several months, and, in December, executed him. Malenkov remained in power for a year and a half, but rapidly became a lame duck. In January 1955 he lost his position as prime minister, and in June 1957, after Malenkov joined the anti-Khrushchev coup, he was expelled from the government and the Party and exiled to Kazakhstan. Many years later he returned to Moscow, and after decades of obscurity died in 1988, eighteen years after Khrushchev, two years after Molotov.

The decade of Khrushchev's flamboyant rule overshadowed the brief interregnum of Beria and Malenkov. But it can be viewed today in a new light. Both Beria and Malenkov were the first among the Kremlin leadership to react to the Soviets' global overcommitment and the danger of nuclear war that Stalin had bequeathed to his successors.

## The Creatures of Terror

The briefest glance at the biographies of both men indicates that they owed their careers not to the Revolution but to Stalin. Beria was born in 1899 in Mingrelia, an ethnic province of Georgia. At the time of the Russian Revolution he graduated from the college of architecture in Baku, Azerbaijan, then worked as a housing inspector for the Baku City Council. He also joined the Communist party and its secret police (ChK). Stalin noticed Beria while on vacation in 1931 (according to the myth in the Caucasus, Beria "saved" Stalin from an assassination attempt that some suspected Beria staged himself) and appointed him first secretary of the Party Central Committee of Georgia and then a party secretary of the entire Transcaucasian Federation. His rise ran parallel to the extermination of the old cadres, along with countless other victims. In 1938 Stalin picked him again from a handful of candidates to replace Nikolai Yezhov as head of the NKVD, the chief mechanism of Stalin's Great Terror.[6]

Malenkov was born in 1902 in Orenburg, an outpost of the Russian empire bordering on the great steppes of Kazakhstan. His ancestors were czarist military officers of Macedonian extraction. His maternal grandfather was an Orthodox priest. During the Revolution Malenkov graduated from high school *summa cum laude* and later became a political commissar on a Red Army propaganda train. In

1925 he graduated from the prestigious Advanced Technological School in Moscow (MVTU). After graduation he worked on the staff of the Orgburo (Organizational Bureau) of the Central Committee's Secretariat, a major instrument of Stalin's emerging dictatorship. Ten years later Stalin picked him to help reshuffle party nomenclature. Malenkov belonged to the circle implementing Stalin's Great Purges, and in 1938 helped Stalin to get rid of Yezhov.[7]

Beria and Malenkov benefited greatly from the purges, remaining in charge of the secret police and cadre selection until Stalin's death. These were the two principal elements of Stalin's "state within a state," a structure of absolute power that helped him first to reach dominance in the Party, and then to reduce the Party itself to an obedient machine. In 1939 Beria and Malenkov became members of the Party's Central Committee, and Malenkov rose to a full member of the Orgburo. In 1939–1941 Beria and Malenkov carried out the "purging" of the newly conquered Baltic lands, Poland and Moldavia, that resulted in the victimization of thousands. Beria, along with Stalin, was responsible for the tragedy of Katyn, in which ten thousand Polish officers, Soviet prisoners of war after the division of Poland between Hitler and Stalin, were murdered.[8]

During the war against Nazi Germany, Beria and Malenkov were both part of the State Committee of Defense (GKO). Their power grew enormously.[9] They became the two most experienced and efficient administrators in Stalin's entourage. When the war ended, both became deputies at the Council of Ministers (Sovmin) and members of its "operational bureau," in many ways an heir to the wartime system of total mobilization.[10] When in August 1945 Stalin finally decided to take up what he perceived to be the American gauntlet and to start a strategic armaments race with the United States, Beria suggested that the NKVD be in charge of the atomic project. Stalin agreed, but after some thought decided that it "must remain under the control of the Central Committee and must work in strict secrecy." He told Boris Vannikov, a minister of war munitions: "This business must be undertaken by the entire Party." Stalin continued, "Malenkov is a secretary of the [Central Committee], he will involve the local party organizations."[11]

From 1945 until Stalin's death, Beria and Malenkov were in charge of the construction of several new enormous military-industrial complexes: one atomic, another dealing with missiles, including cruise missiles, and a third (beginning in 1950) involved with air defense systems. Beria's reports to Stalin in his capacity as curator of the NKVD (later the MVD and MGB) in 1944–1947—the so-called Stalin file, now stored at the State Archive of the Russian Federation—cover a dazzling variety of duties, problems, and bureaucratic interests.[12]

In a word, the two men came to embody the core of Stalin's empire, its military-industrial, administrative-terrorist heart. The projects in which they were involved constituted a significant part of the Soviet underground economy, managed by a coterie of ruthless administrators who were given the titles of MVD-MGB generals. The ideology of these people derived not from Marxism-Leninism but from the "plan"—the fulfillment of production requirements. They, along with top Soviet leaders, got used to wielding power and developed the arrogance and cruelty that it entailed. "Comrades Beria, Malenkov, and Voznesensky behave like supermen," wrote the physicist Petr Kapitsa (then a member of the advisory board of the atomic project) to Stalin in the fall of 1945.[13]

The differences between Beria and Malenkov were as marked as their similarities. Many scientists who worked under Beria, and even Kapitsa, his bitter critic, agreed that he was a formidable administrator in the field of atomic research and development.[14] Yuli Khariton, the scientific director of the first Soviet atomic design bureau, who met Beria often from 1946 to 1953, is of the same opinion. Beria exploited his frightful reputation to energize Stalinist bureaucracies and mobilize scarce resources. "All that Beria was responsible for," commented a Soviet industrialist, "was supposed to function like a Swiss clock: smoothly, reliably, with utter precision."[15]

The same Beria, by his very nature, was a merciless and sly person, reminding one of Machiavelli's *condottieri* and even more of Chicago's Al Capone. He personally tortured and killed in a cold-blooded manner many men and women, innocent victims of the purges.[16] He knew no limits in abject obsequiousness toward Stalin and cruelty toward everyone else. There were only two motives that drove him—power and survival. In his eyes the party ideologues and propagandists were good-for-nothing chatterboxes (*darmoiedi, trepachi)*, potential fodder for the Gulag prisons, like the previous generation of Bolshevik intellectuals. Beria knew very well how cheap ideological slogans were; he even made corrections on the draft of Zhdanov's report for the opening of the Cominform (he suggested calling the Soviet camp

On August 12, 1945, with Germany defeated and Soviet troops blazing into Manchuria, Stalin and his lieutenants were in cheerful spirits, despite news of the obliteration of Hiroshima and Nagasaki by U.S. atomic bombs. From left to right: Anastas Mikoyan, Nikita Khrushchev, Stalin, Georgi Malenkov, Lavrenty Beria, and Vyacheslav Molotov.

While Hitler's armies were still marching eastward, Stalin began to plan for Pax Sovietica after the Second World War. Among his aims was control over the Turkish straits and Poland. Here Stalin is signing the Declaration of Friendship and Mutual Cooperation with the Polish government-in-exile. Second from left is Malenkov then Wladislaw Sikorski; second from right are Wladislaw Anders and Molotov. Moscow, December 1941.

Vyacheslav Molotov was a soldier of the Bolshevik revolution. Standing first on the left, he poses with a rifle as a political commissar aboard the Agitation and Propaganda steamboat *Red Star* in the Volga, summer of 1919. Even though Khrushchev took away his party membership in 1962, Molotov remained a party warrior to the end of his life.

Stalin as a "battle-scarred tiger" and his loyal and low-key "hammer-man," Molotov, approximately twenty years later. By that time, Molotov had become a consummate bureaucrat who had helped Stalin kill most of his comrades-in-arms. For the majority of Soviet citizens, as well as for the outside world, the two men came to represent the new Soviet party state.

Andrei Zhdanov at the podium. Zhdanov's speech at the meeting of the European Communist parties in September 1947 signaled Stalin's reaction to the Marshall Plan and proclaimed the Soviet Union a "bulwark of democracy" against American imperialism.

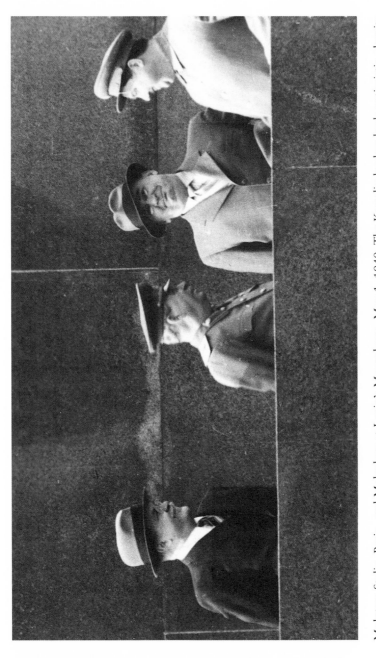

Molotov, Stalin, Beria, and Malenkov at Lenin's Mausoleum, May 1, 1949. The Kremlin leaders look optimistic, despite serious troubles: Stalin "lost" the Berlin blockade to the United States, Molotov's wife had been arrested as a "Zionist agent," and Beria is not at all sure that his atomic project will produce a bomb by the end of August.

A visibly aged Stalin at the Nineteenth Congress of the Communist Party of the Soviet Union, October 1952. With just four months left to live, the Kremlin leader was insisting on the continuation of the Korean War, which he helped unleash in June 1950. He was also plotting a new purge against the Jews, the Kremlin doctors, and his close lieutenants.

The new era in the Kremlin: Stalin is embalmed in the mausoleum along with Lenin, Beria is under interrogation in a military prison, and the first hydrogen bomb was just recently tested. The ruling Kremlin troika of Molotov, Malenkov, and Khrushchev on August 23, 1953.

Georgi Malenkov (left) was the first Soviet leader to claim, in March 1954, that the thermonuclear arms race could mean the end of "world civilization." He was dismissed by Molotov and Khrushchev as weak, and lost his power by the end of 1954. Mikoyan (right) never erred and soon became a loyal supporter of Khrushchev.

Chairman Mao Zedong, Marshal Buganin, and First Party Secretary Khrushchev on October 4, 1954, in Beijing. A visit to the People's Republic of China was a first step in Khrushchev's campaign to fortify Soviet hegemony in the Communist camp and encourage Cold War enemies in the West to start negotiations. Standing behind the leaders are the Soviet ambassador Pavel Yudin and the Chinese foreign minister Zhou Enlai. On the left is Yekaterina Furtseva, Khrushchev's political protégée.

The energetic and pushy Khrushchev emerged as a real leader in the Kremlin's "collective leadership" after his "secret speech" at the Twentieth Party Congress of the CPSU. Khrushchev also began to practice personal diplomacy, traveling to Europe and Asia and agitating for "the end of the Cold War." Here he is leaving Moscow from Byelorussian Station on April 14, 1956. Bidding farewell to him are (left to right) Lazar Kaganovich, Leonid Brezhnev, Malenkov, Nikolai Shvernik, Klement Voroshilov, Mikhail Suslov, and Molotov.

In 1960 Khrushchev vowed support for "movements of national liberation," particularly the Cuban Revolution. Here the Soviet leader, now Chairman of the Council of Ministers, hosts Che Guevara in the Kremlin. Khrushchev was enchanted by Che Guevara, who reminded him of his own revolutionary youth.

Khrushchev with his diplomatic advisors (left to right) Foreign Minister Andrei Gromyko, his personal assistant Oleg Troyanovsky, and the Soviet ambassador in Washington, Mikhail Menshikov, October 1960, New York. The Soviet leader was attending the Special Session of the General Assembly of the United Nations. He closely watched the U.S. presidential elections, hoping that John Kennedy would win and improve relations with Moscow.

"How are you, Mr. Chairman?" Kennedy greets Khrushchev in Vienna on June 3, 1961. Khrushchev valued personal contact with U.S. presidents, but the U.S.–Soviet "summit" in Vienna became a diplomatic disaster. In Khrushchev's eyes Kennedy was weakened by the Bay of Pigs fiasco and, with enough pressure from Moscow, would make concessions in Berlin. During the summit, Kennedy failed to dispel this perception.

In October 1964 Khrushchev was ousted from power and replaced as leader of the Communist party by Leonid Brezhnev, who enjoyed the support of the KGB and the military. The changing of the guard in the Kremlin suited Soviet elites, who sought personal comfort, domestic security, and predictability in international affairs. Here Brezhnev stands with Marshal Rodion Malinovsky, the minister of defense (far left), and young military cadets at a Kremlin banquet commemorating the October Revolution, November 7, 1964.

not only "anti-imperialist" but also "democratic").[17] For him, fear was the best motivator to get things done. In Beria's fiefdoms, from the secret police to the atomic project, there was not a ripple of the ideological storms raging all over the USSR. While Trofim Lysenko and other charlatans, with Stalin's support, were destroying Soviet biology and linguistics, Soviet nuclear physics remained immune, under Beria's protection.[18]

In essence, Beria was an extreme version of the police-state dictator. From his viewpoint (and that was what Stalin liked about him), any problem could be solved by employing sufficient terror and slave labor. The system of the Gulag economy, over which he presided, in his eyes was the best and most efficient part of the Soviet economy. "Veinstein," Beria once said to his subordinate in the Gulag administration, "you are a good worker. But if you had served, say, six years in the camps, you would work even better." Veinstein was one of many police-state engineers, nurtured by Beria, who shared Beria's credo to the end of their days.[19] Andrei Sakharov—then a young physicist working on the Soviet atomic project and later a leading Soviet dissident—driven by liberal ideals, sometimes asked himself later: "What made these people tick? Ambition? Fear? Lust for activity, power? Convictions?" He never came to an answer.[20]

Malenkov was at least in one way a match for Beria, looking at the problems of government pragmatically. But his beliefs were not so crude and primitive. His aide Dmitry Sukhanov later recalled that "Malenkov was free from many ideological dogmas." Malenkov's son Andrei thinks his father viewed himself as a leader of Soviet "technocracy" and an "enlightened autocrat."[21] He was not a man of overpowering dark instincts, but rather a sophisticated and shrewd careerist, half-executioner, half-prisoner of the system he was serving. For his entire career, Malenkov hung on the coattails of a strong leader, lacking character himself or a taste for political fighting. Whereas Stalin's inspiration from ancient Russian history was Ivan the Terrible, Malenkov later liked to imagine himself an elected administrator *(posadnik)* of old Novgorod, a Hanseatic merchant town with republican traditions and a weak executive power.[22] During the war Malenkov did prove himself an able administrator, working with the very best of the young Soviet managers: Alexei Kosygin, a future prime minister, Dmitry Ustinov, a future defense minister, as well as the key administrators of the postwar armament projects Boris Vannikov and Vyacheslav Malyshev. Evidently, Malenkov could treat professionals with respect. After Stalin's death, selected luminaries from the academic elite, among them Sergei Vavilov and Igor Kurchatov, attended parties at Malenkov's home. In a backhanded manner, Khrushchev recognized the technocratic penchant of Malenkov by giving him in his exile a position as director of a power plant.[23]

Working as closely as they did with the dictator, Beria and Malenkov tasted in full measure the darker, tyrannical side of Stalin and soon showed that they were anything but prepared to worship his spirit. Beria was jubilant when he saw Stalin dying. According to one, perhaps apocryphal, story obtained from MVD sources, several weeks after Stalin's death the actor Mikhail Chaureli, who impersonated the Generalissimo in many heroic and pompous movies, came to Beria to show him a new scenario about Stalin. Beria shouted in anger: "Stalin was a scoundrel, a villain, a tyrant! He terrorized all of us, that blood-thirsty devil! This terror was the only source of his power. Fortunately, we got rid of him. So much for that vermin!"[24] Beria's anti-Stalin campaign reflected his struggle for survival, a desire to place on Stalin all the blame for the recent terror.[25]

In April 1953 Beria revealed that the "Kremlin doctors' plot" was a crude frame-up. A secret trial of leading Soviet physicians, some of them Jews, began in September 1952 on Stalin's direct order to the minister of state security, Semyon Ignatiev, and his deputy Mikhail Ryumin. On January 13, 1953, TASS announced that for years there had been a plot to assassinate Soviet leaders, and that this plot was directed by Western intelligence agencies and world Zionism. The anti-Semitic bacchanalia that followed in the Soviet Union greatly contributed to both the fear of war and ideological witch-hunting.

The documents of the Ministry of State Security (MGB) show that Stalin had ordered the arrest of Ignatiev's predecessor, Victor Abakumov, for his failure to find American agents among the doctors. He threatened the MGB with purges until, in September 1952, Ignatiev and Ryumin prepared a falsified "case" indicting the leading professors of medicine in a conspiracy to kill Andrei Zhdanov and other Kremlin leaders. Stalin then sanctioned the torture of the professors: he read the records of their interrogation, made obscene comments on them, and pushed Ryumin, the chief prosecutor on the "case," to stop at nothing to obtain "confessions." Stalin was probably thinking of a new, major "cleansing" of the ranks of the Soviet leadership and state, as well as of the leadership of some Eastern European countries. On December 1, 1952, he gathered his close lieutenants and told them how short-sighted they had been (at that point Khrushchev heard the phrase: "When I die, the imperialists will strangle all of you like a litter of kittens"). Three days later the former General Secretary of the Central Committee of Czechoslovakia, Rudolf Slanski, the former Czech foreign minister, Vladimir Klementis, and some other purged Communist officials were hanged in Prague as "spies." Their bodies were cremated, and the ashes dispersed. Molotov, Mikoyan, Beria, and Malenkov knew very well that the same would have happened to some of them, had Stalin lived longer.[26]

Beria shared with the members of the Central Committee the text of Stalin's instructions to the chief prosecutor, Ryumin, revealing an aging, sick tyrant, motivated by anti-Semitism, cruelty, and a vengefulness bordering on psychosis.[27] "Look at your hero," seemed to be Beria's message to the incredulous and shaken Stalinists. Unlike Khrushchev, who in 1956 denounced Stalin mainly for his crimes against "innocent" Communists, Beria aimed to destroy every vestige of Stalin's authority, every pillar of his myth: in ideology, the world Communist movement, culture and science, military affairs, and foreign policy.

Malenkov never betrayed strong feelings about Stalin after his death. He did not mind getting rid of Stalin's shadow as soon as possible, but, unlike Beria, he had no urgent reasons to exorcise Stalin's ghost. Few in the party and state elite suspected at first that his role in the purges was great or that it lasted until late in Stalin's life. In 1949 Stalin had appointed Malenkov to investigate the "Leningrad affair," in which many top-level state administrators and planners were put into a special party prison in Lefortovo and murdered without trial.[28] Evidently, Malenkov hoped that Stalin's murderous legacy and his part in it could be buried quietly, without excessive publicity.

## Secret Tasks

Stalin assigned Beria and Malenkov the most delicate and secret tasks, which to this day constitute the hidden side of the Cold War. Recent evidence shows that both were part of the intimate circle of the Kremlin's Cold Warriors: along with Molotov, Zhdanov, and Mikoyan, they were members of special Politburo commissions dealing with particularly troubling and complex issues of security, defense, and foreign policy.[29] Together with Zhdanov, the two men were involved in the establishment of the Cominform in September 1947. In addition, Beria maintained his "special" network in the Ministry of Foreign Affairs that included Vladimir Dekanozov and Andrei Vyshinsky. The latter was, as it turns out, as much a creature of Stalin as he was an agent of Beria. A well-educated lawyer, for some years a Menshevik, an opponent of Lenin's party, Vyshinsky had enough malice and cunning not only to survive the great purges but also to become the chief prosecutor of the Bolshevik dignitaries in Stalin's show trials. He was a deputy to Molotov from 1940 to 1949, a foreign minister in 1949–1953, a deputy again, and then a representative in the United Nations until his death in 1954. He clearly shared Beria's notion of power: terrify your rivals and subordinates! In New York he shocked the West with his caustic jeremiads and "unmasking" speeches, well-rehearsed during the Moscow show trials of the 1930s. Back in Moscow, Vyshinsky bullied his subordinates but grovelled before Beria.[30] With the help of Dekanozov and Vyshinsky, Beria watched Molotov and the way he managed key aspects of Soviet foreign policy.

Espionage and "active measures" against Soviet enemies abroad were an important and invisible front of the Cold War, where Beria and Malenkov played significant but still insufficiently documented roles. Most of the mysteries are still closed in the archival vaults of the Russian successors to the former KGB. Beria remained the supervisor of the NKVD with its branches of political intelligence, counterintelligence, and other secret services. He attended wartime conferences of the Big Three at Teheran, Yalta, and Potsdam, in his own words, "in a capacity related to my work," that is, security and espionage.[31] As for Malenkov, in 1938 he became a party supervisor of intelligence organizations. In the fall of 1945 he even chaired a special Politburo commission to reform Soviet intelligence in the wake of the defection of Igor Guzenko, the cipher clerk of the Soviet military attaché in Ottawa, who had betrayed the Soviet spy rings in North America.[32]

It was Beria and Malenkov who, on Stalin's order, in 1939–1940 uprooted extensive espionage networks of the Comintern era and reorganized the military and political intelligence services. Although

Beria reported to Stalin on intelligence findings, he demonstrated his vigilance on possible misinformation at every step. Even the spectacular success of atomic espionage in 1942–1945 did not dispel Beria's doubts. He suspected the West of planting misinformation about the atomic bomb.[33]

Beria and Malenkov were also involved in military industrialization and rearmament, and this caused them to push for maximum exploitation of the occupied territories in Central Europe, particularly for the transfer of German industrial equipment and workers to the USSR. Beria was personally in control of the Department of the Interior (an NKVD offspring) of the Soviet occupational authorities (SMAG).[34] Since late 1944 Malenkov, Beria, and Nikolai Voznesensky supervised the Administration for Soviet Property Abroad. Without the resources taken from Central Europe, Beria could not have finished so soon the deployment of dozens of secret laboratories and whole "closed cities" (in Arzamas, Kyshtym, and other areas).[35] The NKVD set up a huge project in Joachimstahl (Jakhimov) and Erzgebirge, excavating uranium, torium, and mesotorium. A general of the NKVD, Ivan Serov, at Beria's request rounded up German missile specialists and their families to transport them to secret installations in the Soviet Union.

Beria never bothered to ask any Soviet authorities for permission before issuing these orders or to coordinate his policies with them. Nor did he ever care about the "Socialist" future of Germany; and he cared even less for the East German puppets of Moscow.[36] As a result of operations supervised by Malenkov and Beria, East Germany lost 3,500 plants and factories, 1,115,000 pieces of equipment, and 2,000,000 industrial jobs.[37] All this, in addition to the millions of forced refugees, arrests of opposition members, and brutal persecution of intellectuals in Eastern Europe, amounted to a hidden but quite powerful dimension of Soviet foreign policy. It was a traditional policy of the empire, but a more barbaric one. This occupational policy deeply affected millions of people and did irreparable damage to the image of Stalin's Soviet Union in Central Europe.

Both Stalin's lieutenants seemed to have a keen sense of the raw balance of power—the economic and military potential of other states in comparison with the USSR, and their capacity to mobilize this potential. Their intimate knowledge of Soviet military-industrial capabilities told them that the USSR had an economic base vastly inferior to that of the United States (Sakharov recalls Beria frankly admitting this).[38] Beria's administrative experience in armament projects forced him and Malenkov to look for a balance between limited resources and growing commitments—an important prerequisite for a realpolitik approach to foreign policy. Among NKVD reports to Stalin and Molotov, signed by Beria, were those on Iranian oil fields and Bulgarian uranium ore.[39]

Beria's powerful instinct for survival dictated his reactions to international security problems at critical moments for the Kremlin. In June 1941, when the Wehrmacht was cutting into Soviet territory with alarming speed and Stalin remained immobilized in his dacha, Beria was among the first in the Kremlin leadership to seize the initiative. He joined Molotov in the organization of what came to be the State Committee of Defense, the country's center of mobilization.[40] At about the same time he called on his henchman, the NKVD officer and deputy head of intelligence Pavel Sudoplatov, and asked him to send peace feelers out to the Germans through Pavel Stamenov, the Bulgarian ambassador in Moscow and a Soviet agent. In 1960 Sudoplatov, arrested and imprisoned after Beria's fall, spoke about this conversation to the Committee of Party Control and later recalled it (much more vaguely) in his notorious memoirs. Beria told Sudoplatov to pass the following questions on to the Germans through Stamenov: Why did Germany violate the nonaggression pact? On what conditions would Germany be prepared to end the war? Would Berlin be satisfied if the Soviets made territorial concessions, including Ukraine, Byelorussia, the Baltic, Moldavia and Bukovina, the Karelia Peninsula? If not, what additional territories would Germany like to claim? Beria told Sudoplatov (according to the latter's testimony of 1960) that this might help gain two to three months to mobilize the Soviet reserves against German aggression. Beria also said that he had called Molotov and obtained his approval of the scheme.[41] After Stalin recovered from his stupor, however, the idea was dropped: the Kremlin leader knew better that this war was for keeps.

When the German armies were on the doorstep of Moscow in October, and the giant city was in a state of panic, the Politburo gathered for a meeting. Beria, according to one witness, said, "We should leave Moscow. Otherwise, they will smother us all here." Again, he forgot about his proposal once Stalin decided to defend the Soviet capital.[42]

These critical episodes show Beria as an unprincipled desperado whose "realism" sprung from his cowardliness and strong survival instinct. While Stalin could deal with Hitler in 1939, he refused to negotiate with him after his assault on the Soviet Union. For Beria, however, it was only natural to pay ransom to another bandit or to flee the symbolic center of the Russian and Soviet empire under adverse circumstances, in order to save his skin. Some of Beria's far-reaching foreign policy and domestic initiatives after Stalin's death should perhaps be put in line with his reactions in 1941. "He was not interested in matters of high policy," remarked Molotov many years later. "[His philosophy was] that if you are strong enough nobody will touch you."[43] Almost certainly, Beria did not doubt that the imperialist West would destroy the USSR as soon as it was strong enough to do so.

For Molotov and leaders with an ideological commitment, the Cold War was a clash of two antagonistic systems, with geopolitical problems that followed from this main postulate. Their diplomacy was primarily about discovering and exploiting the contradictions between the United States and its Western European allies. For Beria and Malenkov, however, the Cold War was first of all an arms race. The traditional diplomacy of states, coalitions, and alliances had been overshadowed since 1945 by the U.S. atomic monopoly. Beria, along with Stalin, first realized the paramount importance of nuclear weapons for Soviet security. But, while Stalin was burdened with his old interwar experience and still chained to the geopolitical and ideological schemes of the past, Beria was the first among the Kremlin leadership to recognize that the Bomb provided the ultimate answer to all problems of security and international policy.

## Beria and the Bomb

Beria's role in the construction of the atomic bomb was significant. "Many atomic industry veterans believe," wrote Yuli Khariton and Yuri Smirnov, "that if the project had remained under Molotov's leadership, such quick success in carrying out work of such immense scale would not have been possible."[44] In other words, had it not been for Beria and the ruthless Soviet leadership, the Bomb would not have been built in three and a half years, by August 1949. If the first atomic test had not taken place until late 1950 or even 1951, Cold War history might have followed a different course. For example, the synergy created by the test of the atomic bomb in combination with the victory of the Chinese Communist Revolution convinced Stalin and Mao that the international situation was moving in their favor. Without this conviction, they probably would not have supported the aggression of Kim Il Sung against South Korea.

In many ways, Beria approached the unprecedented task of building the Bomb with his usual barbaric methods. He assigned administrators of the Gulag—and hundreds of thousands of prisoners and camp inmates—to the tasks of constructing installations and excavating raw uranium ore.[45] The authors of an inside history of the first Soviet nuclear design laboratory write that Beria "fully ignored" the fact that, though slave labor could build canals and power stations, it could not build the Bomb "and everything related to it."[46] They were mistaken: although the Soviet physicists who designed the Bomb were patriotic and enthusiastic, it was not these characteristics but precisely the unlimited potential for mobilizing and organizing people that enabled Stalin and his lieutenants to start the arms race on the ruins of a devastated country.

Stalin wanted the Bomb as soon as possible, and initially Beria promised to build it earlier than 1949. On December 25, 1946, the first Soviet nuclear reactor started a controlled chain reaction, necessary for production. But by the end of 1947 the cost of the project and mounting technical difficulties made it clear that the deadline had to be moved.[47] That put Beria in a bind. His suspiciousness, cultivated by Stalin's school of politics, was omnipresent: the huge costs of the project drove him mad, and the quiet process of producing weapon-grade plutonium had no visual effects, unlike the testing of a new tank or aircraft. He regularly inspected the nuclear lab (Arzamas-16) and other installations under construction. He traveled on his special train—two comfortable sleepers protected on both sides by armored cars. Most of the time he was disappointed. Once he wanted to see the reactor room. Kurchatov pointed out the risk of radiation. "And how," Beria asked, "can we know that this isn't a deception, not just your fantasy?" Kurchatov had to admit that only detonation of the Bomb would be decisive proof. When the first big reactor for the production of weapon-grade plutonium almost collapsed in August  1948, it took great effort from Kurchatov to dissuade Beria from arresting "the culprits."[48]

On August 29, 1949, a successful test of the first Soviet plutonium bomb (code-named "First Lightning") took place on a testing site at Semipalatinsk, Kazakhstan. Beria's life literally hung on this event. Later, from prison, he wrote to Malenkov: "I will always remember your . . . comradely attitude toward me when I was leaving for Semipalatinsk in a depressed mood, for [reasons that were] well known to you."[49]

After the Bomb exploded, Beria hugged and kissed Kurchatov. "It would have been a great misfortune if it hadn't worked," he said, and all the participants knew what he meant. (Luckily, the first testing failure occurred as late as October 1954, when Beria was no longer alive.) Just moments after the first test Beria was asking the men who had observed the American atomic tests in July 1946 at Bikini: "Did it look like the American one? Very much like it? We didn't screw it up? Kurchatov isn't pulling our leg, is he?"[50]

Beria, along with Stalin, was fully aware of the great political and military significance of the new weapon. On the eve of the test, Beria, in a state of great agitation, told the scientists that "he wanted everything at the test site to be totally destroyed in order to provide maximum terror."[51] His concern that the effect of the Bomb not be less than the effect of the Bikini demonstration betrayed the same assumption: the future role of the USSR in the world would depend on the terrifying yield of its nuclear arsenals.

Since 1946 Beria had known that scientists were developing other, more powerful devices, including the ones based on the principle of thermonuclear fusion—a future "superbomb." Soviet calculations for the first specific design began in the summer of 1949 in Arzamas-16.[52] Sakharov wrote in his memoirs: "Those who held power [in the USSR]—Stalin, Beria, and others—already knew about the potential capabilities of the new [thermonuclear] weapon, and would have stopped at nothing to create it. Any American steps to suspend or permanently cancel the development of a thermonuclear weapon would have been judged as either a sly, deceptive move, or the manifestation of stupidity and weakness. In both cases the reaction [in the Kremlin] would have been unambiguous—not to get caught in the trap and to take immediate advantage of the stupidity of the enemy."[53]

When the first thermonuclear device (Mike-4) was detonated by the United States in November 1952, Beria was in a panic again over this technological breakthrough by the enemy. He increased the pressure on all participants in the Soviet projects. In the words of one witness, Kurchatov's secretary, they worked as if American bombs would start raining on them in a month or two. The first hydrogen bomb test was again scheduled unrealistically early, and had to be postponed until the summer of 1953, because as late as February 1953 there was still a problem with the production of one component of the device.[54]

During the months following Stalin's death, the last obstacles to testing were gone. Beria at that time remained virtually the only person in the Soviet leadership adequately informed about the dynamics of the nuclear project. After Beria was arrested, his subordinates in the atomic project blamed him for trying to turn knowledge about the project into a personal monopoly. According to the new heads of the nuclear project, Vyacheslav Malyshev and Avraamii Zavenyagin, Beria hid the working plan of Arzamas-16 for 1953 "from the government and signed [a whole number of important decisions] single-handedly, taking advantage of his position as chairman of the special [atomic] committee." Malenkov said that Beria "made the decision to organize the explosion of the hydrogen bomb . . . without informing the [Central Committee] and the government."[55]

Malenkov implied that Beria had not kept him informed, and hinted that Beria might have contemplated using his monopoly in the nuclear project as some form of "atomic politics" to help him seize power in the Kremlin. It is absurd to say that Beria could have made a decision to test the first hydrogen bomb single-handedly a month and a half before the test actually took place. Other accusations must be considered with a great deal of caution, but there was a grain of truth to them.[56] Beria, in his July 1 letter to Malenkov from prison, *before* these accusations were made, admitted: "I reported to you in passim and ordered the composition of a detailed report for the government on the state of our atomic affairs. Before the end of this year, [we] are to carry out several blasts, including one super-powerful model equal to 250–300 thousand tons of TNT."[57]

The fact that Beria kept Malenkov and other successors of Stalin uninformed in March–June 1953 on the progress of thermonuclear developments is of extraordinary significance. This gap of knowledge between Beria and his colleagues may explain the difference in their attitude toward the international situation and the balance of power at this crucial moment in the history of the USSR.

Beria had never been an expert in military affairs, and his relationship with most of the military could not have been worse. But he was not indifferent to the prospects of war. Having the Bomb in his pocket must have made Beria scoff at the use of conventional armed forces in the nuclear age. He may have thought that a modern war, should it break out between the Soviet Union and the United States, would be decided not by the general staffs of the warring powers but by their nuclear arsenals. In the early 1950s the location of these arsenals was such that most of the Soviet divisions, along with many cities, would have been turned into smoldering ruins by the planes of the U.S. Strategic Air Command. Therefore, Beria's knowledge of the nuclear situation may have pushed him to prudence and retrenchment in the international arena in the face of a far superior adversary.

According to General Sergei M. Shtemenko, the chief of the General Staff from the end of 1948 until June 1952, Beria "was hardly interested in what we did [in the General Staff]." When Shtemenko showed Beria a mobilization plan for the Soviet army, Beria asked, "Is it a plan of war or not?" Shtemenko explained that it was a plan to deploy the acting armed forces. Beria asked no more questions. Shtemenko asserted that Beria called him only two or three times a year, mostly to consult on some data.[58] Although, like Sudoplatov, Shtemenko is hardly a trustworthy witness, it is possible to argue that Beria's "nuclear education" may have disproportionately shaped his vision of the war danger and future warfare. For the same reason, from Beria's unique perspective, the future position of the Kremlin in the world balance of power was much more promising than it seemed to other successors of Stalin. As he wrote to Malenkov on July 1, the project "was a colossal achievement that our country should be proud of."[59]

The nuclear project also enhanced his already considerable arrogance toward his colleagues. Indeed, it seemed to demonstrate in a most impressive manner the ability of the Soviet system to catch up in the strategic competition with the most powerful capitalist country in the world. The Soviets started from scratch and broke the record of the Manhattan project in construction of the first device. It took four more years to produce a deployable "fission-boosted" thermonuclear bomb, a precursor of the "superbomb." In addition to the Bomb, the military-industrial complexes supervised by Beria produced the prototypes of air defense missiles and cruise missiles—"Berkut" and "Kometa." The design bureaus already aimed at a higher target: ballistic missiles. These developments would turn the USSR into a superpower capable of resisting any enemy.

### The Cold War inside the Kremlin

At a joint session of the Central Committee of the CPSU, the Council of Ministers, and the Presidium of the Supreme Soviet that opened at 8 P.M. on March 5, 1953, the first speaker was the minister of health. He informed the elite audience that Stalin was still alive but that his condition was hopeless. Then Malenkov stated that "the country cannot afford a single hour [without] leadership."[60] The stunned Soviet apparatchiks understood the signal. Nikita Khrushchev, who chaired the session as the acting leader of the Central Committee's Secretariat, recalled: "In the days leading up to Stalin's death, we believed that America would invade the Soviet Union and we would go to war."[61]

Indeed, the deadlock in the Korean War created pressure on the Eisenhower administration to escalate the conflict. Soviet intelligence analysts reported in late 1952 to early 1953 that the U.S. joint chiefs of staff weighed the chances of using atomic bombs against North Korea and the Chinese coastline. Also, long before Stalin's death, the CIA forecast that, in case of "adversities, domestic and foreign . . . the absence of Stalin's prestige and personality might give rise to manifestations of personal rivalry among Politburo members that could result in the rapid disintegration of the Soviet regime."[62] The U.S. Board of Psychological Warfare planned some "active measures" to bring this about. In the end the Eisenhower administration wisely adhered to a wait-and-see policy. But the men in the Kremlin could not bet on such prudence. They saw themselves as surrounded by American bases and expected the worst from their Cold War enemy. A plethora of Soviet intelligence estimates justified this view.[63]

In retrospect, it is clear that Beria and Malenkov had planned a distribution of power in advance. Malenkov became the chairman of the Council of Ministers, the formal successor to Stalin as head of state. Beria assumed control of the Ministry of the Interior (MVD) and merged it with the Ministry of State Security (MGB). Neither of the two dared take the position of General Secretary of the Party. The position was formally abolished, but in fact Khrushchev was left in control of the central party apparat. The three men seized control of Stalin's papers, including his private archive, and called back to service the people he had blackballed—Molotov returned to the post of foreign minister and Marshal Zhukov became deputy minister of defense. It seems that Beria grossly underestimated the importance of the Party Secretariat and expected that with the mechanisms of terror in his hands and the weak Malenkov in the position of head of state, he would have an ideal platform for a future power struggle. In the biggest mistake of his life, he misjudged the abilities of Nikita Khrushchev, then just a dark horse in the new leadership.

Molotov, Malenkov, and Beria immediately moved to switch Soviet foreign policy to a less dangerous track. At Stalin's funeral, Malenkov unveiled a "peace initiative." "There are no contested issues in U.S.-Soviet relations," he proclaimed, "that cannot be resolved by peaceful means."[64] The same day, Malenkov and Molotov spoke with Zhou Enlai, whom Mao sent to pay his last respects to Stalin, about how to stop the Korean War. They did not share Stalin's fatalism about a third world war and were seriously concerned that the new Republican administration of Eisenhower might escalate the war. They also  looked differently at information about a discussion in Washington on the possible use of the atomic bomb in Korea. Stalin was the main obstacle to a compromise between the West, Peking, and Pyongyang on the Korean armistice. But his death unleashed the peace process.[65] According to Soviet sources, during his stay in Moscow "Zhou Enlai urgently proposed that the Soviet side assist the speeding up of the negotiations and the conclusion of an armistice." On March 18 Molotov sent Malenkov and Beria an outline of a new policy on the Korean armistice. The next day it was approved and signed by Malenkov. Two special Soviet envoys went to the Far East: Vassily Kuznetsov, with Zhou, to China, and Yakov Malik to Pyongyang.[66]

In addition, diplomatic relations with Israel, severed at the height of the "doctors' plot," were restored. Earlier, the Presidium, at the  suggestion of Beria, had decided to end the investigation into the "doctors' plot." The new leadership restored relations with Yugoslavia and Greece, which had been broken earlier. They dropped territorial claims to Turkey. Stalin's law of 1947 forbidding marriages between Soviet citizens and foreigners was quietly abrogated, and seven hundred Russian women, who had lived for years as outlaws in Western embassies in Moscow, were allowed to leave the Soviet Union with their husbands.

All these initiatives were the result of the relative consensus in the so-called collective leadership. Even Molotov concurred. But Stalin's successors felt that the crucial battle for leadership was still ahead: some feared it, some wanted to avoid it, some pretended that the status quo sufficed. Very soon Beria and to a lesser extent Malenkov began to move, still within the frame of the "collective leadership," to expand their foreign policy prerogatives. Malenkov used his position as head of state to curb the role of the Party Presidium (Politburo) along with the Party Secretariat. As a result, only those who headed the state structures could take part in substantive discussions of foreign policy, defense, and security issues. Those who remained on the margins included Khrushchev, now the head of the Party Secretariat, Klement Voroshilov, Matvei Saburov, and Mikhail Pervukhin. Obviously, Malenkov believed that, in the tradition of Stalin and Lenin, the head of state, and not the party secretary, should be the chief statesman. This was a mistake that would cost him power in the near future.[67]

After the decision to end the Korean War, Malenkov and Beria started prodding Molotov and his subordinates at the Ministry of Foreign Affairs with persistent demands to change Soviet foreign policy toward a number of countries, including Austria, Iran, and Turkey. Beria chose a much more bold and aggressive tactic of interference into Molotov's domain. Sukhanov, Malenkov's secretary, who attended most of the government sessions in those months, recalls that Beria would suddenly raise important questions, demonstrating his interest in a broad scope of issues. Beria's international initiatives were combined with even more far-reaching proposals on domestic changes. Among them were the proposal to grant amnesty to one million prisoners of the Gulag, approved by the Party Presidium on March 27, and the memoranda of May 8 and May 16, in which Beria proposed canceling Stalin's policies of "russification" and "denationalization" of the "party, Soviet, and economic cadres" in the Baltic republics and Western Ukraine. These, too, were approved by the Presidium on May 20. All these proposals originated in Beria's brain trust, consisting of his assistants Stepan Mamulov, Boris Lyudvigov, and G. Ordyntsev.[68]

Gradually, the tensions behind the facade of the "collective leadership's" consensus on foreign policy began to mount. The increased attempts of Beria and Malenkov to address the less peripheral aspects and issues of Stalin's international legacy clashed with the dogged conservatism of Molotov. The tension was visible on the question of how the Soviet leadership should respond to the initial public gestures of the new U.S. president, Eisenhower, and Churchill. On April 16, Eisenhower appealed to the new Soviet leaders to leave behind the dark legacy of Stalin's foreign policy. Among the conditions that Eisenhower put forward for a détente with the United States were a settlement in Korea, liberalization in Eastern Europe, a treaty of Austrian neutrality, and the issue of German prisoners of war. It is known today that Churchill pushed Eisenhower to agree to a summit with the new Soviet leadership without a specific agenda. However, Eisenhower, under pressure from U.S. Secretary of State John F. Dulles, demurred on this proposal.[69]

On April 24 the Party Presidium held a session to discuss a response to Eisenhower and Churchill. The transcripts are still unavailable, but indirect evidence shows that Molotov regarded Eisenhower's speech (and a much more hard-line speech by Dulles that followed it) as propaganda and provocation. He and the majority of the Presidium, including Khrushchev, still adhered to Stalin's legacy. They were alarmed by the Eisenhower-Dulles doctrine of the "roll-back" of communism and the Soviet position gained in 1945.[70] Beria and Malenkov seemed to be of a different opinion. A new summit, the first since 1945, would have been a powerful means to build up their authority and legitimacy as new Soviet statesmen. The discussion ended in a compromise—an instruction to *Pravda* and *Izvestiia* to publish the full text of Eisenhower's address with a long reply, relatively free of the vituperative rhetoric of the previous years, but decidedly cool on Eisenhower's conditions.[71]

Malenkov urged Molotov to take another look at the Austrian question. Since 1948 Stalin and Molotov had linked the conclusion of the Austrian peace treaty with the German settlement: this small country, occupied by the USSR and three Western powers, remained a pawn of the Cold War. The pragmatic Malenkov, supported in the foreign ministry by Andrei Gromyko, wanted Molotov to begin separate talks on Austria, especially given that in May 1953 the Soviets received a signal from the British about it.[72] A Soviet initiative on the neutrality of Austria would have been a shrewd realpolitik move undercutting the attempts of the Eisenhower administration to integrate West Germany into the military structures of the Western alliance. But Malenkov did not dare to push, and Molotov remained adamant. Five times Malenkov sent a draft of Soviet policy on Austria back to the foreign ministry for "improvement," and five times Molotov sent it again unchanged. On May 28 he argued that "in the present international situation an isolated decision on the issue of an Austrian treaty would be to the Soviet Union's disadvantage." On June 3 he warned Malenkov: "It would be inappropriate to change our stand on such an important issue before we learn about the stand of the three [Western] powers on that and many other issues."[73]

Molotov's position on Austria showed that he could not grasp the realities of the nuclear age. His diplomacy was completely determined by the lessons of the Second World War. For Molotov, the presence of Soviet troops in Austria and communications with them via Hungary and Czechoslovakia represented an important flank in a future war, either against West Germany or against Tito's Yugoslavia.

Yugoslav-Soviet relations also produced tension, this time between Molotov and Beria. A reassessment of the relations between the two countries had quietly begun right after Stalin's death, but Molotov was dead set against a reconciliation with Tito, whom he considered "a right deviationist," a nationalist, and a traitor to the Communist movement. From his viewpoint, a recognition of different roads to socialism would be a heresy. The Presidium ignored Beria's proposals, and instead approved, in June, Molotov's proposal "to establish with Yugoslavia relations of the same type that exist with other bourgeois countries linked with the North-Atlantic aggressive bloc."[74] Beria's patience began to run out. When he received a memorandum on the situation in Yugoslavia from the Committee of Information (an organization linked to Molotov's domain) that repeated the hostile clichés about Tito's capitalist degeneration, he threatened to grind the authors "into dust."[75]

In his conspiratorial and resolute fashion, Beria decided to get around Molotov and the rest of the Kremlin leadership. By the time of his arrest he had prepared a letter to be delivered by illegal Soviet intelligence channels to the Yugoslav prime minister (and formerly Beria's counterpart in the Yugoslav secret police), Alexander Rankovic. The letter stated that "he [Beria] and his friends stand for the

necessity of a fundamental reappraisal and improvement of the relations between the two countries." Beria proposed a secret meeting
with Tito in Moscow or Belgrade, and asked that "nobody, besides
[Rankovic] and Comrade Tito," learn about his secret initiative. A
copy of the letter was later found in Beria's personal safe.[76]

The most explosive foreign policy issue on the Kremlin's spring
agenda was the future of Germany. In expectation of a conclusion of
the General (Bonn) Agreements and European Defense (Paris) Treaty,
which would fully restore the sovereignty of West Germany and
would open the way to West German rearmament, Stalin had sent a
note in March 1952 to the three Western powers proposing that they
agree on a neutral, united Germany. This note caused a big commo-
tion among West German Social Democrats, some of whom blamed
the division of the country on Western policy. To this day some
German scholars and Soviet veteran diplomats believe that the chance
for reunification was real.[77] It is true that Stalin desperately wanted
to prevent a menacing combination of U.S. technology and German
militancy, though he was hardly prepared to sacrifice "his" Germany.
As it turned out, the Western powers took Stalin's initiative as a crude
hoax and proceeded with their plans for West German rearmament.[78]

Stalin then seemed resigned to the idea of a divided Germany. He
told the East German Communist leaders on April 7, 1952: "Irrespec-
tive of any proposals that we can make on the German question, the
Western powers will not agree with them and will not withdraw from
Germany." He said that "the Americans need their army in West
Germany to hold Western Europe in their hands." He acknowledged
that "an independent state is being formed in West Germany" and
prodded the East German Communists to "organize your own state."
For Stalin, the border between the two Germanies became a "dangerous frontier" between the two blocs. "One must strengthen the protection of this frontier," he concluded.[79]

After Stalin's death, many in the Kremlin viewed with fear the
combination of American nuclear superiority and West German rearmament. Of particular concern was the possible acquisition of atomic
weapons by the generals of the former Wehrmacht. How to avert this
development? Beria decided to seize the initiative. He told MVD
General Pavel Sudoplatov, the trusted head of the Bureau of Special
Tasks, that "the Kremlin believed the best way to strengthen our
world position would be to create a neutral, unified Germany run by

a coalition government." He was thinking of some "concessions from [the Soviets]," and was prepared to demote "the Ulbricht government from its central role to a peripheral one." In effect, "East Germany, the German Democratic Republic, would become an autonomous province in the new unified Germany." Beria's plan, according to Sudoplatov, was to "put out feelers" to the Vatican, American German policy circles, and "influential people around West Germany's chancellor, Konrad Adenauer."[80]

Sudoplatov's recollections are not a reliable source for historians. Yet subsequent events proved that Beria had something serious on his mind about Germany and treated the "Socialist GDR" as an expendable asset in the European realpolitik. The motives for this are still not completely clear. Perhaps Beria thought (and if so, with good reason) that the Cold War had started primarily because of the conflict among the Allies on this issue. From this assumption, it logically followed that if some tradeoff could be made on Germany, the Cold War would lose its *casus belli*.

Another burning problem for the new Kremlin rulers was the stability of the GDR. In 1952 Stalin allowed the Communist leadership in East Berlin to start the "construction of socialism"—a policy that quickly led to economic collapse and a flood of refugees to the West. Walter Ulbricht, the general secretary of the SED and the actual leader of the GDR, soon was bombarding Moscow with demands for assistance to cover the deficit of goods and money.[81] The double threat—of West German integration into NATO and the economic collapse of East Germany—was a serious consideration for the Kremlin.

On May 27, 1953, the Kremlin rulers convened for a special session of the Presidium of the Council of Ministers to discuss the problem of the GDR. At that point Beria decided to oppose openly Molotov's stewardship of Soviet foreign policy. The decision-making on the GDR in May–June is still shrouded in mystery, and although Khrushchev, Molotov, and Gromyko recalled this period many years later in great detail, there are significant gaps and discrepancies in the whole story.[82] Molotov approved a draft decision on the GDR prepared by Vladimir Semyonov, the head of the German desk at the foreign ministry. His line was that the Soviet Union should not pay for the mistakes of its East German "friends," and that the "construction of socialism" in the GDR should not serve as a pretext for the remilitarization of West Germany. Molotov's draft recommended that the Soviets "not carry

out a forced policy of the construction of socialism in the GDR." The
foreign ministry also pushed for termination of Soviet occupation of
the GDR, to raise the prestige of its Communist leadership.[83]

Suddenly, Beria cut in first with his own draft. He proposed that
the word "forced" be dropped from the recommendation. Explaining
his position, he said, "We need only a peaceful Germany, it does not
matter to us whether there will be socialism or not." According to
Gromyko, Beria also said with contempt, "What does it amount to,
this GDR? It's not even a real state. It is only kept in being by Soviet
troops."[84]

Beria's proposal must have been prepared in advance. Indeed, before the meeting he asked experts from the Committee of Information
to give him an assessment of the position of the SPD. Malenkov did
not take a stand, yet he seemed to agree with Beria in principle. The
first draft decision of this meeting stated that "the main cause of the
unfavorable situation in the GDR is a course on construction of
socialism, mistaken under present conditions." It decreed disbanding
the collective farms and canceling the policies of "suppressing capitalist elements" in industry, trade, and agriculture.[85] Malenkov's part
in this is unclear. His aide and his son claimed later that Malenkov
had been an advocate of a united, neutral Germany all along. Their
assertions came, however, after German reunification in 1990. The
stronger evidence comes from Khrushchev, who, in his later correspondence and talks with Ulbricht, recalled that there were two, Beria
and Malenkov, who were ready to sell the Socialist GDR for détente
with the West.[86]

Beria's colleagues were not at all ready for such a drastic turnover.
At the Presidium, Molotov strongly objected. He refused to consider
the GDR a bargaining chip in the German settlement. He was convinced that the refusal to build a Socialist state in Germany would
have disoriented Communist forces not only in East Germany but in
all Eastern European states, and that it would eventually lead to a
defection of those states to the West. The discussion threatened to split
the "collective leadership" for the first time. The majority, scared by
this prospect and equally afraid of going against Beria, at Khrushchev's suggestion included Beria's draft in the protocol without
mentioning Molotov's draft. Semyonov, who was also at the meeting
as an advisor, believed later that Khrushchev acted to "deceive" Beria.
This may indeed have been true, as the Presidium's decision allowed

for the draft to be amended by an *ad hoc* group consisting of Molotov, Malenkov, and Beria. This left the final outcome hanging on the intrigues of the key leaders.[87]

Khrushchev, to Molotov's pleasant surprise, was the first to side with him, and this proved a significant step toward his becoming a statesman. Opposing Beria was not safe, yet Khrushchev managed to break the spell of fear. Bulganin, Saburov, and Pervukhin followed Khrushchev's lead. After the session Molotov extended an offer of friendship to Khrushchev, beginning an alliance that lasted for about a year. Beria, feeling he had run into serious opposition, tried one last time, calling Molotov and asking him to withdraw his draft. But Molotov stood firm. "It was a question of principle, and besides, [it was] linked to another issue, where [Germany] would stand in the event of war," Molotov recalled. Beria, true to his glib nature, turned and supported Molotov's position. The superficial consensus in the leadership was restored.[88]

In reality, however, Beria was enraged at Khrushchev and Bulganin, whom he had never considered serious rivals. Later he wrote from prison in a repentant mood that "it came down to unacceptable rudeness and insolence on my part with regard to comrades N. S. Khrushchev and N. A. Bulganin during the discussion on the German question." But, when Ulbricht and Grotewohl had arrived in Moscow to receive new instructions and beg for aid on June 2–4, Beria had yelled at them as if they were his lackeys.[89] Had Beria stayed in power, Ulbricht's days in the GDR leadership would have been numbered.

On June 16–17, the workers' uprisings all over East Germany against the Communist puppet regime proved that the cynical Beria was right: the regime survived only with the help of Soviet tanks. Beria, who stayed in Moscow, called the headquarters of the Soviet high commissioner in Germany, Semyonov, and asked menacingly why he "spared bullets" in dispersing the rioters. He then sent his henchmen, Kobulov and Goglidze, to Berlin to investigate the causes of the uprising. Possible targets for prosecution were Soviet representatives, Semyonov, and Marshal Ivan Chuikov, whom Beria and his people suspected of instigating "the fascist coup" in Berlin! The next target was the SED leadership, which was completely helpless and demoralized by the events. On June 24 the three top Soviet  representatives in Berlin, the head of the General Staff, Vassily Sokolovsky, High Commissioner Vladimir Semyonov, and his deputy

Pavel Yudin, proposed stripping Ulbricht of his state duties and promoting new, energetic people, among them Karl Schirdewan and Rudolf Herrnstadt.[90]

Ulbricht remained in power for twenty more years. Beria's loss of temper (and his simultaneous attempts to replace party cadres in Ukraine and Lithuania) convinced Khrushchev that he was "preparing to grab power" and would spare none of his colleagues. Malenkov, as it turned out, felt the same way, and the two plotted to eliminate Beria.[91] This plot was an exceptionally significant event for the Kremlin rulers and Soviet elites. Beria's dramatic arrest on charges of "state treason" boosted Khrushchev's position. Beria's powerful network was destroyed. Among those arrested were Dekanozov, Merkulov, Beria's brain trusts, and some other MVD generals. Two of Beria's deputies, Ivan Serov and Sergei Kruglov, joined the victors. Many others, who placed their bets on Beria in the power struggle, were shattered. Among the losers was Andrei Vyshinsky. With Beria out of the game, the foreign policy of the Soviet Union became the domain of three people: Molotov, Malenkov, and Khrushchev. It was doomed to be a troubled alliance.

## Malenkov and the Hydrogen Bomb

Malenkov was quickly losing power, whereas Khrushchev was recognized by the party apparatchiks as their new leader. This became visible a mere week after Beria's arrest, when Khrushchev summoned the Plenary Session of the Central Committee to hold extensive hearings on the "Beria affair." Molotov and Khrushchev in unison denounced the "treasonous policies" of Beria, primarily his monopoly on knowledge of the atomic bomb, his secret correspondence with Tito and Rankovic, and his position on the GDR. "For us Marxists," lectured Molotov, "any belief that bourgeois Germany might become peace-loving or neutral" is "illusory" and "signifies a retreat to anti-communism." Khrushchev wondered how a true Communist could even entertain such an idea. "The devil only knows," he said. "Maybe [Beria] was getting cues from the chiefs of foreign intelligence."[92]  Many years later Molotov admitted that it was Khrushchev's Russian patriotism that made him stand for the Socialist GDR: its sacrifice would have meant that "our people had shed their blood in vain" during World War II.[93]

The outcome of the debates on the German question meant a reaffirmation of the old revolutionary-imperial paradigm and the lasting defeat of proponents of a new realpolitik. Gradually the policy of supporting the GDR at any cost began to seem like the only realistic option. From a donor to the Soviet economy East Germany was turning into a major recipient. Khrushchev and other war veterans, unlike the previous generation of Communist believers, saw a triumph of ideology as a redemption for the suffering and losses of the Soviet people during the war against Nazi Germany. They shared Stalin's conviction that imperial expansion was something they deserved, and they believed in it with tremendous passion. These feelings, a generational phenomenon, lasted into the early 1980s, when the Kremlin leaders, Gromyko, Ustinov, and Andropov, thought that nothing could justify the loss of the GDR, the linchpin of the Soviet "Socialist" bloc in Central Europe. Only the passing of this political generation opened the way to the collapse of the Warsaw Treaty and the reunification of Germany.

Malenkov prudently chose to swim with the current. He distanced himself from Beria's position on the GDR and rejected Adenauer's "preliminary conditions" for the German settlement. In his concluding speech at the debates he stressed that neither he nor "anyone alone can dare or wish to be a successor" to Stalin. He repeated Stalin's cliché that the stronger the Soviet Union became, the greater the danger of conflict with the forces of imperialism, and promised the Soviet elites that the Kremlin would make the West respect Soviet strength.[94]

Nevertheless, Malenkov must still have hoped to resume a more pragmatic and less doctrinaire approach to the making of foreign policy. A month later, on August 8, at a session of the Supreme Soviet, Malenkov took a giant rhetorical step away from the revolutionary-imperial doctrine. He said in a nationally broadcasted address, "We consider that there is no objective grounds for a collision between the United States and the USSR."[95] This was a remarkable return to the nonconfrontational vision espoused by Litvinov and Maisky (and the Kremlin leaders) in 1943–1945. Malenkov defended a reorientation of the Soviet economy from its obsession with military production to a larger emphasis on agricultural and consumer sectors. His domestic and foreign reassessments were inextricably tied to international détente.

A new source of confidence fostered Malenkov's new posture—his fresh knowledge about the impending test of the first hydrogen device. It is plausible that Malenkov was undergoing his own "nuclear education" in the light of Soviet nuclear progress—a reappraisal of international realities and of the basic assumptions of Soviet security. After Beria's arrest, the scope of the Soviet nuclear project became known to the rest of the leadership, but Malenkov was in a better position to grasp its significance immediately. On the day of Beria's arrest, Malenkov signed (and presumably prepared in advance) the decree that transformed the Atomic Special Committee into the Ministry of Medium Machine-Building (MSM)—directly subordinate to him as head of state.[96]

Malenkov used his knowledge to impress hundreds of deputies of the Supreme Soviet—and the whole world, for that matter—on August 8, telling them "that the United States no longer has a monopoly on the production of the hydrogen bomb."[97] A successful test of the world's first deliverable hydrogen bomb followed at Semipalatinsk on August 12. This public disclosure of a major military breakthrough before the enemy could learn about it showed that Malenkov understood the changing rules of international diplomacy: not only was secrecy no longer possible, but the very nature of nuclear weapons made their psychological impact as important as their actual stockpile. This announcement, in combination with a new social program benefiting millions of Soviet people, increased Malenkov's popularity. And the successful test more than anything else diminished the fear of war in the country and dispelled the image of a threatening capitalist encirclement of the USSR.

For the first time, a wide circle of state representatives, ministers, and generals joined the scientists and the project managers in watching an ominous blue-black mushroom cloud fill up half the low Kazakh skies. Malenkov did not come, but he called the new head of the atomic program, Vyacheslav Malyshev, immediately from Moscow and asked him to embrace and congratulate Sakharov, the main theoretical father of the bomb, for his "enormous contribution to the cause of peace." Andrei Sakharov, a young Ph.D. in physics, became a "secret" member of the Academy of Sciences. A shower of state prizes, decorations, and promotions fell on all other participants of the project.[98] It seems that all Kremlin inhabitants breathed a sigh of relief—now they had a strong deterrent against the menacing American plans to "roll-back" communism.

On December 8, 1953, Eisenhower, in an address to the United

Nations dubbed "the Atoms for Peace" speech, proposed replacing the arms race with international cooperation on atomic energy. Everyone in Moscow took the speech for what it essentially was: an attempt to deflect the negative reaction produced in Western Europe by the massive introduction of U.S. nuclear arms into NATO troop and war plans. Evidently, Malenkov was preparing his own response to Eisenhower when he was interrupted by reports of a new series of American thermonuclear tests that far surpassed in impact the Soviet "Article." On March 1, 1954, in the Marshall Islands in the Pacific Ocean, the United States had detonated what was then the largest explosion ever created by human beings, a blast with the explosive power of fifteen million tons of TNT, three times the yield scientists had predicted. This test, code-named "Bravo," not only irradiated Japanese fishermen hundreds of miles away from "ground zero" and sent a wave of panic over radioactivity across Japan, but also made it clear that from now on huge metropolitan areas, not just cities, could be obliterated in a matter of seconds. Amid the uproar, press conferences in late March by President Eisenhower and the chairman of the U.S. Atomic Energy Commission, Lewis L. Strauss, for the first time disclosed this stunning fact to the world. "It is possible," writes David Holloway, "that . . . Malenkov too was responding . . . to the demonstration in the Pacific of the terrible destructiveness of thermonuclear weapons."[99]

In a speech on March 12, 1954, to "voters" in the elections to the upcoming session of the Supreme Soviet, Malenkov asserted that a reduction of tensions and negotiations was the only alternative to "the so-called Cold War," that is, "the policy of preparing for a new world war." He said that such a war, "given modern weapons, would mean  the destruction of world civilization."[100] This was a startling blow to the cornerstone of the revolutionary-imperial paradigm: its claim that any war would lead to a crisis in the capitalist world and to the expansion of socialism. In fact, there was no place at all for this paradigm between the two alternatives, catastrophe or détente, outlined in Malenkov's speech. Acknowledgment of new priorities stemming from the thermonuclear danger interfered with the Marxist-Leninist teachings on class struggle and violent Socialist revolutions around the world, a source of Soviet international (and domestic) legitimacy in the eyes of believers. Malenkov's position was edging closer to pacifism than to the accepted Kremlin rhetoric.

The distance between Malenkov and the rest of the Kremlin leadership might be explained by the former's relative freedom from ideological dogma and his habit of looking at issues in a technocratic, problem-solving manner. Also, Malenkov was the only Politburo member who had taken a serious interest in modern physics and had enough sophistication to consider the larger political and philosophical repercussions of the super-weapon. This made him more open to the opinions of very knowledgeable advisors from the Soviet atomic complex.

On April 1, Malenkov, Molotov, and Khrushchev received a remarkable text written by the head of the atomic ministry, Malyshev, and the leading stars of the Soviet atomic project, Igor Kurchatov, Abram Alikhanov, Isaac Kikoin, and Alexander Vinogradov. "Modern atomic practice, based on utilization of the reaction of fusion," wrote the authors, "opens a limitless potential for increasing the explosive power of the Bomb, which makes defense from this weapon virtually impossible. It is clear that the use of atomic arms on a massive scale will lead to the devastation of combatant countries."  The study of the "Bravo" test, argued Malyshev, Kurchatov, and others, showed that "humanity faces the enormous threat of termination of all life on earth." The authors suggested publishing this warning in an article to expose the duplicity of Eisenhower's proposal, which diverted the public's attention from the mortal thermonuclear danger.[101]

It is clear that the text was written after Malenkov's speech and the second American test, "Romeo," on March 27, when an eleven-megaton device was exploded in the Pacific. But it might be the case that by the time of his campaign speech, when Malenkov and his anonymous speech writers were looking for new information and ideas, the essence of this article had become known only to him.

The article corroborated Malenkov's impromptu thesis. Had it been carried through to its logical end, it would have meant acceptance by the two nuclear powers of the great status quo of the new order that emerged in 1945–1953. But the rest of the Kremlin leadership and state, party, and military elites were not ready for this. The speech did not prevent Malenkov's "reelection" to the Supreme Soviet, but in terms of real Soviet politics, it had been self-destructive. Publication of the article, proposed by Malyshev, Kurchatov, and his colleagues, was vetoed, presumably by Khrushchev and Molotov. At a meeting of the Politburo in April, both of them subjected Malenkov to sharp criticism. After that he was forced to repudiate publicly his heresy by making the confident, if hollow, assertion that any atomic aggression by the West would be "crushed by the same weapons" and lead to the "collapse of the capitalist social system."[102]

On January 31, 1955, at the Plenary Meeting of the Central Committee, Malenkov was dismissed from the post of prime minister. Khrushchev criticized his speech on the thermonuclear danger as "theoretically mistaken and politically harmful." Molotov was even more blunt. "A Communist," he said, "should speak not about the 'destruction of world civilization' or about the 'destruction of the human race,' but about the need to prepare and mobilize all forces for the destruction of the bourgeoisie."[103] The Soviet leadership, following the logic of the revolutionary-imperial paradigm, was determined to catch up in nuclear strength with its American adversary without renouncing the goals prescribed by Marxist-Leninist ideology. Not only the Soviet but also the American leadership found Malenkov's thesis politically embarrassing and harmful. The international situation in the fall of 1953 and throughout 1954 was dominated by confrontation and posturing. The Republican administration, both Eisenhower and Dulles, wanted most of all to accomplish the politico-military integration of NATO. They did not believe in negotiations with the "collective leadership," and put pressure on Churchill not to go to Moscow for a tentative summit. In a rude shock to the Kremlin leaders, Adenauer and his conservative coalition had triumphed unexpectedly in the FRG's Bundestag elections, which marked the beginning of political stabilization in West Germany. The Kremlin rulers came to believe that after the GDR riots in June 1953 the U.S. leadership had decided to launch a global propagandist and diplomatic offensive against the Soviet bloc, ranging from Germany to Korea.[104]

 Charles Bohlen, a leading U.S. expert on the Soviet Union and an ambassador in Moscow in 1953–1957, later commented in his memoirs that the failure of the West to engage Malenkov in meaningful negotiations had been a missed opportunity. Malenkov, argued Bohlen, was better suited than Khrushchev to deal with the United States, due to his rationality and culture.[105]

For the same reason, Malenkov's colleagues in the Kremlin came to the opposite conclusion: that he could not represent the Soviet Union abroad because he was too soft, lacked firm principles, and could be cheated by foreign statesmen and diplomats. Molotov recalled that Malenkov "immediately put himself into the hands of the [revisionist] Right on matters of policy and did not behave as befitted a true member of the Central Committee." Since the fall of 1954 Khrushchev had openly argued before other members of the Party Presidium that Malenkov would not be sufficiently tough to succeed in future negotiations with the West. Khrushchev suggested replacing him.[106] It later turned out that only Khrushchev himself could fit the job.

Malenkov lacked the brutal energy of Beria and the charismatic and powerful personality of Khrushchev. He caved in quickly instead of defending his convictions. His repentance in April 1954 was almost certainly not sincere. The threat of thermonuclear catastrophe seemed to follow Malenkov to the end of his life. According to his son, he was keenly interested in the problem of "nuclear winter," the lethal effect of nuclear fallout on the Earth's habitat. There were also rumors that, shortly before his death, the former head of Stalin's cadres sang in a church chorus. These rumors turned out to be false.[107] But even so, Malenkov remains a figure whose qualities are still largely unknown.

## The Survival of the Paradigm

The fall of Beria and the decline of Malenkov did not stop the transformation of Soviet foreign policy, a process that was unleashed after Stalin's death. But the deadlock in the Cold War continued unchallenged by Moscow for another full year. And the man who gained from it was Khrushchev, "a dark horse" whom Beria and Malenkov had unwisely put in charge of the party apparat.

At first Molotov recovered full control over Soviet diplomacy and steered it back to its old course, avoiding fresh and innovative ideas and approaches. In January–February 1954 Molotov represented the Soviet Union at the four-power conference on the German question in Berlin, the first since 1949. There was no unanimity among the Moscow leadership on the tactics to be employed, particularly whether a question of German settlement should be linked to the future of Austria, still occupied by the four victorious powers. Soviet diplomats later recalled that Molotov was the main force behind this linkage.[108] When Western delegations, acting together, pressed him on the issue of Austrian neutrality, Molotov was "knocked off guard" and began to stammer.[109] The conference ended in a complete impasse.

Meanwhile, Khrushchev sensed a new opportunity for diplomacy in the East: Sino-Soviet relations, tried by the Korean War and the mutual suspicions of Stalin and Mao, badly needed rehabilitation and improvement. The Chinese leadership, who quickly realized they could exploit the power struggle in Moscow to their advantage, initiated trade negotiations, trying to get economic aid and concessions that Stalin had earlier denied them. In January 1954, the Chinese premier, Zhou Enlai, invited Khrushchev to come to Beijing on September 30, 1954, for a celebration of the fifth anniversary of the Chinese Revolution. By that time the trade talks were in a deadlock, since the Soviet ministries demanded that their Chinese "friends" pay for Russian supplies in hard currency.[110]

Khrushchev not only agreed to Chinese demands but also surpassed them in "fraternal" generosity. He wanted to cement the Sino-Soviet friendship on the basis of a common cause, the construction of socialism and communism—and who could count pennies when such a high goal was set! The "Khrushchev plan" for the Chinese included 140 large plants for heavy and defense industry, low-interest loans, and even cooperation in the nuclear field. He also proposed returning to the PRC military bases in Lushun (Port-Arthur) and the Soviet-run Manchurian railroad system. Even earlier, at Khrushchev's initiative, the Soviets had sold their share of profitable "joint" concessions in the PRC.[111]

This gift was worth many billions of dollars. Little wonder that opposition to Khrushchev's scheme among technocrats in the economic ministries was very strong. At the last moment one of the oldest Party Presidium members, Klement Voroshilov, rebelled. He called Khrushchev's generosity "an unbearable onus for our people" and drew attention to the condition of the Soviet Union, where "the traces of the terrible war are still visible everywhere." What, Voroshilov asked, would we tell our people? "Russian soldiers went to war with Japan to return the lands lost by czarist Russia during the Russo-Japanese War. And now we are giving them away." Anyone less pushy and persistent than Khrushchev would not have carried this program over these objections. The new leader, however, threatened to cancel his visit if the Presidium sent him to Mao "empty-handed."[112] He made it clear that this Sino-Soviet agreement would be correct both from the viewpoint of Communist principles and from the strategy of the

Cold War. Even though Khrushchev prevailed, hidden opposition to lavish economic assistance to "friends" lingered on in Soviet elites.[113]

The trip to Beijing was a success. Khrushchev's generosity helped him achieve what only Stalin could achieve, owing to his unique status as the Communist pontiff and the leader of the world power that had defeated Germany and Japan. The bonds between the PRC and the USSR seemed stronger than ever. From the high ground of his first international achievement, Khrushchev began to challenge Molotov's position as the highest-ranking Soviet statesman. Early in 1955 he opened secret talks with the Austrian chancellor Karl Raab and, over Molotov's objections, pushed for a compromise. In May 1955 the Austrian State Treaty was signed by four powers in Vienna, and Austria became an island of neutrality in Cold War Europe. Khrushchev insisted on selling Soviet property in Austria (oil refineries and a Danube shipping company) to the Austrians.[114] In April, Khrushchev paid a dramatic visit to Yugoslavia and brought excuses to Tito for his excommunication from the Communist creed in 1948. In July 1955 Khrushchev was already the boss in the Soviet state delegation at the Geneva summit with three Western leaders. In September he dominated the negotiations with Chancellor Adenauer that resulted in the establishment of West German–Soviet diplomatic relations. Finally, at Khrushchev's insistence, the Soviet-Finnish treaty of 1948 was amended to return the Soviet naval base at Porkkala-Udd to Finland.

Khrushchev became a world leader and the proponent of a new Soviet "peace initiative." On the surface, it seemed that, pushed by the logic of the power struggle, he simply seized the initiative dropped by his predecessors, Beria and Malenkov. But Khrushchev's international activities were not only larger in scope, but very different in their basic premises. In 1953 Beria and Malenkov tried to build their reputation as statesmen on the foundation of the new strength of the USSR, its growing atomic and then thermonuclear capabilities. The ideological, revolutionary dimension of Soviet foreign policy was not for them. Beria could never become a leader of the Communist movement because of his odious past, and Malenkov directed his first appeal to the leaders of the capitalist world. His thesis about the mutual interest between the Western powers and the Soviet leadership in averting a nuclear catastrophe was anathema to the Chinese Communists.

Khrushchev, on the contrary, started building his personal diplomacy along the lines prescribed by the revolutionary-imperial paradigm. In his struggle against Molotov, Khrushchev leaned on his position as party secretary (since September 1953 he was a first secretary). He posed as a leader of the international order of Communists that transcended mundane state interests. His early initiatives were meant to dispel the bad odor that Stalin's cynical imperialism had left in the world Communist movement, among the leaders of other Communist countries, such as the People's Republic of China. He got rid of its most obvious vestiges, military bases and "joint" economic concessions on foreign territory; he bent over backwards to demonstrate that Soviet foreign policy stemmed from the noble principles of "fraternal solidarity and internationalism," in contrast with the policies of the colonial powers of the West.

Later, Khrushchev would fully recognize the new realities of the nuclear age and move, on the basis of this recognition, to transform the revolutionary-imperial paradigm and the understanding of the Cold War itself. But all his actions and intentions prove that he was not, unlike Beria and Malenkov, burdened by this paradigm, nor did he want to get rid of it. On the contrary, he managed to save it and adjust it to novel conditions.

The victory of the last true believer in the power struggle was likely, given the mood of Soviet elites at the time. But it was by no means inevitable. The demise of Beria and Malenkov took place roughly at a moment when the Soviet Union began to become a military superpower. At the end of 1953, at the Presidium of the Council of Ministers in the Kremlin, still chaired by Malenkov, the Soviet leadership approved the report of Malyshev about the results of the first hydrogen test. Malyshev promised to produce in two years a megaton nuclear warhead that could be launched toward any part of the globe. To this end, the leaders ordered the Second Main Directorate of the Council of Ministers (another creation of Stalin, Beria, and Malenkov) to build a huge intercontinental ballistic missile that would be able to reach the United States.[115] In August 1957, the head of the Soviet missile-building firm, Sergei Korolyov, tested this missile and, on October 4, it launched the first Sputnik as a peaceful substitute for the megaton device of Sakharov.

The military-industrial complex required huge investments and soon became the central element of the Soviet state and economy. It produced new Soviet elites with a mentality combining the memories of World War II, Soviet patriotism, and shrewd instincts with sophistication and pragmatism. These elites could have become a new power in the Soviet state bureaucracy, with profound and far-reaching consequences for Soviet history and foreign policy. Yet it was a tragic paradox of Stalin's USSR that the most able and resolute leader of those elites, Beria, was a mass murderer and goon, and another leader, Malenkov, could exploit the potential of new technocracy for the peaceful evolution of the Soviet state, but turn out to be a pushover, too prudent to fight for power, a natural loser in the crude political environment of the Kremlin.

The leadership of Khrushchev did not put an end to the rise of these new technocratic elites. But under Khrushchev's rule, they were integrated into the Soviet bureaucracy, sharing power and authority with its more traditional party components, including the legion of party secretaries, a host of ideologues and propagandists, the ranks of Stalin's marshals and generals. The system, under Khrushchev's inspired guidance, managed to subdue the technocratic and pragmatic side of the military-industrial elites, and put their aggressive patriotism and pride to the service of the rejuvenated revolutionary-imperial paradigm. Khrushchev rushed into the Cold War with gusto and for a decade was the driving force behind Soviet international behavior. A new epoch was in the making.

# 6 The Education of Nikita Khrushchev

Khrushchev: By the way, how old are you?
Reston: Forty-eight.
Khrushchev: I think you will live to see the day
a Communist society is built.

Interview with James Reston of the *New York
Times*, October 11, 1957

Nikita Khrushchev inherited the Cold War from Stalin, but his impact on its course was as legendary as his legacy in every aspect of Soviet life. His flamboyant personality, style, and beliefs help explain the most serious crises in U.S.-Soviet relations that held the world in suspense and finally brought it to the brink of nuclear war.

It has long been said that there were two Khrushchevs: the ignorant and crude accomplice of Stalin's criminal system and the man of surprisingly human reactions. The Russian sculptor Ernst Neizvestny, who carved Khrushchev's face in stone on his grave, had one half of the face in white and the other half in black marble, symbolizing Khrushchev's light and dark sides. Khrushchev's role in the Cold War reflected these two sides: in him the revolutionary promise and the imperial, murderous legacy of Stalin were in constant conflict. He could not juggle the paradigm in the cynical and shrewd way Stalin had.

Khrushchev denounced Stalin's crimes at the Twentieth Party Congress in February 1956 because Stalin had offended his sense of justice and of the revolutionary promise. And he attempted to reach a "peaceful coexistence" with the United States because he wanted to divert the resources spent on the Soviet war machine to peaceful

Socialist construction. But both these intentions backfired. The semi-public acknowledgment that Stalin had been a despot and a tyrant dealt an irreparable blow to Soviet Cold War propaganda both in the world Communist movement and among the Soviet elites. The attempt to reach an understanding with Washington precipitated the loss of the Soviets' major geopolitical ally—Communist China. At the same time, Khrushchev's campaign to wind down the Cold War brought about a sharp increase in world tensions, in part because he refused to abandon the revolutionary-imperial paradigm for the sake of "peaceful coexistence" with the West. Incensed by American arrogance and superiority, and proud of Soviet technological achievements, he began using revolutionary nationalism and nuclear threats in the global competition with the United States on a new, unprecedented scale. Yet even when he shook the world with massive thermonuclear tests, he clung to the hope of winding down the Cold War and the arms race, in some kind of glorious truce with the West.

## His Roots and Career

Nikita Khrushchev deceived many people. His chubby appearance misled Stalin, who often ridiculed him as a country bumpkin before his "court." Beria, Malenkov, and Molotov did not perceive him as a serious rival and paid for it dearly, each in his turn. Khrushchev succeeded in pushing all his better-prepared and more high-brow colleagues from power. His Western counterparts had also regarded him at first as a "clowning, crude, unpredictable peasant," only to appreciate him later as an extraordinary and "uniquely clever" leader. Charles Bohlen, the American ambassador in Moscow in 1953–1956, agreed with both estimates, and added that with Khrushchev "there was no meeting point, no common language"; he was culturally incapable of perceiving the Western position.[1]

"I am a child of two epochs," Khrushchev told the Russian poet Evgeny Yevtushenko before his death. "One man inside me understood something and the other shouted something completely different."[2] He was born on April 17, 1894, in Kalinovka, a small Russian village near Kursk, in the great Russian steppe on the border of Ukraine, into a family of poor, illiterate peasants. When Nikita was fourteen, poverty forced his father from the land to the coal mines of the Donbass. Khrushchev spent his childhood and youth doing hard physical work and experiencing all the desperate conditions typical of the industrial stage of capitalism in Russia. Marxist propaganda awakened his political radicalism even before the Russian Revolution. After Lenin seized power in 1917, Khrushchev was elected chairman of the Union of Metal Workers, then joined the Red Army as a political commissar during the Civil War. His first wife died at that time of typhus, leaving him with a daughter and a son. In 1923 he married Nina Kukharchuk, an educated peasant who became a teacher at the local Party's school.

The party organization of the mines of Donbass sent Khrushchev to Moscow in 1929, to study at the Industrial Academy. As luck would have it, another student at the academy at that time was Nadezhda Alliluyeva, Stalin's wife, who brought the energetic Khrushchev to Stalin's attention. From that moment his career took off, and during the purges he ascended to the number two position in the Moscow party organization. In 1939 he became a full member of the Politburo, in 1949 a member of the omnipotent Secretariat. In 1938–1941 and 1944–1949 he was Stalin's party consul in Ukraine. During the Great Patriotic War with the Nazis he was a political emissary of the Kremlin at several fronts, including Stalingrad, and thus was much closer to the horrors of war than other oligarchs.

In September 1953 he became the First Secretary of the Central Committee in Moscow. After a failed coup against him in June 1957, Khrushchev replaced the Politburo and took over the seat of his friend Nikolai Bulganin as chairman of the Presidium of the USSR Council of Ministers. After that he ruled the USSR single-handedly. On October 14, 1964, his colleagues, fed up with his antics and caprices, ousted him. From that time Khrushchev lived in his dacha as a pensioner, under virtual house arrest and bugged by the secret police.

In August 1966 Khrushchev, prodded by his son Sergei, a missile engineer who lost his job along with his father, started to dictate his memoirs. Later Sergei arranged to transport the tapes to the West. The memoirs were published in 1970, creating a sensation, but also uncertainty about their authenticity. Not until twenty years later was the full version of Khrushchev's memoirs published in Russian in Moscow.[3] Khrushchev died on September 11, 1971, at the age of seventy-seven. His grave—he was buried not in the Kremlin wall but in the graveyard of the ancient Novodevichii monastery—became a landmark for Muscovites and visitors to the capital, but soon the authorities closed the whole graveyard to the public. Khrushchev remained a nonperson in the USSR until 1985, when Mikhail Gorbachev and his reformers began to refer to him as their direct predecessor.

Khrushchev's personality was the very opposite of Stalin's. Stalin took each move only after careful reflection and calm calculation. He was a sinister introvert playing a charming host. Khrushchev was impulsive and mercurial. An extrovert, he sometimes acted before thinking and rarely thought in terms of grand conceptions or generalizations. He defined himself as "a man of the earth, of specific tasks, of coal, metal, chemistry, and, to a certain extent, of agriculture."[4] Under Stalin he never dealt with the issues of foreign policy and propaganda. Initially he sought advice from many sides, but more often he improvised himself. If Stalin was a man of iron will and disciplined mind, Khrushchev was a man of enormous intuition and spontaneous reactions, unpredictable for outsiders.

Khrushchev could be both fierce and smart. In the 1930s he denounced dozens of students at his academy; later he took part in the extermination of the Ukrainian intelligentsia—without expressing the slightest remorse later in his memoirs.[5] Yet in 1956 and 1961 he spoke to the party delegates about Stalin's victims as a man whose personal beliefs had been betrayed. Not only Molotov, but also the Malenkovs and earlier the Zhdanovs, considered him an ignorant peasant, yet he was shrewd enough to survive and succeed them. In 1962 he viciously attacked young Russian poets and artists for "ideological misbehavior." But, in his retirement, he grew to like many of them, and they returned his sympathies. He could be warm, humane, a good family man, but also a rude, nasty despot to distinguished politicians and generals. He rendered Gromyko, his foreign minister since 1957, speechless from fear, yet he treated with respect his young foreign policy advisor Oleg Troyanovsky, whose father had worked with Lenin before the Revolution.[6]

Much of Khrushchev's personality was formed during the pre-Stalin years. He was old enough to have glimpsed czarist Russia. At the end of his life he recalled jingoistic Russian propaganda during the First World War whose most popular character was Kuzma Kryuchkov, a Cossack of the Don who was depicted on popular cartoons as killing dozens of German soldiers with his lance. "Stalin featured himself precisely as Kuzma Kryuchkov" in 1945, Khrushchev remembered. "He thought he could walk on water." When Khrushchev decided to heckle a speaker at the United Nations—the infamous banging of his shoe—he recalled that some deputies at the sessions of the Russian State Duma under the last czar had also taken off their shoes and banged them on their desks.[7]

Khrushchev, unlike some other Kremlin leaders and apparatchiks, never sought to distance himself from his peasant roots and pretend to be a new elite. Averell Harriman, during his visit to Moscow in June 1959, became a witness to a bizarre competition in humbleness among the Soviet leaders who obviously emulated Khrushchev's pride in his lower-class ancestors. "I am a plumber," stated Mikoyan. Frol Kozlov, a deputy of Khrushchev's, said that he had been a homeless waif. Gromyko remarked that he was the son of a beggar.[8] In fact, from the 1930s to the 1970s those of peasant descent became the main clay for the new political and administrative elite of the USSR.[9]

This feeling of being linked to the "roots," to the common peasant people of Russia, was a source of Khrushchev's right to rule and a key to his overwhelming self-righteousness. In his own parable, he compared the Kremlin leadership at the time of Stalin's death to a band of thieves in prison. They needed a leader, yet they mistrusted and feared one another. So they elected Pinya, a modest Jewish boy, because they wanted their leader to be weak and malleable. Pinya, however, turned out to be a tough leader. The thieves planned an escape from prison, but no one wanted to go first and risk his life. Pinya said, "You elected me a leader, I will go first." At the end of the story Khrushchev would solemnly proclaim, "I was that Pinya."[10] He saw himself as a simple person who saved the Kremlin leadership from a Stalinist prison cell.

The other source of Khrushchev's self-legitimacy, the foundation of his sense of mission, was the Revolution. Khrushchev was the last "true believer" in the mandate of the Bolshevik Revolution among the post-Stalin generation of Soviet rulers. His adherence to the ideals of the Revolution had little to do with idealistic fanaticism, Marxist theory, or Leninist ideology. But it had a lot to do with the gut feelings about social justice that he had inherited with his peasant roots. Having entered his adult life under the red banners of the Civil War, Khrushchev had never forgotten the promise of the Russian Revolution: a decent life for all who did not have it, peace for people tired of war. He genuinely believed that the old and rotten capitalist world was doomed to perish and that a brave new world would come to replace it. Lenin remained his idol for all his life. He lamented to John Kennedy in Vienna that "he had not had the good fortune of meeting Lenin."[11] The Revolution indeed fulfilled its promise as far as Khrushchev was concerned. The uneducated, but extremely energetic, mercurial leader of the Donbass miners became a new recruit of the top Bolshevik leadership. His shoe-banging at the United Nations, and the expression on his face when he defended Soviet prestige—one of rage and fierce conviction—speaks much more about his system of beliefs than his endless ideological speeches. Looking at him one could understand why the Revolution happened in Russia and what it was for.

Besides the firm foundation of peasant roots and revolutionary beliefs, milestones of the century deeply influenced the impressionable Khrushchev—Stalin's despotism and the Second World War. The role of Stalin in Khrushchev's political career was enormous. Khrushchev himself admitted that for twenty years he looked at politics and the world through Stalin's eyes. One Russian psychiatrist even wrote that Khrushchev had been a latter-day Oedipus who had lived in the shadow of his father, Stalin, and passionately loved "mother" Russia. Later, with "sadistic satisfaction," he had committed parricide at the Twentieth Party Congress.[12] One has to look very hard to find an Oedipus complex in the robust psyche of Khrushchev. But what bursts from all pages of his memoirs is a bitterness that he was "cheated" by Stalin's duplicity. Stalin's crimes and arrogance offended his sense of social justice. For that he could never forgive Stalin. He destroyed Stalin's myth, not with sadistic pleasure, but with great torment and pain. To the end of his life he tried and could not get rid of the dual image of Stalin: a revolutionary and a murderer, a great statesman and a treacherous devil. In 1970 he said to the Politburo member Arvid Pelshe, "I was also infected by Stalin, but liberated myself."[13] He fought against Stalin's system, trying to return it to the fabled "Leninist basics" of the Russian Revolution. He failed, as would Mikhail Gorbachev thirty years later.

The experience of the Second World War also had a tremendous effect on Khrushchev. The unpreparedness of the Stalinist state for war, the slaughter of the Soviet armies, and the occupation of vast territories by the Nazis flabbergasted him. His role in the disastrous defeats of 1941–1942 is murky: later he claimed that he tried to prevent some of them by pointing out dangers to Stalin, but the tyrant was immovable.[14] Having experienced the war, he was later able to liberate himself from Stalin's spell. He strongly felt that people, not the leadership, saved the country and defeated Nazism. "A psychology of slaves," he fumed at the memoirs of the Soviet marshals who praised Stalin's military genius.[15] The war experience had profoundly influenced him in one other way: it prompted him to reject later Stalin's postulate about the inevitability of war. At the same time, Khrushchev, together with millions of Soviets, believed the German threat should never rise again, and his warnings about a revival of revanchism and militarism in Western Germany in the 1950s were deeply felt.

A person of enormous talents, Khrushchev had never received any systematic elementary education beyond Sunday school and Worker's Faculty night lectures. At the Industrial Academy he was engrossed not in his studies, but in the struggle against the "people's enemies." His natural abilities, however, were extraordinary, and for a long time compensated for his "great lack of elementary culture."[16] Khrushchev's mind, quick and imaginative but not disciplined, made his personal diplomacy a permanent gamble. His negotiations with the Austrian delegation about the conclusion of a state treaty, in April 1955, were a breakthrough: at that moment, he recalled, he traded "his boy's pants for adult trousers." Barely a few months later, after the Geneva summit in July 1955 with President Eisenhower, French Prime Minister Guy Mollet, and British Prime Minister Anthony Eden, he was already supremely self-confident. During negotiations with an experienced statesman, Chancellor Adenauer of the Federal Republic of Germany, in September 1955, Khrushchev was blunt and tough, but also rude. At one point he said to Adenauer, "Perhaps my colleagues will say that I am not a diplomat. Indeed, I am not a diplomat . . . If our esteemed, respected partners are not ready to conduct negotiations, [we] can wait—our asses aren't freezing in the wind." The Soviet interpreter changed "asses" to "faces," but the Germans smirked.[17]

Initially, Khrushchev shared Molotov's views and recognized his authority as a world-class statesman. But very soon he began to feel that Molotov's dogmatic inflexibility was constraining him. At the same time, the uncouth flamboyance of Khrushchev increasingly disgusted Molotov. At copious lunches and dinners with foreign leaders, Khrushchev, after several shots of vodka, would reveal the details of inner party life and shared his doubts about Stalin. In Molotov's eyes this was blasphemy. In June 1957, when they clashed, Molotov accused Khrushchev of "undignified" behavior, unworthy of a leader of great power. Khrushchev went to a sauna with a Finnish prime minister in the wee hours and stayed there until dawn![18]

After 1954, Khrushchev found his mentor in Anastas Mikoyan, the only "oligarch" from Stalin's Politburo who survived in the new political environment, an old revolutionary and survivor like Molotov, but also a person of extraordinary flexibility and acumen. Yet very quickly Khrushchev decided he knew enough of foreign policy and the art of diplomacy to manage it more or less by himself. After 1957 he was no less a master of Soviet foreign policy than Stalin had been, and no less than Stalin did he adopt one-man decision-making. In form, he meticulously preserved the Leninist tradition of collective decision-making in the Party Presidium, but in reality he considered himself, as Sergei Khrushchev recalls, his own foreign minister.

Khrushchev saw the foreign policy of other powers through the personalities of their leaders, and he assumed that large, historic events could be arranged through secret channels to these leaders. To establish these channels, he increasingly used the offices of the KGB and personal emissaries, among them his son-in-law Alexei Adzhubei, the chief editor of the major newspaper *Izvestiia,* Mikhail Kharlamov, the head of State Television and Radio, and Yuri Zhukov, a leading commentator of the Party newspaper, *Pravda,* and a cicerone to all important foreign visitors in the Soviet Union. This "light cavalry" served his needs better than the unwieldy foreign ministry, headed by the cautious Gromyko.

Khrushchev's attitude toward foreign leaders was highly emotional and subject to abrupt reassessments. At one moment he could respect and admire Eisenhower, de Gaulle, Adenauer, and Kennedy. And at other moments they filled him with scorn and fury. He was notorious for his fits of rage before foreign audiences. It is impossible to tell when he was sincere and when he was just performing. His intention was to test a person, to establish rapport, and to get things straight, not to plot behind his back. He liked people of initiative and strength, "men of business" with whom he could deal. He was jubilant when he found that they shared some of the same feelings, for instance, mistrust of the Germans.[19] He also trusted his gut reactions more than profiles written by experts. In 1959, when he visited the United States for the first time, New York struck him much less than the prosperous farm of Roswell Garst in Iowa. Garst, like Khrushchev, was a real "master of the land." It seems that the farmer was the first American to win Khrushchev's trust and deep respect.[20]

At first Khrushchev's direction in foreign affairs appealed to the post-Stalin elites. He promised more continuity, respect, and perks to the party apparatchiks and generals than Malenkov and Beria. Yet there was a basic, built-in contradiction between Khrushchev and the majority of the new elites. Khrushchev longed for a more manageable and stable world, but in the name of revolution. This accounts for the inconsistency of his foreign policy. The revolutionary part of Khrushchev's character had led to a number of unpleasant experiences, the apex of which was the Cuban missile crisis. Although he liberated the new elites from terror, he continued to hold many of them in a state of constant uncertainty and suspense. Finally, their patience snapped and they ousted "our dear Nikita Sergeevich."

When finally Khrushchev was betrayed by his comrades, he took his dismissal stoically, though he felt like a peasant father abandoned by his wayward children.

## Khrushchev's View of the Cold War

Khrushchev never thought about the Cold War in systematic terms. His image of it resembled a quilt made from party dogmas, old memories, patriotic pride, and impressions about foreign leaders whom he met.

Khrushchev firmly believed that the USSR had been wronged, mistreated by the United States after the end of the Second World War. Along with Molotov, he stated that the Cold War was a continuation of the policies of isolation, nonrecognition, and intervention that the West had pursued against Soviet Russia since 1917.[21] He was bitter about the devastation and exhaustion of the USSR after World War II, in contrast with American prosperity. He strongly felt that Soviet territorial expansion in 1939–1945 had been justified both by Soviet sacrifices in the war and by ideology, because it contributed to the strength of "Socialist power" and "saved" the occupied peoples from the "capitalist yoke." The partnership that had existed when Roosevelt was alive had made this goal possible, but the postwar Soviet-American clash left the peace settlement unfinished. In late

1961 Khrushchev wrote in a private letter to Kennedy that vestiges of war, "like poisonous plants, give rise to shoots of 'cold war' every hour."[22] There were such vestiges in Greece, Turkey, Korea, and Iran. But the most important ones were the final peace settlement with Germany and Japan—two old enemies of Russia and the Soviet Union.

Khrushchev placed the blame for the U.S.-Soviet confrontation squarely at the door of Western politicians. He took Churchill and Truman to the court of history as warmongers. Khrushchev's opinion of them echoed Molotov's. Churchill was an inveterate enemy of socialism who wanted to "destroy" the Soviet Union.[23] Truman was a narrow-minded politician who came to power by accident, when Roosevelt died. His policy toward the USSR was "provocative" and "simply intolerable." According to Khrushchev, "This arose from his character and mental abilities. A clever president would not have been so abrasive, would not have pitted the Soviet Union against the United States."[24] The Americans violated the Potsdam agreements on Germany. They kicked the Soviets out of Japan unceremoniously, treating them like children. They taught the Soviets a lesson "about the value of the treaties." "If a treaty cannot be fortified by force," Khrushchev told the party elite in July 1953, "then it amounts to nothing, then we would become a laughing-stock, we would be treated [by the West] as naive simpletons."[25]

In Khrushchev's mind, Churchill's initiative of May 1953 to hold an early summit with Stalin's successors looked like a plot to take advantage of Stalin's death by engaging a still unsettled new leadership and "wrenching" out of them "an agreement on certain terms." In 1956, when the crises broke out in Poland and Hungary, he was again looking at the West: "If we let things take their course [in Hungary]," he said to Tito, "then the West will say we are either stupid or weak, and that's one and the same thing."[26]

Nevertheless, Khrushchev did not share Molotov's opinion that the clash with the West had been preordained. In this he had much in common with Marshal Zhukov, his ally and friend until 1957. At the Geneva summit in July 1955, Marshal Zhukov told Eisenhower during a private conversation that he considered the Cold War a product of machinations by "dark forces." He acknowledged that both sides had made mistakes in the past, perhaps "because there was wrong information."[27] Khrushchev blamed Stalin, Molotov, and Beria for the rigid and sometimes erroneous Soviet foreign policy that played into American hands. "We got caught on the [U.S.] hook," he said in retirement. Stalin had overplayed his hand, antagonizing the Americans and the British. Molotov's foreign policy was "obtuse" and "missed simple realities," as when Stalin and he refused to sign a peace treaty with Japan in 1951, thereby acting as the United States expected them to act.[28]

Much of Khrushchev's engagement in the Cold War can be explained by his desire to overcome Stalin's entangled international legacy and by his confidence in his ability to outfox the "dark forces" in the United States—to make them abandon their policies of arrogance, nonrecognition, and strength toward the USSR. Nevertheless, he was haunted by Stalin's aura of statesmanship. The thought that he might somehow lose the strategic periphery of security around the USSR, particularly in Europe, was anathema to him. "There are people in the USSR," he complained to Tito in October 1956, as he sought his support before the Soviet invasion of rebellious Hungary, "who would say: when Stalin was in command, everyone obeyed and there were no big shocks. But since these [bastards] came to power, Russia has suffered the defeat and loss of Hungary."[29] Troyanovsky also had the impression that "Khrushchev constantly feared that the United States would compel the Soviet Union and its allies to retreat in some region of the world," and that Stalin's warnings would then come true.[30] Khrushchev tried to get rid of this specter in a concrete way: in October 1961 he ordered Stalin's corpse to be taken from Lenin's Mausoleum and placed in a deep hole near the Kremlin wall.

The "theoretical" basis of Khrushchev's departure from Stalin's legacy in 1955–1956 was his rejection of the "inevitability of global war" and of the violent revolutionary transition of the world from capitalist to Socialist order. He adopted a broad interpretation of Lenin's doctrine of "peaceful coexistence" between the opposite social systems capitalism and socialism. These innovations, as always with Khrushchev, were linked to his personal experience with the awesome power of thermonuclear weapons and to his realization of the impossibility of war between the nuclear superpowers. The innovations marked a fundamental shift from the thinking of Stalin and Molotov, who saw the Cold War as a prelude to another world war among great powers, to a view of the Cold War as a transitory period between the era of imperialist wars and an era of peaceful economic competition between the two social systems. The future, in Khrushchev's opinion, would be a cold peace perhaps, but hardly the Cold War.

The main problem for Khrushchev was how to accelerate this historic inevitability. At first, when he moved away from Molotov's tutelage, he counted on the ability of Soviet foreign policy to generate "soft power": a reputation as a peace-loving country, friendly to small nations, generous to friends, eager to settle disputes with opponents. He expected this to undermine the "dark forces" in the West and undo U.S.-made anti-Soviet blocs. In March 1956 he told the Danish prime minister, Hans-Christian Hansen, that after Stalin's death the Soviets "convincingly proved our peace-making nature, and we will continue to prove it. Thereby we will shake NATO loose. We will continue to reduce armed forces unilaterally." Then, Khrushchev concluded, "you will find it hard to justify NATO before public opinion." While Molotov seemingly held the same position, he regarded it only as a tactical move to split the Western ranks, to create a cleavage between the forces of American imperialism and "the petty-bourgeois elements" in small nations of Europe.[31] Khrushchev, however, wanted much more: he sincerely hoped to end European polarization.

In those days (1955–1956) Khrushchev believed that a reduction of tensions would result in the capitalists' interest in profitable trading with the USSR. He believed that profit made Western political systems tick, in the United States, West Germany, and Japan. He imagined Wall Street to be an apex of the power pyramid, and Nelson Rockefeller, an heir to the great Rockefeller fortune and governor of New York, to be a shadow ruler behind the official facade of Washington. In 1955 Khrushchev felt that once Soviet embassies in Bonn and Tokyo were opened, crowds of capitalists would throng to them with their proposals to develop trade with Moscow.[32]

Khrushchev looked for partners, Western politicians with common sense and without ideological prejudices against the USSR. In particular, he rested his hopes on a new generation of leaders who, he believed, would acknowledge the Soviets' rightful place in the world.

During this first stage of his career as a statesman, Khrushchev was filled with the enthusiasm of a neophyte. This enthusiasm grew as the Soviet leader expanded his horizons, embarking on intense and widely advertised trips to new lands. Before Stalin's death Khrushchev had been abroad only once: to see conquered Berlin and Vienna in 1945. After Stalin's death there were many trips abroad: in 1954 Khrushchev went to China; in May 1955 to Yugoslavia, then to India, Burma, Indonesia, and so on. He realized there were huge areas outside the old theaters of U.S-Soviet confrontation, pregnant with anticolonial revolutionarism. Khrushchev found himself under the spell of a new wave of revolution and decided to use the immense opportunities of the Third World—actually along the lines of the revolutionary-imperial paradigm. Without noticing a basic contradiction between revolutionarism and détente, Khrushchev wanted to succeed in both. Very soon, however, he began to think that a quiet termination of the Cold War could not be accomplished, inasmuch as policy-making in the United States and other capitalist nations remained in the hands of staunch enemies who could be convinced only by force. Two developments in particular influenced this conclusion. One was the relentless policy of encirclement and roll-back of the Soviet Union conducted by John F. Dulles, whom Khrushchev perceived as the real leader of American foreign policy. The other was a revolt of party oligarchs against Khrushchev and his increasingly autocratic policy-making in June 1957.

The policy of Dulles, from Khrushchev's viewpoint, culminated in the anti-Stalinist revolts in Poland and Hungary in 1956—the revolts that threatened to topple Soviet control over Eastern Europe. Khrushchev was ready to tolerate a national Communist regime relatively autonomous from Moscow in Eastern Europe, as long as it was headed by a strong, trustworthy leader. Khrushchev had known the Polish Communist leader Wladislaw Gomulka since the 1930s. When at the peak of the Polish crisis in October 1956 the furious Soviet leader arrived uninvited in Warsaw and attempted to blackmail the Polish Communist leader by ordering Soviet tanks to move in after him, Gomulka faced Khrushchev down. In the still unpredictable situation, Khrushchev supported Gomulka and stopped the tanks. The Hungarian Communist leader Imre Nagy did not pass the test, however: he did not enjoy Khrushchev's respect (besides, in the 1930s he had been an NKVD agent under the name "Volodya" and reported on his comrades) and was clearly lost in the powerful vortex of popular revolution. After Soviet tanks stormed the Hungarian capital, the Soviet KGB lured Imre Nagy and other members of the Hungarian "revolutionary" cabinet from their asylum in the Yugoslav Embassy and, after a secret trial, shot them.[33]

The Hungarian and Polish affairs had taken Khrushchev aback. He once more viewed the Cold War through the prism of the revolution-ary-imperial paradigm. Once again, it was "them," the enemies out-side and within, against "us." He feared that those Russian writers and artists who challenged official forms of art would develop a Hungarian-type secret society and attempt "to kill the Politburo."[34] The 1956 revolts underscored the fragility of the Socialist camp and cast a long shadow on Khrushchev's optimistic expectations. "Peace-ful coexistence" remained his long-term project, but he learned a lesson about the bipolar and "zero-sum" nature of the Cold War. This lesson came several days after the suppression of the Budapest upris-ing, when Soviet troops in the GDR faced furious crowds of protest-ers. Khrushchev instructed General Andrei Grechko, the army group commander-in-chief, to open fire if necessary.[35] He also dismissed Tito's protests after the execution of Nagy in language similar to Molotov's and Stalin's: the Yugoslavs are splitting the Socialist camp. In his memoirs Khrushchev also maintained that Tito was claiming for himself a special place in the Communist movement after Stalin's death.[36] Soviet-Yugoslav relations became strained once again.

Khrushchev won the power struggle in Moscow in June 1957, but the struggle itself affected his approach to the Cold War. His expec-tation was that now, with the approaching nuclear stalemate, it would be possible to erode the basis of confrontation between the two camps. Molotov, armed as usual with Lenin's quotations, implied that Khrushchev was giving away the initiative in the Cold War and expected too much from negotiations with the United States. Troy-anovsky heard Molotov saying that naiveté in foreign policy is tanta-mount to a crime. Appeasement was another term that could be heard from time to time among Khrushchev's colleagues. Mikoyan had to defend Khrushchev, explaining to the party elite that "[the USSR] once again unfolded the policy of détente, to restore the sympathies of the petty-bourgeois elements" in Western public opinion after the inva-sion of Hungary.[37]

The criticism contributed to Khrushchev's impatience. He needed a foreign policy breakthrough. His newly acquired authority and legiti-macy depended on the success of his personal diplomacy. By the end of the 1950s he had the means to convince the West to accept the terms of "peaceful coexistence." The armaments programs, started by Stalin and chaperoned by Beria and Malenkov, were bearing fruit: the Soviet Union was rapidly becoming a nuclear superpower. It was this factor and the new emerging logic of the nuclear age that, besides Stalin's legacy and Dulles's challenge, shaped Khrushchev's vision of the Cold War.

## The Making of a Nuclear Romantic

It is not clear when Khrushchev grasped the awesome potential of nuclear weapons. Perhaps it was after the test of the first Soviet hydrogen bomb, in August 1953. In September he received a full report on nuclear weapons, saw a documentary about the test, and could not sleep for several days afterward.[38] A nuclear scientist who witnessed the test recalled that, in comparison with the atomic tests of 1949 and 1951, this time "the impact apparently transcended some kind of psychological barrier. The effect of the first atomic bomb explosion had not inspired such flesh-creeping terror, although it had been incomparably more terrible than anything seen in the still recent war."[39] Khrushchev, who had seen the horrors of World War II up close, must have made this comparison as well.

Like Malenkov, Khrushchev included in his orbit some advisors from the Soviet atomic complex. Until his death in February 1960, Igor Kurchatov, the scientific head of the project, played an important role—particularly after November 1955, when the first Soviet multimegaton bomb was detonated—in "enlightening" Khrushchev about the terrible consequences of nuclear war.[40] This relationship undeniably provided Khrushchev with the first lessons of his nuclear education. But as a politician, Khrushchev naturally exploited the scientific advice for his own purposes. He was supportive when Kurchatov and Andrei Sakharov warned the world about the lethal consequences of nuclear fallout. And he brushed off their objections to further radioactive tests when he needed to demonstrate to his opponents that there was real "beef" in his policy of brinkmanship.

The Bomb pushed Khrushchev, as well as his predecessor, Malenkov, to reappraise Stalin's dogmatic view of international relations, revolution, and the road to socialism. In spite of his vigorous criticism of Malenkov's thesis about "the end of civilization," Khrushchev embraced it tacitly before the Twentieth Party Congress, where he proclaimed "peaceful coexistence" with imperialism. In the Kremlin the seriousness of nuclear danger was underscored by the overwhelming air superiority of the United States. On February 4, 1954, the Party Secretariat (the body directly under Khrushchev) sanctioned upgrading underground bunkers and bomb shelters for the military and government. The resulting subterranean "city" spread hundreds of feet deep under party headquarters and the Kremlin, leading for miles away from downtown Moscow. It was expanded again in 1959.[41]

Stalin, despite his interest in the Bomb, had never grasped the new meaning the Cold War acquired in the nuclear age. Khrushchev understood that nuclear bipolarity became the basic feature of the Cold War, as both the Soviet Union and the United States gained the capacity to destroy each other and the whole world. In May 1957 Khrushchev, interviewed by the New York Times, said that "the international tension [the Cold War] apparently boils down in the final analysis to the relations between two countries—the Soviet Union and the United States of America."[42] Khrushchev, for all his later bravado, developed a sense of the ultimate limits imposed by nuclear weapons on statesmanship. Even at the peak of his euphoria about missile technology in late 1957–1958, he sharply distanced himself from Mao's view that nuclear weapons were just a paper tiger in the hands of American imperialists.

Yet the philosophy of prudence and caution went against Khrushchev's grain. As with many optimists, his energy and imagination could not be paralyzed by fear of nuclear war. As he recalled, his nuclear credo since 1953 had been that "we could never possibly use these [nuclear] weapons, but all the same we must be prepared. Our understanding is not a sufficient answer to the arrogance of the imperialists."[43] He felt personally humiliated by American military and technological arrogance. Late in 1955 Khrushchev issued a secret order to the Anti-Aircraft Defense Forces authorizing them to shoot down any aircraft that violated Soviet air space. During the 1950s the Americans lost 130 pilots in the undeclared air-reconnaissance war over Soviet skies. On June 24, 1956, Khrushchev challenged U.S. Air Force Chief of Staff General Nathan Twining during a reception of the American military delegation in Moscow: "Stop sending intruders into our air space. We will shoot down all uninvited guests."[44]

Khrushchev's revolutionary side could not help rejoicing at the thought that, with the advent of nuclear deadlock and missile technology, the end of American arrogance and superiority was within sight. The Geneva summit with Eisenhower greatly influenced Khrushchev's thinking about nuclear deterrence. He understood, in his own words, that "there was not any sort of pre-war situation," and that Americans "feared us as much as we feared them."[45]

Khrushchev learned much from Dulles's rhetoric of "massive retaliation," which, in the Soviets' view, was undisguised nuclear blackmail. In 1961 Khrushchev explained to his party colleagues that he had known all along that John F. Dulles, an advocate of "massive retaliation," was bluffing. Dulles, said Khrushchev, "knew where the brink was [that the Americans] should not overstep, and behaved in a prudent way, taking our resistance into account and seeing that, with sheer force and extortion, they could not get what they wanted."[46] The Soviet leader quickly understood that the nuclear sword cut both ways: the Americans used it to contain communism and, if possible, roll it back. Why shouldn't the Soviets similarly use it to contain American imperialism and, by providing an "atomic umbrella" for the anticolonialism movements, accelerate the roll-back of capitalism?

It first occurred to Khrushchev that nuclear bluff was a good thing in November 1956, during the Anglo-Franco-Israeli-Arab war. He had known very little about the Middle East until 1955, when the Party Presidium decided to supply the Egyptian military-nationalist junta with arms. In June 1956 Dmitry Shepilov, Molotov's successor in the Ministry of Foreign Affairs, went to the Middle East and confirmed that Egypt was the weakest link in Dulles's plan to build an anti-Soviet pact among the Moslem states. At the same time, the consensus in the ministry was that the USSR should try to mediate between Israel and the Arabs.[47] Khrushchev, however, embraced Arab nationalism. He was impressed by the audacity of the Egyptian president, Gamal Abdel Nasser, who set out to nationalize the British-owned Suez Canal. Yet when Israeli and Anglo-French forces launched a surprise attack on Egypt, Khrushchev did not know how to respond. He was busy with the Hungarian uprising, and was under the impression that U.S. opposition to the war was just a show, that the United States in reality was firmly behind its allies against Nasser. As a result, the Kremlin kept an ostentatious silence for several days after the war broke out.

Intercepted cables from foreign embassies in Moscow and other information soon convinced the Kremlin that the Americans had not been informed of the aggression in advance.[48] In the United Nations, John F. Dulles strongly condemned the United States' closest allies. Khrushchev immediately came up with a bold scheme: he persuaded the Presidium to send official letters to the aggressors, threatening them with Soviet military retaliation. Under the circumstances, retaliation could only mean a nuclear strike. Simultaneously, against the doubts of the baffled Molotov, Khrushchev made the Presidium approve a decision to suggest to the United States that they send a joint peace-keeping mission to the Middle East. The Eisenhower administration hastily rejected the offer, but this episode aggravated even further the bad feelings between Washington and its allies.

To his last days Khrushchev believed that this ultimatum was a gem of his diplomacy, a first triumph over American diplomacy in the Cold War.[49] He used this incident to defend his policies when they came under attack from the "antiparty" group in June 1957. Molotov called Khrushchev's thesis on nuclear bipolarity "essentially and tactically wrong." Along with Stalin, Molotov believed that nuclear parity could delay, but not prevent, another world war. Speaking to Soviet elites at the Party Plenum, Molotov railed against the idea that, because of the nuclear stalemate, "allegedly an agreement might be reached between the Soviet Union and the United States of America." By contrast, the new Soviet strength, according to Molotov, would make it easier to drive a wedge into the smallest crack in the antagonistic camp. "Only in this way, placing pressure not only on America but also on other states that distance themselves [from the United States] and are not firmly in the camp of capitalism—only in such a way is it possible to weaken America itself."[50]

Mikoyan defended Khrushchev's postulate that "the question of war or peace nowadays depends on the biggest powers of the two camps in possession of the thermonuclear bomb." "The British and French decided," he said, "that the Russians had gotten stuck in Hungary. So, [they reasoned,] let us strike Egypt, [the Soviets] will not be able to come to its assistance, they cannot fight on two fronts. We will splash the Russians with mud, knock Egypt out, and undermine the influence of the USSR in the Middle East. [But] we found resources both to keep troops in Hungary and to warn the imperialists that, if they would not stop the war in Egypt, we might use missile armaments. Everyone admits that with this we decided the fate of

Egypt."[51] We can safely take this passage as an indication of Khrushchev's thinking at that time.

Soviet generals, plant directors, and regional first party secretaries gave enthusiastic support to Khrushchev's rhetoric of nuclear strength, and he was encouraged to rely on it even more in the future. In August 1957 the Soviet aerospace firm headed by Sergei Korolyov successfully tested R-7 (semyorka), the first intercontinental ballistic missile in the world. Korolyov, a technocrat who dreamed more about space exploration than military deterrence, arranged a show for Khrushchev. On September 7 he invited the First Secretary to attend a second successful test. Khrushchev stood in the launch control center with a broad smile on his face as the gigantic white missile vanished into space. From that moment, Steven Zaloga writes, he became "obsessed with the potential of missile technology."[52]

In the following months Khrushchev took steps to convince the world of Soviet superiority in long-range missiles. He allowed Korolyov, over the objections of the military, to proceed with his pioneer plans of space exploration, and, on October 4, Sputnik stunned the West. Soon afterward, in early 1958, the Soviet leader visited the biggest missile plant, headed by Mikhail Yangel. "If those missiles were already deployed by the Soviet Army," he told the missile designers, "I would guarantee that there would be no third world war."[53] He then made a sensational statement to the world media: the Soviet Union would turn out missiles "like sausages on an assembly line." At the end of 1959 Khrushchev created the Rocket Strategic Forces, at a time when there were only four unwieldy R-7s on a launching pad near Plesetsk in Northern Russia, and the testing of the more sophisticated and deployable missiles was still months away.

In using the nuclear missile bluff, Khrushchev went far beyond what his teacher, John Foster Dulles, had ever done. Most Western analysts had come to view this development as a mastermind coup of realpolitik. Indeed, for many years Khrushchev produced the impression of Soviet strength among the Western public, while actually playing from a position of inferiority. The Americans believed that Khrushchev was now able to play "chicken" with them, and to implement, under the shield of Soviet nuclear deterrence, his expansionist designs, whatever they were.

Yet there was a much stronger and little noticed romantic side to Khrushchev's nuclear bluff. The authors of a profile of the Soviet leader prepared for John Kennedy were correct when they wrote that Khrushchev hoped his missiles would force the West to treat the USSR with respect, promote Soviet national security and the world revolution, "and even perhaps [help] assure universal peace (Soviet style) through disarmament."[54] The nuclear missiles, even before they were deployed, gave Khrushchev a pretext to start implementing his program of moving to the "highest" stage in the construction of communism in the USSR—a pipe dream of the scion of the Russian Revolution. On January 12, 1960, Khrushchev announced that he would reduce the Soviet army by one-third: this time the primary goal was not to impress the West with the Soviets' "peace-loving" nature, but to reduce the burden of the military budget and to save resources for large-scale social and economic programs. The most severe blow fell on the Soviet officer corps in general and on the Soviet navy and naval aviation. Two hundred and fifty thousand officers were forced into retirement in a period of several months, many without adequate compensation, housing, and retraining. Some senior officers were outraged by the cuts and grumbled about "Nikita's folly."[55]

Thus the thermonuclear revolution did shape Khrushchev's thinking and lead him to transform Soviet Cold War policies in several important ways. The Soviet leader began to look at the Cold War as first and foremost a nuclear stalemate between the two superpowers. And though he came to the conclusion that a war between them could not be fought or won, he quickly tried to turn the sword of nuclear deterrence—and even blackmail—on the country that (he believed) had practiced it first, the United States. That became the weapon with which Khrushchev sought to obtain Washington's recognition of the USSR as an equal global power.

Khrushchev's "nuclear education" did not and could not force him to break with his revolutionary background and the revolutionary-imperial paradigm. In his attitude toward nuclear weapons, as well as in his worldview in general, he was torn between the imperatives of world politics and the credo of the ultimate transformation of the world. The realpolitik applications of this education conflicted with and often were overshadowed by his great hope that the nuclear deadlock would make it possible for the USSR to defend and protect the movements of national liberation from the encroachments of the United States and the old European colonial powers. This hope did not bring Khrushchev to more pragmatic, cautious, or restrained behavior in the Cold War. On the contrary, his conviction that the nuclear impasse was a natural prelude to "peaceful coexistence" between superpowers and a favorable environment for the spread of socialism among the new revolutionary-nationalist regimes made Khrushchev more impatient, more bold and crude in his foreign policy calculations. Technological euphoria and nuclear-missile romanticism made him take too lightly the complex Gordian knots tied before and during the Cold War.

The ambiguous lessons that Khrushchev had drawn from the thermonuclear revolution played themselves out in his pressure on Western powers to settle the German question in the late 1950s and early 1960s. In 1920 Lenin and Trotsky had wanted to carry the proletarian revolution into Germany, in the belief that this would ignite a world revolution. Four decades later Khrushchev had a very different set of tasks in Europe and around the world, but his worldview was very much influenced by his revolutionary forebears. He believed that if the question of Germany were settled, that would remove the chief obstacle to the process of negotiating a long truce between the Soviet and the Western bloc and a peaceful transformation of the world from capitalism to socialism—under the long shadow of boundless and deadly nuclear missiles. In both cases the Soviets' focus was Berlin, at the heart of Central Europe. Like the attempt of Lenin and Trotsky to destroy the European system, this attempt was wrought with danger and led Khrushchev to a period of tension, struggle, and loss.

## The Struggle for Berlin

On November 27, 1958, Khrushchev proposed in a public speech that the Western powers sign a German peace treaty that would recognize the existence of two Germanies and "the free city of West Berlin"— free from the presence of Western occupational authorities and their agencies. If the West refused to negotiate, he warned, the Soviet Union would sign a separate peace treaty with the GDR and then all the rights of the Western powers in Berlin and their access routes to the city would be subject to negotiations with the sovereign state of the GDR.[56] This proposal produced a shock in the West, where strategists and the military always feared that the Soviets might repeat Stalin's Berlin blockade of 1948–1949. This time they were not at all sure that a Western airlift could save West Berlin. Their only options were ignominious retreat or military resistance, which, given a sharp geostrategic disparity, might force the United States to use nuclear weapons. For four years the second Berlin crisis kept Europe, the Soviet Union, and the United States in a state of extreme tension.

Despite its sudden development, the Berlin crisis was not accidental. In Khrushchev's eyes the lack of a formal German peace settlement, thirteen years after the end of World War II, was the biggest threat to Soviet security interests in Europe. Since 1955 official Soviet diplomacy in Germany had aimed at consolidation of the status quo and sought a balance between deterrence of Bonn and support of the GDR's sovereignty on the one hand, and attempts at rapprochement with the FRG, against the GDR's objections, on the other. But by the summer of 1958 this policy was in jeopardy. Adenauer's government, as well as the U.S. administration, rejected Khrushchev's offer of the "peaceful coexistence" of two German states allied with the opposing blocs, NATO and the Warsaw Treaty. West Germany remained a pillar of the Western defense alliance against the Soviet Union.

Some analysts warned the Kremlin that Adenauer would soon force Washington to support the "implementation of German reunification on a bourgeois basis."[57] One of the memorandums to the Presidium, sent in December 1956, described the danger of a bilateral settlement between West Germany and Poland behind Moscow's back. Then "the Polish government would no longer be interested in hosting Soviet troops on Polish territory." In the next diplomatic move, Bonn could pick up the old Soviet proposal to withdraw all foreign troops from German territory. The Soviet Union would then have to pull its troops back "not to [the Polish-GDR border], but behind the Soviet state borders." The same memorandum warned of the possible consequences of a reorientation of the Polish economy from the Soviet Union to West Germany, which would turn Poland into "a kind of obstacle" for military and economic communications between the USSR and the GDR. Some intelligence reports gave credibility to these dark forebodings.[58]

The Kremlin greatly feared the possibility of the gradual nuclearization of West Germany. The thought of the Bundeswehr with nuclear weapons, blending with still recent memories of the goose-stepping Nazis, was anathema to the Soviet leaders. On April 25, 1957, in a conversation with the Soviet ambassador Andrei Smirnov, Adenauer did not deny that the FRG might become a nuclear power. Foreign

Minister Heinrich von Brentano added, "If England and other powers have atomic weapons, why should the FRG not have them?" After this, Khrushchev ended all confidential talks with the West German leadership for one year.[59] In the spring of 1958 Mikoyan brought a message from Khrushchev to Adenauer: if the West German Bundestag were to pass a resolution authorizing nuclear armaments, any talks about German reunification would become impossible. Yet as soon as Mikoyan left Bonn, the resolution was passed. Khrushchev received signals that Adenauer, that "old German fox," was using negotiations to gain time for his plans of rearmament to bear fruit and for the West German "economic miracle" to pull the GDR, Poland, and Czechoslovakia out of the Soviet orbit.[60]

Ulbricht and his sympathizers were the second factor in Khrushchev's decision to come up with the German ultimatum. The eldest son of a tailor from Leipzig, Ulbricht worked his way up to a Comintern organizer and, with Stalin's encouragement, first secretary of the Party of German Unity (SED), the Communist boss of the GDR. In 1932 Georgi Dimitrov sharply criticized Ulbricht "for his bureaucratic command methods of leadership, ambition, and stubbornness." The top Soviet diplomats and advisors in East Germany recommended that he be removed in 1953. Ulbricht not only survived, but was even able to humiliate some of his critics. He eradicated all opposition to his personal power inside the SED leadership and succeeded in easing the Soviet ambassador Georgi Pushkin, who objected to his methods and policies, out of Berlin.[61]

The East German leader believed that eradication of capitalism in the Eastern zone was a Communist duty and a precondition for staying in power. Instead of profiting from the proximity to capitalist West Berlin, he wanted to take it over and repeatedly tried to persuade the Soviet leadership to help him in this task. Western observers suspected that the SED leadership began encouraging people to flee to West Berlin in order to give them a pretext to tighten the screws.[62]

Another autocratic ruler of the USSR, more pragmatic and cynical, like Beria and Malenkov, would have reacted to these developments in different ways: by removing Ulbricht or by closing down the border between Western and Eastern sectors of Berlin before starting talks with the West. Khrushchev chose neither. His aims and methods in the crisis were so inconsistent that to this day Western academics and analysts, accustomed to a more systematic manner of thinking and planning, remain confused. As was always the case with Khrushchev, the clue to the behavior that shaped the Berlin crisis and the Cold War itself was in his ambivalent yearnings.

Khrushchev was personally committed to the construction of socialism in the GDR, and he revealed this conviction in his clash with Beria in May 1953. He felt that Ulbricht acted as a *bona fide* Communist in a tough struggle for fulfillment of the old Bolshevik dream: that there would be a German proletarian state in the heart of Europe. Besides, the more Khrushchev feared West Germans as possible heirs to Hitler's Reich, the more he viewed Socialist East Germany as a justification of Soviet war sacrifices. This belief that the Germans could be either Red or Nazi pushed him, against much evidence. He believed in all the Potyomkin villages of Socialist enthusiasm and transformation that Ulbricht staged for him during his official visits. The Germans, he said to Eisenhower, need just ten more years to get used to socialism.[63]

Khrushchev's belief that the Communist system would prevail over capitalism made him reluctant to acknowledge the obvious: that economically the GDR was lagging behind prosperous West Germany and depended on the Soviet Union's subsidies. Khrushchev assumed responsibility for the economic problems of the GDR: he linked them to Soviet confiscatory policies in East Germany and to the USSR's inability to match U.S. aid to the FRG.[64] After the June 1953 revolt in the GDR, Khrushchev became one of the strongest advocates of economic assistance to the Ulbricht regime. "We have fully met the requests of the comrades from the GDR," he told a delegation of Italian Communists in July 1956, "and this will allow them to conduct successfully their struggle with West Germany."[65] In late 1960 he admitted, in a conversation with Ulbricht, his failure in not having "examined the question of the economic liberation of the GDR from the FRG more closely."[66]

Nevertheless, the support of the GDR for Khrushchev was first and foremost a strategic imperative. This became clear when economic assistance to the "Socialist" GDR became an issue in the struggle between Khrushchev and the opposition of Molotov, Malenkov, and Kaganovich. After the defeat of the "antiparty" group, Mikoyan told the party elite that the opposition had emerged during the discussion of a request for three billion rubles in credit for the production of goods the USSR commissioned in the GDR. "Nikita Sergeevich," said Mikoyan, "immediately sensed the political crux of the issue. If we do not strengthen the regime inside East Germany, then our army will be surrounded by fire. And we maintain half a million troops there . . . What will the loss of East Germany mean? We know what it will mean. The options are as follows: we feed the workers of the GDR for free or supply them with work orders; otherwise, we lose the GDR altogether."[67]

The refusal of the Americans to negotiate about the German peace settlement infuriated Khrushchev. He came to think that West German politicians were using the United States to gain power over the GDR and to move to domination in Central Europe. When Walter Lippmann interviewed Khrushchev in Moscow two weeks before the Berlin crisis, he was struck to find the Soviet leader subject to old fears. The First Secretary compared Adenauer to Paul von Hindenburg, the president of the Weimar Republic, who brought Hitler to power in 1933. The U.S. policy, Khrushchev said, "was the same": to pit Germany against the East. The Americans, he finished ominously, "may someday pay with their blood for having encouraged such people" as Adenauer.[68]

The idea of a "free city" was clearly Khrushchev's own and fit his notion of a fair compromise.[69] The Soviet leader persuaded his colleagues in the Kremlin that Berlin was an obvious spot to assume the initiative in the Cold War. The Western powers, he argued, had not taken a single step toward meeting the Soviets halfway. They were pursuing their old policy: arming the Bundeswehr, surrounding the USSR with military bases. The rest of the leadership let themselves be persuaded rather than arguing with the quick-tempered leader.[70] Georgi Pushkin, a former ambassador in the GDR, then the head of the Information Department of the Central Committee, tried to warn Khrushchev of possible risks, but he dismissed them as "nonsense." The leaders of the United States, he said to Pushkin, are not idiotic enough to start fighting over Berlin. Even if the Soviets kicked them out of the city by force, the Americans would not start a war. In anger Khrushchev sent Pushkin away, and soon abolished his analytical department.

Khrushchev decided to gamble in Berlin despite the signs of firmness from Washington. In October 1958, a few months after the forces of the People's Republic of China had started shelling the positions of the Guomindang on offshore islands in the Taiwan straits, Dulles stressed the American commitment to their defense. He drew a parallel between those islands and another tiny island of democracy inside the

GDR—West Berlin. Dulles's comparison was caught and magnified by Ulbricht. "By comparing West Berlin with China's offshore islands," he told the Soviet ambassador, "Dulles himself unmasked the essence of the 'psychological war,' directed from West Berlin." Ulbricht and the GDR president, Otto Grotewohl, spoke about a global imperialist offensive and argued "that, as soon as the issue of the Chinese islands is removed from the front burner, the next will be Germany."[71]

The Far Eastern counterpoint to the developments in Central Europe had considerable influence on Khrushchev's decision-making. Mao Zedong in China was increasingly defiant of the Soviet seniority in the Communist world, and resistant to the Soviet policy of "peaceful coexistence" with imperialism. Khrushchev's legitimacy as the universal Communist leader, unlike his position of power in the Kremlin, had been weakened after his clash with the "antiparty" group. Mao did not conceal his sympathies for Molotov as a senior Communist statesman, and after November 1957 prodded "Comrade Khrushchev" to be tougher and bolder with imperialists now that Sputnik made a world correlation of forces more favorable to the Communist camp. Many years later Oleg Troyanovsky, Khrushchev's foreign policy aide in 1958, recalled his impression that Khrushchev wanted to prove to his Communist colleagues that he was not at all "soft" and "naive" in dealing with the West, and that this contributed to his decision to unleash the crisis around West Berlin.[72]

Khrushchev did not want to seize West Berlin by force, thereby creating a dangerous *casus belli* between NATO and the USSR. But he hoped that the Western part of the city would cease to be the Trojan horse of the West inside the Soviet bloc. At best, he believed it would gradually gravitate toward the GDR. At worst, it would become like Austria, neutral since 1955. He did not look far ahead. Khrushchev was one of many Russian revolutionaries who acted according to Napoleon's motto *"on s'engage, et puis on voit."*[73]

At first, Khrushchev demonstrated the best of his realpolitik talents in trying to lead Western leaders, by hook or by crook, to the negotiating table to discuss a settlement in Europe. Even before the Berlin crisis Khrushchev ordered Gromyko to look into two possibilities: an invitation to Vice President Richard Nixon to come to the Soviet Union, and a meeting "in the United States at the very highest level."[74] But at that time he was still afraid of a rebuff from John F. Dulles, and ordered the KGB to test the possibility of a summit in a quiet way.[75] The pressure on Berlin put the Soviet leader in a position of strength: it helped him to open some doors and ears in Washington. Besides, Dulles was dying of cancer. At Khrushchev's behest, the KGB approached Vice President Richard Nixon with a message that he may come to Moscow, where a deal on Berlin could be settled. In January 1959 Mikoyan brought a similar message to Eisenhower. He even proposed "an end to the cold war."[76] Khrushchev was so certain that only he could reach a diplomatic breakthrough during personal talks with Western leaders that he paid no attention to the negotiations on the German question in Geneva, conducted by Andrei Gromyko in the spring and summer of 1959. Gromyko later complained: "Nikita Sergeevich wanted to be diplomat number one, and this desire made him undercut the Geneva conference and change the course of events."[77]

In September 1959 Khrushchev arrived with great pomp in the United States at the invitation of Eisenhower. He was the first leader of the Soviet Union to visit the bastion of world capitalism, and he was determined to turn this visit into the greatest success of his personal diplomacy. By dramatically disclosing from the podium of the United Nations his plan "for general and complete disarmament in three years," Khrushchev hoped to confirm his reputation as a messenger of world peace and disarmament.[78] Of course, this public triumph provided him with a cushion, should negotiations with Eisenhower over Germany prove unsuccessful.

In the White House many expected a clash between the bombastic Khrushchev and Eisenhower over Berlin. Christian Herter even wanted to appeal to Nina Petrovna, Khrushchev's wife, who "seems to have a much saner outlook on life" (a complete misperception of this woman, who remained a staunch Bolshevik believer to the very end).[79] But Khrushchev dispelled all fears with his controlled, almost serene conduct at Camp David. He wanted respect and recognition. Eisenhower pushed the right buttons by saying that Khrushchev had a chance to become the greatest political figure in history owing to his tremendous power over a monolithic Communist bloc. In comparison, he, Eisenhower, had power only as far as the United States was concerned, and in sixteen months he would be just a private citizen. Eisenhower agreed to come to Russia for a visit. On the substantive side, the U.S. president admitted that the situation in

Berlin was "abnormal" and promised, although in extremely vague terms, to deal with this issue at a summit meeting of the four powers. In return, Khrushchev promised to lift the Soviet ultimatum on a German peace treaty after he returned to Moscow and discussed it with his colleagues in the Presidium.[80]

In Khrushchev's eyes, his meeting with Eisenhower qualified him as the greatest Soviet statesman since Stalin. It was his personal revenge on Molotov. His personal diplomacy was hailed by a host of propagandists as a cornerstone of Soviet foreign policy. Illustrated accounts of his trip to the United States were printed by the millions. Cinema and television cameras turned the trip into a graphic spectacle for thousands of Soviet elites, and many more in the general public.

Surrounded by this aura, Khrushchev arrived in Beijing in early October 1959 to take part in the tenth anniversary of the People's Republic of China. Mao Zedong and the rest of the Chinese leadership were deeply insulted by Khrushchev's decision to come to Beijing via Washington, not the other way around. The reception was cool, and the talks behind closed doors were stormy. All evidence, including some leaks from the still classified minutes of the talks, shows that Khrushchev had firmly put the upcoming summit with Western leaders above all other considerations. According to the Chinese authorities, Khrushchev demanded that the PRC leadership accept "two Chinas." The Soviet leader must have feared that Mao might upstage the summit by unleashing another crisis over the offshore islands. Khrushchev also wanted to defuse a possible flare-up of Sino-Indian hostilities over a territorial dispute. "Whether they [the Indians] penetrated more than five kilometers or less than five kilometers [into China] is unimportant. I take as my example Lenin, who handed over Kars, Ardagan, and Ararat to Turkey."[81]

The Chinese Communists, who considered the territorial integrity of their country very much a part of their revolutionary state-building (in the same way Stalin and Molotov had), were outraged. They openly blamed the Soviet leader for putting his geopolitical scheme—a settlement with the United States—above the Sino-Soviet alliance. The talk degenerated into a screaming match when Khrushchev stood up and yelled at the foreign minister of the PRC, Marshal Chen Yi: "If you think we're time-servers [*vremenschiki*], Comrade Chen Yi, don't give me your hand, because I won't shake it." The marshal responded that he would not shake Khrushchev's hand either, and that his anger did not scare him. "Don't you try to spit on us from up there, marshal," raved Khrushchev. "You haven't got enough spit."[82]

The visit led to the open estrangement of the leadership of the two Communist empires. Khrushchev was genuinely furious: he received more recognition and respect from the leader of the United States than from "the comrades" to whom he had been so generous earlier. He was determined to prove that he, not the Chinese, had been mapping out the right way to communism. After all, a new party program, adopted in 1959 at his insistence and against the cautious advice of economic managers and ideologists, promised to "catch and surpass America" in two decades and to complete the construction of a Communist society in the Soviet Union by 1980. This was, of course, all contingent on the continuation of the decline of tensions and the deceleration of the burdensome arms race between the USSR and the United States.

Yet with the wisdom of hindsight it is clear that the conflicting impulses behind Khrushchev's statesmanship, and of course his character, guaranteed that any problem, even a minor one, would cause him to return to his defiant, confrontational self. Khrushchev's complete dependence on a Communist way of thinking, the legacy of the Comintern, or his commitment to the revolutionary ideals could conflict with his personal diplomacy at any moment. He was reluctant to admit that much of his diplomatic "success" had so far been based on a vague personal understanding with Eisenhower.

Khrushchev's personal diplomacy could not dispel the mistrust and double-play that separated the Kremlin and the U.S. leadership. During the talks at Camp David the Soviet leader never asked the U.S. president to stop the reconnaissance flights of the U-2 spy planes over Soviet territory. During his argument with the Chinese, however, he referred to his policy of shooting down American planes as proof that, despite détente, he intended to be tough with the United States.[83] When, on May 1, 1960, on the eve of the summit, the U-2 piloted by Francis Gary Powers was shot down over the Ural Mountains, Khrushchev showed the world that he was anything but lenient with the West.

## The Revenge of Mr. K

For decades, historians have wondered why Khrushchev, after Francis Gary Powers was shot down, ruined his own successful diplomatic gambits and appeared before the West as a frightening bully, not as a reasonable statesman. From a Western viewpoint, Khrushchev acted irrationally, disastrously. In attempting to understand Khrushchev's actions, some concluded that he had decided in advance that the summit would fail, and was looking for a pretext to blame this on the West. Others pointed out that Khrushchev had to mollify his hard-line critics in the Soviet leadership and outside of it, but especially in China and East Germany.[84]

This is one of the episodes where Khrushchev's personal reactions, observed by witnesses, can be more telling than archival documents. Troyanovsky, a foreign policy assistant of Khrushchev's, recalled many years later that Khrushchev had told him as soon as he had learned about the U-2 that it might ruin the summit in Paris. During the next several days Khrushchev, in Troyanovsky's words, was laying "a kind of trap for the White House," and "did it with relish."[85] The "trap," of course, was to make the U.S. administration lie about the flight, and then to present to the world the evidence of American espionage, including the pilot, Gary Powers, who survived the crash.

Yet Khrushchev did not believe that the U.S. president, who as high commander of the Allied troops in Europe during World War II had greatly impressed Stalin as a man of tact and chivalry, and who was a good host at Camp David, could plan the flight of a U-2 deep into Soviet territory on May Day, the great proletarian celebration. The Soviet leader valued Eisenhower as a partner in future top-level negotiations. He viewed him as a "sober and peaceful" man, opposing the forces of evil, the warmongers in the State Department, the Pentagon, the CIA, Congress, and elsewhere.

The espionage activities of the CIA, like the nuclear rhetoric of the Secretary of State, symbolized for Khrushchev long years of technological inferiority, humiliation, and impotence. Since 1956 the U-2 high-altitude spy plane, designed by Lockheed and operated by the CIA, carried out with impunity many intelligence master strokes, prying open Soviet strategic military secrets. The worst insult for Khrushchev was a U-2 flight on April 9, 1960, on the eve of his birthday and twenty-one days before the fateful May Day mission. The plane photographed the Soviets' three most secret strategic installations: the nuclear test site in Semipalatinsk, the anti-ballistic missiles complex at Sary Shagan, and a space complex at Tyura-Tam (Baykonur). Soviet air defense, headed by Marshal Sergei Biryuzov, three times failed to shoot the plane down, due to bureaucratic sloppiness and sheer bad luck. Khrushchev was furious: the whole machinery of Soviet defense could not strike a single gnat in the sky! He threatened to turn Soviet air defense upside down. Biryuzov answered in despair: if he were a missile himself he would personally fly and blow the damn thing to pieces. Everyone understood that the prestige of the military superpower was at stake in this contest.[86]

The triumph of Soviet technology on May 1 gave Khrushchev an excellent opportunity to teach his arrogant adversaries a lesson: to unmask and compromise them before the whole world on the eve of the summit. Later, on June 6, the Secretariat, at Khrushchev's suggestion, approved a plan of the KGB chairman Shelepin "to make use of this newly complex situation and to carry out . . . measures targeted at further discrediting CIA activity and compromising its leader, Allen Dulles." An impressive array of resources, including psychological warfare, defamation, and complex intelligence operations, was directed to this goal.[87] All this took place after Khrushchev had scuttled the Paris meeting. But it can be argued that, when he was still going to Paris, he hoped Eisenhower might be an easier negotiator, once the hard-liners around him and the U.S. administration as a whole were embarrassed or compromised.

There are some insights into Khrushchev's reaction when Eisenhower took personal responsibility for the reconnaissance flights and refused to discontinue them. Anatoly Dobrynin, at that time in Moscow as the head of the U.S. division in the Ministry of Foreign Affairs, was, along with Troyanovsky, part of Khrushchev's "working group" on the U-2 crisis. He recalled a quarter of a century later that Khrushchev tried to pursue the public fiction that Eisenhower was not responsible for the spy missions. But after Eisenhower's acknowledgment, he was unable to continue dealing with him because that would have meant a public loss of face. Later Khrushchev commented to Dobrynin that he would gladly entrust the education of his children to Eisenhower, because he was "truly an honest man," but he wondered if he understood the responsibilities that accompany political leadership in international affairs. According to Adzhubei, Khrushchev's son-in-law, the Soviet leader felt that Eisenhower had betrayed him, pulled the rug out from under him.[88]

In his memoirs Khrushchev recalled his fear that the Soviet Union would be humiliated. "I was becoming convinced," Khrushchev wrote, "that we might not look dignified." If the Soviet leadership would allow the United States to "spit in [their] faces," that would be tantamount to acceptance of American arrogance. That, in turn, "would have highly damaged our authority in the eyes of world public opinion, especially our friends, Communist parties, and those countries that struggle for independence."[89] No doubt, Khrushchev was thinking about his "friends" in Beijing, including Mao and Marshal Chen Yi.

This was probably the first time Khrushchev could demonstrate that the Americans would not be allowed to "spit in the face" of the Soviet military-industrial complex any longer. His widely publicized anti-American show after May Day had to send a clear message both to adversaries and to friends: the USSR *really* is as strong militarily as Khrushchev had always claimed. The more hype over the latest U-2 incident, the better.

True to form, Khrushchev made up his mind about the summit at the last moment. When he arrived at the airport, with the rest of the Presidium members waiting to see him off, the official instructions of the Soviet delegation still were to make a serious attempt to negotiate with Western powers on Germany, disarmament, and other issues. Suddenly Khrushchev told the Presidium members in the airport waiting-room that he believed the old instructions should be scrapped and that any negotiations with Eisenhower should begin only when he offered excuses for the spy flights.[90]

Did the collapse of personal relations with Eisenhower leave Khrushchev exposed to the hard-liners in Moscow? There was a great deal of secret gloating and hand-rubbing in Moscow. Many in the Central Committee and the Party Presidium began to wonder if "special relations" with the United States were worth the risk of endangering the Sino-Soviet alliance, which at that time had begun to show visible strains. Some felt that this alliance was more important for Soviet foreign policy than peaceful relations with the United States, and that Khrushchev was wrong to jeopardize it by going to Washington before Beijing in the fall of 1959.[91] But there were no serious challenges to Khrushchev inside the Kremlin, as he reversed the vessel of Soviet foreign policy from détente to confrontation. An internal power struggle for a while ceased to be a factor in Soviet foreign policy.

The grumbling and disagreements around the Soviet leader were dwarfed by the collapse of colonial empires, which had been entering its climactic moment just as Khrushchev canceled the Paris summit. The geopolitical avalanche changed almost overnight the map of Asia and Africa. And it enchanted and mesmerized Khrushchev, stirring old memories of the revolutionary passions of the Civil War and the Soviet "Comintern 1920s." The Soviet chairman believed he could seize victory from the jaws of defeat, using the wave of national liberation in Asia, Africa, and Latin America against the bulwarks of the Cold War that had been carefully and at great cost constructed by Eisenhower and Dulles in the 1950s. He did not mind abandoning for a while the role of sober and reasonable world statesman in order to pose more persuasively as a friend of all revolutionaries and "liberated peoples" of the world. From being his own foreign minister, he became a chief Soviet propagandist.

Initially, Khrushchev was rather successful. He shrewdly exploited major problems in the international relations of his greatest enemy, the United States, since 1955. He supported Ghana's leader, Kwame Nkrumah, and Congo's president, Patrice Lumumba, in their fulminations against former West European colonial masters and their "American protectors." His enthusiasm for the Third World peaked as he decided to lead the Soviet delegation at the U.N. General Assembly, making other world leaders and Eisenhower follow suit. The stay in New York in September–October 1960 must have been exhilarating for the revolutionary side of Khrushchev. He enjoyed the atmosphere of a rejuvenated United Nations and listened to fiery rhetoric from the new crop of African and Asian leaders. It seemed as though the old days of the Comintern were back and the idea of the social and political transformation of the world had received a new lease on life on a scale even greater than in 1917–1923.

The Soviet leader "discovered" and embraced the Cuban Revolution. Initially, in 1959 and early 1960, the Soviet leadership did not believe that there could be any chance for "proletarian" revolution on the semicolonial island with a small monoculture economy. The survivors of the old Comintern network in Cuba described Fidel Castro, Che Guevara, and other Cuban revolutionaries as anything but Marxists, and discounted their chances for success. Had Stalin been in the Kremlin, the Soviets would never have assisted the radical Cuban regime. At best, Stalin and Molotov would have tried to trade their role in Cuba for American concessions elsewhere. Khrushchev and his colleagues in the Presidium, however, saw the young Cubans as heroes who had revived the promise of the Russian Revolution, and dared to do it under the very nose of the most powerful imperialist country on earth.[92]

During the summer and fall of 1960, as Khrushchev saw how Castro moved to nationalize American assets in Cuba and institute other "Socialist" measures, his attitude changed from surprise to admiration. During his stormy visit to the U.N. General Assembly, the Soviet leader went to Harlem and publicly hugged and kissed Castro. He came away emotionally committed to the new Cuban regime and its youthful, powerful leaders. In November 1960, when Che Guevara came to Moscow to sell Cuban sugar (on which the United States had declared an embargo), Khrushchev invited him to stand with the leader at Lenin's Mausoleum during festivities commemorating the October Revolution. He also threw around his political weight to ensure that every ton of Cuban sugar was bought by the USSR and its East European allies.[93]

Khrushchev's attachment to Castro's Cuba was the most visible symptom of his "leftist disease" in late 1960 and early 1961. Another symptom was Soviet policy in the Congo. After Lumumba had been assassinated by the military of Katanga, the secessionist Congolese province, an obscure African nationalist was sanctified, on Khrushchev's order, as a world-scale revolutionary martyr. Under Stalin the old collection of official revolutionary martyrs had been replaced by a carefully selected gallery of "Soviet heroes" of the Civil War, collectivization, and the Great Patriotic War against Germany. The African politician symbolized a hero from another epoch, a product of Khrushchev's romantic affair with Third World revolutionarism.

Khrushchev allowed himself to get carried away. Most of the Soviet leadership and elites, seasoned and cynical apparatchiks, were perplexed and startled by Khrushchev's behavior and rhetoric abroad. And, recalls Troyanovsky, who translated for Khrushchev in New York, they were disgusted by the shoe-banging episode in the United Nations, believing that Khrushchev had behaved like a country bumpkin *(muzhik)* who engaged in what looked like a street brawl. Leonid Ilyichev, a secretary of the Central Committee in charge of ideology, told Troyanovsky that "when the first reports" about the shoe incident reached Moscow, he thought it was "some sort of . . . Western propaganda" and "wondered whether those broadcasts should not be jammed."[94]

"I have a feeling," recollects Troyanovsky, "that [Khrushchev's hysterics] began to backfire on him in the eyes, not only of the international public, but also of the public back home."[95] The most important "public" was the Soviet elites. Instead of being a symbol of peaceful prosperity and dignified strength, their leader appeared bellicose and rambling. Remarkably, the first people to betray Mr. K came from the ranks of the KGB and the GRU, the most elite corps of the Cold Warriors (notably, the GRU colonel Oleg Penkovsky, who began to work for British and American intelligence late in 1960). They justified their treason on the ground that Khrushchev's behavior might trigger a third world war.[96]

In November 1960 a conference of Communist and "workers'" parties was held in Moscow. It was the biggest congress in the history of the Communist movement, much bigger than any in the heyday of the Comintern. It was also the last one attended by both the CPSU and the delegation of China's Communist party. Khrushchev defended his authority as a leader of world communism, which was being challenged by his Chinese "friends." On January 6, 1961, Khrushchev made a secret speech to Soviet ideological and propaganda "workers" in which he returned to the language of the Communist millennium that had been the staple rhetoric in the 1920s, re-emerged in Zhdanov's 1947 speech, but was discontinued after Stalin's death. The chairman said that socialism was overtaking capitalism all over the world and expressed a blithe confidence that the Third World would eventually join the Communist camp. Khrushchev insisted that by supporting the "sacred" struggle of colonies and former colonies for independence, the Soviets would be taking a shortcut toward communism and would succeed in "bringing imperialism to its knees." While in the nuclear age war among great powers had become impossible, the "wars for national liberation" remained not only possible, but inevitable, and worthy of support from Moscow. "Communists are revolutionaries," Khrushchev reminded his audience, "and it would be a bad thing if they did not exploit new opportunities."[97]

In this vortex of events the Soviet ruler seemed to have forgotten about the Berlin crisis. But, in fact, he had not. When he met Ulbricht in the Kremlin, during the world Communist conference, he defended his inaction as a tactical pause in order to gain strength before a decisive offensive. Khrushchev argued that it was the right policy, since otherwise it "would have looked as if we had provoked the summit break-up in order to conclude a [separate] peace treaty" with the GDR. "We have not lost the two years," he assured the East German ruler. "We have shaken up their [Western] position." The Soviet foreign policy of solidarity with the national liberation movements against Western powers "brought us a huge success."[98]

The Soviet revolutionary-imperial paradigm saw a spectacular revival in 1960—perhaps the most remarkable in the history of the Soviet Cold War, and certainly the most visible since the advent of the thermonuclear revolution. Khrushchev, like his Bolshevik predecessors, hoped that the groundswell of social transformation even more than Soviet successes in the nuclear arms race and missile technology would demonstrate to the world, and particularly to the United States, that the cause of communism was the wave of the future. But he was prepared, should the American leadership prove slow to recognize new realities, to make full use of the new image of a nuclear superpower that he, as the leader of the USSR, possessed. The stage was set for the decisive chapter in Khrushchev's Cold War: his confrontation with John Fitzgerald Kennedy.

# 7 Khrushchev and the Sino-Soviet Schism

> Soviet physician (reporting to the Soviet leadership): Our scientists now know how to transplant a kidney.
>
> Khrushchev: So couldn't Soviet scientists also perform a brain transplant on Mao Zedong?
>
> Meeting in Moscow, early 1960s

The evolution of Nikita Khrushchev, a leader of the new Soviet elites, was a painful one, for Khrushchev was torn between two opposing desires: to keep faithful to the testament of the Bolshevik revolution and to create a safer international environment for the USSR in the nuclear era. Khrushchev was both the last revolutionary and the first reformer in the Kremlin.

Eventually, when faced with the very real prospect of a nuclear holocaust during the Cuban missile crisis, Khrushchev chose to pursue a truce with the West rather than world revolution, the pragmatic side of his nature prevailing over the revolutionary. Khrushchev's decision proved to be beneficial for Soviet-American relations, but his growing pragmatic bias caused unintended consequences in the East—a prolonged Sino-Soviet confrontation.

The Sino-Soviet split that initially resulted from Khrushchev's pursuit of détente with the United States first became obvious during the Quemoy and Matsu crisis of 1958. This crisis was very different from most other Cold War crises: the major gamblers were not the United States and the USSR, but their allies China and Taiwan. Even when we consider the ambitions of Korea's Kim Il Sung, and his initiative to be at the forefront of events (the very notion of initiative was dead in the Communist camp by 1948, when the Yugoslavs were expelled for being too creative), the Korean War was still a more "classic," more typical, crisis for the bipolar world than the crisis of 1958. Kim Il Sung had persuaded Stalin in April 1950 to sanction his intention to "liberate" the people of South Korea. During the crisis Kim was in constant contact with both Moscow and Beijing. Even though Moscow, from the very beginning, decided not to interfere directly and remained adamant when the defeat of Kim Il Sung appeared imminent, Stalin still controlled the situation. His freedom to maneuver was to a certain extent limited by China, which was more an ally than a satellite, but still both Kim Il Sung and Mao fought Stalin's war.[1]

But the crisis of 1958 was not Khrushchev's war. Not only had the crisis been unleashed by Moscow's main ally at its own risk, but it was also a provocation to the Kremlin to change its new post-Stalin politics (which were regarded in Beijing as a betrayal of the "common cause") and perhaps even to challenge the leadership of the worldwide Marxist empire.[2] The Quemoy and Matsu crisis was therefore of paramount importance as a manifestation of the disintegration of the absolute bipolarity of the early Cold War.

## The Two Towers of Communism

In 1949 Mao Zedong's troops had reluctantly stopped on the banks of the Taiwan Strait. The remnants of the Nationalist forces took refuge on Taiwan, an island protected by its geographic location and also, though indirectly at that time, by American assistance.[3] Mao Zedong did not risk landing there. He needed time and resources. Thus the division of China became a fact.

China had been divided often in the past; its history seemed to follow a cycle of unity, chaos, unity. In 1949 a period of chaos was coming to an end. Mao Zedong's People's Liberation Army was to become the new unifier of China. For Chinese Communists, however, the independence of Taiwan was proof that the new rulers of China, who had promised to change the land completely, still did not have the power to unify the country. That was the challenge for Chinese communism and Mao Zedong in particular. It was up to Mao and other Communist leaders to bring traditional Chinese history to an end.

Yet in August 1958, shortly before Mao Zedong began shelling the islands of Quemoy and Matsu in the Taiwan Strait (which actually was the facade of the crisis), he countered the view of Taiwan as an American springboard in Eastern Asia: "Some of our comrades don't understand the situation. They want us to cross the sea and take over Taiwan. I don't agree. Let's leave Taiwan alone. Taiwan keeps the pressure on us. It helps maintain our internal unity. Once the pressure is off, internal disputes might break out."[4] Later Mao explicitly said that the shells in the Strait were a response to Khrushchev's détente with the United States.[5] In other words, the Taiwan Strait crisis of 1958 had its origins in the Cold War thaw, was a challenge to Khrushchev, and was also connected with the needs of the Communist regime in China.

At a meeting in Beidaihe (the sea resort for Communist China's elites) just a week before the start of the offensive in the Strait, Mao had said: "Both inside the Party and outside it one can see the fear of the West, Americophobia. But who is more afraid? The West is probably afraid of us a bit more [than we are of it]. Both sides have the atomic bomb [here Mao does not yet separate China from the Soviet Union, and at least pretends to believe that he is united with the Soviets, who have atomic weapons], but our population resources are greater. Therefore, they will hardly begin the war. But perhaps they will begin it. We must be ready for it. It is hard to speak for a monopolist capitalist state. Suppose they do strike. Should we be afraid? We are full of burning hatred toward the enemy, and this hardens our hearts and makes us resolute to fight them to the death, to crush them finally, and only then begin our construction. That's why it is useful to say clearly that one should not fear war."[6]

In November 1957, a world conference of Communist and workers parties took place in Moscow. Khrushchev, elated by the success of Sputnik, took the opportunity to promote his new doctrine of "peaceful coexistence." Everyone joined the chorus of speeches on how to avoid war. But, as Khrushchev recalled, "here came Mao Tze-tung, saying we shouldn't be afraid of war."[7]

It was not only the desire to reunite China or to cure the geopolitical vulnerability of the country that motivated Mao to unleash the crisis in 1958; as his words clearly demonstrate, he was responding to the Soviet rapprochement with the United States—a gradual, controversial, but nevertheless visible trend by 1958.

In 1944 Mao himself tried hard to come to terms with America.

Evidence of this can be seen in the minutes of his talks with the Dixie mission (a group of American observers) and the reports sent to Moscow by Petr P. Vlasov (Vladimirov) from his headquarters in Yenan.[8] Mao was even prepared to "soften" Marxism, and the works of the corresponding period reflect this.[9] In 1944–1945 Mao wanted to create the best possible balance of power for China in the international environment: leaning neither toward Moscow nor toward Washington, but using the assistance of both powers to reconstruct a country devastated by the Japanese occupation and civil war. His plans did not succeed because Washington did not take him seriously, and those who did were accused at the very beginning of the Cold War of being pro-Communist.[10] For Mao this was both an end to his hopes and a personal insult. He proclaimed a policy of leaning on the USSR. The decision to enter the Korean War, which he made after serious consideration, was a turning point. By the late 1950s Mao was the strongest advocate of the Cold War in the Communist camp. But China's dependence upon the Soviet Union irked him more and more.

Mao had a very distinctive background when compared with the Communist leaders of Eastern European countries. The latter had been secured in their power by the bayonets of the Soviet army—with the major exception of Yugoslavia's Tito. Mao had been even less dependent on Moscow in the past than Tito: Soviet troops had entered central Yugoslavia, whereas in China they had come only to Manchuria (and their assistance was limited). Mao had been the head of the most powerful independent Communist movement, dating to the 1920s and having experienced armed struggle, party discipline, and government purges in the regions under its control. Unlike most East European Communist apparatchiks, Mao was a great revolutionary, the founder and builder of a new state—he was both a Lenin and a Stalin for China. China had won a Communist victory on its own: the ideology was not introduced into the country by force, but had ripened in the years of chaos and national humiliation and appeared as a saving grace for many. China by 1949 was prepared for an independent Communist crusade. But several factors had prevented that crusade from occurring.

The Cold War system was one of those factors. By 1949 the world was divided into two camps, and China had to lean to one side (the Soviet side) in order to use the USSR's might as a military-political umbrella against the West. In those times of tough confrontation, Mao had no other choice.

Stalin presented another formidable factor. The international essence of Marxism demanded regard for the source of world revolution—Moscow—as the transnational Motherland for all Communist nations. The "fifth column" of Stalin's admirers and informers in the Chinese Communist party was not very strong; a new national ego was by far stronger in China. But in the 1940s and 1950s there were still those Communists—even among the top leadership—who regarded Moscow as the true master. If Mao had defied Moscow openly, the "fifth column" might have tried to replace him with some other leader more loyal to Moscow. It would have been a difficult thing to do, but it would not have been impossible.

After Stalin's death, however, the power of Moscow and its iron fist began to weaken. A totalitarian party state can function at its best—that is, exercising full control over its people and its outer spheres of influence—only with full-scale terror and a leader who completely adheres to the principles of absolute power and control. At the same time, totalitarianism cannot exist forever without changes in attitude and without relaxation of the terror mechanism that usually occurs with the death of the leader.

The new "dominant minority," to use Arnold Toynbee's broad term, emerges after the revolution.[11] Step by step it becomes independent from the revolution and seeks to establish control. The new elite in the postrevolutionary society demand the natural privilege of their high status: personal safety. Also, they want more security in the international arena. They do not want all-out wars, for defeat can undermine their power. The new elite seek some kind of rapprochement with the powerful members of the world community. They can handle crises that are under their full control and do not contradict their goals. This natural tendency became even stronger as the Soviet elite had to live with nuclear weapons and abide by the new rules of nuclear bipolarity.

As a result, by the end of the 1950s Moscow was more inclined to manage international relations in its own interests than to stick to the principles of revolutionarism.

Here was the source of the ideological differences between Moscow and Beijing. Mao was in his prime. His revolutionary absolutism was quite young and could function at its full capacity. The liberties allowed under Khrushchev's thaw in the Soviet Union were unimaginable for Mao because of the total asynchronism of the two societies. In the early 1950s Mao was following something similar to Lenin's New Economic Policy (NEP), while Stalin was turning to forced industrialization and random terror. When Khrushchev and others began to soften the regime, Mao was on the way to tightening control and dragging peasant China into the projects of "Socialist construction." He simply could not afford any rapprochement with the United States, for détente with the West would have inevitably loosened his grip on Chinese society.

The turning point came sometime in 1957–1958, after Khrushchev denounced Stalin as a criminal, and Mao proclaimed his Great Leap Forward policy and unleashed an antirightist campaign. One country shut the doors of concentration camps and the other opened them.[12]

Mao and his followers regarded with disgust and repulsion the attempts of Khrushchev both to promote himself by knocking Stalin off his pedestal and to enhance the security of the USSR by a thaw if not by détente. Moscow was threatening the domestic stability of Mao's regime. Khrushchev was trying to escape the Cold War's embrace, and Beijing decided to check Moscow's preparedness to sacrifice the Cold War to the well-being of the new elites, and even to try to change the course of events. The more Moscow was taken by surprise, the better.

A firm stand on confrontation with the United States was also meant to help Mao secure independence from Moscow; the full independence of the PRC was to be reached through Mao's revolutionary approach to the key issues of world politics.

Only after the death of Stalin did it become possible for Mao to secure China's independence from the Kremlin and even from Moscow's ideological dominance in the Socialist camp, in "the world Communist movement." Moscow could no longer be regarded as a force of revolution. Mao, however, could be considered the bearer of the revolutionary tradition. After all, who was Khrushchev? A party bureaucrat and one of the new elites who had not participated in the Revolution nor in the establishment of the new state. Mao viewed himself as standing higher in the ideological hierarchy of international communism than his Soviet counterparts. In retirement, Khrushchev once angrily exclaimed into a tape recorder: "Mao considered himself God. Karl Marx and Lenin were both in their graves, and Mao thought he had no equal on earth."[13]

In the mid-1950s relations between the two "fraternal" Communist parties, the CPSU and the CCP, still looked excellent.[14] They reached their peak after Khrushchev's personal engagement in Sino-Soviet trade negotiations.[15] Sources from the Moscow archives suggest solid evidence that at that point Mao was demonstrating impressive (but probably not very sincere) trust in Big Brother. The Presidium and Secretariat of the Soviet Central Committee had made a decision on April 17, 1954, to entrust to the party cells of the CPSU in Soviet colleges the supervision and guidance of Chinese students, members of the CCP who studied there.[16] What could be a better example of mutual trust than Beijing's willingness to share control over its students in the USSR with its fraternal party!

The two Communist parties acted in tandem in their diplomacy toward the West. In September 1954, Chinese artillery began to shell the offshore islands of Quemoy and Matsu, occupied by the Nationalist troops. The result was the first "Taiwan crisis," which the Eisenhower administration took as the most serious challenge since the Korean War. In reality, the Chinese leadership launched the offensive primarily "to demonstrate Beijing's refusal to accept a two-China outcome of the civil war."[17] The Soviet leadership expressed their full solidarity with the PRC, in accordance with the terms of the Sino-Soviet treaty, even though at the time they sought to alleviate tensions with the West. Bulganin told the Chinese ambassador in March 1955 that "the foreign policy of the [PRC as well as the Soviet Union] in the Far East has the character of an offensive, which is exemplified by our common position on the Taiwan issues." According to Bulganin, this policy "has been fully justified" both in the East and in the West.[18]

The first "Taiwan crisis" ended abruptly on April 23, 1955, when Chinese Premier Zhou Enlai announced at the Bandung conference the willingness of the PRC to reach a settlement on the two-China issue through negotiations. According to Chinese-American scholars, the Chinese leadership by that time had fulfilled its political task and was looking for a good pretext to end the crisis. But the Soviet factor did play an important role as well. When Chinese Defense Minister Peng Dehuai visited the Soviet Union, Khrushchev allegedly told him that at that moment the United States was still very powerful and, therefore, peaceful negotiations should be encouraged to solve international disputes.[19]

This time the Chinese leadership went along with the Soviet analysis of international trends, and at the Bandung conference Zhou Enlai even attempted to seize the initiative in promoting the principles of "peaceful coexistence." Only in retrospect did it become clear that the Kremlin leadership paid a big price for this "fraternal solidarity." The price was, in part, continuation of the economic assistance to the PRC announced during Khrushchev's trip to China in October 1954. Always negligible under Stalin, Soviet assistance grew a hundredfold, and now corresponded to the canons of "proletarian internationalism"; that is, much of it came at the expense of the Soviet people, and was very beneficial to the Soviets' Chinese "friends." In addition, the Soviets pledged to the PRC leadership full assistance in the creation of a Chinese atomic bomb. On April 27, 1955, the two governments signed an agreement under the unwieldy name "On providing the assistance of the USSR to the PRC in the matter of development of studies on the physics of the atomic nucleus and on the utilization of atomic energy for the needs of the people's economy." According to Khrushchev, "When China asked us for an atomic bomb, we ordered our scientists to receive [Chinese] representatives and to teach them how to produce one." The Soviets provided nuclear know-how for free. "We gave everything to China," recalled Khrushchev. "We kept no secrets from the Chinese."[20]

Khrushchev went out of his way to try to please his Chinese allies. The Central Committee rushed to act on China's slightest complaint. Early in 1958 it censured the popular Soviet magazine *Ogonyok* for publishing an "excessive description" of a planned new Chinese embassy in Moscow. The Kremlin's Chinese "friends" must have complained about what they saw as a security risk.[21] Catering to the whims of comrades, however, could not eliminate the two countries' objective differences. Only eleven years later did the Kremlin organize "people's" protests outside the PRC embassy; in 1958 the Soviet Central Committee tried to show the embassy as much respect as possible—in 1969 it would send students to throw ink bottles at its former allies.

## Mao's Challenge

Khrushchev traveled to Beijing for the first time on September 29, 1954, for the celebration of the fifth anniversary of the Chinese Revolution. A year earlier he had been elected First Secretary of the Central Committee, winning the first round of the power struggle.

On October 3, Sino-Soviet negotiations began. Mao declared that "the international situation in general is favorable to us." Khrushchev stated that imperialism was still pursuing its evil goals. Mao said that if "we" could have twenty peaceful years of construction to develop "our" economy, the threat of war could diminish and, perhaps, go away.[22] At that point the contradiction between postrevolutionary new elites in the USSR and revolution in China had not yet emerged. The Twentieth Congress's debunking of Stalin was yet to happen. In 1954 Khrushchev and Mao still shared the same language, but their evolution was already taking them in different directions; in terms of traditional Marxist language, Mao was leaning left, Khrushchev, right. In 1954 the first Taiwan crisis was not an issue in Sino-Soviet relations.

Khrushchev and his suite had taken a long tour around China. This was particularly important for Khrushchev: the trip to China was one of his first trips abroad, and now he was at last getting a taste of life overseas. One could suggest that, coming from a xenophobic country, Khrushchev was probably shocked by the alien culture. Local authorities had invited their Soviet guests to try a famous Cantonese dish— "Fight of the Dragon and the Tiger"—with the dragon represented by a snake and the tiger by a cat. Only the educated party propagandists Shepilov and Alexandrov tasted the dish. Others refused, and two of the women in Khrushchev's entourage, Furtseva and Nasredinova, burst into tears. The explanation the Chinese interpreter Shi Zhe gives for their abstention is an interesting one in its misperception: "They did not know that the snakes are divided into two types—poisonous and non-poisonous . . . [or] that snake meat is good if we remove the poisonous teeth and poisonous glands."[23] But new—and more important—misperceptions were to come. In four years the situation was to change dramatically, as Khrushchev and Mao drifted further away from their common starting point.

The first omen was the beginning of Mao's Great Leap Forward, which was designed to take China to economic prosperity through revolutionary enthusiasm, without considerable investments and in the absence of modern technology. Moscow was not informed about the timing and nature of the campaign. Ambassador Pavel Yudin in his reports also described the brutal end to the "Hundred Flowers" period of intellectual tolerance. It is not clear what exactly the ambassador reported about the power struggle in Beijing, the terrible famine in the countryside, and Mao's attempts to label his rivals "Soviet agents." But something became known, and for the Kremlin leaders it was like a bolt of lightning. Their first reaction was to search their souls: perhaps they had done something wrong? Khrushchev, among others, believed that "in many areas of our economic relations we had thrust ourselves into China like colonizers. It was Stalin who provided the impetus for China's poor attitude toward the Soviet Union."[24] "For me, China was an independent country with its own traditions and rich culture." At the same time Khrushchev bitterly criticized Mao's revolutionary campaigns. "It was patently clear to us," he wrote, "that Mao Zedong had started down a wrong path that would lead to the collapse of his economy and, consequently, the failure of his politics. We did all we could to influence the Chinese and stop them before it was too late, but Mao thought he was God."[25]

From July 31 until August 4, 1958, Khrushchev was in Beijing for a second time, to test the waters. Already appalled by Mao's domestic revolutionary ardor, he now had to confront the Chairman on international issues. Khrushchev recalled years later a debate he had with Mao by a swimming pool:

Once in Peking, Mao and I were lying next to the swimming pool in our bathing trunks, discussing the problems of war and peace. Mao Tse-tung said to me, "Comrade Khrushchev, what do you think? If we compare the military might of the capitalist world with that of the Socialist world, you'll see that we obviously have the advantage over our enemies. Think of how many divisions China, the USSR, and the other Socialist countries could raise."

I said, "Comrade Mao Tse-tung, nowadays that sort of thinking is out of date. You can no longer calculate the alignment of forces on the basis of who has the most men . . . now with the atomic bomb, the number of troops on each side makes practically no difference to the alignment of real power and the outcome of war. The more troops on a side, the more bomb fodder."[26]

In trying to share with the Chinese Chairman his vision of the new, nuclear geopolitics, Khrushchev failed miserably. He recalled, "Mao replied by trying to assure me that the atomic bomb itself was a paper tiger! 'Listen, Comrade Khrushchev,' he said. 'All you have to do is provoke the Americans into military action, and I'll give you as many divisions as you need to crush them—a hundred, two hundred, one thousand divisions.' I tried to explain to him that one or two missiles could turn all the divisions of China to dust."[27]

Mao retorted: "If there is an attack on the Soviet Union, I would recommend that you offer no resistance . . . Retreat for a year, or two or three. Force your enemy to stretch out his lines of communication. That will weaken him. Then, with our combined strength, we will go for the enemy together and smash him."[28]

Memoirs recently published in China suggest that the exact date of this talk was August 1, 1958.[29]

Khrushchev was appalled. He returned to Moscow wondering what stood behind such reasoning. Mao was a clever man. How could he think this way?

"Politics is a game, and Mao Tse-tung has played politics with Asiatic cunning, following his own rules of cajolery, treachery, savage vengeance, and deceit."[30] This passage reveals Khrushchev's racist perception of Asians, which more than likely strongly influenced his personal relations with the enigmatic and provocative Mao.

## The Grand Provocation

On August 23, 1958, the artillery of the Fujian front of the People's Liberation Army began bombarding two Taiwanese islands—Jinmendao (Quemoy) and Mazudao (Matsu). Quemoy was an archipelago consisting of 12 islands with a combined territory of 17.5 square kilometers, situated 2.5 kilometers from Xiamen (Amoy), a town on the Fujian coast; its military consisted of 65,000 soldiers. The Matsu archipelago consisted of 19 islands with a combined territory of 10 square kilometers, situated across from Fuzhou; its garrison had 10,000 soldiers. In 1958 the stability of the entire world depended upon these 27.5 square kilometers.

The outbreak of the crisis did not come as a total surprise to the Soviet leadership. The Chinese, Khrushchev recalled, said in advance that they wanted to carry out a "new military operation against Chiang Kai-shek. They asked for air cover, long-range and seashore artillery . . . We gave them everything, under the impression that they were contemplating something decisive to liquidate Chiang Kai-shek." Khrushchev even asserted in his memoirs that "at that moment, we did not deter them, but on the contrary considered such actions to be correct, leading to the reunification of China."[31]

To the surprise of the Kremlin leaders, however, the Chinese kept them in the dark about the timing, course, and purposes of their actions. Khrushchev and his colleagues could not understand why Mao suspended the offensive against the islands just at the moment when "the battle began to tilt in favor of the PRC." Perhaps, the Soviet leaders reasoned, they needed military assistance. The Soviets suggested transferring to the battlefront Soviet "fighter-planes, a division of planes or as many as they need." The Chinese spurned the proposal, however. Khrushchev could never understand why the Chinese failed to seize the islands and put an end to the crisis.[32] Only recently have new Chinese and Soviet sources revealed that there was much more to the crisis than the Soviet leadership had realized or wanted to admit.

As soon as the August meeting with Khrushchev ended, Mao said to an associate: "I told him [Khrushchev] that whether or not we attack Taiwan is our domestic affair. He shouldn't try to interfere . . . We will do something on the Taiwan front." Mao's reasoning was clear-cut: "He wants to improve relations with the United States? Good, we'll congratulate him with our guns . . . Let's get the United States involved, too. Maybe we can get the United States to drop an atom bomb on Fujian . . . Let's see what Khrushchev says then."[33]

The outbreak of the crisis in the Taiwan Strait was a challenge to the Soviet Union in that it violated the rules of conduct inside the Socialist camp. Global bipolarity implied tough discipline and hierarchy where the essence of the Cold War—military matters—was concerned. The vassals of the Soviet Union could enjoy a certain amount of privacy and even sovereignty. In an army camp, soldiers have the right to be Catholics or Protestants, Republicans or Democrats—as long as it does not prevent them from obeying the general and being a coherent unit in combat. In the Socialist camp, the Catholic Church could be tolerated in Poland, Eastern European "people's democracies" could permit a private sector to exist in agriculture, and the Chinese could feel free in interpreting Marxism domestically, but the Nationalist rebellion against the interests of the "Socialist camp" was an intolerable danger to Soviet interests.

Mao wanted to establish his total independence from Moscow. The Chinese had been acting on territory they regarded as the domain of their sovereignty. They had always considered the Taiwan issue a domestic affair, and Mao had made a special point of emphasizing this during his talks with Khrushchev on the eve of the crisis.

The Soviet leaders, distracted from their concerns about the annual harvest and even from the discussions of what to do with West Berlin, avidly read every piece of news from China. But not much trickled down to them. Mao spent the days before the crisis, as well as the first days of it, at a resort in Beidaihe. Although August is not the most pleasant time to be in stuffy Beijing, a resort is not the best place for leading a full-scale war; after all, Beidaihe was vulnerable, being situated on the Yellow Sea, with American troops just across the water in Korea. Mao had hardly expected an attack in the Strait to mean an all-out offensive against Taiwan, and he had no intention of ultimately capturing it. Mao's behavior proved again that he did not plan to reunify China, but instead wanted a grand provocation meant to send a message to Khrushchev.

Khrushchev mentions one small but important detail in his memoirs: "There were many incidents which showed that China didn't trust us. An important one occurred when the Chinese carried out their operation against Chiang and the offshore islands of Quemoy and Matsu. Chiang's air force had American equipment, and some of the missiles launched from their fighters against China's aircraft failed to explode and fell to earth. Some in good condition. Our advisors reported this to us. We were naturally interested in new American military weapons, particularly missiles. Here were the Americans sending samples to us via China! We asked China to send us one of the missiles so we could study it and make use of American technology in the common interest of the Socialist countries . . . The Chinese didn't reply . . . We were astonished." Only after plain bullying was the missile sent to a research institute in Moscow.[34] But at the same time Khrushchev must have begun to think in specific terms about cancellation of the joint atomic program with the Chinese.

On the eve of the crisis Mao and Khrushchev (and before that Mao and Soviet Ambassador Yudin) had discussed "joint implementation of several important measures of a defensive nature."[35] The Soviet leader asked for permission to build a radio station in China for Soviet long-range submarines. Chinese sources mention that Khrushchev also asked for Soviet navy submarine bases on Chinese territory and suggested creating a joint fleet.[36] Khrushchev recalls, "Their answer was 'No.' It wasn't long afterward that we got Yudin's coded dispatch about the anti-Soviet attitudes of the Chinese leadership."[37] The embassy report noted later: "Our Chinese friends started to show excessive sensitivity toward the problems of sovereignty and independence of their country, reservations about the measures that used to be taken by both countries jointly."[38]

The principal archival sources on the 1958 crisis are the reports of the Soviet embassy in Beijing and of the consulates general in Shanghai and Harbin. These reports were sent to Foreign Minister Andrei Gromyko and Yuri Andropov, the head of the International Department in the Central Committee. Certainly the information also came to Moscow through KGB and GRU sources that are still beyond our reach, but the foreign ministry channel was still one of the principal avenues for conveying data and analysis.

Any knowledge of the Soviet system of supplying information makes it clear that these sources obfuscated the truth. Soviet diplomats were not encouraged to take sides, and they thought twice before reporting on drastic changes among "friends." So the reports were not just a mirror reflecting the situation in China; they primarily reflected the perceptions and expectations of Moscow's political elites.

In the first weeks of the crisis, the Soviet embassy, responding to pressure from Moscow, increased the flow of information: during 1958, fifty-two reports, more than four hundred minutes of talks, and innumerable cables had been sent to the Soviets.[39] Khrushchev considered Ambassador Yudin, Stalin's favorite philosopher, "a weak administrator and poor diplomat."[40] Now he had to read every word he had signed. The general evaluation of the embassy was that "the Chinese comrades" had "boasted about an easy victory" during the Taiwan crisis, exploiting Mao's thesis that "all imperialists and reactionaries are paper tigers."[41]

The Soviets' main grievance, summarized later in the report of the embassy, was plain: "Taking serious military-political action in the area of Taiwan at the end of August, our Chinese friends, basing their position on the assumption that the solution of the Taiwan issue was solely the domestic affair of China, had not informed the Soviet government beforehand about their plans . . . It would not be entirely correct to regard the solution of the Taiwan issue . . . as purely a domestic affair of China. In the first stage of the development of the Taiwan conflict our Chinese friends have demonstrated a rather simplistic approach to evaluating the degree of urgency of the Taiwan problem and have let the possibility of aggravating the international situation emerge to keep the United States 'on the verge of war' from their side too."[42] The Soviet diplomats could not understand why their

Chinese allies began to wage their own, separate "cold war," but preferred to ascribe it to inexperience and the "simplistic" approaches of their "friends" in Beijing.

After two weeks of uncertainty following the eruption of the crisis, the Kremlin's patience ran out. In early September Gromyko rushed to China to learn about Chinese plans and to restrain the Soviets' "friends" from taking action recklessly.

On September 5, the eve of Gromyko's arrival in Beijing, the Soviet diplomat N. G. Sudarikov, fulfilling a personal errand from Khrushchev, had met with Zhou to test the waters. "I have told him," Sudarikov reported to Moscow, "that the major goal of Comrade Gromyko's visit to Beijing is to inform the Politburo members of the CCP CC about Comrade Khrushchev's message to Eisenhower in connection with the events in the Taiwan Strait, to exchange opinions on this matter."[43]

Zhou understood that it was high time to explain to Moscow China's aims and activities in the crisis: "We had planned to inform the CPSU CC in detail about the situation near Taiwan, about our plans in connection with the military operations and the goals we pursued in beginning these operations." Zhou Enlai asked that Khrushchev be told immediately that since August 23, the artillery of the People's Liberation Army (PLA) "has inflicted several rather strong blows on the Guomindang troops stationed on Quemoy and Matsu islands."[44]

Zhou punctually enumerated the "international and domestic goals" pursued by Beijing in the crisis. By attacking the islands, he said, the PRC wanted the Americans to "get stuck" in Taiwan, "just as they have already 'gotten stuck' in the Middle and Near East." Another goal was to promote "more acute contradictions" between Chiang Kai-shek and Dulles, for Chiang insists on "more active measures toward us, and the Americans will not dare to get involved." The military action was initiated "to prove to the Americans that the People's Republic of China is strong and bold enough and is not afraid of America," and also to probe American allies—Korea, Vietnam, the Philippines, Japan, and Thailand. This list of international goals seemed rather innocent, but when Zhou moved on to domestic goals, his words had more grave connotations for Khrushchev. Zhou said that China's domestic goals were "to raise the combat spirit of our people and their readiness for war, to enhance their feeling of not being afraid of war and their hatred toward American imperialism and its aggressive, insolent foreign policy. We also have to harden our army in combat." Finally, Zhou said: "We did not intend to land on the offshore islands, especially not on Taiwan. That is the cause of the future."[45]

Gromyko met Zhou on September 7. According to the Soviet embassy report, Gromyko "forced the Chinese friends to inform the CPSU CC and the Soviet government more thoroughly about their plans regarding Taiwan." During the talk with Gromyko, Zhou Enlai made a remark that must have sent a shiver down Khrushchev's spine: "Inflicting blows on the offshore islands," Zhou said, "the PRC has taken into consideration the possibility of the outbreak in this region of a local war of the United States against the PRC, and it is now ready to take all the hard blows, including atomic bombs and the destruction of [its] cities." The Soviet Union, according to Zhou, should not take part in the U.S.-Chinese war at that stage, even if the Americans used tactical nuclear weapons. Only if the United States used larger nuclear weapons and risked broadening the war should the Soviet Union respond with a nuclear counterstrike.[46]

Zhou Enlai, clearly on Mao's orders, was actually suggesting that China could draw the Kremlin into a nuclear conflict with the United States! But for the confused Kremlin policy-makers it seemed that the Chinese spurned their nuclear umbrella and were probing the validity of the Sino-Soviet alliance and friendship.

On September 27 Khrushchev, on behalf of the Central Committee, sent a letter to the Chinese leadership that read: "We cannot allow our enemies to develop the illusion that, if the PRC were attacked by the United States or Japan—and these are the most likely adversaries—the Soviet Union would stand by as a passive onlooker. If the enemy were only to imagine such a thing, this would create a very dangerous situation." The Soviet leadership drew on all the proper slogans of proletarian internationalism to prove to the Chinese that a breach of the alliance's unity would have caused "a great calamity for the whole camp of socialism" and would have been "a crime before the world working class, a digression from the sacrosanct basis of communism—the teaching of Marxism-Leninism." The letter concluded: "Our enemies should not have the slightest hope of separating us . . . We can speak for ourselves . . . An attack on China is an attack on the Soviet Union. We also are confident that, in the event of an attack on the Soviet Union, the People's Republic of China would also fulfill its fraternal revolutionary duty."[47]

The grim comedy of misunderstandings between Beijing and Moscow continued. Under pressure from Moscow, the Chinese leadership recognized "the necessity of more deep and thorough planning of their actions toward Taiwan and the offshore islands with regard to the joint and prospective interests of the whole Socialist camp." The embassy report specified the shift in Chinese plans: initially they had planned "liberation of the islands" and now they recognized their mistake and agreed to complete the task of liberating Taiwan and the offshore islands "simultaneously, even if it should take a long time."[48]

Of course the lip service Chinese officials paid to repentance had nothing to do with Mao's real mood. He was triumphant: "The islands [Quemoy and Matsu] are two batons that keep Khrushchev and Eisenhower dancing, scurrying this way and that. Don't you see how wonderful they are?"[49]

On October 2, Mao addressed the diplomats of the Communist bloc with a speech that made the Soviet representatives rush to their cable room in the embassy. Mao gave a "definitive" explanation of China's goals in the crisis. He expressed satisfaction that he had "caught" John Foster Dulles in Taiwan and lectured the audience about the benefits of prolonged brinkmanship as "a means of educating all the peoples of the world, first of all the Chinese people." "There was a time when Hitler also performed the role of 'teacher,' " said Mao, "and thanks to him the peoples of Europe were reeducated . . . Regrettably, there are no more Hitlers, Mussolinis, or Japanese imperialists. Now in their stead 'Mister' Dulles stands out as such a 'teacher.' "[50]

"You see," continued Mao over the laughter of the audience, "without Dulles our life would have been more difficult. He makes our life easier. We always feel he is our 'comrade.' " Mao then voiced his "personal opinion" that the Americans should be kept tied "like thieves" to the defense of Taiwan and the offshore islands as long as possible, "perhaps even three years." "On this issue we spoke with Khrushchev," Mao said. "He sanctioned my opinion."[51]

Mao's speech was a continuation of Sino-Soviet debates on nuclear deterrence and nuclear war. No doubt many in the Kremlin were unhappy to see the Chinese leadership developing their own school of brinkmanship that threatened to draw the Soviet Union into a conflict with the United States. There is no reason to believe that Khrushchev was dismayed by it, however. On the contrary, as his memoirs suggest, he supported nuclear brinkmanship as the means of achieving China's reunification, provided that the policy was fully coordinated with the Kremlin. The nuclear polemics with Beijing, notably, did not shake the Soviet's determination to help the Chinese build their atomic bomb.

At that time the Soviets were still prepared to share some of their atomic secrets with the Chinese. It is difficult to evaluate the progress of the transfer of atomic weapons by August 1958, but the embassy report gives interesting figures: in 1958 in China there were 111 specialists of the Main Department on the Use of Atomic Energy, 43 geologists specializing in finding atomic raw materials, and also two mysterious bodies—Collective no. 1 (specialists of the KGB, consisting of 13 people), and Collective no. 4 (specialists working in the Ministry of National Security of the PRC, consisting of 340 military specialists). It is worth asking the question, what about Collectives no. 2 and no. 3? Why were they missing? Perhaps because they also dealt with atomic matters? In the embassy's report for 1959, we also read that the first Chinese nuclear reactor was built in 1958 and that China was visited by the distinguished nuclear scientists of the USSR—among them I. E. Tamm, A. P. Vinogradov, A. I. Alikhanov, and others.[52]

The tension surrounding the Sino-Soviet atomic program was real, but remained beneath the surface. The Chinese evidently regarded their future bomb as a means to deter the United States during the inevitable war against Taiwan. Some Soviet visitors sharply disagreed. The embassy "informed the Center about the wrong actions" of the academicians Alikhanov and Vinogradov, who strayed from the official Soviet and PRC line on "two Chinas." Perhaps the physicists tried to persuade the Chinese to share their views on the nuclear deadlock and, as its corollary, the international status quo.[53] The Soviet embassy brought official excuses, but the incident was not fortuitous. The day before Mao unleashed the crisis, Eisenhower had publicly invited the Soviets and the British to negotiate a ban on all atomic weapon testing.[54] For Beijing, this was the first sign that a "nuclear club" was being formed, a new international community without Communist China.

The crisis ended as abruptly as it had begun. On October 25, 1958, the Chinese minister of defense declared in an "Appeal to Compatriots on Taiwan Island" that the PLA had received an order to stop firing on even days. On odd days the fire lasted, off and on, for more than twenty years.

It took several months for the Soviets to sort out their feelings and intelligence about what had happened. The Soviet embassy reported in March 1959: "Our Chinese comrades believe that now their goal is to prevent silence in the Taiwan area and by doing so increase the contradiction between Chiang Kai-shek and the United States . . . That is why since October 1958 our friends have taken the tactic of shelling the offshore islands every other day [on odd days]. The situation at the Fujian front as of the end of January 1959 is characterized by stability and monotony."[55] But Sino-Soviet relations, unlike the Fujian front, were never stable and monotonous after the crisis of 1958.

The scar from the crisis was deep on both sides. Sino-Soviet relations continued to worsen, unbeknownst to the outside world and even to many insiders. On October 15 Mao Zedong wrote in a personal letter to Khrushchev that the Chinese leadership had been "deeply moved by your boundless loyalty to the principles of Marxism-Leninism and internationalism."[56] Khrushchev, however, began to rethink the Sino-Soviet nuclear cooperation in the light of recent experiences. Suddenly, he realized that the Sino-Soviet alliance constituted not one happy Communist union, but, from Beijing's perspective, a marriage of convenience, where each sought to satisfy its own needs.[57] When the tactical nuclear bomb was ready and about to be shipped to China, Khrushchev convened the Party Presidium and argued that the Soviets should not act as "docile slaves" committed to the Sino-Soviet agreements while the Chinese violated the very spirit of the alliance. On August 20, 1959, the Kremlin leaders sent a letter to Beijing, informing the PRC leadership that they would not provide them with a prototype of the Bomb. The demise of the Sino-Soviet nuclear program was a tangible blow to China's prospects of developing a nuclear bomb, and it accelerated the unraveling of the Sino-Soviet alliance.[58]

Mao Zedong, left without an atomic device and doubtful about the Soviet nuclear umbrella, had to scale down his ambitions for a while. On October 14, 1959, he told Antonov: "The People's Republic of China is not going to begin a war with the United States of America because of Taiwan. We can wait ten to twenty and even thirty or forty years. In this case we take into account the experience of the Soviet

Union, which for twenty-two years did not take military measures to return the Baltic states to the USSR."[59] The soft language concealed Mao's hatred for his colleagues in the Kremlin who bossed him around just as Stalin once had.

In the first half of 1959, the Chinese unleashed a fierce attack on Tito. It was obvious to the shrewd minds in Moscow that Tito was just a scapegoat for Khrushchev and the new Communist elites in Moscow. For a long period, however, Khrushchev went to great efforts to avoid an outright split of the Communist camp. The unity of this camp was a crucial part of Soviet Cold War ideology that was shared by the vast majority of the new Soviet elites. Initially, the unpleasant facts about the conduct of the Chinese were known only by a few. In 1959, the consul general in Shanghai, A. Elizavetin, assured Moscow that Soviet diplomats in China were "being guided by N. S. Khrushchev's belief that friends should meet more often to shake off the dust that accumulates on their relations—and, as we see it, dust has indeed accumulated on the Soviet-Chinese relations."[60]

## The Road to the Schism

In 1959 and the first months of 1960, Khrushchev had been involved in a complicated tripartite diplomacy, trying to mend fences with the PRC and the United States, two nations that were close to war. His job demanded the brilliant talents and tact of a Metternich, a Gorchakov, or at least a Henry Kissinger. He had none of these. His simple personal diplomacy sometimes amused the Americans, but it invariably insulted the sensitive Chinese. Sometimes Khrushchev, caught between his major ally in Beijing and a principal negotiating partner in Washington, failed even to be consistent. Whatever he did in the West had immediate aftereffects for the Soviet Union in the East. While he spoke about détente at Camp David or in Moscow, Khrushchev felt the icy breath of the Maoist revolution at his back.

In October 1959 Khrushchev arrived in China to commemorate the tenth anniversary of the PRC. Even on the ride from Beijing airport Khrushchev and Mao exchanged views on the world situation. "The major danger for us," Mao said, "comes from West Germany and Japan. America, England, and France stand for the status quo. That is why it is possible to soften relations with these countries in certain cases. And in certain cases one cannot exclude even the possibility of joint actions with these capitalist countries against West Germany and Japan." Had Mao read Khrushchev's mind? Perhaps he was mimicking his "realism," presenting it in his own terms?[61]

Khrushchev still hoped to avoid open tension between the two Communist countries, but at the same time it was already clear to many that Soviet and Chinese interests were drifting apart. The Soviet embassy warned Khrushchev in advance that he was held in ill repute by Mao. After his triumphant trip to the United States and standing ovations in Moscow, the strained hospitality in Beijing made him peevish and testy. Where he had to be delicate, he was bombastic, where tact was required, he was downright rude. In a bugged reception room, alone with the Soviet delegation, he ridiculed his hosts, rhyming their names with Russian obscenities.[62] He did not bother to conceal his condescension for Mao, who, in comparison with him, a world statesman, looked especially parochial. In a deliberate hint, Khrushchev advised the Chinese to get rid of their "old rubber boots." Perhaps he expected "the sober forces" in the Chinese leadership to overthrow Mao? Liu Shaoqi and Zhou Enlai stood as obvious alternatives to the founder of the PRC.

According to Chinese sources, Taiwan was another major issue. But it is unlikely that Khrushchev directly raised the question of "two Chinas," as some scholars suggest; most likely this was the Chinese propaganda interpretation of his thesis that Taiwan was a political reality.[63]

According to Soviet records and Khrushchev's memoirs, however, the real focus of the talks was not a settlement of the Sino-American disputes over the offshore islands, but the growing tension between the PRC and India. After the spring of 1959, when the Chinese military brutally suppressed the separatist rebellion in Tibet, India gave asylum to the Dalai Lama and supported the Tibetan separatists. By the time Khrushchev came to Beijing, the Sino-Indian War, he recalled, "raged on and we had to express our opinion." This led to the heated debate between Khrushchev and Foreign Minister Chen Yi.[64] And it not only put a strain on Sino-Soviet relations, but also laid bare the inner contradiction of the Soviet revolutionary-imperial paradigm in the newly emerging multipolar world. Khrushchev felt, on the one hand, that the USSR had to support the PRC as a Communist power in conflict with a bourgeois state. On the other hand, he did not want the Chinese army to defeat Neru, the leader of the

Non-Aligned movement and a new geopolitical ally of the USSR. He attempted to act as an intermediary. Mao and the Chinese took this as a sign of Soviet perfidy.

The visit was a diplomatic disaster and led the Soviets to question Chinese motives on the broader issues of international relations. After Khrushchev left for Moscow, the embassy stopped sparing the Chinese. "The relaxation of international tension, which occurred thanks to the efforts of the Soviet Union, in particular as a result of N. S. Khrushchev's trip to the United States, has not changed the PRC government's evaluation of China's relations" with the West.[65] The report continued, "The Chinese comrades have recently begun in China's press a one-sided, unprecedented, wide and sharp anti-American campaign."[66] The embassy noted that "after the visit of N. S. Khrushchev to the United States, the anti-American campaign in the Chinese press has widened."[67]

For the first time in the history of the Cold War, the Soviets began to blame their Communist allies for having poor relations with the evil imperialist power—the United States. Even more strange in terms of traditional Cold War dealings was that the Soviet embassy in China, with a sharp sense of what the leadership in Moscow wanted to hear, hinted that imperialist America was more reasonable and predictable than Communist China. "It should be admitted that to bring relaxation to the relations between the PRC and the United States is a task that is rather difficult to fulfill . . . Nevertheless, as has been noted before, the PRC in 1959 did not take any steps from its side to change the situation for the better."[68] "It is necessary to mention that in 1959 in the United States, the voices advocating the necessity of changing the unrealistic American course toward the PRC and of searching for ways to establish contacts with China became more distinct."[69]

The critical mood, however, did not last long. Most Soviet elites blamed Khrushchev for the failure to soothe their Chinese "friends." The Soviet leader, eager to dispel the impression that he was responsible, let his subordinates resume relations with the Chinese. In the whitewashed reports from the embassy his failure looked more and more like success. A quarterly report from the Soviet embassy in Beijing to Moscow, sent on April 12, 1960, briskly spoke about the process of "further improvement" in Sino-Soviet relations "that had begun in the autumn of 1959."[70] The report remarked on "the desire of the Chinese comrades to approach even more seriously the study and use of the experience of the Soviet Union, as well as other Socialist countries in the area of domestic, economic, and cultural construction, and to come to certain conclusions themselves from the active foreign policy pursued by the Soviet government."[71]

The campaign of self-delusion was directed by the new ambassador, S. V. Chervonenko, who arrived with Khrushchev to replace the retired Yudin. Mao, who liked Yudin, avoided Chervonenko, and very quickly the whole embassy found itself in an informational blockade. Finally, the Soviets met with Liu Shaoqi on December 10, 1959. The president of the PRC said that "there is unanimity between our two parties on all principal questions, and the differences on the other questions are only temporary and can be worked out."[72]

In April 1960 the Chinese Communist daily *Renmin Ribao* published the article "Long Live Leninism!"—the opening salvo in the Chinese campaign against Khrushchev's "revisionism" and "appeasement of imperialists." The publication set the embassy to brooding again. "Long Live Leninism!" stressed the inevitability of wars as long as imperialism existed.[73] The embassy's report to Moscow noted "the special position" of the Chinese leadership on "some relevant problems of current international life, such as peaceful coexistence and disarmament."[74] Yet in general, the embassy failed to see in the article the first open challenge to the Soviets' theoretical monopoly on the interpretation of Marxism-Leninism.

By that time Mao's firm intention to introduce his own version of Marxism-Leninism and to reach top status in the hierarchy of the world revolutionary movement was recognized only by a handful of Soviet bureaucrats attuned to changes in party politics. "The cult of personality of Mao Zedong," Yuri Andropov underlined in the embassy's report, "is continuing to develop in the PRC." Khrushchev later commented that this observation opened his eyes. Everything that happened in China later, especially during the "Proletarian Cultural Revolution," was understood by him as an inevitable consequence of one-man tyranny.[75]

Most of the Kremlin leaders still saw no alternative to friendly relations with Beijing. They were dismayed at the thought that Khrushchev's peace overtures to the West might cause a schism. Moscow-watchers were horrified to see the Soviet influence in China rapidly diminishing.

After the U-2 incident in May 1960, the conflict between Khrushchev and Eisenhower produced a strong reaction in the PRC. For five days, fifty-three million people demonstrated all over China.[76] The Chinese leaders declared that "aggression and provocations against the Soviet Union are aggression and provocations against the People's Republic of China, against the Socialist camp in general."[77] These words were similar to the words of Khrushchev during the Taiwan crisis; in both cases the leaders had used conventions of propaganda, not meaning what they said.

This filled many in Moscow with the false hope that new life could be breathed into Sino-Soviet relations. Some were jubilant that now true "class" orientations in Soviet foreign policy could be reasserted in all their clarity and directness.[78] But Khrushchev, with the assistance of diplomatic reports from Beijing, soon found that the real message was different. Mao was telling him that his own anti-Americanism was absolutely correct, whereas Khrushchev's line toward détente was a grave mistake. "But from the very beginning of this campaign," the embassy's report read, "the one-sided nature of China's support of the Soviet Union was obvious." The campaign "pursued the goal of persuading the Party and the people of China that the development of the international situation had proved the correctness of the analysis and estimates of the leadership of the CCP, particularly its conclusions and tactics."[79]

By the beginning of June 1960, the Soviets had made their final assessments. "Having used the aggravation of the international situation after the failure of the Paris summit, the Chinese leaders for the first time directly and openly opposed the foreign policy of the CPSU."[80] In July 1960, Khrushchev decided to withdraw all Soviet specialists from China. The Kremlin leadership sent explanations through the usual party channels citing the intolerable conditions created for the specialists. The Chinese side reacted in a "revolutionary" way. On August 4, meetings to discuss "confidential notes" on the recall of the specialists were to be held throughout China with the participation of Soviet specialists. The Soviet ambassador immediately protested to the Chinese minister of foreign affairs.[81]

On July 26, the embassy, in its "political letter for the second quarter of 1960," had to bury the "further development" of Sino-Soviet relations. "Now it becomes clear that 1958–1959 was the period of a peculiar 'quest' of the Chinese leadership in the area of foreign policy." "The leadership of the CCP had taken a number of 'emphatic' steps toward Japan, [the Nationalists], and the United States supporting them; [they also took steps toward] India and Indonesia that led to a drastic aggravation of the international situation for the PRC and to the decline of its prestige." But, as the ambassador concluded, this did not bother the Chinese, since they "actually deny, at least at this stage, the possibility of peaceful coexistence with the imperialist countries headed by the United States."[82]

Sometime in 1961, Khrushchev decided to stop paying lip service to the vessel of Sino-Soviet friendship that had disappeared in the mist of illusions. To his utter indignation he discovered that "our military men had been printing Mao Tse-tung's works on warfare. I immediately sent for the Minister of Defence and said, 'Comrade Malinovsky, I understand your department is publishing the works of Mao. This is absurd! The Soviet Army crushed the crack forces of the German Army, while Mao Tse-tung's men have spent between twenty and twenty-five years poking each other in the backsides with knives and bayonets.'"[83] He felt at that time that he had been betrayed by Mao. With Mao's personality cult, the ghost of Stalin and his horrible era haunted Khrushchev, even after his forced retirement.

The Cold War, based on the existence of the Eastern monolith, could not remain the same, for one participant in it, notorious for its discipline and unity, suddenly rebelled. This was to alter the geopolitics of the Cold War entirely. For the USSR and China it meant that in the very near future they would have to wage the Cold War on their own, regarding each other as traitors. For the United States it meant two major adversaries instead of one (although Washington failed to understand this until the late 1960s). On the one hand, it was a positive change: the efforts of the USSR and China could neutralize each other. On the other hand, it introduced new uncertainty into the Cold War relationship and made the behavior of the East even less predictable than before.

The Sino-Soviet estrangement during the Taiwan crisis and the growing split afterward underlined the direction in which the Cold War was turning. In 1950 Stalin had, albeit reluctantly, supported the North Korean and then the Chinese "war of liberation" against the United States. In 1958–1959 Khrushchev demonstrated his desire to come to terms with the West, notwithstanding Chinese militant attitudes. Bipolarity was becoming obsolete by 1960, when military cooperation between China and the Soviet Union ended, and the Eastern bloc ceased being a monolith. It was not coincidental that the Sino-Soviet split and Soviet-American détente occurred at the same time. The whole Cold War system began to change as the new elites came to power in the USSR. The spontaneous changes in the revolutionary-imperial paradigm had both split the Socialist bloc and built some bridges between Moscow and the West.

At the dusk of his life, Khrushchev would wearily sigh: "I used to listen to Chinese radio broadcasts. Finally I stopped, because it was simply disgusting to listen. The broadcasts were monotonous repetitions of Mao's sayings—that, and praise for Mao, like prayers. Unfortunately, we followed the same path at the time of Stalin."[84] In the late 1960s Khrushchev, the former leader of the new elites, had seen in China, as in a mirror, the Russian Revolution—and he had shuddered.

# 8 Khrushchev and Kennedy: The Taming of the Cold War

> I laughed. He asked, "What are you laughing
> about?" I said, "What you're talking about
> would lead to war, and I know you're too sensi-
> ble a man to want war." He stopped a minute
> and looked at me and said, "You're right."
>
> Averell Harriman's recollection of a conversa-
> tion with Nikita Khrushchev, October 1959

A perceptive Russian historian, witness to the rise and fall of Khrushchev, once observed that the leader's future biographer "would not escape a chapter featuring another prominent figure, John Kennedy."[1] Khrushchev's relationship with John Fitzgerald Kennedy evolved rapidly and was characterized by periods of friendliness and animosity.

During the U.S. presidential elections of 1960, Khrushchev rooted for the young Democratic candidate and regarded him as a promising partner for future talks. Khrushchev appreciated Kennedy's saying that he would not have sent the U-2 on the eve of the summit and would have apologized to Khrushchev in Paris for the incident. In his memoirs Khrushchev wrote, "I was very glad Kennedy won the election."[2] After the Bay of Pigs Invasion in April 1961, in which a U.S.-sponsored invasion of Cuba failed, Khrushchev began to perceive Kennedy as a "weak president," not entirely in control of the state machinery. He stopped underestimating the U.S. president only after the Cuban missile crisis, in October 1962.[3]

This crisis marked the watershed between the first, virulent stage of the Cold War and the second, long period of truce, when the competition between the two superpowers was constrained by a mutual fear of nuclear force. Just as the new global order had emerged from World War II, this Cold War truce arose out of the labors to avoid a nuclear war in October 1962. Its architects were Nikita Khrushchev and John F. Kennedy. The partnership of these two leaders during the crisis became one of the most remarkable developments in the history of the Cold War.

Despite the wealth of literature covering the crisis, its prelude and aftermath, there is still much uncertainty about Khrushchev's side of the story. How did he come to the conclusion that nothing short of Soviet missiles on Cuban soil would stop U.S. aggression against the Castro regime? What other factors made him risk war for his country and the whole world? Why did he initially underestimate the dangers of the U.S. response to the Soviet deployment, and then, even as the most perilous phase of the crisis passed, continue to make unilateral concessions, infuriating his Cuban friends?

In all the scenarios and analyses of Khrushchev's behavior and thinking one crucial factor has not yet been given the attention it deserves. This factor is Khrushchev himself and how he viewed his competition with Kennedy. This competition was not only about Cuba, although the island did possess tremendous symbolic and emotional significance for the Soviet Chairman; it was also about the status quo of the Cold War and what it implied for the future of the world.

## Sizing Up a Partner

After the debacle of the Paris summit and his conflict with Eisenhower's Republican administration, Khrushchev began to root for the Democratic party and its presidential candidate. As the still unknown Kennedy emerged as the front-runner in the Democratic field, Khrushchev began to view him as a preferred alternative to Richard Nixon. In July 1959, during Nixon's presentation of an American exhibition in Moscow, the Soviet leader clashed with him in a debate on the comparative benefits of socialism and capitalism. Nixon offended Khrushchev by insisting on the superiority of American technology and consumer culture. Thereafter the Chairman branded the U.S. vice president "a McCarthyite."[4] Any candidate would be better than Nixon.

Never before had Khrushchev followed a U.S. presidential campaign so closely. Alexander Feklisov, then the KGB station chief in Washington under the alias "Fomin," recalls that "the *rezidentura* [station] had been instructed to inform the Center periodically about the development of the electoral campaign, and to propose measures, diplomatic, propagandist, or [any] other, to encourage Kennedy's victory." A KGB agent, according to Feklisov, even tried to contact Robert Kennedy, but met a polite rebuff.[5] In the end, Khrushchev did influence the U.S. presidential elections by his belligerent rhetoric, as well as by demonstrating that a constructive U.S.-Soviet dialogue would be impossible so long as Eisenhower or Nixon remained in the White House. Twenty years before the revolutionary leadership of the Islamic Republic of Iran used American hostages to influence a U.S. presidential campaign, Khrushchev did the same by holding captive two pilots of the U.S. reconnaissance plane RB-47, shot down in July 1960 over the Soviet North. Along with fears of the "missile gap," Kennedy successfully exploited the issue of the captive pilots in his barbs against the Eisenhower-Nixon administration.

When Kennedy won the presidential election on November 4, Khrushchev was delighted, and even joked that this was a present to him on the anniversary of the Great October Socialist Revolution. Later, when Khrushchev met Kennedy in Vienna, he did not hesitate to boast that he had helped the Democrat win an extremely narrow race with Nixon.[6]

Yet Khrushchev knew precious little about Kennedy as a man or a politician. Soon after Kennedy was nominated at the Democratic Convention in Los Angeles, the Soviet embassy in Washington sent Khrushchev a profile of the future president. According to the report, "Kennedy, in his general philosophical views, is a typical pragmatist . . . In his political activity he is governed not by any firm convictions but by purely pragmatic considerations, defining his positions in any given concrete circumstances and, most important, in his own interests." Kennedy, the report continued, does not like to go out on a limb politically (he avoided condemning McCarthyism), his liberalism "is rather relative," his position on the relations between the United States and the USSR, "like his position on domestic policy," "is quite contradictory," inconsistent.[7]

The report contained another important passage: "Considering that . . . there is a conflict of 'basic national interests' between the United States and the USSR and that because of this one cannot expect [any] fundamental change in their relations, Kennedy nevertheless grants the possibility of a mutually acceptable settlement . . . on the basis of a joint effort to avoid nuclear war." In the text, found in the Moscow archives, someone underlined the following key sentence: "Kennedy, in principle, is in favor of talks with the Soviet Union, rejecting as 'too fatalistic' the opinion that 'you can't trust' the Soviet Union, that it 'doesn't observe treaties,' and so on."

Khrushchev must have liked what he read. For the first time he was to deal with someone not anchored to a set of hostile, preconceived notions about the USSR and the Russian Revolution. From the report (and, no doubt, many others, sent along from intelligence and diplomatic channels) emerged the portrait of a flexible and prudent politician, attuned to changing circumstances and realities. The biggest question mark was Kennedy's ability to be a leader independent from the will and advice of others. The embassy's profile noted that "Kennedy himself and his supporters now are trying every way possible to create the impression that he is a strong personality of the caliber of Franklin D. Roosevelt," that the Democratic candidate is capable of making "the final decision on serious problems himself, not entrusting this function to his underlings." Yet it also claimed that he "is more of a good catalyst and consumer of others' ideas and thoughts than a creator of independent and original ideas" and "very attached to the institution of advisors."[8]

During his tumultuous stay in New York in the fall of 1960, Khrushchev called the Soviet ambassador Menshikov and his new deputy Georgi Kornienko and asked them if Kennedy would win, and, if so, could he become another Roosevelt? Menshikov answered that Kennedy was an "upstart," he would never make a great leader. Kornienko objected: Kennedy was a truly bright and outstanding politician. His presidency might be a very promising one, although no one knew if he would become another Roosevelt. Several months later Khrushchev met Kornienko in the lobby of the Central Committee in Moscow and said, "You were right about Kennedy, and others were wrong."[9]

Khrushchev was prone to optimistic (and often wishful) thinking, and in the early months after Kennedy's election he had an irresistible temptation to see "his" new president in the best light. He tried many channels to convey to Kennedy that his presidency could open a new era in U.S.-Soviet relations.[10]

On the eve of Kennedy's inauguration, Khrushchev shifted the gears of Soviet foreign policy abruptly toward détente. On January 26 he released the captive American pilots. Khrushchev approved a set of measures to improve Soviet-American public diplomacy that included the creation of an Institute of American Studies in Moscow, granting permission to five hundred elderly Soviet citizens to join their relatives in the United States, payment of honoraria to the American writers whose works were published in the Soviet Union (Moscow pirated books and movies, staying outside all international conventions on copyright), reopening the Jewish theater, reestablishing periodicals closed down by Stalin, and instituting student exchange programs.[11] (Incidentally, this was the second time the issue of Jewish immigration was raised. After the Camp David summit, the KGB had been instructed "to decide positively" on the applications for immigration, with the exception of security risks. The instruction was disregarded after the U-2 incident.)[12]

Communication between the Soviet and the U.S. leader increased daily. The U.S. ambassador in Moscow, Lewellyn (Tommy) Thompson, became a frequent guest of Khrushchev's in the Kremlin. In addition, the Chairman and the Kennedy brothers were able to maintain contact through the GRU colonel Georgi Bolshakov, working in Washington undercover as a press secretary of the Soviet embassy. Soon he, on one side, and Robert Kennedy, on the other, started passing personal messages from one leader to the other. On the Soviet side, the GRU reported to Minister of Defense Malinovsky, who briefed Khrushchev. Mikoyan and Adzhubei, Khrushchev's son-in-law, also knew about Bolshakov's channel. The Soviet ambassador Menshikov did not know about it, however. Foreign Minister Gromyko received only a brief oral summary from Malinovsky, or no information at all.[13]

Other developments put Khrushchev on alert. Kennedy interpreted the Soviet leader's "wars of national liberation" speech in January 1961 as a direct threat to the "free world," a gauntlet that Khrushchev had thrown down and Kennedy had to pick up. On February 6, Robert McNamara, Kennedy's secretary of defense, declared that there was no "missile gap" in favor of the Soviet Union. Yet on

February 27, 1961, Kennedy sent a letter to Khrushchev, proposing an early summit meeting. Khrushchev agreed to meet in Vienna, Austria. Immediately thereafter, the usual presummit fever gripped Khrushchev and infected Soviet officials. In Washington, Feklisov told his contact from the *Washington Post* that some agreements might be possible at the upcoming meeting, among them a compromise on the stalled test-ban talks.[14]

Once again, however, an unpredictable event broke the presummit mood. On April 17, CIA-trained and financed counterrevolutionary volunteers ("contras") launched an operation to overthrow Castro's regime. The offensive ended in disaster; the result was a major loss of prestige for the United States, not only among the countries of Latin America, but also among its NATO allies.

There is some indication that Khrushchev had been forewarned about the Bay of Pigs Invasion. On February 14, 1961, the Soviet leader had perused an annual report of the KGB's chairman, Alexander Shelepin, marked "Top Secret—Highly Sensitive." Shelepin proudly enumerated, among the main achievements of Soviet intelligence, obtaining "evidence of preparations by the United States for an economic blockade of and military intervention against Cuba."[15]

One American historian suggests that Khrushchev knew about the invasion, but speculates that he miscalculated its timing.[16] But Castro's border troops were well prepared, tipped off by Moscow (and the *New York Times,* for that matter). The Chairman had clearly learned about "Operation ZAPATA." The real question is why he kept silent on this matter in his correspondence with Kennedy until the offensive was under way.

The incident took place at a time when Khrushchev—like Stalin at the end of World War II—was at the peak of his power and faced alone a pivotal moment in world history. It still did not appear that complications with the Chinese Communists would result in the "loss of China." At the same time, the Soviet sphere of influence included a growing number of Third World countries. Indicators of growth in the Soviet economy were still counted in the double-digits. On February 21, a much more advanced Soviet intercontinental ballistic missile, R-16 (SS-7), had been tested successfully, and Khrushchev ordered its mass production and the construction of underground silos.[17] On April 12, just days before the Bay of Pigs Invasion, the Soviet space program achieved its biggest triumph, sending the Soviet military pilot Yuri Gagarin around the Earth in a spaceship—making him the first human being to travel around the globe. As a shrewd politician, Khrushchev had to know that worse things might ensue in Cuba, but as a revolutionary romantic, mesmerized by the tide of events that seemed to flow in the Soviet Union's favor, he pushed this knowledge to the back of his mind.

Khrushchev learned of the contras' invasion on his sixty-seventh birthday. By noon of the next day the Chairman had sent a letter to Kennedy, after receiving the approval of the Party Presidium, warning that the Cuban events jeopardized "the peace of the whole world," and admonishing the U.S. president "to avoid the irreparable." Khrushchev was blunt and direct about the Soviet position—the Cuban people and their government would get "all necessary assistance to repel the armed attack." To this Khrushchev added a veiled threat: if the flame of military conflict in the Caribbean continued to burn, then "a new conflagration may flare up in another area."[18] It required no special analysis to understand that by "another area" Khrushchev meant West Berlin.

When Kennedy refused to engage the U.S. Air Force and Marines to save the Cuban contras, Khrushchev had reason to believe that his diplomacy of deterrence had worked again, as it had in the Suez crisis of 1956. This time, however, the victory was more significant, and the taste of triumph was unmitigated. Cuba's closeness to the United States could be compared to Hungary's geographical proximity to the USSR, yet in 1961 the United States failed to achieve what the Soviet Union had done in 1956—prevent a breach in its sphere of influence.

Even more than in the U-2 affair, Khrushchev tended to attribute the responsibility for the Bay of Pigs not to Kennedy but to his underlings, "the dark forces" who had vested interests in the arms race and an ideological commitment to the Cold War. On April 10, 1961, in conversation with Walter Lippmann, Khrushchev personalized these forces, reducing them to one name: "Rockefeller."[19] He was referring to the governor of New York, Nelson Rockefeller, a scion of one of the wealthiest capitalist dynasties in the United States. On March 10 the KGB reported to Khrushchev and the Party Secretariat that a special slander campaign would be directed at "the reactionary militarist group in U.S. ruling circles—[Nelson] Rockefeller, [Lauris] Norstad, A. Dulles, E. [J. Edgar] Hoover, as well as their allies in pushing an aggressive course in other countries."[20]

Khrushchev believed that the young and inexperienced president had been "taken in" by these circles. According to Troyanovsky, there was a sigh of relief in the Kremlin when the Bay of Pigs incident was over, but also almost a feeling of pity for Kennedy's discomfiture. Old Ike, at least, would have brought the Cuban affair to its successful completion.[21]

On the eve of the summit in Vienna, scheduled for June 3–4, Khrushchev convened a special session of the Politburo (Presidium) and told his colleagues that he intended to exert as much pressure as possible on Kennedy. He believed that after the Bay of Pigs incident he would be able to force the young and inexperienced American president to make concessions, in particular on Berlin. When Mikoyan tried to argue that a reasonable and constructive dialogue with Kennedy would be more likely to improve Soviet-American relations, Khrushchev exclaimed that the favorable situation must be exploited. The rest of the Kremlin leadership, who knew little about Kennedy and the course of secret diplomacy, supported Khrushchev.[22]

## The Chairman's Miscalculation

Khrushchev met with Kennedy in Vienna as a prima donna meeting a first-time starlet. "I heard you were a young and promising man," Khrushchev greeted the forty-three-year-old president.[23] The difference in age was almost a quarter of a century. This generation gap grows into an abyss, if one thinks of all the milestones of Russian history as well as the personal experience that had shaped Khrushchev, and of which Kennedy had only a limited understanding. The only two links between the leaders were World War II and the nuclear polarization of the Cold War.

Kennedy's main goal in his meeting with Khrushchev was to suggest a retreat from the Cold War, the broadening of the zone of neutrality between the two established blocs. Something along these lines had been proposed in the United States by Walter Lippmann and advocated by Maxim Litvinov in 1944.[24] Kennedy did not believe it would be feasible to change the status quo in divided Europe or in the Far East. Therefore he spoke in very general terms about the desirability of informal cooperation to prevent the spread of bipolar competition into the Third World. He told Khrushchev he would not object to having more Socialist Yugoslavias, Indias, or Burmas—the nonaligned countries that would not affect the existing geostrategic balance be-tween the two superpowers. Kennedy also targeted Laos, where a struggle was on among the Communist guerillas, the pro-American strongman, General Phoumi Nosavan, and a neutral group. In Ken-nedy's opinion, if both superpowers could convince their respective clients to move toward neutrality in Laos, the country might provide a model for settlement in future Third World conflicts.

Kennedy's attitude was in striking contrast to Eisenhower and Dulles's strategy of encirclement of the USSR and their antagonism to the idea of neutrality in the Cold War, in Europe and elsewhere. But to Khrushchev it seemed as if the U.S. president were suggesting to the First Secretary of the Communist Party of the USSR that he renounce his beliefs in the revolutionary transformation of the world and the path to socialism and communism.

For two days the leaders were engaged in an academic and mis-guided dialogue on the history of the Cold War. They spoke about the issues of war, peace, and revolution, but the most important things at the summit were left unsaid.[25] The two men's encounter was similar to an immortal scene written by the great French satirist François Rabelais—"the debate" between the stiff British scholar and the jester Panurgue. In the end, Khrushchev (Panurgue) overwhelmed Kennedy (the scholar)—not by the force of argumentation, but by his formida-ble temperament and vigor. Some American observers, interestingly, attributed Kennedy's setback at the summit to his physical handicap, a bad back.[26]

Khrushchev, however, was not a mere jester or an idle talker. He was guided by the dictates of Communist ideology and his profound convictions. His passionate view of history and the world was very different from the detached and slightly fatalistic outlook of the U.S. president. Khrushchev was ready to meet the level of historical dis-cussion offered by the Harvard graduate. He even did his homework and mastered the art of historical parallels. A century and a half earlier in Vienna, he reminded Kennedy, Czar Alexander I had presided over the "Holy Alliance," a reactionary concert of rulers who wanted to put the genie of national revolutions back into the bottle.[27] In vain! The world order envisioned in 1815 eventually broke down as a result of revolutionary outbursts. The revolutionary situation in the world today, Khrushchev explained, had nothing to do with the Soviet Un-ion. It was just a response to a Western "Holy Alliance" led by the

United States and organized by John Foster Dulles to protect the status quo. But in fact America itself, continued Khrushchev, had been born in a war of national liberation. The Soviet Union should not reach agreement at the expense of other people; such an agreement could not bring peace.

While lecturing Kennedy, Khrushchev repeatedly pressed salt into his wounds by raising the Bay of Pigs fiasco. Although Castro is not a Communist, Khrushchev said, "you are well on the way to making him a good one." Indeed, having initially come to power with little sympathy toward the Communist sectarians in Cuba, Castro, under heavy American pressure, decided to lean toward the Socialist camp. Khrushchev saw the United States at this moment as a power historically on the wane. Washington could shore up its faltering global positions only through the use of military force, building "dams against the flow of ideas."[28]

Today it is hard to believe that the Secretary of the Communist party could launch these criticisms with the complete confidence of a man riding the crest of history. Yet Kennedy succumbed to this onslaught. He took a defensive line, arguing that when systems "are in transition," be it from feudalism to capitalism, or from capitalism to communism, "we should be careful, particularly today, when modern weapons are at hand." The president admitted that social transformation could not be stopped by force, and if the Shah of Iran resisted change he would perish like Fulgencio Batista, the last ruler of Cuba before Castro's revolution. It is dangerous when superpowers, capable of destroying each other, involve themselves in violent social change. Such involvement might lead to "miscalculations" with catastrophic consequences. Our judgments of events may not always be correct, he said, and as an example, he confessed that the Bay of Pigs affair was his "mistake."[29]

Kennedy's words had the opposite effect of what he had hoped to achieve. In Khrushchev's opinion, the United States had an unchallenged capability of nuclear blackmail for a decade, and American politicians had been teaching the Soviet Union by example how to behave. Secretary of State Dulles had not worried in those days about the danger of "miscalculations." And now, just when the Soviet Union acquired the means of retaliation, the Americans changed their approach: they began to view the Soviet leader as a child playing with fire. "Miscalculation!" Khrushchev burst out in anger. "All I ever hear from your people and your news correspondents and your friends in Europe and every place else is that damned word." The United States, he continued, simply wanted the USSR "to sit like a schoolboy with his hands on his desk." "We don't make mistakes." (Stalin made them, but we will not.) "We will not make war by mistake."[30]

After the first day of talks, Khrushchev's advisors, who waited for his return in front of the Soviet embassy, asked him about his impressions of Kennedy. Khrushchev waved his hand dismissively. Kennedy, he said, was no match for Eisenhower; he lacked the broad horizons and the statesmanship of the earlier president.[31]

Even on the second day of talks Kennedy hesitated to use his aces against Khrushchev: he never mentioned that Soviet missile forces were lagging disastrously behind those of the United States, and he hardly played on the eruption of the Sino-Soviet conflict. Both developments were corroborated to the American side by Oleg Penkovsky before the Vienna summit.[32] In a familiar Cold War pattern, crucial intelligence did not affect the important meeting. Instead, Kennedy said that "they" in the U.S. administration "regard the present [state] of power between Sino-Soviet forces and the forces of the United States and Western Europe as being more or less in balance."[33] Khrushchev found these words both pleasing and mocking. The Chairman had long tried to convince everyone that the balance of power between the two superpowers could not be measured on scales, that the exact number of missiles "did not matter anyway."[34] But he also knew that by the Vienna summit there could be nothing resembling joint "Sino-Soviet forces."

Again, both leaders operated on a completely different plane. Kennedy viewed the nuclear deadlock through the prism of geopolitics, as an invitation to a more cautious and prudent policy for both superpowers, perhaps even a kind of partnership between them. He felt he was offering a fair deal from a position of substantial strategic superiority (in terms of deliverable nuclear warheads). But Khrushchev saw this as a recognition by the leader of the most powerful imperialist country that the forces of socialism had now caught up with the forces of the old world. As a true believer, he took it as another sign that the imperialist camp was doomed and in retreat. For the rest of the meeting the Soviet leader was on the offensive, acting increasingly arrogant.

At last Khrushchev turned to the question of Germany. One of his main expectations was that Kennedy and his advisors would divorce their position on the German question from the "policy of Adenauer," would look at it from what Khrushchev knew was a common ground between the superpowers—mistrust of German militarism.[35] The Chairman received confusing signals: at one point U.S. Ambassador Thompson told him that the Americans "would rather deal with the Russians" in Central Europe than "leave it to the Germans," and added, "I refuse to believe that your Germans are any better than ours." Khrushchev laughed and, reaching over the table, said impulsively, "Let's shake on that."[36]

In Vienna, however, Kennedy did not show any signs of flexibility. He explained to Khrushchev America's vital interest in maintaining the present status of West Berlin. The Soviet leader insisted that he had come to Vienna to reach some agreement with Kennedy similar to "the interim agreement" that he had discussed with Eisenhower. The USSR, he said, was prepared to accept such an arrangement even now. "Now" was the key word. Khrushchev would accept no delay. The alternative would be a separate peace treaty with the GDR.[37]

Kennedy ignored the message and the hint about an interim agreement. The president acted on advice received from de Gaulle: it should be left to the Soviet leader to press for change in Central Europe. But unlike de Gaulle, who always believed Khrushchev was merely bluffing in Berlin, Kennedy was not so sure.[38] The Soviet Chairman grew impatient. He told Kennedy how many lives the USSR had lost in the war with Germany and reminded him that his own son had been one of those killed. Finally he snapped. "Perhaps the USSR should sign a peace treaty [with the GDR] right away and get it over with," he said. The Soviet Union would "never, under any conditions, accept U.S. rights in West Berlin after a peace treaty had been signed." In the frenzy of brinkmanship Khrushchev said that the USSR would not start a war, but if the United States was going to unleash war, then let it be now, before the development of even more destructive weapons. This passage was so reckless that it was not included in either Soviet or American records of the conversation.[39]

Khrushchev, of course, was bluffing. But again Kennedy did not call the Chairman's bluff. Khrushchev left the meeting saying that "if the United States [refused] an interim agreement," Moscow would sign the peace treaty in December. "It will be a cold winter," said Kennedy.[40] These were the last words Khrushchev heard from the president. They never met again.

Some in the Kennedy administration were convinced that the president had reinforced the impression of his weakness that had arisen from the Bay of Pigs fiasco.[41] They were correct. The outcome of the Vienna summit encouraged Khrushchev to launch the most serious campaign of brinkmanship around Berlin. Years later he said he "could tell" that Kennedy was a reasonable man, interested "in avoiding conflict with the Soviet Union." He was sure that Kennedy would not start "a war over Berlin."[42] Upon returning from Vienna he ordered the publication of a confidential Soviet memorandum to the U.S. administration restating the ultimatum of 1958 on West Berlin. This time Khrushchev threatened to sign a separate treaty with the GDR by the end of 1961, and he pulled all stops to prove that he meant it.

The Chairman miscalculated: the pressure he put on Kennedy pushed him to the limits of bluff and nuclear rhetoric, but failed to change the position of the United States on the German question. Khrushchev's words and actions did, however, result in the most heated summer and fall since the beginning of the Cold War in Europe.

## Brinkmanship and the Wall

Confident as he was that the revolutionary-imperial paradigm would lead the USSR from one historic victory to another, Khrushchev soon discovered that in Berlin and Germany as a whole, social forces that elsewhere seemed to justify Soviet optimism threatened to undo Soviet geopolitical positions. In the spring of 1961 the flight of people from the GDR to West Germany via Berlin and the resulting economic disruption created a situation in which the East German Communist regime might collapse without a single shot fired from the Western side. Ironically, it was the very same crisis, unleashed by Khrushchev, that destroyed the status quo in East Germany and sent a wave of panic through the population of the GDR: many fled, fearing that the gate to the West would eventually close. The Soviet embassy in Berlin informed Moscow on a weekly basis about this human exodus, and in April 1961 calculated that during the 1950s the population of the GDR was reduced by 1.2 million.[43]

The seriousness of the situation was not lost on Khrushchev's entourage. One of his speechwriters, however, an expert on Germany, showed his black humor, saying that soon there would be no one left in the GDR, except Ulbricht himself.[44] Experts observed that the USSR's "friends" in the GDR received more Soviet assistance per capita than West Germany received from the Americans.[45] The embassy reported that West Berliners and Western tourists were buying a huge number of goods in East Berlin, profiting from subsidized prices and the favorable ratio between the DM and the mark of the GDR. The longer the GDR suffered, the higher the bill for the Soviet economy and morale.

Ulbricht himself brought this naked truth to Khrushchev's attention. Since October 1960 he had been asking for "emergency aid," claiming that the Bonn government was about to sever a trade agreement with the GDR. He requested 50 million dollars in cash and compensation for the consumer goods that the GDR refused to buy in West Germany. Later the Soviets learned that total losses of hard currency for 1961 amounted to 540 million DM.[46] In November, when Ulbricht attended the world Communist forum in Moscow, Khrushchev invited him to the Council of Ministers. Alexei Kosygin, a leader of Gosplan (the State Planning Committee at the Council of Ministers), complained that the requests of the GDR created difficulties for the Soviet economy. The hundreds of tons of butter and meat that the GDR asked for, he said, were in extremely short supply in the Soviet Union itself.[47]

Khrushchev was uneasy about Ulbricht's growing appetite. When the East German leader asked him to send Soviet *Gastarbeitern,* or seasonal labor, to the GDR, Khrushchev snapped: "We won the war," he reminded the East German Communist. "Our workers will not clean your toilets."[48] He refused to touch the Soviet gold reserve to get the GDR out of trouble. "Don't encroach on our gold, don't thrust your hands into our pockets," he said.[49] But, his temper notwithstanding, Khrushchev remained generous toward his East German "friends," since their collapse would mean a Soviet defeat in the Cold War.

Ulbricht knew this as well. Like the Chinese Communists, he did not conceal his critical attitude toward Khrushchev's foreign policy, and he put increasing pressure on the leader to change his priorities. He called the plan to disarm within three years "demoralizing palaver" and was shocked by drastic reductions of Soviet troops in the GDR. The U-2 affair and the debacle of the Paris summit allowed him to argue for tougher, decisive actions in West Berlin. East German activists, according to a Soviet diplomat, were ready to storm West Berlin "tomorrow"—naturally in the rear guard of Soviet tanks.[50] At the meeting in November, Ulbricht made it clear to Khrushchev that another détente with the United States, at the expense of the interests of the GDR, would be a disaster. "What will happen in 1961?" he asked Khrushchev after Kennedy was elected to the White House. "We cannot repeat our campaign in favor of a peace treaty as we did before the Paris summit . . . We can only do this in the event that we actually achieve something." When Gromyko accused him of provocative conduct toward West Germany, Ulbricht pretended not to hear.[51] The GDR government prepared detailed plans for a "purge" from West Berlin of "a number of persons and organizations hostile to the GDR."[52] At a minimum, Ulbricht wanted to control all intersectoral traffic in the city and to discourage his people from looking for jobs in capitalist sectors of the city.

Khrushchev initially used the threat of a separate peace treaty with the GDR to jolt Western powers out of complacency on the German question. He was an angler, holding Adenauer and the Western powers on his hook. But suddenly Ulbricht directly involved himself in the affair, and the Chairman had to face the truth: if he signed a separate peace treaty with the GDR, the situation in Berlin could become explosive. Ulbricht's "impatience" with the status quo in the city would lead to Western economic sanctions against the whole Soviet bloc, as well as retaliation from both sides.

The only way out of this impasse would be to protect the Soviet sphere of influence by forcefully closing the loophole through which people and resources escaped to West Berlin. The German experts at the ministry of foreign affairs, and Mikhail Pervukhin, the Soviet ambassador in the GDR, wrote that the closing of the border would be difficult technically and damaging politically, but "with the exacerbation of the political situation," dividing Berlin "could be necessary."[53] Until after the Vienna summit Khrushchev still hesitated to take this route to stabilizing the GDR. For him it meant an effective renunciation of his grand diplomacy. The border closing would render absurd his idea of Berlin as a free city. It would be a colossal propaganda defeat for the Communist system in its competition with capitalism. In other words, the political damage appeared forbiddingly high.[54]

It took another ultimatum—this time Ulbricht's—to make Khrushchev reassess his priorities. After the meeting in Vienna Ulbricht urged Khrushchev to convene a summit of the leaders of the Warsaw Treaty Organization to discuss the situation in the GDR. The previous such meeting, in March, had been inconclusive. Khrushchev deferred unpleasant decisions in expectation of the coming meeting with Kennedy. This time, however, Ulbricht was determined not to let Khrushchev's preoccupation with Soviet-U.S. relations get in the way of a favorable settlement for the GDR. In early July he asked the Soviet ambassador to report to the Kremlin that "if the present situation of open borders remains, collapse is inevitable"; Ulbricht made it clear that he "refuses all responsibility for what would then happen."[55]

The decision to build the Wall to separate the GDR from West Berlin was the benchmark of Khrushchev's statesmanship; although something like it was expected, the decision was made spontaneously, coming as a surprise to friends and foes alike. In his memoirs Khrushchev described how the plan unfolded. "I spoke to Pervukhin, our ambassador in Germany, about the establishment of border control." The Soviet ambassador was ill prepared for the operation. "He gave me a map of West Berlin. The map was very poor." Khrushchev then asked Pervukhin to share the idea with Ulbricht, "and also to ask Marshal Ivan I. Yakubovsky [the commander of the Soviet troops in Germany] to send me a new map." When Pervukhin disclosed the strategy to Ulbricht, he "beamed with delight." To the surprise of the Soviet ambassador, the GDR chief immediately laid out a detailed plan of action: barbed wire and fencing must be set along the entire border, the U-Bahn and S-Bahn to West Berlin must be stopped, and the main Friedrichstrasse train station should be divided by a glass wall. Ulbricht even had a code name for the operation: "Rose."[56]

At about the same time, on July 25, the day President Kennedy publicly announced military mobilization to meet a Soviet challenge in Berlin, Khrushchev invited the president's disarmament advisor, John J. McCloy, on a diplomatic mission to Moscow, to fly to his spacious resort at Pitsunda, on the Black Sea. The next morning the Soviet leader staged a spectacle for his visitor, one minute playing the "man of peace," and the next the tough leader. He wanted to send McCloy back to Washington scared and pleading for a compromise. The following day Kennedy's envoy cabled from the U.S. embassy in Moscow that, although "the situation is probably not yet ripe for any negotiation," it is "too dangerous to permit it to drift into a condition where lack of time for balanced decision-making could well lead to unfortunate action."[57] "I know he [McCloy] reported accurately," Khrushchev smugly commented to the Communist leaders.[58]

The Warsaw Treaty allies gathered in secrecy in Moscow on August 3. A transcript of Khrushchev's speeches from the meeting was found in the party archives in Moscow in the summer of 1993. Khrushchev's message was rambling and incoherent. The situation was slippery, he told the group, but as long as he, Khrushchev, was in control, it could be managed. True to his nature, Khrushchev waved the bloody shirt of revolutionary rhetoric. "I wish we could give imperialism a bloody nose!" he said to the Communist leaders. He even compared the risk of signing a separate peace treaty with the GDR to the risk that the Bolsheviks had taken in 1917 when they seized power in Russia.[59]

In his speech of July 25, Kennedy "declared war on us and set down his conditions," said Khrushchev. He told the audience how McCloy (who of course had known about the speech, being a messenger from the White House) first pretended he had not heard about it, but then tried to convince the Soviet leader that "Kennedy did not mean it, he meant to negotiate."[60] Khrushchev shared with the Communist leaders his confusion about the seemingly odd nature of U.S. politics. The American state, he said, is "barely governed." Kennedy himself "hardly influences the direction and development of policies."[61] Power relations in the United States were characterized by chaotic infighting among factions, where the "faction of war" was still greater than the "faction of peace." "Therefore anything is possible in the United States," Khrushchev admitted. "War is . . . possible. They can unleash it. The situation in England, France, Italy, and Germany is more stable." Khrushchev even had to admit, contrary to much of his previous rhetoric, that German militarism was much more under check than U.S. militarism![62]

The new U.S. president was no match for the huge military-industrial complex that his predecessors had nourished. Khrushchev expressed sympathy for the young, inexperienced Kennedy, who, for all his best intentions, was "too much of a lightweight." The U.S. state *(gosudarstvo)* "is too big, powerful, and it poses certain dangers."[63] At this moment Khrushchev seriously questioned whether Kennedy would be able to keep "the dark forces" of his country at bay while he negotiated for a long truce.

Khrushchev's uncertainty about Kennedy's power and character did not stop him from employing his two favorite political tools—nuclear brinkmanship and strategic deception. On July 10 Khrushchev hosted a meeting for the leaders and scientists of the Soviet nuclear complex to announce an end to the nuclear moratorium. To those who listened to the First Secretary, the decision was unmistakably linked to the Berlin crisis. The best scientists from Arzamas-16, Yakov Zeldovich and Andrei Sakharov, informed Khrushchev that they were eager to test a "new idea," a 100-megaton thermonuclear bomb. Khrushchev jumped at the suggestion. "Let this terrible weapon become the Sword of Damocles hanging over the imperialists' necks," he said to the assembly.[64]

The image of a superbomb and nuclear missiles as the ultimate expression of Soviet power had always remained of paramount importance to the Kremlin ruler, along with the arguments borrowed from the arsenal of Marxist-Leninist "teaching" on revolutionary change. He once told the U.S. ambassador that if he got down on his knees and prayed in a "Holy Orthodox Church" for peace, the West would not believe him. But if he walked toward the West with "two missiles under my arms, maybe I'd be believed."[65] After Vienna the Chairman made the nuclear threat his ultimate argument. From July on he methodically shocked NATO diplomats in Moscow by briefing them in a casual manner on how many hydrogen bombs he thought would be assigned to the task of burning their home countries to the ground. Khrushchev relied on the West Europeans' outrage at the idea that they might be forced to die for the sake of two and a half million Germans in Berlin.

Khrushchev also turned the summer of 1961 into a hot season for the KGB masterminds of deception. On July 29, KGB Chief Shelepin sent a memorandum to the Chairman containing a vast array of proposals to create "a situation in various areas of the world that would favor dispersion of attention and forces by the United States and their satellites, and would tie them down during the settlement of the question of a German peace treaty and West Berlin." The multifaceted deception campaign, Shelepin claimed, would "show the ruling circles of Western powers that unleashing a military conflict over West Berlin could lead to the loss of their position not only in Europe but also in a number of Latin American, Asian, and African countries."[66]

The first part of the plan ought to have appealed to Khrushchev's sense of solidarity with "wars of liberation." Shelepin advocated measures "to activate by the means available to the KGB armed uprisings against pro-Western reactionary governments." The subversive activities began in Nicaragua, where the KGB plotted an armed mutiny through an "internal revolutionary front of resistance," in coordination with Castro's Cubans and with the "Revolutionary Front Sandino." Shelepin proposed making "appropriations from KGB funds in addition to the previous assistance of 10,000 American dollars for the purchase of arms." The plan also envisaged the instigation of an armed uprising in El Salvador, and a rebellion in Guatemala, where guerilla forces would be given $15,000 to buy weapons.[67]

The campaign extended to Africa, to the colonial and semicolonial possessions of the British and the Portuguese. The KGB promised to help organize anticolonial mass uprisings of the African population in British Kenya and Rhodesia and Portuguese Guinea, by arming rebels and training military cadres.[68]

In the Far East, Shelepin suggested "bringing to the attention of the United States, through KGB channels, information about existing agreements among the USSR, the PRC, the DPRK [North Korea], and the DRV [North Vietnam] about joint military actions to liberate South Korea, South Vietnam, and Taiwan should armed conflict erupt in Germany."[69]

Shelepin planned "to cause uncertainty in the government circles of the United States, England, Turkey, and Iran about the stability of their positions in the Middle and Near East." He offered to use established KGB connections with the head of the Kurdish guerillas, Mulla Mustafa Barzani, "to activate the movement of the Kurdish populations of Iraq, Iran, and Turkey for creation of an independent Kurdistan that would include the provinces of the aforementioned countries." Barzani would be given the necessary aid in arms and money.[70]

Shelepin's grand plan was also directed against NATO installations in Western Europe and aimed "to create doubts in the ruling circles of Western powers regarding the effectiveness of military bases located on the territory of the FRG and other NATO countries, as well as in the reliability of their personnel." Shelepin contemplated working with the secret service of the GDR and Czechoslovakia to carry out "active measures . . . to demoralize" military servicemen in the FRG (by agents, leaflets, and brochures), and even terrorist attacks on depot and logistics stations in West Germany and France.[71]

Shelepin suggested intensifying a campaign of deception aimed at exaggerating the Soviet strategic arsenal. He wanted to convince the West that Soviet land forces were now armed with new types of tanks "equipped with tactical nuclear weapons"; that there was "considerable advancement in the readiness of rocket forces and . . . an increased number of launching pads—resulting from the Soviets' supply of medium-range solid-fuel ballistic missiles and the transfer of launching pads from stationary positions to mobile launching positions on highways and railroads, which secure high maneuverability and survivability"; that the Soviet Navy had acquired a number of nuclear submarines with solid fuel "Polaris" missiles; that the Soviet air defense and Air Force had grown much stronger.[72]

Khrushchev approved the report and sent it to his deputy Frol Kozlov. On August 1 it was, with minor revisions, passed as a Central Committee directive. The KGB and the ministry of defense were also instructed to work out more "specific measures and present them for consideration" to the Party Presidium.[73]

The well-documented campaign of brinkmanship and disinformation that this directive supported reveals that Khrushchev took very seriously the military might of the United States and NATO. At the same time, the Soviet leader was acting in the belief that the blend of disinformation, nuclear bluffing, and the utilization of the "movements of national liberation" around the globe, including in the United States' backyard, Latin America, would create a preponderance of power for the USSR and convince the enemy to back away from a final showdown. This combination of cynical manipulation and revolutionary readiness to stand up to the imperialists produced a very dangerous moment. Khrushchev's rhetoric and the KGB disinformation activities were designed to deter the West, but instead they sowed the seeds of mistrust and uncertainty in a dangerously polarized world. They exacerbated the danger of armed conflict in Central Europe, not to mention the wars by proxies in the Third World.[74]

On August 13, two and a half million West Berliners and a quarter of a million East Berliners who crossed the internal border every day were separated by barbed wire from East Berlin. A month later workers began to build a cement wall. For a while Khrushchev basked in the seeming success of the operation. The U.S. administration resisted the public uproar over the Wall, especially in West Germany, and did nothing. The disintegration of the GDR, economically and politically, was stopped and reversed. There was no longer the possibility of a quiet *Anschluss* of the GDR to West Germany. Adenauer's foreign policy, based on this tacit expectation, lost credibility among the Social-Democratic opposition leaders, including the mayor of West Berlin, Willy Brandt. They were angry at the United States, which seemed to pay only lip service to the idea of German reunification, and in reality was relieved when the Wall was built. Soon the opposition leaders began to contact Soviet representatives and search for new ways of dealing with the problems of the dismembered nation.[75]

Kennedy did, indeed, feel that the Wall was preferable to a war over Berlin.[76] He authorized his Secretary of State, Dean Rusk, to begin secret communications with Gromyko on the Berlin situation. Khrushchev noticed and appreciated this move. During his vacation in September he summoned Bolshakov, his GRU messenger, to his Black Sea resort in Pitsunda and handed him a long letter addressed to Kennedy, with a modified proposal for the "free city" of West Berlin. Khrushchev suggested that secret correspondence could be a means for ending the stalemate on the German question. He invited Kennedy to Moscow. Kennedy's reply came on October 16, shortly before the Party Congress. He declined Khrushchev's proposal, but agreed to continue a personal exchange of views through a confidential channel.[77]

The construction of the Wall, for all the vitality it gave to the Soviet sphere of influence in Central Europe, remained an ideological and propaganda defeat for Khrushchev in the struggle "between the two systems." The Soviet leader could not admit this, however, particularly not on the eve of the Twenty-second Party Congress, where he wanted to renounce Stalin's cult, bury the ghosts of the "antiparty group," and respond in kind to the challenge from Beijing. For this reason, Khrushchev still pretended that the Wall was not an alternative to, but just a preparation for, the inevitable signing of a separate peace treaty with the GDR.[78]

Late in October, when the Party Congress approved Khrushchev's leadership and the Chinese delegation left Moscow in anger and dismay, Khrushchev delayed the deadline indefinitely. But not before he dramatically confronted American hard-liners. On October 21, when the Party Congress was still in full swing, Deputy Secretary of Defense Roswell Gilpatric announced to the public that the "missile gap" was a myth, and, in fact, the United States had vast strategic superiority over the Soviet Union. Simultaneously, Khrushchev learned from intelligence sources that Lucius Clay, a veteran of the Berlin blockade, whom Kennedy appointed as a commander of the Western garrison in Berlin, was making preparations to tear down the barbed wire between the Western and Eastern parts of the city.

In Khrushchev's eyes, this was a game between him and "the dark forces" to see who would call the other's bluff first. He informed his diplomatic advisors that he was sending Marshal Ivan Konev, a fierce and trigger-happy war veteran, to Berlin with "full authority" to fight back, if the Americans dared to storm the border.[79] In reality his instructions to the military were much less belligerent. American military jeeps should be let through the border, he said, as they had been before the Wall. And if the Americans moved in tanks, Soviet tanks should block their advance right across the border. Khrushchev seemed to be sure that the Americans would not risk a military clash over Berlin, and he was right. The famous tank stand-off lasted at Checkpoint Charlie on Friedrichstrasse for two days, where the Wall still had not been erected. Finally Kennedy "blinked": there was some kind of exchange (which is still classified) between him and Khrushchev, probably through Robert Kennedy and Bolshakov. The president was looking for a way out of the dangerous impasse. Khrushchev ordered Konev to pull the Soviet tanks back. The American tanks followed their example within twenty minutes.[80]

Khrushchev also sent a powerful nuclear signal to Washington at 11:32 A.M. on October 30, when a 50-megaton nuclear bomb was dropped from a Soviet plane at an altitude of 7.5 miles over the testing site in Novaya Zemlya. The flash of light from the monstrous explosion was visible at a distance of 700 miles, and a gigantic, swirling mushroom cloud rose as high as 50 miles. The bomb had been designed to yield only half of its potential. Had its maximum yield been tested, it would have generated a firestorm engulfing an area larger than the state of Maryland. When the telegram proclaiming the success of the test arrived at the Kremlin, Khrushchev and Minister of Defense Malinovsky presented this news to the delegates of the Party Congress as the Soviets' "crushing" response to the imperialists' talk of strategic superiority.[81]

The Berlin crisis of 1961 did not convert Khrushchev to the idea of a permanent truce. While Kennedy's ministers and advisors rehashed the prospect of a nuclear response to the Soviet blockade of West Berlin, no one in the Kremlin was thinking about the possibility of nuclear war.[82] This certitude was not undermined by Khrushchev's episodic uneasiness about the confusion of American politics. The events of the crisis did not shake his belief in his ability to use deliberate pressure and even brinkmanship in his diplomacy. With his approval, the KGB and the Ministry of Defense continued their operations directed at the "strategic deception" of the West.[83] He still regarded himself as capable, as John Foster Dulles had been, of reaching the brink without falling over it. Equally important, Khrushchev had still not made up his mind about Kennedy. Was he an educated wimp or a challenger capable of being Khrushchev's partner? In August Khrushchev told his Communist allies that, frightened by the possible consequences of the crisis, "people close to Kennedy are beginning to pour cold water [on the engine of military escalation] like a fire brigade."[84]

But the signs of American belligerence in October made Khrushchev think that perhaps the military, which was very influential in Washington, was putting some pressure on Kennedy. In a second personal letter to Kennedy, the First Secretary expressed the hope that the two would "plant a new orchard" on the ashes of the Cold War.[85] But what if "the dark forces" in the Pentagon, the CIA, and the State Department drew Kennedy into another Cold War adventure? The more Khrushchev thought about it, the more he worried that the hard-liners in America would take revenge by invading Cuba. And so he fixed his eyes on the island in the Caribbean Sea that could drastically change the geopolitics of the Cold War.

## The Missiles in Cuba, the Riots in Russia

Operation "Anadyr," the code name for deployment of the Soviet missiles in Cuba that led to the showdown with the United States in October 1962, proved to be the most dangerous moment of the Cold

War. Most details about the Soviet side of the crisis became known only recently, when ex-Soviet generals declassified the operation, which promised to deliver troops and missiles to the "Island of Liberty." They described in great detail how the ships deluded their American escorts, what the soldiers on those ships and in Cuba wore, ate, spoke, and wrote in their letters.[86] The cost of the operation, according to CIA estimates, amounted to one billion 1962 U.S. dollars.[87]

Many still cannot grasp the fact that the lives of millions of Americans, Soviets, and indeed all people hung on one single thread, controlled by two mortal men, John F. Kennedy and Nikita Khrushchev.[88] Had either one of them pulled too hard, the crisis could have escalated into war. It is no surprise that the reasonable Harvardian felt he was on the brink of an abyss. What is remarkable, however, is that Khrushchev, the gambler of the decade, panicked and capitulated.

Why did Khrushchev send missiles across the ocean to America's backyard and put his purported "partner," Kennedy, in such a terrible bind? Recently, an American scholar has suggested that "his motivations for this initiative, like the motivations for his threats against Berlin, should not be attributed to any single policy aim; more likely, he intended the move as a bold stroke that would alleviate pressures from several directions."[89] At the time of the crisis there were two interconnected problems being considered by the American government and experts: strategic balance and Berlin. Many in the Kennedy administration, especially the Pentagon's civilian officials, were obsessed with numbers of missiles, comparison of strategic arsenals, and war scenarios, a consequence of the major shift from Eisenhower-Dulles's "massive retaliation" to the new doctrine of "flexible response." They believed the Soviet leader had decided to rectify in one move the "missile gap" in favor of the Soviet Union and, once in a position of strength, to push the Western powers out of West Berlin. There could be only one response to this challenge: to liquidate the Soviet missiles in Cuba or force the Soviets to remove them under the threat of global war.[90]

This analysis underestimates two aspects of Khrushchev's beliefs. First, he was convinced that there was no third alternative between "peaceful coexistence" and all-out war between the Soviet Union and "the imperialists." Therefore, he saw the size of both sides' nuclear arsenals as important, but not crucial, to tipping the scale in international relations, not to mention the historic competition of the two systems. Second, he was fervently dedicated to preserving revolutionary Cuba against a possible U.S. invasion for the sake of the victorious march of communism around the globe and Soviet hegemony in the Communist camp. It was not the temptation to use the Cuban Revolution as a chance to improve the Soviet position in the strategic balance of the superpowers that brought the Soviet missiles to San Cristobal, Cuba; rather, it was a new strategic capability that emboldened Khrushchev to launch an overseas operation to save the Cuban Revolution.[91]

The reverse would have been true of Stalin and Molotov: they would not have cared about the revolutionary process in the Caribbean unless it were directly linked to an increase in Soviet might. It is very hard to imagine that, from the "realist" and cynical platform, either Stalin or Molotov would have risked confrontation thousands of miles away from the fortress of the USSR. But Khrushchev was doing exactly that and even relished in advance how the United States would have to swallow "the same medicine" it had for a decade administered to the Soviets—enemy missiles in its backyard. Khrushchev believed that because the Americans had extended their influence into Europe, the Soviets had the right to extend theirs into the zone of the Monroe Doctrine.[92]

Despite the firm belief of an entire generation of American policymakers and some prominent historians that Khrushchev's gamble in Cuba was actually aimed at West Berlin, there is little evidence of that on the Soviet side. True, many facts seem to indicate that Khrushchev and those around him used the Soviet leverage over West Berlin to deter the Kennedy administration from a Cuban invasion. During the crisis, there was pressure on Khrushchev to use this leverage. The new Soviet ambassador, Anatoly Dobrynin, recommended from Washington that the leader "hint unequivocally to Kennedy" about "our possible repression of Western powers in West Berlin (as a first step—the organization of a blockade of ground access routes, with aerial communication left intact, in order not to create a pretext for an immediate clash)." The KGB chief in Washington, Feklisov (Fomin), actually used this leverage when he talked with John Scali, his channel to the White House.[93] But we also know that when Vassily Kuznetsov, the first deputy of Gromyko, a cautious and pragmatic diplomat, reminded Khrushchev of this possibility at the height of the crisis, the Chairman barked at him: "We are here trying to get ourselves out of this *avantyura* [reckless gamble] and now your are pulling us into another one!"[94]

What pushed Khrushchev into his worst *avantyura* was not the pragmatic search for the well-being of the Soviet empire. On the contrary, it was his revolutionary commitment and his sense of rivalry with the United States. From this perspective, the Cuban adventure was linked to the Berlin crisis. Khrushchev's fear of losing Cuba was similar to his concern about the survival of the GDR. The geopolitical stake of the Soviets in East Germany was incomparably higher than that in Cuba, but what mattered for Khrushchev was to preserve the impression of communism on the march, which, in his opinion, was critical to dismantling the Cold War on Soviet terms. The loss of Cuba would have irreparably damaged this image. It would also have meant the triumph of those in Washington who insisted on the roll-back of communism and denied any legitimacy to the USSR. Khrushchev decided to leap ahead, despite the terrible risk, as he had done at the Twentieth Party Congress, revealing Stalin's crimes against the Party and communism. In September, when Troyanovsky was alone with Khrushchev in his study, he told the Chairman that the Cuban enterprise was far too risky. "It is too late to change anything," said the leader of the USSR. Troyanovsky felt that his boss was a man driving out of control, gathering speed, and rushing God knows where.[95]

Khrushchev's daredevil attitude was not completely shared by many other Soviet elites. Even earlier, in July 1961, Oleg Penkovsky had reported to his Western handlers that higher Soviet officials grumbled: "If Stalin were alive, he would do everything quietly, but this fool is blurting out his threats and intentions and is forcing our possible enemies to increase their military strength."[96] The new gamble was "quiet," but the risk was enormous. Mikoyan and Gromyko were aware of it and initially voiced their concern that the reaction of the United States to the introduction of Soviet troops and missiles in Cuba would be fierce. The question of nuclear war was even raised at the Council of Defense, the special standing body consisting of key Politburo members and government officials. Khrushchev knew that he was taking a huge responsibility and wanted to share some of it with his subordinates. All members of the Politburo and the Secretariat took part in the final meeting of the Defense Council on May 24, 1962, when the minister of defense, Malinovsky, laid out the details of "Anadyr." On the list of speakers were Kozlov, Brezhnev, Mikoyan, Georgi Voronov, Dmitry Polyansky, Otto Kuusinen. The Chairman made everyone sign the directive to start the operation. When some members of the Secretariat of the Central Committee argued that they just did not know enough about the problem, Khrushchev dismissed their objections. They had to sign off, too.[97]

The blueprints for Operation "Anadyr" were still on the table of the Presidium-Politburo when Khrushchev's prestige, which had already fallen among the military and other elite cadres of the Party and the state, faltered among the Soviet general public, including workers and peasants. On May 31 the Soviet Chairman spoke on the radio announcing that the state-controlled prices on meat, sausages, and butter would be doubled. At the same time the minimal individual plan for workers was increased, in effect reducing the guaranteed disposable income of millions. After three years of rhetoric about "overtaking the United States" and the soon-to-be abundance of goods, the economic (one is tempted to say imperial) overstretch was catching up with Khrushchev. Earlier he had saved the Ulbricht regime by sending carloads of Soviet food to the GDR. Now he had to ask his subjects to diminish their food rations.

A close aide tried to persuade Khrushchev not to stick out his neck, to order someone else to make the announcement. Khrushchev answered: If not me, who else will take the heat? This was the same Khrushchev who had risked denouncing Stalin before the Communist universe and its enemies, and sending missiles across the Atlantic Ocean. An inveterate fighter for the future of utopia, he dismissed the pragmatic advice, at great cost to his political future.[98]

The announcement produced widespread discontent. Leaflets and graffiti protesting the cutbacks appeared in and around Moscow, Leningrad, and many industrial centers of Ukraine, Georgia, Latvia, Southern Russia, the Urals, and Siberia. The KGB reported to the Politburo numerous calls to strike. In many instances protesters were outraged over economic aid to Soviet satellites and "progressive regimes." In their reports the KGB informers preserved some voices of that moment:

*Azovsky, worker from Moscow:* Our government sends out gifts, feeds others, and now we have nothing to eat, so they are trying to solve their problems at our expense.

*Zaslavsky, actor:* We will not die, but we should be ashamed to look abroad. If they could only stop boasting that we are overtaking America.

*Kolesnik, driver from Archangel:* Life goes from bad to worse. Kennedy will be doing the right thing if he drops an atom bomb on the Soviet Union.[99]

The accountants of the KGB computed that "in the first half of 1962, 7,705 anti-Soviet leaflets and anonymous letters were distributed . . . twice as many as in the analogous period of 1961." Most of them were aimed at Khrushchev. "After a long period," the impassive KGB record read, "anonymous documents again are distributed praising the participants of the antiparty group. There is a dramatic increase in the number of letters containing terrorist intentions regarding the leadership of the Party and the government."[100]

On June 1–3 in Novocherkassk, the former capital of the Don Cossacks that was now occupied by machine-building plants, the Soviet Communist regime was overthrown by thousands of workers, women, and children. The crisis of the Kremlin's legitimacy was so acute that Khrushchev sent his most able troubleshooter, Anastas Mikoyan, and the second-ranking man in the Party, Frol Kozlov, to Novocherkassk. Soon half of the Politburo gathered there hastily, along with senior KGB officials. Early on the morning of June 2, Kozlov called Khrushchev, who had stayed in Moscow, and received his permission to fire on the rebellious crowd.[101]

That same day Khrushchev was on the radio again, addressing a meeting of Cuban and Soviet youths. He wandered back and forth, from the imperialists threatening the Castro regime to the Novocherkassk rioters, whom he denounced (without mentioning the place of the riot) as "antisocial elements who spoil our lives," as "grabbers, loafers, and criminals." He called for the employment of Civil War methods to deal with dissenters. By then Mikoyan and Kozlov had failed to talk the people of Novocherkassk into submission. Khrushchev must have learned that the workers of the Novocherkassk locomotive plant had painted a chilling slogan on one of their engines: "Khrushchev's flesh for goulash." That day the Red Army moved its tanks into Novocherkassk and restored order. Twenty-three protesters, most of them aged eighteen to twenty-five, were shot dead, and eighty-seven were seriously wounded. Hundreds were arrested; a dozen "instigators" were court-martialed and shot.[102]

The man in charge of the Novocherkassk massacre was the commander of the North Caucasian military district, Army General Issa A. Pliyev. Born on the Caucasian borderland and resembling a character from Leo Tolstoy's *Cossacks,* this brave cavalryman had led many fierce charges against the Germans and the Japanese. Despite being a trained cavalryman, Pliyev was a man of great reserve. He waited for Khrushchev's personal authorization to move tanks and armored personnel carriers into Novocherkassk, and then he held back fire, waiting for another order from Khrushchev to shoot. When the order was issued, his troops dispersed the crowd with machine guns.[103]

When the czarist officers would put down peasant revolts, the czars would promote them to higher ranks or called them to the Court. A grateful Khrushchev had a better idea for Pliyev. He appointed him head of the provisional contingent of Soviet troops in Cuba, seven thousand miles from Moscow. The Soviet leader personally instructed Pliyev, who knew more about horses than missiles, what to do with the latter once they were deployed on the island. The rocket division of medium-range R-12s and R-14s (some of which Khrushchev had once compared to "sausages") could be used only on the personal order of Nikita Sergeevich. Khrushchev told Pliyev he could use the tactical missiles, called *Luna* (Moon), exclusively in the event of a U.S. sea landing, to prevent the larger missiles from falling into the enemy's hands.[104] When the crisis erupted and the U.S. joint chiefs of staff proposed a preventive strike on the Soviet installations in Cuba, Pliyev had a nuclear option at his discretion.[105]

The guns of Novocherkassk and the missiles of San Cristobal entrusted to the general by Khrushchev were the means of deterrence and retaliation. Did the Chairman realize that the latter could trigger nuclear war? If he did, then the chances of failure in Novocherkassk and Cuba must have seemed infinitesimal to him. He did not believe that Novocherkassk could be a harbinger of the fall of the Soviet order. Nor did he imagine that six *Luna* missiles in Pliyev's hands could bring about a nuclear holocaust. The whole experience of the Berlin crisis assured him he could stay in control. But this time he pushed his luck too far.

Again, as after the revolutions of 1956 in Poland and Hungary, Khrushchev had to build back the muscles of the Stalinist state he sought to dismantle. On July 19 he ordered the KGB to mobilize its reserves for possible future riots on a large scale. Special rapid deployment forces were to be created for "guarding official buildings, communications, banks, and prisons." The situation was so serious that the KGB leadership solemnly "warned" all its officials that the "stepping up of the struggle" against anti-Soviet elements did not mean the reversal of de-Stalinization.[106]

Khrushchev's attention was also riveted on several Soviet ships in the open sea. Those ships were transporting 42 missiles to Cuba and 42,000 Soviet officers and soldiers to protect them. In a separate operation, 3 ships, *Indigirka, Alexandrovsk,* and *Archangel,* set out from the Kola Peninsula in the North with a cargo of 164 nuclear charges on board. They passed the British Isles and the Bahamas, and on October 4 the first of the ships, *Indigirka,* arrived at Port Mariel in Cuba.[107]

In September, just as one year before, the Chairman was vacationing at his Black Sea resort and fetched the GRU colonel Bolshakov, his messenger to the Kennedy brothers. This time the Chairman wanted to know if the Americans would go to war with Cuba in the near future. Bolshakov said it was a possibility. "We in Moscow want to know everything," urged Khrushchev. But he did not tell Bolshakov (or Ambassador Dobrynin in Washington) anything about the missiles on their way to Cuba. Perhaps he even used Bolshakov's channel to mislead Kennedy.[108] Some later thought that Khrushchev's belief in secrecy was misplaced. But it is unimaginable that the Soviet leader, given his view of Kennedy and his political surroundings, could even contemplate a public announcement that he was sending missiles and thousands of Soviet troops over an ocean dominated by the U.S. Navy.[109] His plan was to announce his "deterrent" to Kennedy only after the November mid-term elections in the United States. Even if there were tremendous pressure on Kennedy to do something, Khrushchev reasoned, the president had enough common sense to be daunted by the threat of nuclear war over Cuba.[110] According to the schedule, the missiles were to be operational on October 25–27. Just two weeks before that, a tropical storm in the Caribbean subsided, clouds melted over San Cristobal, and a U-2 flew over unfinished Soviet missile installations. Khrushchev was not alarmed. He was so sure of his success that he did not even bother to tell Gromyko, who flew to New York to attend the U.N. General Assembly, to prepare convenient explanations in case the whole plot became public.

Gromyko met with Kennedy and repeated the official lie: there were not and would not be any "offensive weapons" in Cuba. Kennedy already knew about the missiles but gave no sign of it. Gromyko and Khrushchev felt encouraged: the U.S. president, whatever he knew about the Soviet operation, seemed to prefer keeping silent about the build-up in Cuba until the mid-term elections were over. The Soviet foreign minister reported to Khrushchev that "the situation was satisfactory in general." "The government, as well as the ruling American circles as a whole, are astonished at the boldness of the action of the Soviet Union in rendering assistance to Cuba." And in these new circumstances, he concluded, "a military *avantyura* of the United States against Cuba is next to impossible."[111] The minister reported what Khrushchev wanted to hear.

While Soviet soldiers in Cuban T-shirts worked around the clock to finish the rocket positions, and some higher officers in charge of "Anadyr" played tennis or hid from the scorching sun, the crisis exploded.

## The Moment of Truth

The "black week" of October 1962 forced Khrushchev to make a fateful choice: between hegemony in the Communist world and peaceful accommodation with the United States. Before the crisis the Soviet Chairman believed the two goals were compatible, provided that the United States respected Soviet nuclear power. But during the crisis Khrushchev lost his faith in the nuclear deterrent: chaos and uncertainty overpowered the audacious ruler. Vassily Kuznetsov, the same diplomat who had proposed a counterattack in Berlin, later remarked that "Khrushchev shit his pants."[112] In his first letters to Kennedy (October 23 and 24), Khrushchev tried to cover his dismay with unabashed bravado, although he was gripped with fear as he read KGB reports from Washington informing him that the U.S. military was pushing Kennedy toward a military showdown in the Caribbean.[113] He believed that Kennedy was too weak to stem the onslaught of the hard-liners. Some Soviets, including Ambassador Dobrynin (who replaced Bolshakov as chief messenger), attempted to get a "fair deal" from Kennedy by trading the Soviet missiles for the U.S. missiles in Turkey. But as soon as the brink seemed too close, Khrushchev was prepared to accept any terms of settlement.[114]

This happened for the first time on the night of October 25–26, when Khrushchev received erroneous intelligence reports that the U.S. invasion of Cuba was imminent. The next morning Khrushchev dictated a conciliatory letter to Kennedy that did not mention the missiles in Turkey. We must prevent the invasion, and later return to the missiles in Turkey, he explained to Kuznetsov and the other assistants who stayed with him on the night watch in the Kremlin. This "later" came in a few hours. As soon as Khrushchev realized that the reports were false and must have been planted deliberately by the Americans, he sent another letter to Washington in which he insisted on inclusion of the Turkish missiles in any deal over Cuba. For a moment, pride and arrogance again took the upper hand over prudence: he could not look weak in the eyes of his subordinates.

But on October 27 another war scare gripped Khrushchev. Through a failure in the chain of command, Soviet air defense shot down a U-2 over Cuba. Major Rudolf Anderson, Jr., the pilot, was killed. Cries of revenge reverberated all over the United States. Castro shouldered responsibility for the shooting. But at that moment Khrushchev understood that nuclear war could result from a simple accident. He told Malinovsky to send a ciphered message to Pliyev categorically forbidding any use of nuclear weapons. At the same time, at his request twenty-three key Kremlin officials, including the Presidium and Secretariat members, gathered in his dacha at Novo Ogarevo and stayed there all day and night discussing what to do if an American attack were imminent.

The final wave of panic shook the Kremlin on Sunday, October 28, when Khrushchev feared that Kennedy would make another speech on national television at noon, announcing the U.S. invasion of Cuba. As it turned out, this was just a replay of his quarantine speech. Khrushchev immediately accepted Kennedy's terms—a unilateral withdrawal of "all Soviet offensive arms" from Cuba. A courier was sent from Novo Ogarevo at breakneck speed, beating the Moscow traffic, to the State Broadcasting Committee to announce the concessions on the radio. At 6:00 P.M. Moscow time, only two hours before the rebroadcasting of Kennedy's address, the whole world was listening to Khrushchev's submission. The Soviet military immediately began to dismantle missile sites and prepare them for the long trip back to the Soviet Union (nuclear warheads for missiles were evacuated later, by December 1). In his haste Khrushchev even forgot to consult with Castro.[115]

In an instant the Soviet leader seemed to have forgotten how fiercely he had just recently reacted to minor slights to Soviet honor. He also forgot about the pride and prestige of Castro and his revolutionary friends. He acted in the chillingly "realist" manner of Stalin: walking over the egos and bodies of those who had helped in the implementation of his grandiose designs, but then just happened to be in the way of retreat. Khrushchev further infuriated Castro when he single-handedly made two more concessions to Kennedy: he withdrew from Cuba Soviet IL-28 tactical bombers, his "comradely aid" to the Cuban army, and finally all Soviet troops with the exception of one training brigade. Only on November 20, after the Soviet withdrawal was complete, did Kennedy order the lifting of the U.S. blockade around Cuba. He reneged on his promise, made through confidential channels, to make a public pledge of nonaggression against Cuba. The Irishman from Boston left the boastful Russian from Kalinovka hanging on the ropes.

The making and handling of the Cuban missile crisis tarnished Khrushchev's reputation among well-informed members of the Soviet elite, and certainly among his allies. The rift between the Soviet military corps and Khrushchev, produced by his drastic cuts in early 1960, had grown deeper during the hasty withdrawal of Soviet troops from Cuba. Khrushchev ordered his military to put all missiles on the decks of Soviet ships so that U.S. pilots could count them. For the Soviet generals and admirals this was a humiliation they could not forgive Khrushchev even many years later.[116]

Humiliated, Castro refused to cooperate with the U.N. inspectors who had to supervise the dismantlement of Soviet installations in Cuba. A new fissure appeared in the Soviet alliance system: relations with Cuba deteriorated to such an extent that Castro was thinking about taking the side of Beijing in the great opposition within the Socialist camp. Khrushchev sent Mikoyan to Havana just as Mikoyan's wife, Ashkhen, was dying in a hospital in Moscow. Khrushchev wanted Mikoyan to show Castro his secret correspondence with Kennedy during the crisis and tell him that, in his view, the crisis ended in a "victory of socialism"—Cuba was saved, and the crisis did not end in a nuclear war that might have led to the destruction of not only capitalist but Communist countries.[117]

But the flowery rhetoric about "proletarian solidarity" rang hollow in the ears of the Cubans, who were disgusted at finding themselves impotent onlookers in the superpowers' deadly waltz. The fiery Ernesto (Che) Guevara felt betrayed. He told Mikoyan that the outcome of the crisis "baffled" the revolutionaries of Latin America, and had already led to their split into pro-Moscow and pro-Beijing factions. In his opinion, "two serious mistakes"—bargaining with the United States and retreating openly—undercut good chances of "seizing power in a number of Latin American countries."[118] Fidel Castro also barely concealed his rage at being treated like a puppet in the grand game. He wondered wryly why Moscow swapped the Soviet missiles for the U.S. missiles in Turkey, not for an American base in Guantanamo. Ten days later, when Mikoyan came to tell him about Khrushchev's decision to take IL-28 bombers back, Castro interrupted his long-winded explanation: "Why explain the rationale? Just say bluntly what the Soviet government wants."[119]

Another fissure appeared in the Warsaw Treaty, as a result of Khrushchev's failure to inform East European leaders about "Anadyr." A Rumanian ambassador secretly told Washington officials that his government dissociated itself from Khrushchev's actions that had just led to the confrontation and similar steps that might produce another such crisis in the future.[120]

In light of these developments, the Soviet leader chose what seemed to be the only strategy: he posed as a great "peacemaker" and tried to utilize the new chemistry between Kennedy and himself for the benefit of "peaceful coexistence." If you cannot defeat the enemy, try to win him over. Khrushchev quickly forgot his ambivalence about Kennedy. He convinced himself that Kennedy was a leader of world stature, wise and magnanimous, in a word, "another Roosevelt." In Vienna he had shrugged off Kennedy's lecture on "miscalculations," believing that it would force him to swallow Soviet missiles in his backyard. Now he praised Kennedy's reserve. "My role was simpler than yours," he wrote in a letter to the U.S. president, "because there were no people around me who wanted to unleash war."[121]

In the aftermath of the crisis, Khrushchev felt an irresistible temptation, in a sort of catharsis, to offer Kennedy a grand deal. He commented with satisfaction that Nixon, Kennedy's strongest Republican rival, was "pinned down to the mat" in California's elections, and predicted that Kennedy would be reelected to a second term. "Six years in world politics is a long period of time," he wrote, "and during that period we could create good conditions for peaceful coexistence."[122] The Soviet Chairman consistently referred to three issues that were high on his postcrisis agenda: a nonaggression pact between NATO and the Warsaw Treaty Organization, disarmament, and a German peace treaty. This was his "orchard" to replace the "poisonous plants" of the Cold War.

Quietly, Khrushchev abandoned his grandiose plan for general and complete disarmament, which had been designed to win propaganda contests, and returned, instead, to the old Soviet proposals that Moscow had put forward on May 10, 1955—the first serious production of the emerging Soviet arms control bureaucracy. The Soviet leader also suggested reaching a quick agreement on the banning of all nuclear tests, although he still resisted the idea of on-sight inspections as a channel for Western espionage.[123]

As Khrushchev was retreating in the fields of the Cold War, he tried to save face. In his inimitable style—naiveté blended with arrogance—he proposed that the superpowers jointly pressure Chancellor Adenauer. "Should you and we—two great states," Khrushchev wrote only twenty days after the U.S.-Soviet clash, "submit, willingly or unwillingly, our policy, the interests of our states, to an old man who both morally and physically has one foot in the grave?"[124]

The Soviet leader continued to believe that cooperation with the United States and the support of revolutionary regimes were not mutually exclusive goals. Khrushchev, in correspondence with Kennedy, called the Cuban revolutionary leaders "young, expansive people; in a word, Spaniards," but he took very seriously their questioning his credentials as the world Communist leader.[125] The prospect of Cuba's defection to the side of Beijing could strengthen China's claim to hegemony in the Communist world and was simply intolerable to the Chairman. During the next several months the Soviet leader made it one of his priorities to mend fences with Castro, and convince him of his sincere friendship—with vodka, bear hugs, a visit to the supersecret silo of intercontinental ballistic missiles, and more billions of rubles from the Soviet state coffer.[126] The comparative reading of Khrushchev's letters to Kennedy and Castro provides a fascinating insight into the widening gap between the revolutionary legacy and pragmatic considerations in the mind of the Kremlin leader. He tried with obvious sincerity to convince the Cuban leader that Soviet economic and military assistance to Cuba was dictated by "internationalist duty," not by "mercantile goals." He mentioned more than once that Soviet leaders understood the Cuban Revolution as a validation of Russia's revolutionary experience—it was part of the same struggle against the West; it reflected the same difficulties in creating a "new society." In a spirit of Communist camaraderie, Khrushchev wrote to Castro: "What could be more sublime, from the point of view of fulfilling proletarian internationalist duties, than the actions undertaken by our country on behalf of another Socialist country, on behalf of the common Marxist-Leninist cause?"[127]

This battle cry was more faint than those Khrushchev had uttered before he built the Wall in Berlin. In his unique way, he believed he could make the objectives meet under a happy banner of "peaceful coexistence." To Kennedy he proposed cooperation to defuse the potential sources of the Cold War crises. At the same time he believed this cooperation could be beneficial to the Communist cause. In the short term, it would safeguard revolutionary Cuba and, possibly, would lead to U.S. recognition of the People's Republic of China. In the long term, it would promote stability for economic competition between the two systems—a competition in which (as Khrushchev never doubted) socialism would prevail. In his correspondence with Castro the Soviet leader explained that peaceful coexistence with the United States allowed them to gain time. "And gaining time is a very important factor," he explained, "because the correlation of forces is everyday more favorable to socialism."[128] Before his own colleagues, hastily convened to approve the deal with Kennedy, Khrushchev again used the term "peace of Brest-Litovsk," a notorious treaty that Lenin had signed with the German militarists in 1918 to win time for world revolution.[129]

By the end of the crisis, Khrushchev began to lean on the idea of joint management of the world with the United States much more than his Communist creed and his—albeit very crude—sense of social justice permitted. The Cuban missile crisis did not convert him from the Communist Saul into the peace-building Paul. Still, Khrushchev's truce with Kennedy after the crisis was not a marriage of convenience, as had been the agreement between Stalin and Hitler in 1939. It was not another "Yalta," like Roosevelt's concessions to Stalin in 1945. It was a step toward peace, not war. The taming of the Cold War, fifteen years after its inception, and almost a decade after Stalin's death, finally happened.

## The Heirs to the "Long Truce"

Two years later, Khrushchev's colleagues conspired against him and ousted him from power. The plot's masterminds belonged to the new, post-Stalin nomenclature; they represented the highest echelons of party and state office-holders who quickly became the established Soviet elites. "The old man" (Khrushchev celebrated his seventieth birthday in April 1964) seemed to be the last obstacle on their way to a comfortable, stable existence, free from purges, the reshuffling of cadres, and risky international games. The rest of society, recalls Khrushchev's son Sergei, was equally tired of the old leader and his incessant, heavy-handed experimentation in search of a "Communist paradise." One group of conspirators emerged around Leonid Brezhnev—Mikhail Suslov, Nikolai Podgorny, and Dmitry Polansky. These men enjoyed the support of regional party secretaries, marshals, and leaders of the military-industrial complex, whose careers had started with Stalin's "revolution from above" and skyrocketed during the Second World War. Another group consolidated itself around Alexander Shelepin, the former head of the Young Communist League and the KGB, who relied on younger cadres recruited into the Party's nomenclature after the Second World War.[130]

At the heart of the anti-Khrushchev conspiracy was the new elites' yearning for personal security; their focus, therefore, was on domestic politics. Most of them had experienced the shock of the German invasion in 1941–1942 and lived for years in the shadow of American nuclear superiority. As a result, they also strongly believed that their personal security was linked to the prevention of war and the creation of a more stable and predictable international environment. Yet only the most pragmatic, cynical, and sophisticated among them understood that in order to reach this goal they should curb the domain of the revolutionary-imperial paradigm, which complicated any accommodation with the United States.

Among the conspirators, Shelepin seemed to be close to this understanding. At the secret session of the Presidium that convened in October 1964 to relieve Khrushchev of his duties, Shelepin attacked the key moments of Khrushchev's foreign policy. As Shelepin recalled a quarter of a century later, he "pointed out big foreign policy mistakes, as a result of which our country was on the brink of war three times in one decade (the Suez, Berlin, and Cuba crises)." Shelepin blamed Khrushchev for sabotaging the Paris summit in May 1960, particularly for his demand that Eisenhower bring excuses for the U-2 episode. "There will always be spies," he recalled, "and the same [demand] could be made of Eisenhower in another place and at another time."[131]

Khrushchev, in his reply, defended his confrontational tactics in his relations with the West. He said that he "was and would be proud" of his role in the Suez crisis. As for the Berlin crisis, he admitted that he had "made a mistake" in underestimating Western resolve to stay in West Berlin, but added that he "was proud that everything had ended so well."[132] The majority of the Presidium understood all too well, however, that serious discussion of the fallen leader's "mistakes" could lead to some fundamental questions about the nature and direction of Soviet foreign policy. In particular, the debates about the Cuban missile crisis would reopen fresh wounds to Soviet prestige, and could even, to everyone's horror, leak outside the Soviet Union. Consequently, any critic could be blamed then or later for exposing Soviet weaknesses to the enemy.

No wonder that, by tacit agreement, the Kremlin leadership silenced criticism of Khrushchev's foreign policy at the Plenum of the Central Committee, the representative forum of the party and state elites. Mikhail Suslov, who was a keynote speaker at the Plenum, praised the "correct line of the Party in international affairs."[133] As after Stalin's death, the new leadership preferred to preserve and protect the continuity of Soviet foreign policy and, implicitly, the foundation of this policy—the revolutionary-imperial paradigm.

The new leaders chose Khrushchev's son-in-law, Alexei Adzhubei, as a scapegoat. They branded his trips abroad and, indirectly, the personal diplomacy of Khrushchev as "damaging." The anti-Khrushchev attack was primarily targeted at his agricultural policies, restructuring of the party apparatus, and other domestic issues. "In his instructions to agricultural workers, Khrushchev leaped from one extreme to another," said Suslov. "His was not a leadership, but simply a merry-go-round."[134]

Privately, the members of the new Soviet elite must have used the same words when recalling the dramatic events of both the Berlin crisis and the Cuban missile crisis. Khrushchev had endangered their lives without any real necessity. Taking Khrushchev's settlement with the United States with a sigh of relief, they nevertheless detested the way it was reached. During the Cuban missile crisis the USSR had to pay for Khrushchev's ideological nostalgia. The Soviet elites' mixed feeling of survival and humiliation made them later spend huge resources on reaching strategic parity with the United States and building a "blue-water" navy—to undercut the lasting image of U.S. superiority.

Khrushchev's successors abandoned his rabid revolutionarism, but by no means did they abandon his dream of emerging from the Cold War as a superpower second to none, the leader of the growing Communist camp. This time, however, the changing of the guard in the Kremlin propelled to the top not the strongest among equals, but rather the blandest and weakest. Shelepin, who under different circumstances could have continued the trend toward the realpolitik that was aborted with the downfall of Beria and Malenkov, lost miserably to Leonid Brezhnev, who was supported by the vast majority of Soviet elites. Years later, long a pensioner, Shelepin remarked that Brezhnev was good-for-nothing in comparison with his predecessor: "Khrushchev was a character with a political gift, intuition." The former omnipotent KGB chairman and party secretary complained that letting Brezhnev take the helm was "a very big mistake by the Party."[135]

The departure of the last man from Stalin's cohort, the establishment of the conservative Soviet elites, and the end of the most terrifying period in the Cold War ushered in a new era for the Soviet leadership. Khrushchev's heirs felt increasingly safe under the protection of thousands of nuclear weapons, and longed for domestic and foreign legitimacy and recognition. The Cold War was at a standstill, a "long truce" dawned, and the character of the Kremlin's leader no longer seemed to be a matter of life and death for the elites of the USSR.

# Postmortem: Empire without Heroes

The leaders of the Kremlin waged the Cold War in the hope of preserving the Soviet empire, the empire that millions of Soviet people had defended with their lives during the Second World War. Yet almost as soon as the last of these leaders died, the Cold War ended and the Soviet Union itself collapsed.

It is now clear that the generational change in the Soviet leadership strongly influenced the history of the Cold War. The generation that had grown up under the merciless hand of Joseph Stalin was trained to lead the Soviet Union to victory. But its successors came to realize, first grudgingly, that there could be no military victory in the Cold War. After decades of rivalry, the new elites conceded to themselves that the USSR had lost the political and economic competition with the United States and could not continue unreformed under the burden of its own inner contradictions.

For those who conceive of the despotic Soviet regime as static, consistent, and expansionist at all times, we have argued otherwise. Like all political systems, even the one built by Stalin had a human face and limitations. Three major factors shaped the Kremlin's view of the post–World War II order and later of the Cold War: the personalities of the key Soviet leaders, their peculiar blend of ideological and geopolitical motivations, which we have labeled the revolutionary-imperial paradigm, and the policies of the West, primarily the United States.

Of these three factors, the Soviet leadership was by far the most dynamic and variable. Soviet leaders possessed impressive qualities and suffered terrible delusions and weaknesses. They could be brutal and unreasonable but also prudent, cautious, and patient. Raised in an autocratic state, they were influenced by its dictates and in turn challenged them. Not all of the leaders were die-hard dogmatics. Their whims and innovations, complexes and phobias, shaped a malleable view of the Cold War from the Soviet shore. Sometimes they even enjoyed more flexibility in their roles than their Western counterparts. Yet the messianic prescriptions of revolutionary-imperial ideology loomed large in the political environment in which Soviet leaders struggled, rose, and fell. Ideology was neither the servant nor the master of Soviet foreign policy. But it was the *delirium tremens* of Soviet statesmen, the core of the regime's self-legitimacy, a terrifying delusion they could never shake off.

It is tempting to lay total blame for the Cold War on the delusions of Stalin and his lieutenants. A closer look at the Cold War from the Soviet side reveals, however, that they were not the only culprits in the conflict. We cannot disregard other, complex factors, such as the crass nature of power politics, choices of U.S. and British policy-makers, and the deeper causes of hostility and mistrust between dictatorship and democracy in an uncertain world. Stalin, notwithstanding his reputation as a ruthless tyrant, was not prepared to take a course of unbridled unilateral expansionism after World War II. He wanted to avoid confrontation with the West. He was even ready to see cooperation with the Western powers as a preferable way of building his influence and solving contentious international issues. Thus, the Cold War was not his choice or his brainchild.

The arrangements at Yalta for Eastern Europe, and the critical victories of the Red Army in the Allies' ultimate triumph over the Axis powers, led Stalin to expect that the cooperative regulation of international relations would be possible. For this, by 1945, Stalin was ready to diminish the role of ideology in his postwar diplomacy with the West to a minimal level. He was ready to observe the limits on Soviet spheres of influence in Europe and Asia, and he was prepared to keep in power "transitional" regimes in Eastern Europe that would be acceptable to the West. That did not mean that Stalin would cease to be the dreadful dictator and the pontiff of the Communist world. It did mean, however, that the Kremlin leader believed he needed years of peace in order to bring the USSR from its wartime destruction, when six out of the fifteen Soviet republics were occupied and devastated by the Germans, to the status of an economic and military superpower.

After the death of Roosevelt, which signaled the end of the wartime bonds of amity between Stalin and the Western leaders, and particularly after the atomic bomb was dropped on Hiroshima, Stalin began to have increasing doubts about postwar cooperation. His probes in Turkey and in Iran, "gray areas" between the Soviet and British zones of influence, had evoked fierce resistance on the part of the United States. Step by step, the revolutionary-imperial paradigm began to resurface in Stalin's thought and actions.

Stalin's foreign and domestic priorities were limited in nature, and yet they led to tension with the West. Stalin wanted not only to restore order and strength to a country torn apart by war, but also to maximize the fruits of victory. He refrained from flying red flags all over the Soviet spheres of domination, yet he was determined to exploit Central Europe for his rearmament program. The brutality of the Soviet regime and Stalin's cruel, scheming, and maniacally suspicious nature, which served these ends, looked first unacceptable and then sinister to the West.

Stalin's road to the Cold War, in the years from 1946 to 1950, was strewn with miscalculations. He did not want to provoke American and British "imperialism," yet he overreacted to any perceived threat of it in Germany and in Eastern Europe. In response to the Marshall Plan, Stalin began to consolidate a Soviet security zone in Eastern Europe by ruthless police methods and intensive Communist propaganda. Trying to stop Western separatist policies in Germany, he triggered the Berlin blockade crisis. Stalin's biggest diplomatic triumph in the chilling years after the Second World War was an alliance with Communist China in February 1950. Yet this strategic success did not survive the Korean conflict, where the Kremlin leader grossly misjudged the international situation and, by sanctioning the North Korean aggression, subjected the Koreans, his Chinese ally, and the rest of the world to a bloody and protracted war that contained the real danger of a global conflagration. In short, Stalin's postwar foreign policy was more defensive, reactive, and prudent than it was the fulfillment of a master plan. Yet instead of postponing a confrontation with the United States and gaining a much-needed respite for recovery, he managed to draw closer to it with every step. The explanation of this seeming paradox can best be found in Stalin's mentality as well as in his increasing reliance on the logic and dictates of the revolutionary-imperial paradigm to which he had committed himself.

It is no secret that Stalin ran Soviet foreign policy more or less single-handedly, without the benefit of advice from his close circle of friends. Molotov and Zhdanov, two oligarchs at Stalin's side, never acted on their own while Stalin was alive. These men, their perceptions and activities, point to the real source of the impressive achievements, yet ultimate folly and debacle, of Soviet foreign policy under Stalin—the totalitarian way in which it was conceived, directed, and implemented. Molotov's diplomacy was exactly what Stalin hoped Soviet diplomacy could be: a combination of blunt pressure and exploitation of "imperialist contradictions" among Western countries. Molotov was always prudent and even more cautious than Stalin. He had a strong sense of how far the Soviets could probe Western strength and resolve. For Molotov, the growth of Soviet power was the most certain and infallible road toward the global triumph of the Communist order. Disastrous miscalculations, policies that cost millions of lives, were just tactical slips en route to ultimate triumph and mattered little to him. After Stalin's death, Molotov became the guardian of the revolutionary-imperial paradigm that his predecessor and idol sought to shape and that was embodied in the conquests of the USSR during the Second World War.

Zhdanov's activities testify to his subservient role as a keeper of ideological orthodoxy in Soviet foreign policy under Stalin. Zhdanov cannot be associated with a "party diplomacy" or anything distinct from the diplomacy of Stalin and Molotov. All attempts of the Communist party's propaganda staff to expand its responsibilities came to naught in the face of Stalin's personal diplomacy. Zhdanov, however, became one of the main and most talented players, when in the summer of 1947 Stalin decided to use Communist propaganda and ideology to legitimize Soviet control over Eastern Europe and resuscitate the Comintern's "fifth column" throughout Western Europe. Through Zhdanov, Stalin announced the concept of "two camps" and accepted the worldview of Manichean bipolarity long before this bipolarity acquired its deadly nuclear reality. Until his premature death, Zhdanov remained an obedient keeper of the ideological goals that only Stalin had the power to implement.

Stalin cast a long shadow on the Cold War from the Soviet shore and on the foreign policy of his successors. The challengers to Stalin's legacy, Beria, Malenkov, and finally Khrushchev, fought against the West, and had to face the formidable military threat of the United States, rearmed and bristling with nuclear weapons as a result of Stalin's provocations in Berlin and Korea. But, equally, they fought against Stalin's immortality, the enormous burden of protecting his legacy inside the Soviet Union and worldwide. All their strategies for détente with the United States were severely constrained and eventually shattered by America's hard line, but also by the determination of the vast majority of Soviet elites to prevent a roll-back of Soviet power and influence in the world. The only possible course, in this climate, was to achieve a truce with the West from a position of strength.

It is tempting to argue that, in this sense, the Cold War tensions and the revolutionary-imperial paradigm, shared by most of Stalin's successors, fed off each other. The magnitude of the U.S. challenge served to unite the Soviet leadership and elites in their determination to spare no resources in fending off the war threat. Also, it may explain why, long after Stalin was dead, there was no outbreak of mass discontent in the Soviet Union over the issue of "guns versus butter": most in that generation of Russians, Ukrainians, Byelorus, and others, having experienced the Nazi invasion, did not question the Kremlin's military and foreign policies, so long as they appeared to provide protection, however illusory, against the nightmare of another major war.

Yet, Stalin's death changed much in the Cold War from the Soviet side. None of his successors could afford to wage the Cold War with the same large-scale mobilization of resources. Nor were most of them as ruthless as Stalin had been. The stories of Beria's and Malenkov's brief rise to power provide new pages in this little-known story. Both men were prepared to reduce Soviet external commitments as much as possible and to wed a future Soviet foreign policy, not to ideological messianism, but to a Soviet nuclear arsenal. Beria, czar of the Soviet atomic project, was the first among Stalin's lieutenants to become aware of the awesome power of nuclear energy. Malenkov was the second, and it was he who made the first far-reaching conclusion about the futility of nuclear conflict that threatened the whole ideological construct of Soviet foreign policy. Beria and Malenkov quickly lost power in the Kremlin, however, and the possibility of the transformation of Soviet foreign policy to a more pragmatic and less messianic direction immediately after Stalin's death was never fulfilled. Neither of them had the personality or the credentials required to bring such a great task to fruition.

In Beria's case, perhaps a unique one, an attempt to make an important concession in Germany ran aground because the majority of Stalin's successors and other influential Soviet elites did not want to sacrifice Stalin's empire or their ideological messianism. They perceived their main adversary, the United States, to be guided by its own blend of messianic anti-communism and national arrogance, to which the Soviet Union could not submit. It is unlikely in this atmosphere of mistrust and competition after Stalin's death that there were significant "missed opportunities" to avoid the nuclear arms race and the Cold War enmity, as some have claimed. Again, responsibility for the continuation of the Cold War should not rest solely on Stalin's successors; rather, it should be shared with Eisenhower, Dulles, and others in the West whose priorities had always been to increase Western military strength and stare the Soviets into unilateral concessions.

Important changes were occurring in the USSR after Stalin's death. Revolutions dissipate their energies as their elites age and die off. Like the rings of a tree, the younger the elites of a revolutionary regime are, the further they are from the original shoot. Revolutionary regimes pass through inexorable phases of youth, maturity, and declining old age, and their adherents do the same. In the 1930s Stalin destroyed a revolutionary core of the Soviet leadership and filled the hollow space with followers of his personality cult. Molotov and Zhdanov in particular acted as Stalin's clones in foreign policy and international propaganda. But after Stalin's death this void was reopened and other vital forces further from the center of the Soviet power structure flowed in. Khrushchev was able to leap to power over the heads of the younger, more pragmatic, and cynical pretenders, Beria and Malenkov, and became the last "true believer." Only after his ouster did the vestiges of Stalin's leadership wane.

Nikita Khrushchev was simultaneously driven by a new-found Soviet pragmatism and by a personal commitment to the revolutionary-imperial paradigm. In his more reasonable, pragmatic incarnation, he conclusively ended Stalin's reign of terror. He allowed new Soviet elites to emerge and consolidate into a permanent strata of the political hierarchy. And he recognized the bipolarity of the nuclear world, as a source of new opportunities for Soviet foreign policy, but also as an ultimate constraint.

At the same time the vocation of Khrushchev as ideologue, and his fiery but uncultivated persona, greatly helped aggravate the Cold War in the late 1950s and early 1960s. As the first undisputed Soviet leader after Stalin, Khrushchev adapted the revolutionary-imperial paradigm to the age of nuclear missiles and anticolonial movements. His grandstanding performance with the U.S. leadership and solemn commitment to support "movements of liberation" with Soviet power led him to the brink of war during the Cuban missile crisis, a significant watershed in the Cold War.

A major and unexpected schism inside the Communist camp was a major result of the Cold War. Communist China had been developing autonomously and out of sync with the USSR. The rise and fall of the Sino-Soviet "friendship" was not caused by a personal feud between Mao and Khrushchev, but the two personalities did matter. They represented two postrevolutionary powers in transition. In Khrushchev's case, it was the transformation of Stalin's regime into a deeply conservative society, ruled by increasingly pragmatic, cautious, and self-interested elites. In Mao's case, it was the transformation of a revolutionary process into the institutions of an authoritarian state. The main features of the Cold War, a nuclear deadlock and the necessity of détente with the West, finally caused the Sino-Soviet split. This split ushered in a new stage of the Cold War—with greater geopolitical diversity, new ideological winds, and a new generation of statesmen.

Khrushchev's tumultuous statesmanship came to an abrupt halt shortly afterward. His successor, Leonid Brezhnev, was the incarnation of the postrevolutionary new elites whose expansionism was driven by great power commitments (and often by stupidity and fear), rather than by ideology, ruthless determination, and cunning. Though the revolutionary-imperial paradigm was still alive, leading to the Soviet engagement in Angola, the Horn of Africa, and finally in Afghanistan, it was in its death throes.

The gallery of portraits of Soviet "statesmen" in the Cold War pales in comparison with the one of American and West European "wise men," even if one makes allowance for a tinge of adulation and triumphalism in the case of the latter. The authors must admit that, in addition to the intellectual and investigative energy required, this book demanded a great deal of reserve. There is no blade of historical analysis sharp enough to separate the pragmatism of Soviet leaders (or their idealism) from their butchery, or their bold foreign policy steps from their moral and intellectual debauchery. All these leaders reflect the shades of Soviet totalitarian darkness.

Yet the truth is that these men did not have a master plan for global domination. The most loathsome of them were closer to a cynical realpolitik than to the idea of world revolution. Stalin did not mind pushing the United States from Eurasia and dominating the whole continent, but his resources were limited and forced him to be a prudent, cautious practitioner of geopolitics. And Khrushchev, who threatened to "bury" the capitalist West, in reality had much more immediate interest in the confirmation of the USSR's great power positions through détente, and in fending off ideological challenges from the leadership of Communist China.

The Soviet leaders' caution and sense of limits helped at times to prevent the escalation of the Cold War into a global carnage. But their ideological arrogance and penchant for associating the national interests of their country with the logic of the revolutionary-imperial paradigm more than once brought the world perilously close to deadly confrontation. It also pushed the USSR down the road to economic overextension and, ultimately, imperial fatigue and decay. There is no one on the Soviet side to praise. Stalin's empire left no heroic statesmen to posterity. It did, however, leave a rubble of shattered peace and savaged biographies to a potentially democratic Russia. Through this rubble looms a ray of hope for Russia and the world. Whatever may happen behind the walls of the Kremlin in the future, the generation of Stalin's followers that inhabited it, and the revolutionary-imperial paradigm that guided them in the past, are dead. They will not come back.

Notes

Index

★

# Notes

Preface

1. John Lewis Gaddis, *The Long Peace: Inquiries into the History of the Cold War* (New York: Oxford University Press, 1987).

2. Among the most authoritative volumes based on pre-glasnost information are: Adam B. Ulam, *Expansion and Coexistence: The History of Soviet Foreign Policy, 1917–1973,* second edition (New York: Praeger, 1974); *The Rivals: America and Russia since World War II* (New York: Viking Press, 1971); *Stalin: The Man and His Era* (New York: Viking Press, 1973); Vojtech Mastny, *Russia's Road to the Cold War: Diplomacy, Warfare, and the Politics of Communism, 1941–1945* (New York: Columbia University Press, 1979); William Taubman, *Stalin's American Policy* (New York: Norton, 1982). Books from the glasnost era include Robert Conquest, *Stalin: Breaker of Nations* (London: Weidenfeld and Nicolson, 1991); Adam Ulam, *The Communists: The Story of Power and Lost Illusions, 1948–1991* (New York: Macmillan, 1992); Walter Laqueur, *Stalin: The Glasnost Revelations* (New York: Macmillan, 1990), chap. 9; Michael Beschloss, *Kennedy and Khrushchev: The Crisis Years* (New York: Harper-Collins, 1991). The most recent volumes based fully or partly on material from the newly opened archives are Norman Naimark, *Russians in Germany: The History of the Soviet Zone of Occupation, 1945–1949* (Cambridge, Mass.: Harvard University Press, 1995); and David Holloway, *Stalin and the Bomb: The Soviet Union and Atomic Energy, 1939–1956* (New Haven: Yale University Press, 1994). An impressive array of new documents from the former Eastern bloc and scholarly comments on them have been published on a regular basis since 1992 in *The Bulletin of the Cold War International History Project,* ed. James G. Hershberg, Woodrow Wilson International Center for Scholars, Washington, D.C., as well as in Working Papers of the same project.

3. Dmitri Volkogonov, *Stalin: Triumph and Tragedy* (London: Weiden-

feld and Nicolson, 1991), a translation from the Russian original published in 1988 by Novosti Publishers.

Prologue: The View from the Kremlin, 1945

1. See Robert C. Tucker, "Sovietology and Russian History," in *Post-Soviet Affairs*, vol. 8 (July–September 1992), pp. 175–196.

2. See a good compilation of various viewpoints in Thomas G. Paterson and Robert J. McMahon, *The Origins of the Cold War*, third edition (Lexington, Mass.: D. H. Heath and Co., 1991).

3. For a comparison between Lenin's thinking and "hegemonic realist theory," see Robert Gilpin, *War and Change in World Politics* (New York: Cambridge University Press, 1981), pp. 91–95; William Curti Wohlforth, *The Elusive Balance: Power and Perceptions during the Cold War* (Ithaca: Cornell University Press, 1993), p. 35.

4. For alternative definitions of ideology, see Karl Marx and Frederick Engels, *Selected Works*, vol. 1 (Moscow: Progress Publishers, 1973), pp. 16–80; Karl Mannheim, *Ideology and Utopia: An Introduction to the Sociology of Knowledge* (London: Routledge, 1991); Louis Althusser, *For Marx* (London: Allen Lane, 1969); Raymond Aron, *The Opium of the Intellectuals* (London: Greenwood, 1977); Leon P. Baradat, *Political Ideologies* (Englewood Cliffs, N.J.: Prentice Hall, 1984).

5. Geoffrey Parker, *Western Geopolitical Thought in the Twentieth Century* (New York: St. Martin's Press, 1985); Wohlforth, *The Elusive Balance*, pp. 18–31.

6. See this view in Karl Marx, *Capital* (New York: Vintage Books, 1977), pp. 91–93.

7. Natalia Lebedeva and Mikhail Narinsky, "Rospusk Kominterna [Dissolution of the Comintern]," *Mezhdunarodnaia zhizn*, no. 5 (1994), pp. 80–88; and "Rospusk Kominterna v 1943 godu [Dissolution of the Comintern in 1943]," *Mezhdunarodnaia zhizn*, no. 7–8 (1994), pp. 33–40. For debate about the Western response to Stalin's security demands during the war, see Amos Perlmutter, *FDR and Stalin: A Not So Grand Alliance, 1943–1945* (Columbia, Mo.: University of Missouri Press, 1993), pp. 211–217; Lloyd G. Gardner, *Spheres of Influence: The Great Powers Partition Europe, from Munich to Yalta* (Chicago: Ivan Dee, 1993); Warren Kimball, *The Juggler: Franklin Roosevelt as a Wartime Statesman* (Princeton: Princeton University Press, 1994), pp. 84–104, 191–198.

8. David Reynolds, ed., *The Origins of the Cold War in Europe: International Perspectives* (New Haven: Yale University Press, 1994), p. 2.

9. See also Andres Stephanson's chapter in Reynolds, *The Origins of the Cold War in Europe*, pp. 24–25.

1. Stalin: Revolutionary Potentate

1. Dmitri Volkogonov, *Stalin: Triumph and Tragedy* (London: Weidenfeld and Nicolson, 1991), p. 5; Robert C. Tucker, *Stalin in Power: The Revolution from Above, 1938–1941* (New York: Norton, 1990), p. 3; Quotations from George F. Kennan, *Memoirs, 1925–1950* (Boston: Little, Brown and Co., 1967), p. 279; Valentin Berezhkov, *Kak ia stal perevodchikom Stalina* (Moscow: DEM, 1993), p. 214 [translated and published as *At Stalin's Side* (Secaucus, N.J.: Carol Publishing Group, 1994)].

2. A. T. Rybin, *Riadom s Stalinim* [At Stalin's side: memories of Stalin's bodyguard] (Moscow, 1994); see also his *Stalin i Zhukov* [Stalin and Zhukov] (Moscow, 1994); see Walter Laqueur, *Stalin: The Glasnost Revelations* (New York: Scribner's, 1990), p. 150, for Stalin's health after the war; see Dmitri Volkogonov, *Lenin: A New Biography* (New York: The Free Press, 1994), for Stalin's vacations after the war.

3. Stalin to Eketerina Dzhugashvili, 14 March 1934, Stalin's personal collection in the Archive of the President of the Russian Federation (hereafter APRF), f. 45, op. 1, d. 1549, p. 46, in *Iosif Stalin v obiatiiakh semyii: Iz lichnogo arkhiva* [Joseph Stalin in his family's embrace: from the personal archive] (Moscow: Rodina, Edition Q, 1993), p. 17.

4. See these "images" of Stalin in Adam Ulam, *Stalin: The Man and His Era* (New York: Viking Press, 1973); Robert Conquest, *Stalin: Breaker of Nations* (London: Weidenfeld and Nicolson, 1991). See Laqueur, *Stalin;* Robert C. Tucker, *Stalin as Revolutionary: A Study in History and Personality, 1879–1929* (New York: Norton, 1973); see also his *Stalin in Power.*

5. Leon Trotsky, *Stalin* (Benson, Vt.: Chalidze Publications, 1985); Roy Medvedev, *Let History Judge: The Origins and Consequences of Stalinism* (New York: Vintage Books, 1973); Volkogonov, *Stalin;* Daniil Andreev, *Roza Mira* [The rose of the world] (Moscow, 1993), pp. 229–247.

6. Karl Marx and Frederick Engels, *The Communist Manifesto,* in *Selected Works,* vol. 1 (Moscow: Progress Publishers, 1973), pp. 124–125, 137.

7. J. V. Stalin, "About the Communist Party of Poland," 3 July 1924, in *Sochineniya* [Works] (Moscow: Politizdat, 1947), vol. 6, p. 265.

8. *XIV s'ezd Vsesoyuznoy Kommunisticheskoy partii (b): Stenographicheskiy otchet* [Stenographic report on the fourteenth congress of the communist party of the USSR] (Moscow-Leningrad, 1926), p. 26.

9. Archive of the Foreign Policy of the Russian Federation, Moscow (hereafter AVP RF), f. 100, op. 12, d. 4, papka 14.

10. Yuri Modin, with Jean-Charles Deniau and Aguieszka Ziarek, *My Five Cambridge Friends: Burgess, Maclean, Philby, Blunt, and Cairncross, by Their KGB Controller* (New York: Farrar, Straus and Giroux, 1994);

Harvey Klehr, John Earl Haynes, and Fridrikh Igorevich Firsov, *The Secret World of American Communism* (New Haven: Yale University Press, 1995); *Neizvestnaia Rossiia: XX vek* [Unknown Russia: the twentieth century], vol. 2 (Moscow: Istoricheskoiie naslediie, 1992), p. 323; Alexander Feklisov, *Za okeanom i na ostrove: Zapiski razvedchika* [Overseas and on the island: notes of an intelligence officer] (Moscow: DEM, 1994), pp. 105–106.

11. Interview with Mikhail A. Milstein, Moscow, 31 January 1990.

12. Mikhail Lozovsky to Zhdanov, late October 1946, Russian Center for the Preservation and Study of Documents of Contemporary History (hereafter RTsKhIDNI), f. 17, op. 125, d. 391, pp. 140–141.

13. *Rodnik,* no. 4 (1989).

14. Younger Communists did not welcome this. Interview with Boris N. Zanegin, 12 October 1990, Moscow.

15. Felix Chuev, *Sto sorok besed s Molotovym: Iz dnevnika F. Chueva* [One hundred and forty conversations with Molotov: from the diary of F. Chuev] (Moscow: TERRA, 1991), p. 90. For the English-language version see *Molotov Remembers: Inside Kremlin Politics. Conversations with Felix Chuev,* ed. Albert Resis (Chicago: Ivan Dee, 1993).

16. Sergei N. Goncharov, John W. Lewis, and Xue Litai, *Uncertain Partners: Stalin, Mao, and the Korean War* (Stanford, Calif.: Stanford University Press), pp. 2–6.

17. Felix Chuev heard this story from A. I. Mgeladze, the former first secretary of the Communist party of Soviet Georgia. Molotov confirmed and augmented it. See Chuev, *Sto sorok besed,* p. 14.

18. This fact is cited in Tucker, *Stalin in Power,* p. 351.

19. Modin, *My Five Cambridge Friends,* pp. 78, 79–80.

20. Volkogonov, *Stalin,* p. 410.

21. Oleg Rzheshevsky, "Vizit A. Idena v Moskvu v dekabrie 1941 g. Peregovori s I. V. Stalinim i V. M. Molotovym [The talks between A. Eden with Stalin and Molotov in Moscow in December 1941]," *Novaia i noveishaiia istoriia,* no. 2 (1994).

22. Leo Tolstoy, *Sobranie sochinenii* [Collection of works], vol. 20 (Moscow, 1964), p. 94.

23. An entry of 22 June 1939 from the diary of A. Soloviev, *Neizvestnaia Rossia: Vek XX,* vol. 4, pp. 203–204.

24. Tucker, *Stalin in Power,* p. 3; Ronald Grigor Suny, "Making Sense of Stalin: Some Recent and Not-So-Recent Biographies," *Russian History,* 16, no. 2–4 (1989), pp. 435–448.

25. *Pravda,* 21 December 1994.

26. Karen Horney, *Neurosis and Human Growth* (New York-London, 1950), p. 87.

27. Svetlana Alliluyeva, *Dvadtsat' pisem k drugu* [Twenty letters to a friend] (Moscow, 1990), pp. 130, 181, 183.

28. Joseph Stalin, "Pismo com. Demianu Bednomu [A letter to com. Demian Bedny]," in *Sochineniya* (Moscow: Politizdat, 1947), vol. 6, p. 273.

29. Tucker, *Stalin in Power*, pp. 51–52.

30. Stalin said this on 14 May 1947. Konstantin Simonov, "Glazami cheloveka moego pokoleniia: Razmishleniia o I. V. Staline [With the eyes of a person of my generation: reflections on I. V. Stalin]," *Znamia*, no. 3 (1988), pp. 59–60.

31. Chuev, *Sto sorok besed*, p. 75.

32. Andrei M. Alexandrov-Agentov, *Ot Kollontai do Gorbacheva* [From Kollontai to Gorbachev] (Moscow: Mezhdunarodniie otnosheniia, 1994), p. 39.

33. Boris Bazhanov, *Vospominaniia byvshego sekretaria Stalina* [Memoirs of Stalin's former secretary] (St. Petersburg, 1992), p. 56; Volkogonov, *Stalin*, pp. 101–124.

34. Modin, *My Five Cambridge Friends*, pp. 79–80, 131, 137.

35. Sergo Beria, *Moi otets—Lavrentii Beriia* [My father—Lavrenty Beria] (Moscow: Sovremennik, 1994), p. 234.

36. Modin, *My Five Cambridge Friends*, p. 115.

37. Strobe Talbott, ed., *Khrushchev Remembers* (Boston: Little, Brown and Co., 1970), p. 299.

38. Alan Bullock, *Stalin and Hitler: Parallel Lives* (New York: Knopf, 1992).

39. Horney, *Neurosis*, p. 176.

40. Milovan Djilas, *Conversations with Stalin* (New York: Harcourt, Brace, Jovanovich, 1962), pp. 73, 74.

41. Chuev, *Sto sorok besed*, p. 67.

42. Alliluyeva, *Dvadtsat' pisem k drugu*, p. 176; Chuev, *Sto sorok besed*, p. 271.

43. Vladimir Karpov, *Marshal Zhukov: Opala* [Zhukov in disfavor] (Moscow: Veche, 1994), pp. 80–83.

44. Elena Zubkova, "Obshchestvennaia atmosphera posle voiny (1945–1946) [The postwar social mood (1945–1946)]," *Svobodnaia mysl*, no. 6 (1992), pp. 8–9.

45. Georgi Kornienko, *Kholodnaia voina: Svidetelstvo ieie uchastnika* [The Cold War: a witness's memoir] (Moscow: International Affairs, 1994), p. 18.

46. Jerrold Schecter and Anatoly Luchkov, eds., *Khrushchev Remembers: The Glasnost Tapes* (Boston: Little, Brown and Co., 1991), p. 144.

47. Molotov, in conversation with Chuev, confirmed this episode. See Chuev, *Sto sorok besed*, p. 103.

48. Hugh D. Phillips, *Between the Revolution and the West: A Political Biography of Maxim M. Litvinov* (Boulder, Colo.: Westview Press, 1992); Vojtech Mastny, "The Cassandra in the Foreign Office," *Foreign Affairs*, vol. 54 (January 1976); Chuev, *Sto sorok besed*, p. 98.

49. Ivan Maisky, *Memoirs of a Soviet Ambassador: The War, 1939–43* (New York: Scribner's, 1967), pp. 378, 380; Litvinov to Molotov, 3 August 1943, AVP RF, f. 06, op. 6, papka 14, d. 149a, pp. 1–8, 27–29; Alexei Filitov, "Problems of the Postwar Order in Soviet Conceptions of Foreign Policy during the Second World War," a paper presented at the Nono Colloquio Internationale di Cortona, "The Soviet Union and Europe in the Cold War (1943–1953)," Cortona, Italy, 23–24 September 1994, pp. 3–5.

50. I. Maisky to V. M. Molotov, 11 January 1944, AVP RF, f. 06, op. 6, papka 14, d. 145, pp. 1–41.

51. AVP RF, f. 06, op. 6, papka 14, d. 145, pp. 3, 4–5, 8–9, 23–26, 34–40.

52. Protocol no. 6 of the commission on the preparation of peace treaties and the postwar settlement (hereafter the Litvinov Commission), July 1944, AVP RF, f. 06, op. 6, papka 14, d. 141, pp. 23–24, 35.

53. M. M. Litvinov, "Zapiska o mezhdunarodnoi organizatsii bezopasnosti [Memorandum about an international security organization]," July 1944, AVP RF, f. 06, op. 6, papka 14, d. 144, p. 22.

54. M. M. Litvinov, "O perspektivakh i vozmozhnoi baze Sovetsko-Britanskogo sotrudnichestva [On the prospects and a possible foundation for Soviet-British cooperation]," 15 November 1944, AVP RF, f. 06, papka 14, d. 143, pp. 53–55.

55. AVP RF, f. 06, papka 14, d. 144, pp. 22, 28, 44.

56. AVP RF, f. 06, op. 6, papka 14, d. 145, pp. 11, 15, 40–41.

57. I. Maisky, G. Arkadiev, "Osnovniie linii reparatsionnoi programmi SSSR [The main guidelines for the reparations program of the USSR]," AVP RF, f. 06, op. 7, papka 18, d. 183, pp. 54, 62; AVP RF, f. 06, op. 7, papka 18, d. 181, p. 51; Maisky to Stalin, 19 December 1944, AVP RF, f. 06, op. 6, papka 17, d. 169, pp. 73–74; Filitov, "Problems of the Postwar Order," p. 26. For Molotov's statement about the "pittance," see Chuev, *Sto sorok besed*, p. 87.

58. AVP RF, f. 06, op. 6, papka 14, de. 145, pp. 27, 39.

59. *Molotov Remembers*, p. 51.

60. *Foreign Relations of the United States: The Conferences at Malta and Yalta, 1945* (Washington, D.C.: GPO, 1955), pp. 378, 973–974, 982, 984, 976; Mastny, *Russia's Road*, pp. 239–266; Remi Nadeau, *Stalin, Churchill, and Roosevelt Divide Europe* (New York: Praeger, 1990), pp. 133–146.

61. Nadeau, *Stalin, Churchill, and Roosevelt Divide Europe*, pp. 141–143.

62. Kornienko, *Kholodnaia voina*, pp. 18, 21–22; Kornienko heard about

Stalin's positive attitude toward the U.N. Charter from Andrei Gromyko, then Soviet ambassador to the United States. Interview with Kornienko, 22 November 1989, Moscow.

63. I. V. Stalin, "Rech na predvybornom sobranii izbirateley Stalinskogo izbiratelnogo okruga g. Moskvy [Speech at a meeting of Stalin's electoral district of Moscow]" (Moscow: Politizdat, 1946), p. 6.

64. Microfiche collection of State Department documents, Ohio University Library, PtB, reel 2.

65. For an analysis of Kennan's cables in early 1946 see John Lewis Gaddis, *Strategies of Containment: A Critical Appraisal of Postwar American National Security Policy* (Oxford: Oxford University Press, 1982), pp. 19–21; Tucker, *The Soviet Political Mind: Stalinism and Post-Stalin Change*, revised edition (New York: Norton, 1971), p. 91; William Taubman, *Stalin's American Policy*, pp. 135–136; Hugh Thomas, *Armed Truce: The Beginning of the Cold War, 1945–1946* (New York: Atheneum, 1987), chap. 1; William O. McCagg, Jr., *Stalin Embattled, 1943–1948* (Detroit: Wayne State University Press, 1978), esp. pp. 217–237; Albert Resis, *Stalin, the Politburo, and the Onset of the Cold War, 1945–1946*, The Carl Beck Papers in Russian and East European Studies, 701 (Pittsburgh: University of Pittsburgh Press, 1988), pp. 14–19, 22–23.

## 2. Stalin and Shattered Peace

1. Arthur M. Schlesinger, Jr., "Origins of the Cold War," *Foreign Affairs*, 46 (October 1967), reprinted in Thomas G. Paterson and Robert J. McMahon, *The Origins of the Cold War*, third edition (Lexington, Mass.: D. H. Heath and Co., 1991), p. 34; Adam Ulam, *The Rivals: America and Russia since World War II* (New York: Viking Press, 1971), p. 27; William Taubman, *Stalin's American Policy* (New York: Norton, 1982), pp. 8, 9, 21, 129; William O. McCagg, Jr., *Stalin Embattled, 1943–1948* (Detroit: Wayne State University Press, 1978); Werner G. Hahn, *Postwar Soviet Politics: The Fall of Zhdanov and the Defeat of Moderation, 1946–1953* (Ithaca: Cornell University Press, 1982), p. 183; Gavriel D. Ra'anan, *International Policy Formation in the USSR: Factional "Debates" during the Zhdanovschina* (Hamden, Conn., 1983).

2. Quoted in Robert Conquest, *Stalin: Breaker of Nations* (London: Weidenfeld and Nicolson, 1991), p. 271.

3. "Svergnut vlast nespravedlivosti . . ." *Neizvestnaia Rossiia: XX vek* [Unknown Russia: the twentieth century], vol. 4 (Moscow: Izdatelstvo obiedineniia 'Mosgorarkhiv,' 1993), pp. 468–475 (publication of the NKVD report, stored at GARF, f. 9401, op. 2, d. 134, pp. 180–188).

4. See Yelena Zubkova, *Obschestvo i reformi, 1945–1964* [Society and reforms, 1945–1964] (Moscow: Rossiia molodaiia, 1993), pp. 16–44.

5. Cited in Mikhail Narinsky, "The USSR and the Berlin Crisis, 1948–1949," a paper presented at the conference "The Soviet Union and Europe in the Cold War, 1943–1953," Cortona, Italy, 23–24 September 1994, p. 3.

6. Hottelet published the content of his conversations with Litvinov in the *Washington Post*, 21–25 January 1952. On the significance of this conversation see Taubman, *Stalin's American Policy*, pp. 132–133; Vojtech Mastny, "The Cassandra in the Foreign Office," *Foreign Affairs*, vol. 54 (January 1976). On Truman's reaction see the Microfiche collection of State Department documents, Ohio University Library, PtB, reel 2.

7. Molotov in Felix Chuev, *Sto sorok besed s Molotovym: Iz dnevnika F. Chueva* [One hundred and forty conversations with Molotov: from the diary of F. Chuev] (Moscow: TERRA, 1991), p. 97. Valentin Berezhkov, a former interpreter for Stalin and Molotov, claims that he heard Mikoyan saying that Litvinov was killed in a car ambush; Valentin Berezhkov, *Kak ia stal perevodchikom Stalina* (Moscow: DEM, 1993). We cited this information in our contribution to David Reynolds, ed., *The Origins of the Cold War in Europe* (New Haven: Yale University Press, 1994), p. 66. Litvinov actually died of natural causes in January 1953. We thank Vojtech Mastny for bringing this mistake to our attention.

8. David Holloway, *Stalin and the Bomb: The Soviet Union and Atomic Energy, 1939–1956* (New Haven: Yale University Press, 1994), p. 370.

9. Vojtech Mastny, *Russia's Road to the Cold War: Diplomacy, Warfare, and the Politics of Communism, 1941–1945* (New York, 1979), pp. 222, 223.

10. See this point in Alexei Filitov, "Problems of the Postwar Order in Soviet Conceptions of Foreign Policy during the Second World War," a paper presented at the conference "The Soviet Union and Europe in the Cold War (1943–1953)," Cortona, Italy, 23–24 September 1994, p. 23.

11. Protocol no. 6 of the Litvinov Commission, discussion on the memorandum about an international security organization, July 1944, AVP RF, f. 06, op. 6, papka 14, d. 141, pp. 35 and 40, and d. 143, p. 53.

12. Taubman, *Stalin's American Policy*, pp. 9, 99.

13. *Neizvestnaya Rossiya*, vol. 2, pp. 297–323.

14. On postwar uncertainty and fears see Melvyn P. Leffler, *A Preponderance of Power: National Security, the Truman Administration, and the Cold War* (Stanford: Stanford University Press, 1992), pp. 1–10, 49–53.

15. James M. Goldgeier, *Leadership Style and Soviet Foreign Policy: Stalin, Khrushchev, Brezhnev, Gorbachev* (Baltimore: The Johns Hopkins University Press, 1994), pp. 17–51.

16. Chuev, *Sto sorok besed,* pp. 78, 79.

17. A. Lavrent'eva, "Stroiteli novogo mira," *V mire knig,* no. 9 (1970), p. 4; quoted in David Holloway, *Entering the Nuclear Arms Race: The Soviet Decision to Build the Atomic Bomb, 1939–1945* (Washington, D.C.: The Wilson Center, 1979), p. 41; see also Steven Zaloga, *Target America: The Soviet Union and the Strategic Arms Race, 1945–1964* (Novato, Calif.: Presidio, 1993), p. 29.

18. Holloway, *Stalin and the Bomb,* pp. 115, 129.

19. Ibid., pp. 85–86, 90, 102–103, 115; see also Zaloga, *Target America,* pp. 11–12.

20. Interview with Vladimir Geraschenko, a banking expert under Stalin (and the father of Viktor Gerashchenko, the head of the Russian State Bank in 1991–1994). We are grateful to Vladimir Batyuk, who provided us with a copy of the interview.

21. This document was declassified by the KGB and prepared for publication in *Voprosi istorii iestestvoznaniia i tekhniki,* no. 3 (1993), reprinted in Pavel Sudoplatov and Anatoli Sudoplatov with Jerrold L. and Leona P. Schecter, *Special Tasks: The Memoirs of an Unwanted Witness—a Soviet Spymaster* (Boston: Little, Brown and Co., 1994), pp. 457, 474–475.

22. Jerrold Schecter and Anatoly Luchkov, eds., *Khrushchev Remembers: The Glasnost Tapes* (Boston: Little, Brown and Co., 1991), p. 81; Holloway, *Stalin and the Bomb,* p. 125.

23. Maisky to Molotov, 11 January 1944, AVP RF, f. 06, op. 6, papka 14, d. 145, pp. 9, 38–39.

24. Svetlana Alliluyeva, *Dvadtsat' pisem k drugu* [Twenty letters to a friend] (Moscow, 1990), pp. 143–144; Khariton, in Yuli Khariton and Yuri Smirnov, *Mifi i realnost sovetskogo atomnogo proekta* [Myths and reality of the Soviet atomic project] (Russian Federal Nuclear Center: Arzamas-16, 1994), p. 64.

25. The text of the cable may be found in the Library of Congress, Harriman Papers, box 181; cited in Holloway, *Stalin and the Bomb,* p. 128.

26. A different reading of Stalin's words and feelings is in Holloway, ibid., p. 129.

27. The meeting took place around 18–19 August 1945. S. G. Kocheriants, N. N. Gorin, "Stranitsi istorii iadernogo tsentra 'Arzamas-16' [Pages from the history of a nuclear center]" (Arzamas-16: VNIIEF, 1993), pp. 13–14; see also Liudmila Goleusova, "Kak vsio nachinalos . . . [How everything started]," *Mezhdunarodnaia zhizn,* no. 6 (1994), p. 136.

28. The full text of Kurchatov's notes, written after the meeting, is reproduced in *Voprosi istorii estestvoznaniia i tekhniki,* no. 2 (1994), pp. 123–124; see also Yuri Smirnov, "Stalin i atomnaia bomba," ibid., pp. 128–129;

translated excerpts appeared in the *Bulletin* of the Cold War International History Project (Washington, D.C.: Woodrow Wilson International Center for Scholars), hereafter the *Bulletin* of CWIHP, no. 4 (1994), p. 5.

29. On the debates in Western political circles see McGeorge Bundy, *Danger and Survival: Choices about the Bomb in the First Fifty Years* (New York: Random House, 1988), pp. 151–152, 154–155; the quotation is from a cable to Moscow, sent by a Soviet ambassador in Washington, in Scott Parrish, "A Diplomat's Report," *Bulletin* of CWIHP, no. 1 (Spring 1992), p. 21.

30. Stalin to D. Pishevari, 8 May 1946, AVP RF, f. 06, op. 7, papka 34, d. 544, pp. 8, 9; quoted in Natalia Yegorova, "'Iranskii krizis,' 1945–1946 gg," *Novaiia i noveishaiia istoriia*, no. 3 (May–June 1994), p. 41.

31. Yegorova, " 'Iranskii krizis,' " p. 42.

32. Alexander Feklisov, *Za okeanom i na ostrove: Zapiski razvedchika* [Overseas and on the island: notes of an intelligence officer] (Moscow: DEM, 1994), p. 149 (the information was passed on by Klaus Fuchs on 19 September 1945); Chuev, *Sto sorok besed*, p. 81; American calculations are in David Alan Rosenberg, "U.S. Nuclear Stockpile, 1945 to 1950," *Bulletin of the Atomic Scientists* (May 1982), pp. 25–30; and "Nuclear Notebook: U.S. Secrets Revealed," *Bulletin of the Atomic Scientists* (March 1993), p. 48.

33. Daniil Andreev, *Roza mira* [The rose of the world] (Moscow, 1993), pp. 237–238; Odd Arne Westad, *Cold War and Revolution: Soviet-American Rivalry and the Origins of the Chinese Civil War, 1944–1946* (New York: Columbia University Press, 1993), p. 118.

34. Valentin Falin, a letter to Vladislav Zubok, 11 November 1993; Wladimir S. Semjonow, *Von Stalin bis Gorbatschow: Ein halbes Jahrhundert in diplomatischer Mission, 1939–1991* (Berlin: Nicolai, 1995), pp. 200–201, 206.

35. R. C. Raack, "Stalin Plans His Post-War Germany," *Journal of Contemporary History*, no. 28 (1993), pp. 62–63.

36. The thorough treatment of all these issues is in Norman M. Naimark, *The Russians in Germany: The History of the Soviet Zone of Occupation, 1945–1949* (Cambridge, Mass.: Harvard University Press, 1995). See also Norman Naimark, "'To Know Everything and to Report Everything Worth Knowing': Building the East German Police State, 1945–1949," Working Paper no. 10, Cold War International History Project, Woodrow Wilson International Center for Scholars, August 1994; Manfred Wilke, "Nach Hitler kommer wir: Die Planungen der Moskauer KPD-Fuerung 1944/45 fuer Nachkriegsdeutschland," unpublished paper, September 1994.

37. Chuev, *Sto sorok besed*, p. 87; *Molotov Remembers: Inside Kremlin*

*Politics. Conversations with Felix Chuev,* ed. Albert Resis (Chicago: Ivan Dee, 1993), p. 60.

38. Semjonow, *Von Stalin bis Gorbatschow,* pp. 210–221, 232.

39. Ibid., pp. 250–252.

40. Mikhail Narinsky, "SSSR i plan Marshalla: Po materialam Arkhiva Prezidenta RF [The USSR and the Marshall Plan: the materials from the presidential archives of the Russian federation]," *Novaiia i noveishaia istoriia,* no. 2 (March–April 1993), p. 18; see also Scott D. Parrish and Mikhail Narinsky, "New Evidence on the Soviet Rejection of the Marshall Plan, 1947: Two Reports," Working Paper no. 9, CWIHP (March 1994).

41. Minutes of this visit and conversation with Stalin on 9 July 1947 were printed in *Bohemia: A Journal of History and Civilization in East Central Europe,* no. 32 (1991).

42. "The Transcript of the Meeting of Com. I. V. Stalin with the Leadership of the Party of Socialist German Unity, W. Pieck and O. Grotewohl, 26 March 1948," APRF, f. 45, op. 1, d. 303, p. 34; cited by Mikhail Narinsky, "The USSR and the Berlin Crisis, 1948–1949," a paper presented at the conference "The Soviet Union and Europe in the Cold War, 1943–1953," Cortona, Italy, 23–24 September 1994, p. 14.

43. "Memuari Nikiti Sergeevicha Khrushcheva," *Voprosi istorii* (hereafter MNSK), 10 (1993), p. 63; Valentin Falin, *Politische Erinnerungen* (Munich: Droemer Knaur, 1993), p. 338. Falin discovered documentation of this in 1958, when he worked as an assistant to Soviet Foreign Minister Andrei Gromyko.

44. Chuev, *Sto sorok besed,* p. 90.

45. *Khrushchev Remembers,* p. 368; Chuev, *Sto sorok besed,* p. 104. In the English version of *Molotov Remembers,* the key word "national" is omitted (p. 75). Meanwhile, this describes what Molotov (and allegedly Stalin) had thought at the time about Kim Il Sung's motives.

46. A ciphered cable from Stalin to T. Shtykov (the Soviet ambassador in North Korea), 30 January 1950, translated and published in the *Bulletin* of CWIHP, no. 5 (1995), p. 9; Kathryn Weathersby, "Korea, 1949–1950: To Attack, or Not to Attack? Stalin, Kim Il Sung, and the Prelude to War," ibid., pp. 2–3.

47. "O Koreiskoi voine 1950–1953 gg. i peregovorakh o peremirii (Information from the archives of the Ministry of Foreign Affairs of the USSR to the Central Committee, 9 August 1966)," TsKhSD, f. 5, op. 58, d. 266, pp. 122–131, translated and published by Kathryn Weathersby, "New Findings on the Korean War," *Bulletin* of CWIHP, no. 3 (Fall 1993), pp. 15–18; "The Soviet Role in the Early Phase of the Korean War: New Documentary Evidence," *Journal of American-Asian Relations,* vol. 2, no. 4 (Winter 1993), pp. 440–446; and her "Korea—1949–1950," pp. 2–3.

48. Bruce Cumings, *The Origins of the Korean War,* 2 vols. (Princeton: Princeton University Press, 1981, 1990).

49. "O Koreiskoi voine," p. 122; *Bulletin* of CWIHP, no 3, p. 16.

50. Sergei N. Goncharov, John W. Lewis, and Xue Litai, *Uncertain Partners: Stalin, Mao, and the Korean War* (Stanford, Calif.: Stanford University Press, 1993), pp. 14–15; Shi Zhe, *Zai Lishi Juren Shenbian Shi Zhe Huiyilu* [Beside great historical figures: the memoirs of Shi Zhe] (Beijing, 1991), p. 459; see also Gordon Chang, *Friends and Enemies: The United States, China, and the Soviet Union, 1948–1972* (Stanford, Calif.: Stanford University Press, 1990).

51. This was the only time, to our knowledge, when Mao gave the Soviets a detailed "story" of his relations with Stalin. "Iz dnevnika P. F. Yudina: Zapis besedi s tovarischem Mao Tsedunom 31 marta 1956 [From Yudin's diary: memorandum of a conversation with Comrade Mao Zedong, 31 March 1956]," TsKhSD, f. 5, op. 30, d. 163, pp. 88–99, published in *Problemi Dalnego Vostoka,* 5 (1994); A. Grigoriev and T. Zazerskaya, "Mao Tsedung o kitaiskoii politike Kominterna i Stalina [Mao Zedong on the Chinese policy of the Comintern and Stalin]," *Problemi Dalnego Vostoka,* 5 (1994), p. 105.

52. The intricate story of Soviet involvement in separatism in Xinjiang is partially described in Linda Benson, *The Ili Rebellion: The Moslem Challenge to Chinese Authority in Xinjiang, 1944–1949* (Armonk, N.Y.: M. E. Sharpe, 1990); Aichen Wu, *Turkestan Tumult* (New York: Oxford University Press, 1984).

53. Westad, *Cold War and Revolution,* pp. 173–174; Chen Jian, "The Sino-Soviet Alliance and China's Entry into the Korean War," Cold War International History Project, Working Paper no. 1 (June 1993), p. 9; see also Chen Jian, *China's Road to the Korean War: The Making of the Sino-American Confrontation* (New York: Columbia University Press, 1994). On inviting Chiang, see AVP RF, f. 100, op. 32, papka 122, d. 1, p. 4.

54. Stalin to Dimitrov on the Greek rebellion, in "Rospusk Kominterna," *Mezhdunarodnaia zhizn,* 5 (1994).

55. S. L. Tikhvinskii, "Perepiska I. V. Stalina s Mao Tsedunom v ianvare 1949 g. [Correspondence of I. V. Stalin with Mao Zedong in January 1949]," *Novaiia i noveishaiia istoriya,* no. 4–5 (1994), pp. 133–139; on the Mikhoyan visit, see Goncharov, Lewis, and Litai, *Uncertain Partners,* pp. 38–44.

56. Goncharov, Lewis, and Litai, *Uncertain Partners,* pp. 61–72; Stalin's words quoted in ibid., p. 71; Chen Jian, "The Sino-Soviet Alliance," p. 8.

57. Goncharov, Lewis, and Litai, *Uncertain Partners,* p. 87.

58. Quotations from Shi Zhe, *Zai Lishi Juren,* pp. 434–437. For another interpretation of these and other sources see Goncharov, Lewis, and Litai, *Uncertain Partners,* p. 86. Other sources on the Mao-Stalin talks are: Shi

Zhe, "I Accompanied Chairman Mao," and N. T. Fedorenko, "The Stalin-Mao Summit in Moscow," *Far Eastern Affairs* no. 2 (Moscow, 1989).

59. "Zapis besedi tovarischa Stalina I. V. s predsedatelem tsentralnogo narodnogo pravitelstva Kitaiskoi narodnoi respubliki Mao Tse-Dunom 16 dekabria 1949 [Transcript of the meeting of Com. Stalin with the Chairman of the Central People's government of the People's Republic of China, Mao Zedong, 16 December 1949]," APRF, f. 45, op. 1, d. 331, pp. 9, 10, 14. A copy of this and other documents, unless otherwise noted, are on file at the National Security Archive, Washington, D.C.

60. Quoted in Yudin, "Zapis besedi s tovarischem Mao," *Problemi Dalnego Vostoka,* 5 (1994), pp. 105–106; "Zapis besedi s tovarischem Mao," APRF, f. 45, op. 1, d. 331, pp. 11, 12.

61. Shi Zhe, *Zai Lishi Juren,* p. 459.

62. "Zapis besedi I. V. Stalina s predsedatelem tsentralnogo narodnogo pravitelstva Kitaiskoi Narodnoi Respubliki Mao Tse-Dunom [Transcript of a conversation of I. V. Stalin with the Chairman of the Central People's Government of the People's Republic of China, Mao Zedong]," 22 January 1950, APRF, f. 45, op. 1, d. 329, pp. 29, 30, 32.

63. Goncharov, Lewis, and Litai, *Uncertain Partners,* pp. 121–127; Yudin's diary, "Zapis besedi s tovarischem Mao," *Problemi Dalnego Vostoka,* 5 (1994), p. 106.

64. Goncharov, Lewis, and Litai, *Uncertain Partners,* pp. 68, 74; Ivan Baibakov (the MGB) and Mikhail Kapitsa (the MFA), interpreters during the Stalin-Mao negotiations, speak about Stalin's betrayal of the Comintern network of informers in 1950; they were interviewed for "Messengers from Moscow: The East Is Red." Documentary. Copyright of Parraclough Carey Production, Ltd., Pacem Production, Ltd.

65. Yudin to Stalin via Roschin, a ciphered cable, 4 October 1950, APRF, f. 45, op. 1, d. 329, p. 108; Yudin's diary, "Zapis besedi s tovarischem Mao," *Problemi Dalnego Vostoka,* 5 (1994), pp. 106–107.

66. The transcripts of the meeting cannot be found. The quotations are taken from Stalin to Roshchin via Vyshinsky, a ciphered telegram, 14 May 1950, translated and published in the *Bulletin* of CWIHP, no. 4 (1994), pp. 60–61.

67. Dean Acheson, "Crisis in Asia: An Examination of U.S. Policy," Department of State *Bulletin,* 23 January 1950, pp. 111–118; Goncharov, Lewis, and Litai, *Uncertain Partners,* pp. 101–103, 142; Shtykov to Vyshinsky [for Stalin], a ciphered cable, 28 January 1950, APRF, the "Korean dossier," pp. 118–121.

68. Roschin to Filippov (Stalin), a ciphered cable, 13 May 1950, and Stalin to Roschin via Vyshinsky, 14 May 1950, trans. in *Bulletin* of CWIHP, no. 4 (1994), pp. 60–61.

69. Yudin to Moscow on his conversation with Mao on 31 March, a ciphered cable, 20 April 1956, APRF, the "Korean dossier," p. 157.

70. Weathersby, "To Attack or Not to Attack?" p. 3.

71. Stalin, ciphered cable (on the Inchon landing), 18 September 1950; a cable from Shtykov to Gromyko with the letter from Kim Il Sung and Pak Hong-yong, 30 September (delivered to Stalin after midnight on 1 October), APRF, f. 45, op. 1, d. 347, pp. 43, 44–45.

72. A cable from Filippov (Stalin) to the Soviet ambassador in Beijing for immediate transfer to Mao Zedong and Zhou Enlai, 1 October 1950, APRF, f. 45, op. 1, d. 334, pp. 97–98; Alexander Mansurov, "The Korean War Could Have Ended in Mid-October 1950: New Evidence from the Russian Archives," in *Bulletin* of CWIHP, no. 6 (Fall 1995).

73. Holloway, *Stalin and the Bomb,* pp. 285–288.

74. A cable from Mao to Stalin, 2 October 1950, APRF, f. 45, op. 1, d. 334, pp. 105–106. In an extensive analysis of the Chinese sources on the PRC's entry into the Korean War, one historian concludes that on 2 October Mao Zedong and the Standing Committee of the Politburo of the CCP decided in favor of intervention, and on 4–5 October Mao passed this decision through the reluctant Politburo. This stands in stark contrast to the picture Mao presented to Stalin in their correspondence. See Chen Jian, *China's Road to the Korean War: The Making of the Sino-American Confrontation* (New York: Columbia University Press, 1994), pp. 172–184.

75. Stalin to Kim Il Sung via Shtykov (informing him of the Stalin-Mao correspondence), 7 October 1950, APRF, f. 45, op. 1, d. 347, pp. 65–66.

76. Shi Zhe, *Zai Lishi Juren,* pp. 495–498; Goncharov, Lewis, Litai, *Uncertain Partners,* pp. 187–191; Shu Guang Zhang, *Deterrence and Strategic Culture: Chinese-American Confrontations, 1949–1958* (Ithaca: Cornell University Press, 1992), pp. 98–99; Chen Jian, *China's Road to the Korean War,* pp. 199–200, 204.

77. The records of the Stalin-Zhou talks, stored at the Archive of the President of the Russian Federation, are still unavailable, but they are quoted verbatim in Mansurov, "The Korean War Could Have Ended." Mansurov himself argues that Zhou disobeyed Mao's instructions and bluffed in Sochi—a very far-fetched hypothesis, given the history of the Zhou-Mao relationship. See also Shi Zhe, *Zai Lishi Juren,* pp. 495–499; Chen Jian, *China's Road to the Korean War,* pp. 197–200. Shi Zhe's account of the Stalin-Zhou talks is corroborated by new Soviet evidence.

78. Ibid.

79. The reference to the Politburo decisions is in Mansurov, "The Korean War Could Have Ended"; *Khrushchev Remembers,* p. 147; a cable from Pheng Xi (Stalin) to Kim Il Sung, 13 October (this cable mentions the

instructions in question, sent on a previous day), APRF, f. 45, op. 1, d. 347, p. 75.

80. Pheng Xi to Kim Il Sung, 13 and 14 October, APRF, f. 45, op. 1, d. 347, pp. 74, 77.

81. Goncharov, Lewis, and Litai, *Uncertain Partners*, p. 195.

82. Mark Trachtenberg, *Strategy and Diplomacy* (Princeton: Princeton University Press, 1990), pp. 115–126; Leffler, *A Preponderance of Power*, pp. 361–374.

83. Boris N. Slavinsky, "San Frantsisskaia konferentsiia 1951 g po mirnomu uregulirovaniiu s Iaponiiei i Sovetskaia diplomatiia: Noviie dokumenti iz arkhiva MID Rossii [The San Francisco Conference of 1951 on the peace settlement with Japan and Soviet diplomacy: new documents from the archive of the Ministry of Foreign Affairs of Russia]," *Problemi Dalnego Vostoka*, no. 1 (1994), pp. 80–99, especially p. 99.

84. Kim to Stalin via Razuvayev, a ciphered cable, 17 July 1952, APRF, f. 45, op. 1, d. 348, p. 65.

85. Stalin to Mao Zedong via Krasovsky, a ciphered cable, 5 June 1951, APRF, f. 45, op. 1, d. 337, p. 17.

86. "Zapis besedi tovarischa Stalina I. V. s Zhou Enlaiem [Transcript of conversations of Stalin with Zhou Enlai]," 20 August and 19 September 1952, APRF, f. 45, op. 1, d. 329, pp. 66, 67, 68.

87. Ibid., pp. 68, 84, 93.

88. Shtemenko (General Staff) to A. N. Poskryobyshev (Stalin's secretary) on the losses of aircraft, 9 December 1951, APRF, f. 3, op. 65, d. 829, p. 70; "Zapis besedi tovarischa Stalina I. V. s Zhou Enlaiem [Transcript of conversations of Com. Stalin and Zhou Enlai]," 3 September 1952, APRF, f. 45, op. 1, d. 329, p. 84. According to Soviet military sources, the U.S. Air Force lost 4,000 planes in Korea, 2,000 of them in battle. The "Korean air force," that is, the Soviets, and the Chinese "volunteers" lost 1,000 planes in battle and 400 more in various accidents. B. S. Abakumov, "Sovetskiie liotchiki v nebe Korei [Soviet fighters in Korean skies]," *Voprosi istorii*, no. 1 (1993), p. 139. These figures differ considerably from Western calculations, and the actual numbers and ratio of losses remain a disputed issue.

89. Mao Zedong to Stalin via Semyonov (the chief Soviet military advisor in Korea), a ciphered cable, 17 December 1952, and Stalin to Mao via Semyonov, a ciphered cable, 27 December 1952, APRF, f. 45, op. 1, d. 343, pp. 105, 106, 115.

90. MNSK, *Voprosi istorii*, 6 (1993), p. 87.

91. *Neizvestnaia Rossiia: XX vek* [Unknown Russia: the twentieth century] (Moscow: Istoricheskoie nasledie, 1992), vol. 1, p. 275.

92. "Zapis besedy tov. I. V. Stalina s deiatelem respublikanskoi partii SShA Garoldom Stassenom 9 aprelia 1947 goda [The record of a conversa-

tion of Comrade Stalin with a member of the U.S. Republican party, Harold Stassen]," (Moscow: Politizdat, 1947), pp. 32–33, 34.

93. "Zapis besedi tovarischa Stalina s Zhou Enlaiem [Transcript of a conversation of Stalin and Zhou Enlai]," 19 September 1952, APRF, f. 45, op. 1, d. 329, pp. 94, 97.

94. Conquest, *Stalin: Breaker of Nations,* p. 281.

95. I. V. Stalin, *Ekonomicheskiye problemy socializma v SSSR* [Economic problems of socialism in the USSR] (Moscow: Politizdat, 1953), pp. 30, 32.

96. "Zapis besedi tovarischa Stalina I. V. s Zhou Enlaiem [Transcript of conversations of Stalin and Zhou Enlai]," 20 August 1952, APRF, f. 45, op. 1, d. 329, p. 68.

97. "The Development of Soviet Military Strategy, Operational Art and Tactics after the Second World War," a chapter in a manuscript, the Institute of Military History, Moscow, pp. 420–421.

98. *Special Tasks,* pp. 334, 335.

99. "On Some Issues of the Foreign Policy of the New U.S. Administration," memorandum of the Committee of Information to I. V. Stalin, 31 January 1953, AVP RF, f. 595, op. 6, d. 769, vol. 12, p. 223.

100. *Interview I. V. Stalina s korrespondentom "Pravdy" otnositelno rechi g. Cherchillya 13 marta 1946 g.* [Interview of Stalin with correspondents of *Pravda* regarding the speech of Mr. Churchill] (Moscow: Politizdat, 1946), p. 4; I. V. Stalin, *Beseda s korrespondentom "Pravdy"* [Conversation with a correspondent of *Pravda*], 2 Sept. 1951 (Moscow: Politizdat, 1951), p. 13.

101. MNSK, *Voprosi istorii,* no. 6 (1993), p. 86.

3. Molotov: Expanding the Borders

1. "O razvedyvatelnoi deiatelnosti organov gosbezopasnosti nakanune napadeniia fashistskoi Germanii na Sovetskii Soiuz [On the intelligence activity of the Soviet state security organizations on the eve of the Nazi aggression against the Soviet Union]," *Izvestiia TsK KPSS,* 4 (1990); "Taina 'Kenta': Sud'ba sovetskogo razvedchika A. M. Gurevicha [The 'Kent's' mystery: the life and fate of the Soviet intelligence agent Anatoly Gurevich]," *Novaiia i noveishaia istoriia,* 5 (1993), pp. 100–115.

2. APRF, f. 56, op. 1, d. 1161, pp. 147–160, published in Mikhail Narinsky, "Kreml i Komintern v 1939–1941 godakh [The Kremlin and the Comintern in 1939–1941]," *Svobodnaia mysl,* no. 2 (1995), p. 20. The correspondence between Molotov and Stalin during the talks is in AVP RF, f. 59, op. 1, p. 338, d. 2314, pp. 11–18, published in S. A. Gorlov, "Peregovory V. M. Molotova v Berline v Noiabre 1940 goda [V. M. Molotov's talks in Berlin in November 1940]," *Voenno-Istoricheskii Zhurnal,* no. 6–7 (1992). See also G. N. Sevostianov, "Poezdka V. M. Molotova v Berlin v

noiabre 1940 g. [Molotov's trip to Berlin in November 1940]," *Novaia i noveishaia istoriia,* no. 9 (1993); and "On the Eve (Vyacheslav Molotov's talks in Berlin in November 1940)," *International Affairs,* no. 7 (1991).

3. AVP RF, f. 59, op. 1, papka 338, d. 1214, pp. 32–33.

4. AVP RF, f. 59, op. 1, papka 338, d. 1214, p. 39; see also "On the Eve," p. 85.

5. Valentin Berezhkov, *Kak ia stal perevodchikom Stalina* (Moscow: DEM, 1993), p. 53.

6. Felix Chuev, *Sto sorok besed s Molotovym: Iz dnevnika F. Chueva* [One hundred and forty conversations with Molotov: from the diary of F. Chuev] (Moscow: TERRA, 1991), p. 32.

7. AVP RF, f. 048z, op. 11, p. 82, pp. 4, 1–5; see also S. A. Gorlov, "Peregovory V. M. Molotova v Berline v Noiabre 1940 goda," *Voenno-Istoricheskii Zhurnal,* no. 6–7 (1992), pp. 47–48.

8. Larisa Vassilyeva, *Kremlyovskiie zheni* [The Kremlin wives] (Moscow, 1993), pp. 314–315.

9. Ibid., p. 342.

10. Chuev, *Sto sorok besed,* p. 20.

11. Derek Watson, "The Early Career of V. M. Molotov," *CREES Discussion Papers, Soviet Industrialisation Project Series,* University of Birmingham, no. 26 (1986), pp. 34–35; Steven Merrit Miner, "His Master's Voice: Viacheslav Mikhailovich Molotov as Stalin's Foreign Commissar," in Gordon A. Craig and Francis L. Loewenheim, eds., *The Diplomats, 1939–1979* (Princeton: Princeton University Press, 1994), pp. 65–100.

12. Chuev, *Sto sorok besed,* p. 107.

13. Ibid.

14. Molotov to John Foster Dulles, Livingston T. Merchant Papers: Correspondence and Related Material. Seeley Mudd Library, Princeton, box 2, folder: Berlin Conference, 1954. The best collection of documents about this phase of Molotov's life is Lars T. Lih, Oled V. Naumov, and Oleg V. Khlevniuk, eds., *Stalin's Letters to Molotov, 1925–1936* (New Haven: Yale University Press, 1995).

15. See *Stalin's Letters to Molotov, 1925–1936.*

16. N. T. Fedorenko, "Zapiski diplomata: Rabota s Molotovym," *Novaiia i Noveishaiia Istoriia,* no. 4 (1991), p. 79.

17. Vassilyeva, *Kremlyovskiie zheni,* p. 322.

18. Chuev, *Sto sorok besed,* p. 312.

19. Another one, perhaps, was Lazar Kaganovich, who defended Stalin's rule in the face of imminent ouster from the leadership circles in June 1957.

20. Milovan Djilas, *Conversations with Stalin* (New York: Harcourt, Brace, Jovanovich, 1962), pp. 69, 70.

21. Ibid., p. 70.

22. Chuev, *Sto sorok besed*, p. 30.

23. Ibid., p. 69.

24. Ibid., p. 93.

25. Chernenko spoke about this at a Politburo meeting, 12 July 1984. See the translated transcript in the *Bulletin* of CWIHP, no. 4 (Fall 1994), p. 81.

26. Vladimir Yerofeev, "Ten Years of Secretaryship," *International Affairs*, 9 (1991), pp. 107–108.

27. TsKhSD, fund KPK (Party Control Commission), "Delo Molotova," 13/76, vol. 2, p. 74.

28. Berezhkov, *Kak ia stal*, pp. 162, 212.

29. Ibid., p. 360.

30. Fedorenko, "Zapiski," pp. 79–80.

31. Yerofeev, *International Affairs*, 9 (1991), p. 106.

32. Berezhkov, *Kak ia stal*, pp. 221, 223.

33. Chuev, *Sto sorok besed*, p. 95.

34. Fedorenko, "Zapiski," p. 76; interview with Vladimir I. Yerofeev, 14 August 1992, Moscow.

35. As noted by Melvyn Leffler, "U.S. Estimates of Soviet Capabilities, 1945–1953," presentation at the Peace Research Institute, Oslo, 28 October 1993.

36. Chuev, *Sto sorok besed*, p. 99.

37. Yuri Modin, with Jean-Charles Deniau and Aguieszka Ziarek, *My Five Cambridge Friends: Burgess, Maclean, Philby, Blunt, and Cairncross, by Their KGB Controller* (New York: Farrar, Straus and Giroux, 1994), p. 137.

38. Ibid., pp. 142–143; Vladislav Zubok, "Soviet Intelligence and the Cold War: The 'Small' Committee of Information in 1952–1953," *Diplomatic History* (Winter 1995).

39. Chuev, *Sto sorok besed*, p. 31.

40. Ibid., pp. 97, 98.

41. Ibid., p. 29.

42. Fedorenko, "Zapiski," p. 78.

43. Chuev, *Sto sorok besed*, p. 86.

44. Ibid., p. 77.

45. Ibid., p. 75.

46. Ibid., p. 65.

47. Ibid., p. 85.

48. Ibid., p. 77.

49. MNSK, *Voprosi istorii*, no. 8 (1993), p. 76.

50. Chuev, *Sto sorok besed*, pp. 91–92.

51. On the more complicated attitude of Russian right-wing nationalists toward Stalin, see Walter Laqueur, *Stalin: The Glasnost Revelations* (New

York: Scribner's, 1990), p. 243ff.; see also Laqueur, *Black Hundred: The Rise of the Extreme Right in Russia* (Russian edition, Problems of Eastern Europe, 1994), pp. 222–223.

52. Chuev, *Sto sorok besed,* p. 90.

53. Ibid., p. 18.

54. "O levatskom predlozheniii Molotov ob obrazovanii Konfederatsii sotsialisticheskich gosudarstv, veduschei k podrivu vliianiia sotsialisticheskogo lageria v OON [On the leftist proposal of Molotov to establish a confederation of socialist countries, undermining the influence of the socialist camp in the UN]," TsKhSD, fund KPK, "Delo Molotova," 13/76, vol. 10, pp. 2–7.

55. Chuev, *Sto sorok besed,* p. 78.

56. Ibid., p. 18.

57. "K voprosu ob istorii sovetsko-turetskiikh otnoshenii v 1944–1948 godakh [On the historical question of Soviet-Turkish relations in 1944–1948]," a review prepared by the Historic-Diplomatic Directorate of the Ministry of Foreign Affairs of the USSR, Zemskov I. N., TsKhSD, fund KPK, "Delo Molotova," 13/76, vol. 8, p. 13. The best background for this story from the Western side is in Bruce R. Kuniholm, *The Origins of the Cold War in the Near East* (Princeton, N.J.: Princeton University Press, 1980), pp. 257–264.

58. AVP RF, f. 059, op. 1, papka 338, d. 2315, pp. 29–39; "On the Eve," *International Affairs,* no. 7 (1991), p. 85.

59. Litvinov to Stalin, Molotov, "O perspektivakh i vozmozhnoi baze sovetsko-britanskogo sotrudnichestva [On the prospects and a possible foundation of Soviet-British Cooperation]"; "K voprosu o prolivakh [On the issue of the straits]," 15 November 1944, AVP RF, f. 06, op. 6, papka 14, d. 143, p. 52; d. 149, pp. 62, 63.

60. Stalin's conversation with Churchill and Eden, 17 October 1944, *Vestnik,* no. 4 (1995), p. 152. Stalin's discussion of the Montreux Convention at Yalta is in *Foreign Relations of the United States* (hereafter *FRUS*), *The Conferences at Malta and Yalta, 1945* (Washington, 1955), pp. 903–904; the reaction of Churchill is in ibid., p. 328. For the Soviet version of the Molotov-Sarper talks, see "K voprosu ob istorii sovetsko-turetskiikh otnoshenii," TsKhSD, fund KPK, "Delo Molotova," 13/76, vol. 8, p. 13; the version that the Turks reported to Western capitals is in *FRUS: The Conference of Berlin (The Potsdam Conference), 1945,* vol. 1 (Washington, 1960), pp. 1017–1018.

61. Kuniholm, *The Origins,* pp. 260–264.

62. Chuev, *Sto sorok besed,* pp. 102–103.

63. "The U.S.S.R.," George Kennan wrote from Moscow in October 1945, "has remained remarkably inactive with regard to Turkey." Quoted

in Melvyn Leffler, *A Preponderance of Power: National Security, the Truman Administration, and the Cold War* (Stanford, Calif.: Stanford University Press, 1992), pp. 78–79.

64. Modin, *My Five Cambridge Friends*, p. 120.

65. Eduard Mark, "The War Scare of 1946 and Its Consequences," an article submitted for publication in *Diplomatic History* (we are grateful to Eduard Mark for making this material available to us).

66. Kuniholm, *The Origins*, pp. 359–382; Chuev, *Sto sorok besed*, p. 103, as quoted by David Holloway, *Stalin and the Bomb: The Soviet Union and Atomic Energy, 1939–1956* (New Haven: Yale University Press, 1994), p. 169.

67. Chuev, *Sto sorok besed*, p. 78.

68. The official memorandum about the meeting bore no traces of the clash. "Zapisi besedi V. M. Molotova s presidentom SShA Garri Trumenom [Records of conversations of V. M. Molotov with U.S. president Harry Truman]," 22 and 23 April 1945, AVP RF, f. 06, op. 7, papka 43, d. 677, pp. 49–51; Chuev, *Sto sorok besed*, p. 81; also on this episode see Andrei Gromyko, *Pamyatnoie* (1990, 2nd edition), pp. 258–259.

69. Modin, *My Five Cambridge Friends*, pp. 118, 192; Georgi Kornienko, *Kholodnaia voina: Svidetelstvo ieie uchastnika* [The Cold War: a witness's memoir] (Moscow: International Affairs, 1994), p. 31.

70. Gromyko, *Pamyatnoie*, vol. 1, p. 275; Holloway, *Stalin and the Bomb*, pp. 116–117; Modin, *My Five Cambridge Friends*, p. 193.

71. Vladimir V. Shustov, "A View on the Origins of the Cold War and Some Lessons Thereof," in Geir Lundestad and Odd Arne Westad, eds., *Beyond the Cold War: New Dimensions in International Relations* (Oslo: Scandinavian University Press, 1993), p. 32.

72. Leffler, *A Preponderance*, pp. 38–39.

73. Soviet transcript of the London meeting, AVP RF, f. 6, op. 7, papka 43, d. 678, pp. 69, 70.

74. Ibid., AVP RF, f. 6, op. 7, papka 43, d. 678, pp. 71–72, 74–75.

75. *FRUS*, vol. 2 (1945), pp. 164–165; a detailed description of the London talks can be found in William Taubman, *Stalin's American Policy* (New York: Norton, 1982), pp. 116–118; Chuev, *Sto sorok besed*, p. 103.

76. Taubman, *Stalin's American Policy*, p. 118.

77. Molotov to Stalin, Beria, Mikoyan, Malenkov, Vyshinsky, Dekanozov, a ciphered telegram, 19 September 1945, TsKhSD, fund KPK, "Delo Molotova," 13/76, vol. 2, pp. 43–49.

78. AVP RF, f. 059, op. 15, papka 76, d. 445, pp. 140–141, and f. 059, op. 15, papka 11, d. 59, pp. 21–23; Shustov, "A View on the Origins," pp. 30–31.

79. Taubman, *Stalin's American Policy*, pp. 128–165.

80. Leffler, *A Preponderance*, p. 48.

81. Chuev, *Sto sorok besed*, p. 86.

82. "Zapis besedi Molotova s Matiasom Rakosi," 29 April 1947, RTsKhIDNI, f. 17, op. 128, d. 1019, p. 8.

83. RTsKhIDNI, f. 17, op. 128, d. 1019, pp. 14–15.

84. RTsKhIDNI, f. 17, op. 128, d. 1019, pp. 16–17, 22.

85. Modin, *My Five Cambridge Friends*, p. 131.

86. Leffler, *A Preponderance*, pp. 119–120.

87. Modin, *My Five Cambridge Friends*, p. 131; memorandum from Andrei Smirnov to Molotov, Vyshinsky, and Malik, 3 October 1947, AVP RF, op. 9, papka 45, d. 673, pp. 15–16, 21.

88. On the "high policy" versus the rest, see Wladimir S. Semjonow, *Von Stalin bis Gorbatschow: Ein halbes Jahrhundert in diplomatischer Mission, 1939–1991* (Berlin: Nicolai, 1995), pp. 218–219, 222–223; memorandum from Andrei Smirnov to Molotov, 19 June 1947, AVP RF, f. 059, op. 9, papka 632, d. 43, p. 14.

89. N. V. Novikov, *Vospominaniia diplomata* [Memoirs of a diplomat], 1938–1947 (Moscow: Politizdat, 1989), pp. 352–353.

90. *Origins of the Cold War: The Novikov, Kennan, and Roberts "Long Telegrams" of 1946* (Washington, D.C.: United States Institute of Peace, 1991), p. 7.

91. Ibid., p. 7.

92. Ibid., pp. 8–9.

93. Ibid., p. 10.

94. Tarasenko to Molotov, 6 October. Secret. Received by A. Panyushkin and F. Orekhov. Copies sent to Stalin, Molotov, Beria, Mikoyan, Zhdanov, Malenkov. AVP RF, f. 6, op. 9, papka 57, d. 67, pp. 22, 23–24.

95. Chuev, *Sto sorok besed*, p. 88.

96. Vladimir I. Yerofeev, a member of Molotov's staff at that time. Interview with Vladimir I. Yerofeev, June 1991, Moscow.

97. Chuev, *Sto sorok besed*, p. 76.

98. On the growing opposition to American aid to Russia in some influential U.S. "circles," see George C. Herring, Jr., *Aid to Russia, 1941–1946: Strategy, Diplomacy, and the Origins of the Cold War* (New York: Columbia University Press, 1973).

99. Byrnes to N. V. Novikov, AVP RF, f. 06, op. 8, papka 794, d. 47, p. 9; Herring, *Aid to Russia*, pp. 254–255.

100. AVP RF, f. 06, op. 9, papka 214, d. 18, pp. 1–12.

101. Interview with Vladimir Gerashchenko, an expert in the Soviet delegation in Paris, Moscow, July 1991 (we are grateful to Vladimir Batyuk for bringing this interview to our attention).

102. Molotov to Moscow, a ciphered telegram, 29 June 1947; Vyshinsky

to Molotov, ciphered telegram, 30 June 1947, APRF, f. 3, op. 63, d. 270, pp. 54, 59–60, quoted from Mikhail Narinsky, *Novaia i noveishaia istoriia,* no. 2 (March–April 1993), pp. 14–15. On William Clayton's role in the preparation and negotiations for the Marshall Plan, see Wilson D. Miscamble, *George F. Kennan and the Making of American Foreign Policy, 1947–1950* (Princeton, N.J.: Princeton University Press, 1992), pp. 51–52, 54, 56; see also *FRUS: The Conferences at Malta and Yalta.* Novikov's report of 26 August 1947 on the Marshall Plan is quoted in Novikov, *Vospominaniia diplomata,* p. 394; see also his cable in *Mezhdunarodnaiia Zhizn,* no. 5 (May 1992), p. 121.

103. Acheson to Truman, letter of 28 May 1953, Dean Acheson Papers, S. 1, box 30, f. 391, Sterling Library, Yale University.

104. Leffler writes that U.S. and British officials "assumed that Molotov wanted to sabotage the Marshall Plan." They were not ready for a different scenario. *A Preponderance,* p. 184.

105. Molotov to Stalin, a ciphered telegram, 1 July 1947, in Narinsky, *Novaia i noveishaia istoriia,* p. 15.

106. Chuev, *Sto sorok besed,* p. 88.

107. Mikhail Narinsky, "The Soviet Union, Finland, and the Marshall Plan," in Jukka Nevakivi, ed., *Finnish-Soviet Relations, 1944–1948* (Finland: University of Helsinki, 1994), pp. 91–94.

108. Chuev, *Sto sorok besed,* p. 88.

109. Leffler, *A Preponderance,* pp. 198–199.

110. Modin, *My Five Cambridge Friends,* p. 155.

111. Chuev, *Sto sorok besed,* p. 88.

112. Ibid., p. 89.

113. *Molotov Remembers,* pp. 353, 360.


4. Zhdanov and the Origins of the Eastern Bloc

1. L. Y. Gibianski, "Kak voznik Kominform: Po novim arkhivnim materialam [How the Cominform emerged: the new archival materials]," *Novaiia i noveishaia istoriia,* 4 (July–August 1993), p. 131.

2. Kollontai to Zhdanov, 1 November 1947, RTsKhIDNI, f. 77, op. 2, d. 108.

3. Felix Chuev, *Sto sorok besed s Molotovym: Iz dnevnika F. Chueva* [One hundred and forty conversations with Molotov: from the diary of F. Chuev] (Moscow: TERRA, 1991), p. 323; Svetlana Alliluyeva, *Dvadtsat pisem k drugu* [Twenty letters to a friend] (New York: Harper & Row, 1967), p. 179.

4. William O. McCagg, Jr., *Stalin Embattled, 1943–1948* (Detroit:

Wayne State University Press, 1978); Gavriel D. Ra'anan, *International Policy Formation in the USSR: Factional "Debates" during the Zhdanovschina* (Hamden, Conn.: Archon Books, 1983).

5. Harrison Salisbury, *The 900 Days: The Siege of Leningrad* (New York: Harper & Row, 1969), pp. 135, 128, 145–149.

6. Svetlana Alliluyeva, *Tolko odin god* [Only one year] (New York: Harper & Row, 1969), p. 333.

7. Interview with Boris Ponomarev, 15 July 1990, Moscow; Wladimir S. Semjonow, *Von Stalin bis Gorbatschow: Ein halbes Jahrhundert in diplomatischer Mission, 1939–1991* (Berlin: Nicolai, 1995).

8. RTsKhIDNI, f. 77, op. 3, d. 54; quoted in part in Dmitri Volkogonov, *Stalin: Triumph and Tragedy* (London: Weidenfeld and Nicolson, 1991), p. 554.

9. Vojtech Mastny, *Russia's Road to the Cold War: Diplomacy, Warfare, and the Politics of Communism, 1941–1945* (New York: Columbia University Press, 1979), pp. 133–144.

10. Tatyana Androsova, "The Allied Control Commission in Finland, 1944–1947: Zig-Zags in the Tactical Line," in Jukka Nevakivi, ed., *Finnish-Soviet Relations, 1944–1948* (Finland: University of Helsinki, 1994), p. 52; Maxim Korobochkin, "Soviet Policy toward Finland and Norway, 1947–1949," the Norwegian Nobel Institute Working paper, Oslo, 20 October 1994, p. 8.

11. RTsKhIDNI, f. 77, op. 3, d. 54, p. 4; *Molotov Remembers: Inside Kremlin Politics. Conversations with Felix Chuev*, ed. Albert Resis (Chicago: Ivan Dee, 1993), p. 10.

12. Nevakivi, *Finnish-Soviet Relations*, pp. 169–190.

13. Melvyn Leffler, *A Preponderance of Power: National Security, the Truman Administration, and the Cold War* (Stanford, Calif.: Stanford University Press, 1992), p. 80; Luise L'Estrange Fawcett, *Iran and the Cold War: The Azerbaijan Crisis of 1946* (Cambridge, England: Cambridge University Press, 1992), pp. 58–59.

14. Fawcett, *Iran and the Cold War*, p. 40.

15. Memorandum of L. Baranov to Molotov, 12 March 1946, RTsKhIDNI, f. 17, op. 125, d. 848, pp. 18–21.

16. RTsKhIDNI, f. 17, op. 125, d. 988, pp. 81–82.

17. Suslov to Zhdanov, 1 June 1946, "O polozhenii, organizatsionnoi strukture i blizhaishikh zadachakh Otdela vneshnei politiki TsK KPSS [On the position, organizational structure, and immediate tasks of the department of foreign policy of the CC CPSU]," RTsKhIDNI, f. 17, op. 128, d. 846, pp. 53–65.

18. RTsKhIDNI, f. 17, op. 128, d. 64, pp. 50–51.

19. Ibid., pp. 55–61.

20. RTsKhIDNI, f. 17, op. 125, d. 377, pp. 1, 35, 36; d. 378, pp. 1–2, 76–85.

21. Suslov to Zhdanov, 1 June 1946, "O polishenii, organizatsionnoi strukture i blizhaishikh zadachakh Otdela vneshnei politiki TsK VKP (b)," RTsKhIDNI, f. 17, op. 128, d. 846, pp. 56, 63.

22. RTsKhIDNI, f. 17, op. 128, d. 846, p. 51.

23. Interview with Ponomarev, 15 June 1990, Moscow.

24. Diary of N. Palgunov (director of TASS), to Zhdanov and Dekanozov, conversation with Eddie Gilmore, a Moscow correspondent of the Associated Press, 9 October 1946. RTsKhIDNI, f. 17, op. 125, d. 427, pp. 55–56.

25. RTsKhIDNI, f. 17, op. 128, d. 94, p. 246, Bulleten informatsii TsK VKP(b). Voprosi vneshnei politiki, "Burzhuaznie politicheskiie partii SShA [Bourgeois political parties of the United States]," no. 15(39), 15 August 1946.

26. I. V. Stalin, Sochineniya, vol. XVI, pp. 35–43, 45–46.

27. Peter J. Stavrakis, Moscow and Greek Communism, 1944–1949 (Ithaca: Cornell University Press, 1989), p. 49.

28. Ra'anan, International Policy Formation, pp. 65–66; Milovan Djilas, Conversations with Stalin (New York: Harcourt, Brace, Jovanovich, 1962), p. 150; Stavrakis, Moscow and Greek Communism, p. 191.

29. Haris Vlavianos, Greece, 1941–1949: From Resistance to Civil War (Oxford: Macmillan, 1992), p. 72.

30. Leffler, A Preponderance of Power, pp. 143–144.

31. "Beseda Zhdanova s Zakhariadisom [Conversation of Zhdanov with Zachariades]," 22 May 1947, RTsKhIDNI, f. 17, op. 128, d. 1019, pp. 35–36.

32. Ibid., p. 36.

33. L. Baranov to M. Suslov, 16 June 1947, RTsKhIDNI, f. 17, op. 128, d. 1068, p. 107.

34. Stavrakis, Moscow and Greek Communism, pp. 149–150.

35. L. Ya. Gibiansky, "The 1948 Soviet-Yugoslav Conflict and the Formation of the 'Socialist Camp' Model," in Odd Arne Westad, ed., The Soviet Union in Eastern Europe, p. 30.

36. RTsKhIDNI, f. 77, op. 3, d. 89, pp. 1–2, 7. Handwritten notes, revisions, and drafts of Zhdanov's letter to Torez; final draft, 2 June 1947.

37. Gibiansky, "The 1948 Soviet-Yugoslav Conflict," p. 45.

38. Zhdanov to Stalin, "Dokladnaia zapiska o predpolagaimoi programme soveschaniia deviati communisticheskikh partii v Polshe [On the probable agenda of the conference of nine Communist parties in Poland]," RTsKhIDNI, f. 77, op. 3, d. 90, p. 12.

39. "Beseda Zhdanova s chlenami TsK compartii Finliandii Pessi, G. Kuusinen o politicheskoi obstanovke v Finliandii, 30 June 1947

[Zhdanov's conversation with the Communist party of Finland Central Committee members Pessi and G. Kuusinen on the political situation in Finland]," RTsKhIDNI, f. 77, op. 3, d. 88, p. 11.

40. "Beseda Zhdanova s Pessi i Kuusinen [Conversation of Zhdanov with Pessi and Kuusinen]," 1 July 1947, RTsKhIDNI, f. 77, op. 3, d. 36, pp. 17, 18.

41. RTsKhIDNI, f. 77, op. 3, d. 92, pp. 48–49.

42. Korobochkin, "Soviet Policy toward Finland and Norway," 11–22.

43. Gibiansky, "Kak voznik Kominform," pp. 146–147. Another author believes that the "two camps" emerged so late because "the Soviet leadership had still not decided on a new framework which could guide their response to the Marshall Plan." Scott Parrish, "The Turn Toward Confrontation: The Soviet Reaction to the Marshall Plan, 1947," in *New Evidence on the Soviet Rejection of the Marshall Plan, 1947: Two Reports*, Working Paper no. 9, The Cold War International History Project, the Woodrow Wilson Center, Washington, D.C. (March 1994), p. 35.

44. RTsKhIDNI, f. 77, op. 3, d. 98, p. 3.

45. Recollections of Jakub Berman, in Teresa Toranska, *"Them": Stalin's Polish Puppets* (New York: Harper & Row, 1987), pp. 283–284.

46. RTsKhIDNI, f. 77, op. 3, d. 98, pp. 6–11.

47. Ibid., pp. 47, 52, 63.

48. RTsKhIDNI, f. 77, op. 3, d. 91, p. 46.

49. Ibid.

50. Gibiansky, in Westad, ed., *The Soviet Union in Eastern Europe*, p. 41.

51. Gibiansky, "The 1948 Soviet-Yugoslav Conflict," p. 34; RTsKhIDNI, f. 77, op. 3, d. 99, p. 8; d. 102, pp. 11–12.

52. Zhdanov to Zecchia, RTsKhIDNI, f. 17, op. 128, d. 1101, p. 185.

53. Gennadi Kostyrchenko, *V Plenu u krasnogo faraona: Politicheskiie presledovaniia evreev v SSR d posledneie stalinskoie desiatiletiie. Dokumentalnoie issledovaniie* [In the prison of the red pharaoh: political persecutions of Jews in the USSR in the last decade of Stalin. Documentary investigation] (Moscow: Mezhdunarodniie otnosheniia, 1994), pp. 309–312, 335–339.


5. Beria and Malenkov: Learning to Love the Bomb

1. There were, however, some accurate predictions. See Peter Grose, *Gentleman Spy* (Boston: Houghton Mifflin, 1994), p. 350.

2. "Pattern of Current Soviet Behavior," IR-6278, 21 April 1953, p. 26, OSS/State Department Intelligence Reports, a microfilm collection; "Career and Views of G. M. Malenkov," IR-6242, 6 August 1993, ibid., pp. 3, 5; Grose, *Gentleman Spy*, p. 350.

3. Gromyko, *Pamyatnoie* (Moscow: Progress Publishers, 1990), vol. 1, p. 241.

4. David J. Dallin, *Soviet Foreign Policy after Stalin* (Philadelphia: Lippincott, 1961), p. 122; Deborah W. Larson, "Crisis Prevention and the Austrian State Treaty," *International Organization,* vol. 41 (Winter 1987), pp. 58, 33; see also Robert C. Tucker, "Research Note on Stalin's Death," paper presented to the U.S.-Soviet seminar on the Cold War, Athens, Ohio, October 1988; and Matthew Evangelista, "Cooperation Theory and Disarmament Negotiations in the 1950's," *World Politics,* no. 42 (July 1990), pp. 502–529.

5. Amy Knight, *Beria: Stalin's First Lieutenant* (New York: Knopf, 1993).

6. A. Antonov-Ovseenko, "Kariera palacha," in V. F. Nekrasov, *Beria: Konets karieri,* pp. 4–139; Knight, *Beria,* pp. 36–94.

7. Andrei Malenkov, *O moem otse Georgii Malenkove* [About my father, Georgi Malenkov] (Moscow, 1992), p. 13; Andrei Malenkov, interview with William Taubman and Vladislav Zubok, 18 January 1993, Moscow.

8. *Izvestiia,* 10 November 1992.

9. *Khrushchev Remembers: The Glasnost Tapes,* ed. Jerrold Schecter and Vyacheslav Luchkov (Boston: Little, Brown and Co., 1990).

10. Yu. N. Zhukov, "Borba za vlast v rukovodstve SSSR v 1945–1952 godakh [Power struggle in the Soviet leadership in 1945–1952]," *Voprosi istorii,* no. 1 (1995), pp. 23–24.

11. The meeting between Stalin and Vannikov is described by S. G. Kochariantz and N. N. Gorin, *Stranitsi istorii iadernogo tsentra Arzamas-16* [The history of the nuclear center Arzamas-16] (Arzamas-16: VNIIEF, 1993), pp. 13–14, cited in Yuri N. Smirnov, "Stalin u Atomnaia bomba," *Voprosi istorii estestvoznaniia i tekhniki,* no. 2 (1994), pp. 126–127.

12. See V. A. Kozlov and S. V. Mironenko, eds., *Archive of Contemporary Russian History, Volume 1. The "Special" Files for I. V. Stalin: From Materials of the Secretariat of the NKVD-MVD of the USSR, 1944–1953: A Catalogue of Documents* (Moscow: Blagovest, Ltd., 1994).

13. Petr Kapitsa, *Pisma o nauke* [Letters on science] (Moscow: Moskovsky rabochii, 1989), p. 243.

14. Ibid., pp. 244–245.

15. Vladimir N. Novikov, "'Shefstvo' Berii," in *Beria: Konets kar'eri,* p. 237.

16. Antonov-Ovseenko, "Kariera palacha," p. 5.

17. RTsKhIDNI, f. 77, op. 3, d. 94, pp. 193, 194, 196, and 175, 180, 186; cited in Grant Adibekov, *Kominform i poslevoennaia Evropa, 1947–1956* [The Cominform and postwar Europe] (Moscow: Rossiia Molodaia, 1994), pp. 49–50.

18. *Andrei Sakharov: Facets of a Life* (collection of reminiscences) (Hong

Kong: Edition Frontiers, 1991), p. 48 (memoirs of L. V. Altshuler); Yuli Khariton and Yuri Smirnov, "The Khariton Version," *Bulletin of the Atomic Scientists,* vol. 49, no. 4 (May 1993), p. 27.

19. Interview with Boris Veinstein, *Izvestiia,* 2 January 1993, p. 10.

20. Andrei Sakharov, *Vospominaniia* [Memoirs] (New York: Chekhov, 1990), p. 182.

21. "Stalin Moved His Fingers . . . ," interview with Dmitry Sukhanov, *New Times,* no. 48 (1991), p. 34; Malenkov, *O moem otse,* p. 103; interview with Andrei Malenkov, 19 January 1993, Moscow.

22. Elena Zubkova, "Lideri i sudbi: 'Posadnik' Georgia Malenkova [Leaders and destinies: the 'Posadnik' of Georgi Malenkov]," *Svobodnaia misl* (1991), p. 183.

23. "Stalin Moved His Fingers . . . ," pp. 33–34; Malenkov, *O moem otse,* p. 61.

24. Yu. Kunavin, "Ia vipolnial prikaz Berii [I carried out an order from Beria]," *Golos Rodini,* no. 42 (October 1990). Reprinted in *Beria: Konets kar'eri,* p. 257.

25. Knight, *Beria,* pp. 179–180.

26. On the "doctors' plot," see Gennadi Kostyrchenko, *V plenu u krasnogo faraona: Politicheskiie presledovaniia evreev v SSSR d posledneie stalinskoie desiatiletiie. Dokumentalnoie issledovaniie* [In the prison of the red pharaoh: political persecutions of Jews in the USSR in the last decade of Stalin. Documentary investigation] (Moscow: Mezhdunarodniie otrnosheniia, 1994), pp. 289–357; see also the English-language version, *Out of the Red Shadows: Anti-Semitism in Stalin's Russia* (New York: Prometheus Books, 1995), and Arkady Vaksberg, *Stalin against the Jews* (New York: Alfred A. Knopf, 1994), pp. 247–278.

27. Beria submitted this initiative to the Party Presidium on 3 April 1953, *Istochnik* 4 (1994); Constantin Simonov, "Glazami cheloveka moego pokoleniya (Razmishleniya o I. V. Staline) [With the eyes of a man of my generation: reflections on Stalin]," *Znamya,* no. 3 (March 1988), pp. 114–115.

28. "Ob antikonstitutsionnoi praktike 30–40-kh i nachala 50-kh godov. Osobaia Papka [On the anticonstitutional practice of the 1930–1940s and early 1950s. Special file]," *Vestnik Arkhiva Prezidenta Rossiiskoi Federatsii,* no. 1 (1995), p. 127; "Posledniaia 'antipartiinaiia gruppa' [The last antiparty group]," stenographic report on the June 1957 plenum of the CC CPSU, *Istoricheskii arkhiv,* no. 3 (1993), pp. 21–26; no. 4 (1993), p. 74.

29. Vladislav M. Zubok's interview with ret. Lt. Gen. Mikhail Milstein (GRU), 20 January 1990, Moscow, and with ret. Lt. Gen. Sergei A. Kondrashev (KGB), 23 October 1993. In December 1945 Stalin created a new foreign policy commission of the Politburo that consisted of himself,

Molotov, Beria, Mikoyan, Malenkov, and Zhdanov. Yu. N. Zhukov, "Borba za vlast v rukovodstve SSSR v 1945–1952 godakh [The power struggle in the leadership of the USSR in 1945–1952]," *Voprosi istorii,* no. 1 (1995), p. 24.

30. Gromyko, *Pamyatnoie,* vol. 2, pp. 508, 510; see also Vladimir Sokolov and Arkady Vaksberg, "The People's Commissar Andrei Vyshinsky," *International Affairs* (Moscow), no. 7 (1991), pp. 94–105.

31. Beria to Malenkov, 1 July 1953, APRF, f. 3, op. 24, d. 463, published in *Istochnik,* 4 (1994), p. 7.

32. Interview with Mikhail A. Milstein, 20 January 1990, Moscow.

33. David Holloway, *Stalin and the Bomb: The Soviet Union and Atomic Energy, 1939–1956* (New Haven: Yale University Press, 1994), pp. 82–95, 103–108, 222–223; see also Michael Dobbs, "The Soviets' Secret Bombshell," *Washington Post,* National Weekly Edition, 12–18 October 1992, pp. 10–11; V. Kulishov, "Klaus Fuks: Konets atomnomu sekretu [The end of the atomic secret]," in *Professia razveschik* [Profession: a spy] (Moscow: Politizdat, 1992), pp. 132–143.

34. A. Filitov, "Problems of the Postwar Order in Soviet Conceptions of Foreign Policy during the Second World War," paper presented at a conference on the Soviet Union and Europe in the Cold War, 1943–1953, Cortona, Italy, 23–24 September 1994, pp. 33–36.

35. Norman Naimark, *The Russians in Germany: A History of the Soviet Zone of Occupation, 1945–1949* (Cambridge, Mass.: Harvard University Press, 1995), particularly pp. 206–250; see also "The Soviet Missile Triumphs Had Their Beginning in Germany" (recollections of B. E. Chertok, prepared by Boris Konovalov), *Izvestiia,* no. 56, 6 March 1992.

36. Interview with Radomir Bogdanov, the deputy director of the Institute of U.S. and Canada Studies (and a colonel in the KGB), July 1988, Moscow.

37. A. A. Kuznetsov (a secretary of the CC CPSU in charge of administrative organs], remarks at a meeting of the Department of Propaganda in the Central Committee, 9 December 1946, RTsKhIDNI, f. 17 (Tekhsecretariat), op. 121, d. 640, p. 5; also see Rainer Karlsch, *Allein Bezahlt? Die Reparationsleistungen der SBZ/DDR, 1945–1953* (Berlin: Links Verlag, 1993), pp. 87–90, 228–238.

38. Sakharov, *Vospominaniia,* p. 196.

39. GARF, Stalin's file, d. 66, pp. 151–158, d. 92, pp. 166–174.

40. "Lavrenty Beria: Pisma iz tyuremnogo bunkera [Letters from a prison bunker]," *Istochnik,* 4 (1994), p. 7. This is supported by the logbook of visits to Stalin on 22 June, published in *Izvestiia TsK KPSS,* no. 6 (1990), p. 216.

41. Pavel Sudoplatov to the Party Control Commission, 11 October 1960. TsKhSD, the Party Control Commission, 13/76, vol. 1, p. 30. This fact is mentioned in Pavel Sudoplatov and Anatoly Sudoplatov, with Jerrold Schec-

ter and Leona Schecter, *Special Tasks* (Boston: Little, Brown and Co., 1994), pp. 145–147.

42. Recollections of Vasilii Pronin, the chairman of the Executive Council of the Moscow Soviet in 1941, "Gorod u linii fronta [The city at the frontline]," *Moskovskiie novosti,* n. 21, 26 March–2 April 1995, p. 14.

43. Felix Chuev, *Sto sorok besed s Molotovym: Iz dnevnika F. Chueva* [One hundred and forty conversations with Molotov: from the diary of F. Chuev] (Moscow: TERRA, 1991), pp. 334–335.

44. "The Khariton Version," p. 26.

45. The two most prominent men assigned these tasks were Nikolai Pavlov, the former chief of state security for the Saratov region, and Vassily Makhnev, the former administrator of a concentration camp in Kolyma, and then a chief of Beria's personal chancellery.

46. Ludmila Goleusova, "Kak vsio nachinalos [How it all began]," the fiftieth anniversary of the first nuclear center, *Mezhdunarodnaia zhisn,* 6 (1994), p. 136.

47. Ibid., p. 142. Goleusova mentions a decision of the Council of Ministers on 21 June 1946 that had set the earlier deadline for the Bomb's testing.

48. Steven Zaloga, *Target America: The Soviet Union and the Strategic Arms Race, 1945–1964* (Novato, Calif.: Presidio Press, 1993), p. 49; interview with Igor Golovin, 20 January 1993; Leonard Nikishin, "They Awakened the Genie," *Moscow News,* 41 (1989); Igor Golovin, "Kurchatov: Scientist, Man of the State, Person," a paper for the Kurchatov anniversary, January 1993, Moscow, p. 10.

49. Beria to Malenkov, 1 July 1953, *Istochnik,* 4 (1994), p. 6.

50. Interview with Golovin, 20 January 1993, Moscow.

51. Nikishin, "They Awakened the Genie"; "The Khariton Version," p. 26.

52. Holloway, *Stalin and the Bomb,* pp. 294–297.

53. Sakharov, *Vospominaniia,* p. 136.

54. Interview with Igor Golovin, 20 January 1993, Moscow.

55. Transcript of 3 July 1953 CC CPSU Plenum, *Izvestiia TsK KPSS,* no. 1 (1991), pp. 204–206, 144; for the English translation, see D. M. Sickle, ed., *The Beria Affair* (Commack, N.Y.: Nova Sciences Publishers, Inc., 1993), pp. 84, 7–8.

56. Vladislav Zubok and Yuri Smirnov, "Nuclear Weapons after Stalin's Death: Moscow Enters the H-Bomb Age," *Bulletin* of CWIHP, 4 (Fall 1994), p. 17.

57. *Istochnik,* 4 (1994), p. 6.

58. Shtemenko to Khrushchev, 21 July 1953, TsKhSD, f. 5, op. 30, d. 4, pp. 46–47; *Neizvestnaia Rossiia: XX vek,* vol. 3, p. 51.

59. *Istochnik,* 4 (1994), p. 6.

60. "Posledniaia 'otstavka' Stalina [The last 'resignation' of Stalin]," *Istochnik*, no. 1 (1994), Moscow, pp. 105–109.

61. *Khrushchev Remembers*, pp. 100–101.

62. The report on the JCS discussion is in "On Some Issues of the Foreign Policy of the New U.S. Administration," memorandum of the Committee of Information at the Ministry of Foreign Affairs to I. V. Stalin (and other members of the Politburo), 31 January 1953, AVP RF, f. 595, op. 6, d. 769, vol. 13, p. 223. The pressures to escalate and go "nuclear" were very great at that time in the United States; see McGeorge Bundy, *Danger and Survival: Choices about the Bomb in the First Fifty Years* (New York: Random House, 1988), pp. 238–242; Marc Trachtenberg, *History and Strategy* (Princeton: Princeton University Press, 1991), pp. 129–130 (with reference to the JCS discussion); Melvyn Leffler, *A Preponderance of Power: National Security, the Truman Administration, and the Cold War* (Stanford, Calif.: Stanford University Press, 1992), pp. 486–487. On the CIA forecast of destabilization after Stalin, see "The Succession of Power in the USSR," ORE 9, 13 January 1948, Central Intelligence Agency, NARA, RG 263, box 1, f. 34, p. 1.

63. "Komitet informatsii—I. V. Stalinu [Memorandum of the Committee of Information to I. V. Stalin]," AVP RF, f. 595, op. 6, d. 769 (hereafter KI), vol. 7, p. 224; vol. 10, p. 177. For details, see V. M. Zubok, "Soviet Intelligence and the Cold War: The 'Small' Committee of Information, 1952–1953," Working paper no. 4, Cold War International History Project, the Woodrow Wilson International Center for Scholars, Washington, D.C.

64. *Pravda*, 12 March 1953.

65. Vladislav M. Zubok, "Soviet Intelligence and the Cold War: The 'Small' Committee of Information, 1952–1953," *Diplomatic History*, vol. 19, no. 3 (Summer 1995), pp. 459–460; Kathryn Weathersby, "New Findings on the Korean War," *Bulletin* of CWIHP, no. 3 (Fall 1993), p. 15.

66. "On the Korean War, 1950–1953, and the Armistice Negotiations," 9 August 1966 (an official history sent to the Soviet leadership from the foreign ministry, TsKhSD, f. 5, op. 58, d. 266, pp. 130–131; see also a handwritten note from Molotov to Malenkov and Beria, 18 March 1953, and the decision of the Council of Ministers of the USSR of 19 March 1953 (the question of the Ministry of Foreign Affairs) with the attached letter to Mao Zedong and Kim Il Sung, APRF, f. 3, op. 65, d. 830, pp. 60–82.

67. Plenary Meeting of the CC CPSU, July 1953, stenographic record, first session, *Izvestiia TsK KPSS*, no. 1 (1991), pp. 161–162; interview with Dmitry Sukhanov (Malenkov's deputy, in 1953–1955 the head of the Chancellery of the CC CPSU Presidium), June 1990, Moscow.

68. *Istochnik*, 4 (1994), p. 11; Knight, *Beria*, pp. 184–189; Sukhanov in "Stalin Moved His Fingers . . . ," p. 34. Information about Beria's brain trust is from Merkulov to Khrushchev, TsKhSD, f. 5, op. 30, d. 4, p. 68, Sudopla-

tov et al., *Special Tasks*, p. 59, and an interview with Dmitry Sukhanov, June 1990, Moscow.

69. "The Chance for Peace," *Department of State Bulletin*, vol. 28, no. 722, 27 April 1953, pp. 599–603.

70. Zubok, "Soviet Intelligence and the Cold War," p. 461.

71. *Pravda*, 25 April 1953; *Istochnik*, 4 (1994), p. 12.

72. A. I. Kuznetsov to N. V. Shvernik, "Ob antipartiinikh deistviiakh Molotova V. M. v oblasti vneshnei politiki [On the antiparty activities of V. M. Molotov in the area of foreign policy]," report of the Commission of Party Control prepared in early 1960, in the collection of the Commission of Party Control of the CC CPSU, TsKhSD, fund KPK, "Molotov file," 13/76, vol. 3, p. 7.

73. TsKhSD, fund KPK, "Molotov file," 13/76, vol. 3, pp. 7, 112–113; quoted in Sergei Kiselev and Yuri Malov, "The Soviet Leader's Foreign Policy Mentality (1953–1957)," a working paper presented at a conference in Moscow, 13–15 January 1993, p. 14.

74. Boris Starkov, "Sto dnei 'Lubianskovo Marshala' [The one hundred days of the marshal from Lubyanka]," *Istochnik*, 4 (1993), p. 86.

75. Interview with Georgi Kornienko (then an analyst at the KI), 22 November 1989, Moscow.

76. *Izvestiia TsK KPSS*, vol. 1 (1991), p. 143.

77. Rolf Steininger, "Eine Chance zue Wiedervereinigung? Darstellung und Dokumentation auf der Grundlage unveröffentlicher britischer und amerikanischer Akten [Chance for reunification? Exposition and documents based on the release of British and American documents]," *Archiv für Sozialgeschichte*, Beiheft 12, Bonn 1985; the opposite view is in Gerhard Wettig, "Die Deutschland-Note vom 10: Maerz 1952 auf der Basis diplomatischer Akten des russischen Aussenministeriums," *Deutsche Archiv*, no. 7 (1993), pp. 786–805. Among the Soviet veterans are Vladimir Erofeyev, a former interpreter of Stalin's, interview with V. M. Zubok, July 1990, Moscow; Valentin Falin, *Politische Erinnerungen* [Political reminiscences] (Hamburg, 1993), pp. 310–314, and also his letter to V. M. Zubok, 11 November 1993; telephone conversation with Sergei Kondrashov, 23 October 1993.

78. Rolf Steininger, "John Foster Dulles, the European Defense Community, and the German Question," and Hans-Jürgen Grabbe, "Konrad Adenauer, John Foster Dulles, and West German-American Relations," in Richard H. Immerman, ed., *John Foster Dulles and the Diplomacy of the Cold War* (Princeton: Princeton University Press, 1990), pp. 79–108 and 109–132; Thomas Shwartz, *America's Germany: John J. McCloy and the Federal Republic of Germany* (Cambridge, 1991), pp. 115–158; James G. Hershberg, *James B. Conant: Harvard to Hiroshima and the Making of the Nuclear Age* (New York: Knopf, 1993), pp. 650–686.

79. Minutes of a conversation between Comrade Stalin and the leaders of

the SED W. Pieck, W. Ulbricht, and O. Grotewohl, *Bulletin* of CWIHP, no. 4 (1994), p. 48.

80. Sudoplatov et al., *Special Tasks,* pp. 363–364.

81. Victor Baras, "Beria's Fall and Ulbricht's Survival," *Soviet Studies,* vol. 27, no. 3 (July 1975), p. 381. Much of the recent data on the episode are in James Richter, "Pre-examining Soviet Policy Towards Germany in 1953," *Europe-Asia Studies,* vol. 45, no. 4 (1993), pp. 671–691.

82. MNSK (1992), no. 2–3, pp. 93–94; Chuev, *Sto sorok besed,* pp. 332–335; Gromyko, *Pamyatnoie,* vol. 2, pp. 505–507; Wladimir S. Semjonow, *Von Stalin bis Gorbatschow: Ein halbes Jahrhundert in diplomatischer Mission, 1939–1991* (Berlin: Nicolai, 1995), p. 290.

83. Gromyko, *Pamyatnoie,* vol. 2, p. 506.

84. Gromyko, *Pamyatnoie,* vol. 2, p. 506; on Beria's position see Boris Starkov, "Sto dnei 'Lubianskovo Marshala,' " pp. 85, 86; *Izvestiia TsK KPSS,* vol. 1 (1991), p. 163.

85. *Istoricheskii arkhiv,* no. 2 (1994), p. 88.

86. Richter, "Re-examining Soviet Policy," p. 677; Hope M. Harrison, "The Bargaining Power of Weaker Allies in Bipolarity and Crisis: The Dynamics of Soviet-East German Relations, 1953–1961" (Ann Arbor: University Microfilms International, 1994), pp. 48–52; Gerhard Wettig, "Zum Stand der Forschung ueber Berijas Deutschland politik im Fruhjahr 1953 [On the state of research on Beria's German policy in the spring of 1953]," *Deutschland Archiv,* vol. 26, no. 6 (1993), pp. 674–682.

87. *Istoricheskii arkhiv,* no. 2 (1994), p. 88; Chuev, *Sto sorok besed,* p. 334; Semjonow, *Von Stalin bis Gorbatschow,* p. 291.

88. Chuev, *Sto sorok besed,* p. 334; Nikita Khrushchev, "Aktsiia [Action]," in Nekrasov, *Beria: Konets kar'eri,* p. 263.

89. *Istochnik,* no. 4 (1994), p. 5; *Izvestiia TsK KPSS,* vol. 1 (1991), pp. 157–158.

90. Sokolovsky, Semyonov, and Yudin to Molotov and Bulganin, "O sobitiiakh 17–19 iunia 1953 g. v Berline i GDR i nekotorikh vivodakh iz etikh sobitii [On the events of 17–19 June 1953 in Berlin and the GDR and on some conclusions drawn from these events]," AVP RF, f. 06, op. 12a, papka 51, d. 301, pp. 34–35, 46; also Christian Ostermann, "New Documents on the East German Uprising of 1953," *Bulletin* of CWIHP, no. 5 (1995), pp. 15–16; Semjonow, *Von Stalin bis Gorbatschow,* pp. 295, 298.

91. MNSK (1992), no. 2–3.

92. *Izvestiia TsK KPSS,* vol. 1 (1991), pp. 213, 157, 163.

93. Chuev, *Sto sorok besed,* p. 336.

94. *Izvestiia TsK KPSS,* vol. 2 (1991), pp. 197, 199.

95. *Izvestiia,* 9 August 1953.

96. Holloway, *Stalin and the Bomb,* p. 306.

97. *Izvestiia,* 9 August 1953.

98. Sakharov, *Vospominaniia,* p. 232.

99. Smirnov and Zubok, "Nuclear Weapons after Stalin's Death," p. 15; Holloway, *Stalin and the Bomb,* p. 337.

100. *Pravda,* 13 March 1954.

101. V. Malyshev, I. V. Kurchatov, A. I. Alikhanov, I. K. Kikoin, and A. P. Vinogradov, "Dangers of Atomic War and the Proposals of President Eisenhower," draft of an article for the open press, 1 April 1954, TsKhSD, f. 5, op. 30, d. 126, pp. 39, 40, 41.

102. Further research, unfortunately, did not produce any record of discussion on this remarkable document; *Izvestiia,* 27 April 1954.

103. See Andrei Malenkov, *O moem otse,* pp. 115–117; Yu. V. Aksiutin and O. V. Volobuev, *XX s'ezd KPSS: Novatsii i dogmy* [The twentieth congress of the CPSU: innovations and dogmas] (Moscow: Politizdat, 1991), pp. 60–61; L. A. Openkin, "Na istorichestom pereput'e [At a historical turn]," *Voprosy istorii KPSS,* 1 (1990), p. 116; Holloway, *Stalin and the Bomb,* pp. 338–339.

104. Zubok, "Soviet Intelligence," p. 468; Falin, *Politische Erinnerungen* (Munich: Droemer-Knaur, 1993), pp. 321–322.

105. Charles E. Bohlen, *Witness to History, 1929–1969* (New York: Norton, 1973), p. 370.

106. Chuev, *Sto sorok besed,* p. 337; Openkin, "Na istoricheskom," p. 53.

107. Interview with Andrei Malenkov, 20 January 1993, Moscow.

108. TsKhSD, fund KPK, "Molotov's file," 13/76, vol. 3, p. 9.

109. Minutes of Livingston Merchant, in Seeley Mudd Library, Princeton University, Livingston T. Merchant Papers, Correspondence and Related Material, box 2, folder: Berlin Conference (February–March 1954).

110. K. M. Koval, "Peregovory I. V. Stalina s Chou Enlaem v 1953 g. v Moskve i N. S. Khrushcheva s Mao Tze Dunom v 1954 g. v Pekine [Negotiations of I. V. Stalin with Zhou Enlai in 1953 in Moscow and between N. S. Khrushchev and Mao Zedong in 1954 in Beijing]," *Novaya i noveishaia istoriia,* no. 5 (1989), pp. 107–108.

111. Ibid., p. 113. The joint concessions were "Sovkitneft [Soviet-Chinese oil]," "Sovkitmetall [Soviet-Chinese metal]," and others. They were liquidated by the decision of the CC CPSU Presidium on 31 July 1954, *Istoricheskii arkhiv,* no. 2 (1994), p. 87.

112. Koval, "Peregovory," pp. 111–113.

113. Khrushchev in Port-Arthur, "Memoirs of Mikhail Belousov" (at that time the chief of the special division of the MVD of the USSR in the 39th Far Eastern Army), *Neizvestnaia Rossiia: XX vek,* 3 (1993), p. 385.

114. Vladislav Zubok, "Soviet Foreign Policy in Germany and Austria

and the Post-Stalin Succession Struggle, 1953–1955," paper delivered for the conference "The Soviet Union, Germany, and the Cold War: New Evidence from Eastern Archives," in Essen, Germany, 28–30 June 1994, pp. 22–23.

115. Holloway, *Stalin and the Bomb,* p. 332; Sakharov, *Vospominaniia,* pp. 238–239.

## 6. The Education of Nikita Khrushchev

1. Charles E. Bohlen, *Witness to History, 1929–1969* (New York: Norton, 1973), p. 370. On Khrushchev's political biography, policies, and views, see Herbert Dinerstein, *War and the Soviet Union* (New York: Praeger, 1959); Adam Ulam, *Expansion and Coexistence: Soviet Foreign Policy, 1917–1973,* second edition (New York: Praeger, 1974); Michel Tatu, *Power in the Kremlin: From Khrushchev to Kosygin* (New York: Viking Press, 1968); James G. Richter, *Khrushchev's Double Bind: International Pressures and Domestic Coalition Politics* (Baltimore: Johns Hopkins University Press, 1994); Fedor Burlatsky, *Khrushchev and the First Russian Spring* (New York: Scribner's, 1991); Sergei N. Khrushchev, *Khrushchev on Khrushchev* (Boston: Little, Brown, 1990); see also his *Nikita Kruschev: Krizisi i raketi. A Look from Inside* (Moscow: Novosti, 1994), vol. 1–2; Alexei Adzhubei, *Those Ten Years* (Moscow: Sovetskaia Rossiia, 1989).

2. Quoted in Stephen F. Cohen and Katrina van den Heuvel, *Voices of Glasnost: Interviews with Gorbachev's Reformers* (New York: Norton, 1989), p. 264. See also Richard Ned Lebow and Janice Gross Stein, *We All Lost the Cold War* (Princeton, N.J.: Princeton University Press, 1994), p. 51.

3. Khrushchev, *Khrushchev on Khrushchev.* The most recent and complete Russian version of the memoirs of N. S. Khrushchev is "Memuari Nikiti Sergeevicha Khrushcheva [MNSK]," *Voprosi istorii,* no. 2–12 (1990); no. 1–12 (1991); no. 1–3, 6–9, 11–12 (1992); no. 2–12 (1993); no. 1–12 (1994); no. 1–6 (1995).

4. MNSK (1990), no. 2, p. 91.

5. S. N. Ponomaryov, "Nikita Kruschev: Nachalo kar'eri. Dokumental'nii ocherk [Khrushchev: the early career. A documentary essay]," *Neizvestnaia Rossiia: XX vek* (Moscow, 1993), vol. 3, pp. 133–139.

6. For a good historiographical essay that incorporates recent Soviet-Russian revelations of "glasnost," see David Nordlander, "Khrushchev's Image in the Light of Glasnost and Perestroika," *Russian Review,* vol. 52, no. 2 (April 1993), pp. 248–264.

7. MNSK (1991), no. 9–10, p. 80; no. 10, p. 76.

8. Conversation between N. S. Khrushchev and Governor Harriman, June 23, 1959, Harriman papers, Library of Congress, Manuscript Division.

9. T. P. Korzhikhinz, Yu. Figatner, "Sovetskaya nomenklatura: Stanovleniie, mekhanizmi deistviia," *Voprosi istorii,* no. 7 (1993), p. 32.

10. Ernst Neizvestny, *Govorit Neizvestny* [Neizvestny speaks] (Moscow, 1992), pp. 16–17.

11. "Transcripts of the Vienna Summit," 3 June 1961 (lunch), on file at the National Security Archive, Washington, D.C.

12. A. Belkin, *Pochemu mi takiie?* [Why are we like this?] (Moscow, 1993), pp. 103, 110–111.

13. Stenographic report of a conversation with Com. N. S. Khrushchev in the Party Control Committee of the CC CPSU, 10 November 1970, *Istochnik,* no. 4 (1994), p. 71.

14. MNSK (1990), no. 8, p. 67; no. 10, pp. 87–98.

15. MNSK (1990), no. 8, p. 75.

16. Neizvestny, *Govorit Neizvestny,* p. 13.

17. MNSK (1993), no. 8, p. 80; "Peregovory mezdu pravitelstvennimi delegatsiiami SSSR i GFR: Nepravlennie stenogrammi zasedanii [Unedited transcripts of negotiations between the state delegations of the USSR and the FRG]," AVP RF, f. 06, op. 14, papka 14, d. 206, pp. 30–31, 35; Rostislav Sergeev, who translated the meeting, in an interview with V. M. Zubok, Moscow, 25 June 1994.

18. "Posledniaia 'antipartiinaia' gruppa" [The last antiparty group]," stenographical report of the June (1957) Plenum of the CC CPSU, *Istoricheskii arkhiv,* 4 (1993), p. 7.

19. Khrushchev sensed it, incorrectly, in U.S. Ambassador Lewellyn: Thompson to the State Department, cable no. 2887, 24 May, noon. We would like to thank William Burr of the National Security Archive for bringing this document to our attention.

20. John F. Kennedy Library, President's Office Files: Country Files: USSR, box 126, f. 4; MNSK (1993), pp. 5, 81.

21. MNSK (1991), no. 9–10, p. 82.

22. Khrushchev to Kennedy, 13 December 1961, p. 9. The correspondence was declassified by the Kennedy Library in Boston in 1993; available at the library and on file at the National Security Archive, Washington, D.C.

23. Strobe Talbott, ed., *Khrushchev Remembers* (Boston: Little, Brown and Co., 1970), p. 68.

24. MNSK (1991), no. 9–10, p. 80.

25. Quotation from the June 1953 CC CPSU Plenary meeting, in *Izvestiia TsK KPSS* (1990), no. 1, p. 157.

26. MNSK (1992), no. 8–9, p. 69; Veljko Micunovic, *Moscow Diary* (New York: Doubleday, 1980), p. 133.

27. Eisenhower-Zhukov meetings, 20 and 23 July 1955, transcripts made by O. Troyanovsky, TsKhSD, f. 5, op. 30, file 116, pp. 107–131; *FRUS,*

*1955–1957,* vol. V (Washington, D.C.: Government Printing Office, 1988), p. 409.

28. MNSK (1991), no. 9–10, pp. 82, 84, 85.

29. Micunovic, *Moscow Diary,* p. 134.

30. Oleg A. Troyanovsky, *Nikita Khrushchev and the Making of Soviet Foreign Policy,* paper presented at the Khrushchev Centenary Conference, Brown University, 1–3 December 1994, p. 38.

31. "Zapis besedy Bulganina, Khrushcheva, Mikoiana i Molotova s premier-ministrom i ministrom inostrannikh del Danii Khansenom [Memorandum of a conversation of Bulganin, Khrushchev, Mikoyan, and Molotov with the prime minister and the minister of foreign affairs of Denmark, Hansen]," 5 March 1956, TsKhSD, f. 5, op. 30, d. 163, p. 33. Molotov had spoken about this in his speech at the June 1957 CC CPSU Plenary meeting, *Istoricheskii arkhiv,* 4 (1994).

32. Oleg A. Troyanovsky, interview with V. M. Zubok, Moscow; Rostislav Sergeev, interview with V. M. Zubok, 25 June 1994, Moscow.

33. Leo Gluchovsky, "Poland, 1956: Khrushchev, Gomulka, and 'Polish October,'" Janos M. Rainer, "The Yeltsin Dossier: Soviet Documents on Hungary, 1956," and Johanna Granville, "Imre Nagy, aka 'Volodya'—A Dent in the Martyr's Halo?" in *Bulletin* of CWIHP, no. 5 (1995).

34. Neizvestny, *Govorit Neizvestny,* p. 17.

35. Victor Karyagin, "Berlin after the War," *International Affairs,* no. 7 (1991), p. 88.

36. MNSK (1994), no. 4, p. 85.

37. Troyanovsky, *Nikita Khrushchev and the Making of Soviet Foreign Policy,* p. 9; "Posledniaia 'antipartiinaia' gruppa," p. 33.

38. Mohammed Heikal, *Sphinx and Commissar: The Rise and Fall of Soviet Influence in the Arab World* (London: Collins, 1978), p. 129; David Holloway, *Stalin and the Bomb: The Soviet Union and Atomic Energy, 1939–1956* (New Haven: Yale University Press, 1994), p. 339.

39. N. A. Vlasov, "Desiat' let riadom s Kurchatovym [Ten years alongside Kurchatov]," in M. K. Romanovsky, ed., *Vospominaniia ob akademike I. V. Kurchatove* (Moscow: Nauka, 1983), cited in Holloway, *Stalin and the Bomb,* p. 307.

40. Igor Golovin, "Kurchatov: Scientist, Man of the State, Person," a paper for the Kurchatov anniversary, January 1993, Moscow, p. 15.

41. TsKhSD, f. 5, op. 4, d. 31; cited in Alexander Volkov and Marina Kolesova, "Soviet Reaction to U.S. Nuclear Policy (1953–1962)," a paper presented at a conference on the Cold War, Moscow, 13–15 January 1993.

42. *Pravda,* 14 May 1957.

43. Heikal, *Sphinx and Commissar,* p. 129.

44. G. A. Mikhailov and A. S. Orlov, "Tainy 'zakrytogo neba' [The mys-

teries of the 'closed skies']," *Novaiia i noveishaiia istoriia*, no. 6 (1992), pp. 99–100.

45. MNSK (1992), no. 8–9, p. 76.

46. Khrushchev's talk at the conference of the first secretaries of Central Committees of Communist and workers' parties of Socialist countries, 4 August 1961, TsKhSD, translated by Zubok, *Bulletin* of CWIHP, no. 3 (1993), p. 60.

47. "Beseda Nasera i Tovarisha Shepilova 18 Iyunia 1956 [Memo of conversations between Nasser and Shepilov, 18 June 1956]"; memorandum of the Committee of Information at the foreign ministry of the USSR on the positions of Western powers, Israel, and Arab countries on the issue of the Arab-Israeli conflict, 5 October 1956—AVP RF, f. 595, op. 6, papka 789, vol. 77, pp. 83–91.

48. Georgy Kornienko, interview with V. M. Zubok, 1989, Moscow.

49. MNSK, 1992, no. 8–9, p. 99.

50. "Posledniaia 'antipartiinaia' gruppa," *Istoricheskii arkhiv*, no. 4 (1993), pp. 4, 5.

51. Ibid., p. 36.

52. Steven J. Zaloga, *Target America: The Soviet Union and the Strategic Arms Race, 1945–1964* (Novato, Calif.: Presidio Press, 1993), pp. 146–147.

53. Vladimir Platonov, "Schit i mech Satani: Strategicheskoe oruzhiie Mikhaila Yangelia," *Sovershenno Secretno* (Moscow), no. 1 (1993), p. 11.

54. "Khrushchev: The Man, His Manner, His Outlook, and His View of the United States," background paper, 25 May 1961, John F. Kennedy Library, President's Office Files: Country Files: USSR, Vienna Meeting, box 126, f. 9.

55. See Thomas M. Nichols, *The Sacred Cause: Civil-Military Conflict over Soviet National Security, 1917–1992* (Ithaca: Cornell University Press, 1993), pp. 71–83; and Jerrold L. Schecter and Peter S. Deriabin, *The Spy Who Saved the World: How a Soviet Colonel Changed the Course of the Cold War* (New York: Scribner's, 1992), pp. 109, 141. The GRU colonel Oleg Penkovsky was an important source of information for the American government on the rift between Khrushchev and the senior military, which would grow in 1961. The materials of his debriefings by Western handlers in April–May, July, and September 1961 in London have been declassified.

56. Jack M. Schick, *The Berlin Crisis, 1958–1962* (Philadelphia: University of Pennsylvania Press, 1971), pp. 8–9. The recent research on the origins of the crisis and the Soviet-East German dynamics is in Hope Harrison, "Ulbricht and the Concrete 'Rose' ": New Archival Evidence on the Dynamics of Soviet-East German Relations and the Berlin Crisis, 1958–1961," Working paper no. 5, Cold War International History Project, Washington, D.C., May 1993; see also Hope Harrison, "New Evidence on Khrushchev's

1958 Berlin Ultimatum," *Bulletin* of the CWIHP, no. 4 (Fall 1994), pp. 35–39.

57. Report of the Committee of Information to the Presidium CC CPSU, 28 December 1956, AVP RF, f. 595, op. 6, d. 789, vol. 77, pp. 558, 559.

58. Report of the Committee of Information to the Presidium CC CPSU, 20 November 1956, AVP RF, f. 595, op. 6, d. 789, p. 437; TsKhSD, f. 5, op. 49, d. 17, pp. 46–47, 59. TsKhSD, f. 5, op. 64, d. 578, pp. 17–18.

59. "Ob itogakh poezdki A. I. Mikoyana v FRG [On the results of the trip of A. I. Mikoyan to the FRG]," TsKhSD, f. 5, op. 64, d. 578, pp. 24–26.

60. RTsKhIDNI, f. 17, op. 128, d. 717, pp. 28–29.

61. Carola Stern, *Ulbricht: A Political Biography* (London, 1965), p. 96. A recent, profound analysis of Ulbricht-Soviet relations in the 1950s and early 1960s is in Harrison, "Ulbricht and the Concrete 'Rose.' "

62. U.S. intelligence official, quoted in Honore M. Catudal, *Kennedy and the Berlin Wall Crisis: A Case in U.S. Decision Making* (Berlin: Berlin Verlag, 1980), p. 49.

63. *Khrushchev Remembers, Glasnost Tapes*, p. 161. Eisenhower recalled this in Paris; see L. Merchant papers, handwritten remarks on 15 May, Mudd Manuscript Library, Princeton University.

64. *Khrushchev Remembers, Glasnost Tapes*, p. 164.

65. N. S. Khrushchev, transcript of a conversation with a delegation of the Italian Communist party, 10 July 1956, *Istochnik*, no. 2 (1994), pp. 89–90.

66. Record of a meeting of Comrade N. S. Khrushchev with Comrade W. Ulbricht, 30 November 1960, AVP RF, f. 0742, op. 6, p. 4, papka 43, p. 9.

67. "Posledniaia 'antipartiinaia' gruppa," *Istoricheskii arkhiv*, no. 4 (1993), pp. 28, 29.

68. Notes taken during an interview with Khrushchev, 24 October 1958, Walter Lippmann papers, Yale University, Sterling Library, Series YII, box 239, f. 27.

69. On Khrushchev's central role in this, see Harrison, "New Evidence on Khrushchev's 1958 Berlin Ultimatum," p. 36.

70. Troyanovsky, *Nikita Khrushchev and the Making of Soviet Foreign Policy*, p. 15.

71. Valentin Falin, *Politische Erinnerungen* (Munich: Droemer-Knaur, 1993), p. 336. M. Pervukhin in conversation with Ulbricht, 26 September 1958, TsKhSD, f. 5, op. 49, d. 76, pp. 23–24; M. Pervukhin's conversation with Ulbricht and Grotewohl, 2 October 1958, op. 49, d. 82, pp. 200–204.

72. Oleg A. Troyanovsky, interview with V. M. Zubok, 9 March 1993, Washington, D.C.

73. Ibid. See also Troyanovsky's presentation at the Khrushchev Centenary Conference, Providence, R.I., 2 December 1994.

74. TsKhSD, card index of incoming documents from the Ministry of Foreign Affairs to the Central Committee, nos. 4554 and 4556.

75. Dwight D. Eisenhower Library (DDEL), Ann Whitman File (Papers of Eisenhower as President), International Series, box 46.

76. Michael Beschloss, *Kennedy and Khrushchev: The Crisis Years* (New York: Harper-Collins, 1991), p. 154; V. Kuznetsov to M. Suslov, 21 January 1959, TsKhSD, f. 5, op. 30, d. 300, pp. 1–8; Mikoyan's Call on the President, 17 January 1959, Dwight D. Eisenhower Library, Ann Whitman File, International Series, box 49. Oleg Troyanovsky confirms that the purpose of Mikoyan's visit was to tell Eisenhower that Moscow's deadline on Berlin was not the final word, *Nikita Khrushchev and the Making of Soviet Foreign Policy*, p. 17.

77. According to Valentin Falin, *Politische Erinnerungen* (Munich: Droemer-Knaur, 1993), p. 342.

78. He also competed on this ground with the rhetoric of other Western leaders, including Adenauer, who persistently communicated through Soviet contacts his desire to talk about "disarmament," AVP RF, f. 0757, op. 3, papka 17, d. 3, p. 48.

79. Larisa Vassilieva, *Kremlevskiie zheny* [Kremlin wives] (Moscow: Vagrius, 1993), pp. 417–457.

80. "The President's Private Conversation with Khrushchev," John F. Kennedy Library, President's Office Files: Country File: USSR, box 126, folder 3; Mark Trachtenberg, *Strategy and Diplomacy* (Princeton: Princeton University Press, 1990), pp. 202–204; William Burr, "Eisenhower's Search for Flexibility: Strategy and Diplomacy during the Berlin Crisis, 1958–1960," working paper.

81. Quoted from Volkogonov, *Lenin,* p. 453. Xue Mouchong, a senior PRC archivist, in his talk at the Woodrow Wilson International Center for Scholars, Washington, D.C., 31 January 1995.

82. Volkogonov, *Lenin,* p. 454.

83. Ibid., p. 454.

84. L. Thompson to Herter, 7 October 1960, Dwight D. Eisenhower Library, White House Office, Office of the Staff Secretary, International Series, box 15, folder 11; Raymond Garthoff, interview with V. M. Zubok, 2 May 1989, Washington, D.C.; Livingston T. Merchant papers, diary entry for 7 May 1960, correspondence and related material, box 7, folder 2; George Kennan papers, box 31, letter to Chip Bohlen, 17 February 1960, both in the Mudd Manuscript Library, Princeton University.

85. Troyanovsky, *Nikita Khrushchev and the Making of Soviet Foreign Policy,* pp. 23–24.

86. Interview with Maj. Gen. Boris Surikov, then in the Soviet air defense forces; Mihailov and Orlov, "Tainy," pp. 105–107; on the U-2 intelligence operation, its results, and Dulles's role, see Peter Grose, *Gentleman Spy* (New

York: Houghton Mifflin, 1994), pp. 470–478; on Dulles's career, see, besides Grose, Wayne G. Jackson, *Allen Welsh Dulles as Director of Central Intelligence,* 26 February 1953–29 November 1961, declassified with deletions in 1994, copy available from the CIA History Office and on file at the National Security Archive, Washington, D.C.

87. Shelepin to CC CPSU, 7 June 1960, TsKhSD, f. 4, op. 13, d. 65, pp. 13–14, in Special Dossier of the Secretariat of the Central Committee, 153/30c from 14.VI.60. The KGB document and other details of this operation were covered in Vladislav Zubok, "Spy vs. Spy: The KGB vs. the CIA, 1960–1962," *Bulletin* of CWIHP, no. 4 (1994), pp. 23–26; see also Vitaly S. Lelchuk and Yefic I. Pivovar, "Mentalitet Sovetskogo Obshchestva i Kholodnaya Voina [The mentality of Soviet society and the Cold War]," *Otechestvennaya Istoria,* no. 6 (November–December 1993), pp. 70–71.

88. Dobrynin-[George] Shultz meeting, notetaker: Jack Matlock. An e-mail message from Matlock to Donald R. Fortier, National Security Archive, 9 April 1986, declassified according to the Freedom of Information Act and on file at the National Security Archive, Washington, D.C.; Alexei Adzhubei's interview with George Colburn for a documentary, "Dangerous Years," aired on the Discovery Channel, October 1991.

89. MNSK (1993), no. 10, pp. 51–52.

90. Troyanovsky, *Nikita Khrushchev and the Making of Soviet Foreign Policy,* p. 25.

91. Troyanovsky, interview with V. M. Zubok, 9 March 1993, Washington, D.C.

92. Interview with Georgi Kornienko, May 1990, Moscow; A. E. Alexeev (the first Soviet ambassador in Havana), at the Conference on the Cuban Missile Crisis, Moscow, September 1994.

93. Nikolai Leonov (a KGB veteran), *Likholetie* [Lean years] (Moscow: Mezhdunarodnie Otnoshenia, 1995), p. 61.

94. Troyanovsky, *Nikita Khrushchev and the Making of Soviet Foreign Policy,* p. 27.

95. Ibid.

96. Penkovsky's first attempt to contact Western intelligence services took place in August 1960. See the materials of Penkovsky's debriefings, particularly on 18–25 July 1961, declassified by the CIA. On the dangerous activities of the KGB at that time, see Zubok, "Spy vs. Spy," pp. 25–30; David Wise, *Mole Hunt: How the Search for a Phantom Traitor Shattered the CIA* (New York: Avon Books, 1994), pp. 58, 61–62.

97. The "wars of national liberation speech" was never published in full in the USSR, but quickly became known in the West. Quoted from Beschloss, *The Crisis Years,* p. 60.

98. "Zapis besedi tovarischa N. S. Khrushcheva s tovarishem V. Ulbrikh-

tom 30 noiabria 1960 goda [Memorandum of a conversation between Comrade Khrushchev and Comrade Ulbricht, 30 November 1960]," AVP RF, f. 0742, op. 6, papka 43, d. 4, pp. 8–9.

## 7. Khrushchev and the Sino-Soviet Schism

1. For a description of the Soviet and American efforts in China during the Stalin era, see Odd Arne Westad, *Cold War and Revolution: Soviet-American Rivalry and the Origins of the Chinese Civil War, 1944–1946* (New York: Columbia University Press, 1993); Nancy Bernkopf Tucker, *Patterns in the Dust: Chinese-American Relations and the Recognition Controversy, 1949–1950* (New York: Columbia University Press, 1983); Michael Shaller, *The U.S. Crusade in China, 1938–1945* (New York: Columbia University Press, 1979); Lewis McCarroll Purifoy, *Harry Truman's China Policy: McCarthyism and the Diplomacy of Hysteria, 1947–1951* (New York: New Viewpoint, 1976); David Mayers, *Cracking the Monolith: U.S. Policy against the Sino-Soviet Alliance, 1949–1955* (Baton Rouge: Louisiana State University Press, 1986). The Korean War from the Chinese and Soviet perspective is discussed in Sergei N. Goncharov, John W. Lewis, and Xue Litai, *Uncertain Partners: Stalin, Mao, and the Korean War* (Stanford: Stanford University Press, 1993).

2. The Taiwan crisis of 1958 is discussed in a number of Western publications. See, for example, David Zagoria, *The Sino-Soviet Conflict, 1956–1961* (New York: Atheneum, 1964), pp. 200–221; Thomas E. Stolper, *China, Taiwan, and the Offshore Islands* (Armonk, N.Y.: M. E. Sharpe, 1985), pp. 117–131.

3. See June M. Grasso, *Truman's Two-China Policy: 1948–1950* (Armonk, N.Y.: M. E. Sharpe, 1987).

4. In Li Zhisui, *The Private Life of Chairman Mao: The Memoirs of Mao's Private Physician* (New York: Random House, 1994), p. 262.

5. Ibid., p. 270.

6. *Vystupleniya Mao Tse-duna, ranee ne publikovavshiesya v kitayskoy pechati* [Mao Zedong's talks withheld from publication in the Chinese press], 2nd issue (Moscow: Progress, 1975), p. 304.

7. MNSK (1993), no. 2, pp. 89–90.

8. See John S. Service, *The Amerasia Papers: Some Problems in the History of U.S.-China Relations* (Berkeley: University of California Press, 1971); D. Barrett, *Dixie Mission: The United States Army Observer Group in Yenan, 1944* (Berkeley: University of California Press, 1970); P. P. Vladimirov, *Osoby raion Kitaia, 1942–1945* [A special region of China] (Moscow: APN, 1973).

9. See Mao Zedong, *O novoi demokratii,* Izbrannye proizvedeniya v 5

tomakh (Beijing: Izdatelstvo literatury na inostrannykh iazykakh, 1967–1969), vol. 4, pp. 447–448.

10. See Service, *The Amerasia Papers;* Purifoy, *Harry Truman's China Policy,* pp. 151–188.

11. Arnold Toynbee, *A Study of History* (London: Oxford University Press, 1955), vol. 1, p. 54.

12. See the direct proof of this in Mao's words, quoted by Li Zhisui in *The Private Life of Chairman Mao,* p. 262. K. Pleshakov and D. Furman, "Obshchee i osobennoye v socialno-politicheskom i ideologicheskom razvitii KNR i SSSR [Generic and specific features in the social, political, and ideological evolution of the PRC and the USSR]," *Mirovaya economica i mezhdunarodnye otnosheniya,* no. 12 (1989).

13. *Krushchev Remembers: The Glasnost Tapes,* p. 153.

14. See Western scholarship on the subject predating the new archival findings: David Floyd, *Mao against Khrushchev: A Short History of the Sino-Soviet Conflict* (New York: Praeger, 1964); R. K. I. Quested, *Sino-Russian Relations: A Short History* (Boston: G. Allen and Unwin, 1984); Raymond Garthoff, ed., *Sino-Soviet Military Relations* (New York: Praeger, 1966).

15. See Chapter 6.

16. Secretariat of the CPSU CC, protocol no. 75, 17 April 1954, TsKhSD, Kartoteka Sekretariata TzK KPSS, 10371.

17. See Qiang Zhai, *The Dragon, the Lion, and the Eagle: Chinese-British-American Relations, 1949–1958* (Ohio: Kent State University Press, 1994), p. 175; on the U.S. strategic view of the crisis, see Gordon H. Chang, *Friends and Enemies: The United States, China, and the Soviet Union, 1948–1972* (Stanford, Calif.: Stanford University Press, 1990), pp. 129–142.

18. "Zapis besedi N. A. Bulganina s Poslom KNR v SSSR Liu Qiao," 19 March 1955, TsKhSD, f. 5, op. 30, d. 116, p. 19.

19. Chang, *Friends and Enemies,* p. 137; Qiang Zhai, *The Dragon,* pp. 173–174.

20. The documentary collection "The USSR-PRC (1949–1983): Documents and Materials, Part I, 1949–1963" (Moscow: Historical-Diplomatic Division of the Ministry of Foreign Affairs of the USSR, 1985), pp. 145–146, 147–148; MNSK (1993), no. 3, p. 77; for the Chinese side, see John W. Lewis and Xue Litai, *China Builds the Bomb* (Stanford, Calif.: Stanford University Press, 1988), pp. 62–63, 105–106.

21. Komissiya TzK KPSS po voprosam ideologii, cultury i mezhdunarodnylh partiynykh svyazey, protocol no. 3, 6 February 1958, TSKD, Kartoteka Sekretariata TzK KPSS, 10371.

22. Shi Zhe, *Zai Lishi Juren Shenbian Shi Zhe Huiyilu* [Beside great historical figures: the memoirs of Shi Zhe] (Beijing, 1991), p. 572.

23. Ibid., p. 579.

24. *Khrushchev Remembers: The Glasnost Tapes,* p. 142; MNSK (1993), no. 3, p. 86.

25. Ibid., pp. 143, 153.

26. *Khrushchev Remembers,* pp. 469–470; MNSK (1993), no. 2, pp. 90–91.

27. *Khrushchev Remembers,* pp. 469–470.

28. Ibid.

29. Li Yueran, "Some Recollections from When I Was Working at the Side of Premier Zhou Enlai," in *Xin Zhongguo Waijiao Fengyun* [The main diplomatic events of new China] (Beijing, 1990), pp. 173–175.

30. *Khrushchev Remembers,* p. 461.

31. MNSK (1993), no. 2. p. 81.

32. Ibid.

33. Li Zhisui, *Waijiao wutai shang de xin zhongguo lingxiu* (Beijing: Jiefangjun chubanshe), p. 262.

34. *Khrushchev Remembers: The Glasnost Tapes,* p. 151.

35. "Otchet posolstva SSSR v Kitayskoy Narodnoy Respublike za 1958 god [The report of the embassy of the USSR in the PRC, 1958]," TsKhSD, f. 5, op. 49, d. 134, p. 81.

36. Li Yueran, "Some Recollections," pp. 168–169; Li Zhizui, *The Private Life of Chairman Mao,* p. 262.

37. *Khrushchev Remembers,* p. 472. Mao's response to the joint fleet proposal was that the fleet should have Soviet ships and Chinese captains.

38. "Otchet posolstva SSSR v Kitayskoy Narodnoy Respublike za 1959 god [The report of the embassy of the USSR in the PRC, 1959]," TsKhSD, f. 5, op. 49, d. 240, p. 117.

39. Ibid., p. 245.

40. *Khrushchev Remembers,* p. 465.

41. TsKhSD, f. 5, op. 49, d. 134, p. 72.

42. Ibid., p. 84.

43. "Zapis besedy s premierom Gosudarstvennogo Soveta KNR Zhou En-laem 5 centyabrya 1958 g. [The minutes of a talk with Prime Minister Zhou Enlai, 5 September 1958]," TsKhSD, f. 5, op. 49, d. 133, pp. 1–8.

44. Ibid.

45. Ibid.

46. "Otchet posolstva SSSR v Kitayskoy Narodnoy Respublike," f. 5, op. 49, d. 134, p. 84; *Sbornik dokumentov SSSR-KNR (1949–1983), Part I* (Moscow: The Historical-Diplomatic Division of the Ministry of Foreign Affairs of the USSR, 1985), p. 232; "Zapis besedy s premierom Gossoveta KNR Zhou En-laem 10 centabrya 1958 [The minutes of a talk with Prime Minister Zhou Enlai, 10 September 1958]," TsKhSD, f. 5, op. 49, d. 133, p. 3.

47. *Sbornik dokumentov SSSR-KNR (1949–1983), Part I,* pp. 232–233.

48. TsKhSD, f. 5, op. 49, d. 134, pp. 85, 168.

49. Li Zhisui, *The Private Life of Chairman Mao*, p. 270.

50. "Zapis besedy tov. Mao 2 oktiabria 1958 na vstreche s shestyu dele-gatsiiami sotsialisticheskikh stran, nakhodiashchikhsia v KNR [Mao's meeting with six delegations of the Socialist countries on a visit to the PRC]," TsKhSD, f. 5, op. 49, d. 128, pp. 234–235.

51. Ibid.

52. "Otchet posolstva SSSR v Kitayskoy Narodnoy Respublike za 1959 god [The report of the embassy of the USSR in the PRC, 1959]," TsKhSD, f. 5, op. 49, d. 240, p. 117; for the little we know about Sino-Soviet cooperation, see Litai, *China Builds the Bomb*, pp. 63–64.

53. TsKhSD, f. 5, op. 49, d. 240, p. 88.

54. Chang, *Friends and Enemies*, p. 192. Eisenhower proposed a meeting in late October in New York.

55. TsKhSD, f. 5, op. 49, d. 134, p. 170.

56. *Sbornik Dokumentov SSSR-KNR (1949–1983), Part I*, p. 233.

57. MNSK (1993), no. 2, p. 82.

58. MNSK (1993), no. 3, p. 78; Litai, *China Builds the Bomb*, pp. 64–65.

59. "Iz dnevnika Antonova S. F. Zapis besedi s Mao Tse Dunom ot 14 oktiabria 1959 [Mao's conversation with S. Antonov, 14 October 1959]," TsKhSD, f. 5, op. 49, d. 233, p. 88. This document is published in *Problemi Dalnego Vostoka* [The issues of the Far East] (Moscow), no. 5 (1994), pp. 103–110.

60. "Otchet Generalnogo Konsulstva SSSR v Shanghaye za 1959 god [The report of the USSR consul general in Shanghai, 1959]," TsKhSD, f. 5, op. 49, d. 240, p. 111.

61. "Iz dnevnika Antonova," TsKhSD, f. 5, op. 49, d. 233, p. 95.

62. Interview with Yuri Shvedkov, member of the delegation, February 1990, Moscow.

63. Chang, *Friends and Enemies*, pp. 212–213, 342.

64. MNSK (1993), no. 3, pp. 69–70; see also Chapter 6.

65. "Otchet Generalnogo Konsulstva SSSR v Shanghaye," TsKhSD, f. 5, op. 49, d. 240, p. 171.

66. Ibid.

67. Ibid., p. 199.

68. Ibid., p. 198.

69. Ibid., p. 200.

70. "Ob osnovnykh momentakh vnutrenney zhizni, vneshney politiki KNR i sovetsko-kitaiskikh otnosheniy v I kvartale 1960 g. [On the key issues of PRC domestic life, its foreign policy, and Sino-Soviet relations, first quarter of 1960]," p. 1, TskhSD, f. 5, op. 49, d. 340, p. 2.

71. Ibid., p. 2.

72. Ibid., p. 46.
73. Ibid., p. 3.
74. Ibid., p. 64.
75. Ibid., pp. 48, 49; MNSK (1993), no. 3, pp. 78–81.
76. Ibid., pp. 53–54.
77. Ibid., p. 53.
78. Interview with Oleg Troyanovsky, 2 May 1993, Washington, D.C.
79. "Ob osnovnykh momentakh vnutrenney zhizni," TsKhSD, f. 5, op. 49, d. 340, p. 54.
80. Ibid., p. 54.
81. Ibid., pp. 64, 65.
82. "Politicheskoye pismo posolstva SSSR v KNR za II kvartal 1960 g. [Political report of the USSR embassy in the PRC, second quarter of 1960]," TKSD, f. 5, op. 49, d. 340, pp. 53, 87.
83. *Khrushchev Remembers,* p. 471.
84. *Khrushchev Remembers: The Glasnost Tapes,* p. 160.

8. Khrushchev and Kennedy: The Taming of the Cold War

1. Mikhail Gefter, *Iz tekh i etikh let* [On the past and present years] (Moscow: Progress, 1991), p. 335.
2. Strobe Talbott, ed., *Khrushchev Remembers* (Boston: Little, Brown and Co., 1970), p. 458.
3. Interview with Oleg Troyanovsky, 30 March 1993, Washington, D.C.
4. *Khrushchev Remembers,* p. 367.
5. Alexander Feklisov, *Za okeanom i na ostrove: Zapiski razvedchika* [Overseas and on the island: the notes of an intelligence agent] (Moscow: DEM, 1994), pp. 199–200, 201.
6. Sergei N. Khrushchev, *Nikita Kruschev: Krizisi i raketi* [Nikita Khrushchev: crises and missiles] (Moscow: Novosti, 1994), pp. 88–89, 89–90.
7. The profile of Kennedy was sent by Chargé d'Affaire M. Smirnovsky to Gromyko on 26 July 1960. Gromyko sent it to Khrushchev on 3 August 1960 with a note: "This is of interest." TsKhSD, f. 5, op. 30, d. 335, pp. 92, 93, 96, 100. Translated passages are from the full text published in the *Bulletin* of CWIHP, no. 4 (1994), pp. 65–67.
8. TsKhSD, f. 5, op. 30, d. 335, pp. 103–105, 106, 107; the *Bulletin* of CWIHP, no. 4 (1994), p. 67.
9. G. M. Kornienko, "Novoie o Karibskom krizise [New facts on the Cuban missile crisis]," *Novaya i noveishaya istoriya,* 3 (1991), p. 82. Kornienko had told Arthur M. Schlesinger, Jr., about this episode; see Schlesinger, *A Thousand Days: John F. Kennedy in the White House* (Boston: Houghton Mifflin, 1965), p. 378.

10. One channel was, via Walt Rostow, Abrasimov to Gromyko (for Khrushchev), 8 February 1961, TsKhSD, f. 5, op. 30, d. 365, pp. 19, 26–27, 29. On a channel via Alexander Korneychuk, Khrushchev's friend, see "Zapiska Sovetskikh obshchestvennikh deiatelei ob itogakh poezdki v ShA [Report of Soviet public figures on the results of the trip to the United States]," sometime late November 1960, TsKhSD, f. 4, op. 16, d. 944, st. 172/15 (special dossier of the Secretariat of the Central Committee) for 24 January 1961, pp. 30, 36.

11. "Zapiska Sovetskikh obshchestvennikh deiatelei"; Boris Ponomarev to the Central Committee, 19 January 1961; the Secretariat's decision on the proposals, 27 January 1961, in TsKhSD, f. 4, op. 16, d. 944, pp. 27, 38–39, 40–53, st. 172/15 for 24 January 1961.

12. TsKhSD, f. 4, op. 16, d. 944, pp. 41–42.

13. Anatoly Dobrynin, *In Confidence: Moscow's Ambassador to America's Six Cold War Presidents (1962–1986)* (New York: Random House, 1995), pp. 52–54; V. Zubok's interview with Alexei Adzhubei, July 1990, Moscow.

14. Michael Beschloss, *Kennedy and Khrushchev: The Crisis Years* (New York: Harper-Collins, 1991), pp. 65–66, 78, 80–81, 83–84. Feklisov told Robert Estabrook, the editorial page editor of the *Washington Post;* Estabrook memo to the president, 20 March 1961, JFKL-NSF:CO:USSR, box 176.

15. "Otchet Komiteta Gosudarstvennoi Bezopasnosti pri Sovete Ministrov SSSR sa 1960 [The report of the Committee of State Security at the Council of Ministers of the USSR for the year 1960]," 14 February 1961, st. 179/42c (special dossier of the Secretariat), dated 21 March 1961, TsKhSD, f. 4, op. 12, d. 74, p. 147.

16. Beschloss, *The Crisis Years*, p. 88.

17. Vladimir Platonov, "Shchit i mech 'Satani': Strategicheskoye oruzhie Mikhaila Yangelia," *Sovershenno Sekretno*, no. 1 (1993), p. 12.

18. The letter was handed by Vladimir Semyonov to the American chargé d'affaires in Moscow, Edward Freers, at 12:15 P.M.; a collection of Khrushchev-Kennedy correspondence, declassified in 1993, is available on file at the National Security Archive, Washington, D.C.

19. "Khrushchev to Lippmann—Face to Face," *New York Herald Tribune*, 17 April 1961.

20. KGB to CC CPSU, 10 March 1961, in st. 199/10c (special dossier of the Secretariat), dated 3 October 1961, TsKhSD, f. 4, op. 13, d. 74, p. 149.

21. Interview with Oleg Troyanovsky, then a foreign policy aide of Khrushchev's, 30 March 1993, Washington, D.C.

22. Dobrynin, *In Confidence*, pp. 43–44, 45.

23. Memorandum of a Conversation at the Vienna Meeting between the

President and Chairman Khrushchev, 3 June 1961, 12:45 P.M., John F. Kennedy Library, POF:CO:USSR, box 126, folder 12, p. 1.

24. See Chapter 1, and Walter Lippmann, *U.S. War Aims* (Boston, 1944).

25. Troyanovsky, interview with V. M. Zubok, 27 May 1993, Moscow.

26. Beschloss, *The Crisis Years,* pp. 206, 235.

27. Memorandum of a Conversation at the Vienna Meeting, 3 June 1961, 12:45 P.M., box 126, folder 12, pp. 3–4.

28. Ibid., p. 4; Memorandum of a Conversation at the Vienna Meeting, 3 June 1961, 3:00 P.M., box 126, folder 12, p. 3; Beschloss, *The Crisis Years,* p. 196.

29. Memorandum of a Conversation at the Vienna Meeting, 3 June 1961, 3:00 P.M., box 126, folder 12, p. 2; ibid., 3 June 1961, 12:45 P.M., p. 6.

30. Ibid., 3 June 1961, 12:45 P.M., p. 6; Beschloss, *The Crisis Years,* pp. 196–197.

31. Interview with Oleg Troyanovsky, 30 March 1993, Washington, D.C.

32. The first successful satellite reconnaissance of *Discoverer* was accomplished by the CIA in August 1960, *Corona: America's First Satellite Program,* ed. Kevin C. Ruffner, History Staff Center for the Study of Intelligence, Central Intelligence Agency, Washington, D.C., 1995, pp. 22–24. The transcripts of the CIA debriefings of Penkovsky, July 1961, are on file at the National Security Archive, Washington, D.C.

33. Memorandum of a Conversation at the Vienna Meeting, 3 June 1961, 12:45 P.M., box 126, folder 12, p. 6.

34. Ibid., 3 June 1961, 3:00 P.M., p. 9.

35. In the documents of the CC CPSU Secretariat, we found some of these signals on the new flexibility of the Kennedy circle (Arthur M. Schlesinger, Jr., Walt W. Rostow). See Vladislav M. Zubok, "Khrushchev and the Berlin Crisis," CWIHP Working paper no. 6, p. 17.

36. This portion was excised from the published version; see Thompson to State Department, Telegram from the Embassy in Moscow, 24 May 1961, *FRUS: Berlin Crisis,* pp. 66–69. We thank William Burr from the National Security Archive for bringing this to our attention.

37. Memorandum of a Conversation at the Vienna Meeting, 4 June 1961, 10:15 A.M., box 126, folder 12, pp. 17, 18.

38. Cyril Buffet at the conference on the Berlin crisis, Woodrow Wilson International Center for Scholars and the Nuclear History Project, Washington, 21 May 1993.

39. *FRUS: Berlin Crisis,* 1961–1963, XIV, pp. 87–94. G. M. Kornyenko, "Upushchennaia vozmoshnost: Vstrecha N. S. Khrushcheva i J. Kennedi v Vene v 1961 g. [The missed opportunity: the meeting of N. S. Khrushchev and J. Kennedy in Vienna in 1961]," *Novaiia i noveishaia istoriia,* no. 2 (1992), p. 101.

40. Memorandum of a Conversation at the Vienna Meeting, 4 June 1961, 3:15 P.M., box 126, folder 12, p. 3.

41. Dean Rusk, *As I Saw It,* ed. Daniel L. Papp (New York: Norton, 1990), pp. 220–221; Theodore C. Sorensen, *Kennedy* (New York: Harper & Row, 1965), p. 549; Arthur M. Schlesinger, Jr., *A Thousand Days: John F. Kennedy in the White House* (Boston, 1965), p. 361, and *Robert Kennedy and His Times* (Boston: Houghton Mifflin, 1978), p. 427. On other sources and the essence of the debate, see Richard Ned Lebow and Janice Gross Stein, *We All Lost the Cold War* (Princeton: Princeton University Press, 1994), pp. 23, 71, 408–410.

42. *Khrushchev Remembers,* p. 458; *Khrushchev Remembers: The Last Testament* (Boston: Little, Brown and Co., 1974), trans. and ed. Strobe Talbott, pp. 562–572.

43. From the diary of V. Suldin, the first secretary of the Soviet embassy in the GDR, TsKhSD, op. 49, d. 380, pp. 13–14, 47, 70–72, 92–93; "On the Issue of the Exodus of the GDR Population to West Germany" (embassy's materials), 7 April 1961, TsKhSD, op. 49, d. 380, p. 60.

44. Interview with Oleg Troyanovsky, 30 March 1993, Washington, D.C.

45. By 1962 Soviet loans to the GDR amounted to 6.8 billion deutsche-marks; Yuri Andropov to the Presidium of the Central Committee, Report of the International Department, 16 March 1962, TsKhSD, f. 4, op. 18, d. 103, p. 129.

46. Pervukhin to Gromyko, 6 December 1961, AVP RF, f. 082, op. 57, por. 388, papka 119, p. 32.

47. Memorandum of a Conversation of Comrade N. S. Khrushchev and Comrade W. Ulbricht, 30 November 1960, AVP RF, f. 0742, op. 6, por. 4, papka 43, pp. 18, 19, 20, 21.

48. MNSK (1993), no. 10, p. 68.

49. AVP RF, f. 0742, op. 6, por. 4, papka 43, p. 13.

50. First secretary of the embassy in the GDR (A. Avalduev) on his conversation with O. Neumann, member of the SED Central Commitee, 9 June 1960, TsKhSD, f. 5, op. 50, d. 226, p. 122.

51. AVP RF, f. 0742, op. 6, por. 4, papka 43; ibid., p. 12.

52. Yu. Kvitsinsky, conversation with P. Papist, 21 October 1960, TsKhSD, op. 49, d. 288, p. 278.

53. Yuli Kvitsinsky's recollections, in Hope M. Harrison, "Ulbricht and the Concrete 'Rose' ": New Archival Evidence on the Dynamics of Soviet-East German Relations and the Berlin Crisis, 1958–1961," Working paper no. 5, CWIHP, Washington, D.C. (May 1993), p. 39; letter from Ambassador Pervukhin to the minister of foreign affairs of the USSR, Comrade A. A. Gromyko, 4 July 1961, AVP RF, referentura po GDR, op. 6, por. 34, papka 46.

54. Harrison, "Ulbricht and the Concrete 'Rose' "; Zubok, "Khrushchev and the Berlin Crisis," p. 20.

55. A younger Soviet diplomat, Yuli Kvitsinsky, was present at this meeting and described it in Julij A. Kwitzinskij, *Vor dem Sturm: Erinnerungen eines Diplomaten* (Berlin: Siedler Verlag, 1993), p. 179; quoted in Harrison, "Ulbricht and the Concrete 'Rose,' " p. 47.

56. Harrison, "Ulbricht and the Concrete 'Rose,' " pp. 47, 51; MNSK (1993), no. 10, p. 69; Kwitzinskij, *Vor dem Sturm,* pp. 179–180.

57. Beschloss, *The Crisis Years,* p. 263.

58. The conference of the first secretaries of the Central Committee of Communist and workers parties of Socialist countries for the exchange of views on questions related to the preparation and conclusion of a German peace treaty, 3–5 August 1961 (transcripts of the meeting were found in the miscellaneous documents of the International Department of the Central Committee), TsKhSD (hereafter, Transcripts), p. 144. Khrushchev hinted more than once that the KGB services intercepted cables sent by foreign embassies in Moscow. Excerpts of the document were translated by V. Zubok and published in *Bulletin* of CWIHP, no. 3 (Fall 1993), pp. 59–61.

59. Ibid., p. 178.

60. Ibid., pp. 142, 143.

61. Ibid., p. 157.

62. Ibid., pp. 157, 158.

63. Ibid., p. 159.

64. An account by Sakharov and Zeldovich to Yuri Smirnov, who then worked on Sakharov's research team in Arzamas-16. Interview of V. M. Zubok with Smirnov, Antibes, France, 26 June 1993. This story contradicts the version of Andrei Sakharov, *Vospominaniia* [Memoirs] (New York: Chekhov, 1990), pp. 285–290. According to Smirnov, Sakharov at that time was still an enthusiast of nuclear testing. The opposition and the clash with Khrushchev happened later.

65. 27 January 1959, "Memorandum of Henry C. Ramsay on Ambassador Thompson's Remarks at the Planning Board, 13 January 1959." Declassified by the U.S. Department of State on 24 February 1995, on file at the National Security Archive, Washington, D.C. We would like to thank William Burr of the National Security Archive, who brought this document to our attention.

66. Shelepin to Khrushchev, 29 July 1961, in st. (special dossier of the Secretariat of the CC CPSU), 191/75gc, 1 August 1961, TsKhSD, f. 4, op. 13, d. 81, p. 130; see Vladislav M. Zubok, "Spy vs. Spy," the *Bulletin* of CWIHP, no. 4 (1994), pp. 28–29.

67. TsKhSD, f. 4, op. 13, d. 81, p. 131.

68. Ibid., pp. 131–132.

69. Ibid., p. 132.

70. Ibid.

71. Ibid., p. 133.

72. Ibid., pp. 133–134.

73. Ibid., pp. 128–129.

74. See Zubok, "Spy vs. Spy," p. 31.

75. Timothy Garton Ash, *In Europe's Name: Germany and the Divided Continent* (New York: Random House, 1993), pp. 51, 59–62.

76. See Beschloss, *The Crisis Years*, pp. 310–312.

77. Khrushchev to Kennedy, 29 September 1961; Kennedy to Khrushchev, 16 October 1961, *FRUS: Berlin Crisis*. Declassified copies of the letters are available at the National Security Archive, Washington, D.C.

78. Khrushchev's opening speech, 3 August, Moscow, Transcripts, p. 3.

79. MNSK (1993), no. 10, p. 69; Valentin Falin, *Politische Erinnerungen* (Munich: Droemer-Knaur, 1993), pp. 345–346.

80. MNSK (1993), no. 10, pp. 69–70. For traces of the secret exchange during the confrontation, see Beschloss, *The Crisis Years*, p. 335, and Khrushchev's letter to Kennedy, 9 November 1961, p. 9, National Security Archive, Washington, D.C.

81. Viktor Adamsky and Yuri Smirnov, "Moscow's Biggest Bomb: The 50-Megaton Test of October 1961," the *Bulletin* of CWIHP, no. 4 (1994), pp. 3, 19; *XXII s'ezd kommunisticheskoi partii sovetskogo soiuza: Stenograficheskii otchet* [Twenty-second Congress of the CPSU, stenographic report] (Moscow: Gospolitizdat, 1962), vol. 1, p. 50; vol. 2, pp. 571–573.

82. Interview with Oleg Troyanovsky, 28 May 1993, Moscow; Dobrynin, *In Confidence*, p. 45.

83. Ivashutin and Malinovsky to CC CPSU (Khrushchev), 10 November 1961, in st (special dossier of the Secretariat), 2/35c, 14 November 1961, TsKhSd, f. 4, op. 14, d. 1, pp. 10–14; Zubok, "Spy vs. Spy," pp. 29–30.

84. Transcripts, p. 144; Honore M. Catudal, *Kennedy and the Berlin Wall Crisis: A Case Study in U.S. Decision Making* (Berlin: Berlin Verlag, 1980), p. 201.

85. Interview with Oleg Troyanovsky, 28 May 1993, Moscow; Khrushchev to Kennedy, 9 November 1961, *FRUS: Berlin Crisis*, p. 9.

86. In the sea of publications it is important to emphasize the recent revelations: James G. Blight and David A. Welch, *On the Brink: Americans and Soviets Reexamine the Cuban Missile Crisis*, 2nd edition (New York: Noonday, 1990); Bruce J. Allyn, James G. Blight, and David A. Welch, eds., *Back to the Brink: Proceedings of the Moscow Conference on the Cuban Missile Crisis, January 27–28, 1989*, CSIA Occasional paper no. 9 (Latham, Md.: University Press of America, 1992); Arthur M. Schlesinger, Jr., "Four

Days with Fidel: A Havana Diary," *New York Review of Books,* vol. 39, no. 6, 26 March 1992; Anatoly Dokuchaev, "100-dnevnyi yadernyi kruiz [One hundred days of nuclear travel]," *Krasnaya zvezda* (Moscow), 6 November 1992; also see Dokuchaev's "Operatsia 'Anadyr' [Operation 'Anadyr']," *Krasnaya zvezda,* 21 October 1992; Gribkov, "Karibskii krizis (Caribbean Crisis)," *Voenno-Istoricheskii Zhurnal* (Moscow), no. 10–12 (1992), no. 4 (1993); Gen. Anatoly I. Gribkov and Gen. William Y. Smith, *Operation Anadyr: U.S. and Soviet Generals Recount the Cuban Missile Crisis,* ed. Alfred Friendly, Jr. (Chicago: Edition Q, Inc., 1994).

87. Beschloss, *The Crisis Years,* p. 388.

88. Mark Kramer, "Tactical Nuclear Weapons, Soviet Command Authority, and the Cuban Missile Crisis"; James G. Blight, Bruce J. Allyn, and David A. Welch, "Kramer vs. Kramer," in the *Bulletin* of CWIHP, no. 3 (Fall 1993), pp. 40–41.

89. James Richter, *Khrushchev's Double-Bind: International Pressures and Domestic Coalition Politics* (Baltimore: The Johns Hopkins University Press, 1994), p. 194; the discussion of the "reinforcing objective" is in Lebow and Stein, *We All Lost the Cold War,* pp. 60–62.

90. Among the strong believers in this hypothesis are Walt W. Rostow and Adam Ulam; V. Zubok's interview with John Auslund, Oslo, Norway, November 1993.

91. Interview with Oleg Troyanovsky, 28 May 1993, Moscow.

92. *Khrushchev Remembers,* p. 494; interview with Oleg Troyanovsky, 28 May 1993, Moscow.

93. Dobrynin to Gromyko, 23 October 1962. From the collection of AVP RF, pp. 7–8. A. Feklisov's recollections of his meetings with Scalia, in "Neizvestnoie o razviazke Karbiskogo krizisa [Reminiscences of Alexander Feklisov, the chief of the KGB station in Washington in 1962]," *Voienno-Istoricheskii Zhurnal,* no. 10 (1989); also his presentation at the Conference on the Cuban Missile Crisis: New Evidence from the Archives, September 1994, Moscow.

94. Interview with Oleg Troyanovsky, 28 May 1993, Moscow.

95. Troyanovsky, "Nikita Khrushchev and Soviet Foreign Policy," p. 101.

96. Penkovsky's debriefings, second phase: July–August in London. July 18–19, p. 14, the collection of the National Security Archive, Washington, D.C.; see also Jerrold L. Schecter and Peter S. Deriabin, *The Spy Who Saved the World: How a Soviet Colonel Changed the Course of the Cold War* (New York: Scribner's, 1992), pp. 209, 241.

97. *Operation Anadyr,* p. 14.

98. Interview with Oleg Troyanovsky, 28 May 1993, Moscow.

99. "Information of V. E. Semichastny, the Chairman of the KGB, to the

Central Committee on the Reaction of the Population," 2 June 1962, in "Novocherkasskaia tragediia, 1962 [The Novocherkassk tragedy, 1962]," *Istoricheskii arkhiv*, no. 1 (1993), pp. 114, 116.

100. Information from the KGB to the Central Committee, special dossier, top secret, 25 July 1962, in "Novocherkasskaia tragediia, 1962," *Istoricheskii arkhiv*, no. 4 (1993), pp. 170–171.

101. A. V. Tretetskii, "Novocherkassk: Iyun 1962 goda [Novocherkassk: June 1962]," *Voenno-Istoricheskii Zhurnal*, no. 1 (1991), p. 70. The group of top officials included Alexandre Shelepin, Andrei Kirilenko, Kozlov, Mikoyan, Ilyichev, Dmitry Polyansky, and Piotr Ivashutin.

102. *Pravda*, 3 June 1962; *Istoricheskii arkhiv*, no. 1 (1993).

103. Pliyev received authorization to use arms from Kirilenko and Shelepin on 1 June, after Kirilenko's telephone conversation with Khrushchev. The decision was approved by Mikoyan and Kozlov the next day, and also, by phone, by the minister of defense, Malinovsky. A. V. Tretetskii, "Novocherkassk," pp. 69, 72.

104. Gribkov, "Karibskii krizis," p. 31; Mark Kramer, "The 'Lessons' of the Cuban Missile Crisis for Warsaw Pact Nuclear Operations," the *Bulletin* of CWIHP, no. 5 (1995), pp. 110, 112.

105. For a discussion of whether this threat was real or exaggerated, see Kramer, "Tactical Nuclear Weapons"; Blight, Allyn, and Welch, "Kramer vs. Kramer."

106. "Predlozheniia Khrushcheva i drugikh ob usilenii borbi s vrazhdebnimi proiavleniiami antisovetskikh elementov: Vypiska iz protokola N. 42 zasedaniia Prezidiuma TsK ot 19 iulia 1962 g. [Khrushchev's proposal of July 19]," the Central Committee of the CPSU, top secret, special dossier, TsKhSD, f. 89, op. 6, doc. 22, pp. 1–2. Also cited from this file are the draft order of the KGB chief and the collective proposals of the leadership of the state police—surveillance, prosecution, and the penitentiary system (Shelepin, Semichastny, Ivashutin, Zakharov, Tikhunov, Rudenko, Mironov), ibid., pp. 10, 11, 15.

107. Based on the account of Col. Nikolai Beloborodov, at the Conference on the Cuban Missile Crisis of 1962, New Evidence from the Archives, Moscow, 27–29 September 1994; see also *Operation Anadyr*, pp. 62–63. Beloborodov was responsible for the transportation and storage of all nuclear munitions on Cuba.

108. Col. V. T. Roshchupkin, "Moskva hotela znat' vse [Moscow wanted to know everything]," *Voenno-Istoricheskii Zhurnal*, no. 9 (1992), pp. 59–60; Dobrynin, *In Confidence*, p. 54.

109. For a discussion of this issue, see Lebow and Stein, *We All Lost the Cold War*, p. 80; Kornienko at the Conference on the Cuban Missile Crisis of 1962, Moscow, September 1994.

110. Dobrynin, *In Confidence,* p. 72.

111. Gromyko to the CC CPSU, 19 October 1962, from the declassified collection of the AVP RF, on file at the National Security Archive, Washington, D.C.

112. Georgi Kornienko, "Novoie o Karibskom krizise," *Novaiia i noveishaia istoriia,* no. 3 (May–June 1991), p. 85; Kornienko, interview with Zubok, April 1990, Moscow.

113. Kornienko, "Novoie o Karibskom"; Feklisov, "Neizvestnoie o razriadke Karibzkogo krizisa."

114. Dobrynin, *In Confidence,* pp. 86–91.

115. Oleg Troyanovsky, "Karibskii krizis: Vzgliad iz Kremlia [The Caribbean crisis: a view from the Kremlin]," *Mezhdunarodnaiia zhizn,* no. 3–4 (1992), p. 174. On the Soviet nuclear charges stored in Cuba, see the account of Beloborodov, the Conference on the Cuban Missile Crisis of 1962, Moscow, 27–29 September 1994.

116. Beloborodov and Gribkov at the Conference on the Cuban Missile Crisis, September 1994, Moscow.

117. Memorandum of a conversation between A. I. Mikoyan and Fidel Castro, Oswaldo Dorticos Torrado, Raul Castro, Ernesto Guevara, Emilio Aragones, and Carlos Rafael Rodriguez, 4 November 1962. From the collection of AVP RF, pp. 1–17; published in *Bulletin* of CWIHP, no. 5 (Spring 1995), pp. 94–101.

118. Memorandum of a conversation between A. I. Mikoyan and Oswaldo Dorticos, Ernesto Guevara, and Carlos Rafael Rodriguez, 5 November 1962, evening, from the collection of AVP RF, pp. 20–21.

119. Memorandum of a conversation between A. I. Mikoyan and F. Castro, 12 November 1962, from the collection of AVP RF, p. 5.

120. Raymond Garthoff, "When and Why Romania Distanced Itself from the Warsaw Pact," *Bulletin* of CWIHP, no. 5 (1995), p. 111.

121. Khrushchev's letter to Kennedy of 30 October 1962, from the collection of Khrushchev-Kennedy correspondence, declassified by AVP RF in 1991, published in *Problems of Communism* (Spring 1992), Special Edition, p. 65. Copies of the originals are on file at the National Security Archive, Washington, D.C.

122. Letter to Kennedy of 11 November 1962; letter to Kennedy of 10 December 1962; *Problems of Communism,* pp. 84, 114.

123. Letter to Kennedy of 11 November 1962; letter to Kennedy of 30 October 1962; *Problems of Communism,* pp. 65, 83, 84.

124. Letter to Kennedy of 10 December 1962; *Problems of Communism,* p. 116.

125. Letter to Kennedy of 22 November 1962; *Problems of Communism,* p. 108.

126. Khrushchev's letter to Castro of 31 January 1963, esp. pp. 3–4, 7, 11.

127. Letter to Castro of 31 January 1963, p. 10.

128. Letter to Castro of 31 January 1963.

129. Personal interview with Boris Ponomarev, a long-term chief of the International Department of the Central Committee, Moscow, 5 June 1990. The meeting took place in Novo-Ogarevo, the Party retreat near Moscow.

130. Sergei Khrushchev, *Nikita Khrushchev: Kriziski i raketi*, vol. 2, pp. 468–469.

131. "Beseda s Shelepinim A. N. i Semichastnym V. E. [Conversation between Shelepin and Semichastny]," 27 March and 22 May 1989, *Neizvestnaia Rossiia: XX vek* [Unknown Russia: the twentieth century], vol. 1 (Moscow: Istoricheskoiie Naslediie, 1992), pp. 281–282.

132. Ibid., p. 283.

133. "Kak snimali Khrushcheva [How Khrushchev was deposed]," the materials of the Plenum of the Central Committee of the CPSU, 14 October 1964, *Istoricheskii arkhiv*, no. 1 (1993), p. 10.

134. Ibid., pp. 11–13.

135. "Beseda s Shelepinim," *Neizvestnaia Rossiia*, pp. 288, 290.

# Index